MW01038650

ECONOMIC SANCTIONS AND INTERNATIONAL LAW

In recent years sanctions have become an increasingly popular tool of foreign policy, not only at the multilateral level (at the UN), but also regionally (the EU in particular) and unilaterally. The nature of the measures imposed has also changed: from comprehensive sanctions regimes (discredited since Iraq in the 1990s) to 'targeted' or 'smart' sanctions, directed at specific individuals or entities (through asset freezes and travel bans) or prohibiting particular activities (arms embargoes and export prohibitions). Bringing together scholars, government and private practitioners, *Economic Sanctions and International Law* provides an overview of recent developments and an analysis of the problems that they have engendered. Chapters examine the contemporary practice of the various actors, and the legality (or otherwise) of their activities. Issues considered include the human rights of persons targeted, and the mechanisms established to challenge their listing; as well as, in cases of sanctions imposed by regional organisations and individual states, the rights of third States and their nationals. The book will be of interest to scholars and practitioners of international law and politics.

Volume 62 in the series Studies in International Law

Studies in International Law

Recent titles in this series

Democratic Statehood in International Law: The Emergence of New States in Post-Cold War Practice
Jure Vidmar

International Law and the Construction of the Liberal Peace
Russell Buchan

The OIC, the UN, and Counter-Terrorism Law-Making: Conflicting or Cooperative Legal Orders?
Katja Samuel

Statelessness: The Enigma of the International Community
William E Conklin

The Reception of Asylum Seekers under International Law: Between Sovereignty and Equality
Lieneke Slingenberg

International Law and Child Soldiers
Gus Waschefort

The Contractual Nature of the Optional Clause
Gunnar Törber

Non-State Actors in International Law
Edited by Math Noortmann, August Reinisch and Cedric Ryngaert

The Rule of Law at the National and International Levels: Contestations and Deference
Edited by Machiko Kanetake and André Nollkaemper

Human Rights Obligations of Non-State Armed Groups
Daragh Murray

Security and International Law
Edited by Mary E Footer, Julia Schmidt and Nigel D White

For the complete list of titles in this series, see 'Studies in International Law' link at www.hartpub.co.uk/books/series.asp

Economic Sanctions and International Law

Edited by
Matthew Happold and Paul Eden

OXFORD AND PORTLAND, OREGON
2016

Hart Publishing
An imprint of Bloomsbury Publishing Plc

Hart Publishing Ltd
Kemp House
Chawley Park
Cumnor Hill
Oxford OX2 9PH
UK

Bloomsbury Publishing Plc
50 Bedford Square
London
WC1B 3DP
UK

www.hartpub.co.uk
www.bloomsbury.com

Published in North America (US and Canada) by
Hart Publishing
c/o International Specialized Book Services
920 NE 58th Avenue, Suite 300
Portland, OR 97213-3786
USA

www.isbs.com

First published 2016

British Library Cataloguing-in-Publication Data
A catalogue record for this book is available from the British Library.

ISBN: HB: 978-1-84946-590-8
ePDF: 978-1-78225-472-0
ePub: 978-1-78225-473-7

Library of Congress Cataloging-in-Publication Data

Names: Happold, Matthew. | Eden, Paul, 1964–

Title: Economic sanctions and international law / edited by Matthew Happold and Paul Eden.

Description: Oxford ; Portland, Oregon : Hart Publishing, 2016. | Series: Studies in international law | Includes bibliographical references and index.

Identifiers: LCCN 2016020805 (print) | LCCN 2016021061 (ebook) | ISBN 9781849465908 (hardback : alk. paper) | ISBN 9781782254737 (Epub)

Subjects: LCSH: Economic sanctions. | Sanctions (International law)

Classification: LCC KZ6373 .E265 2016 (print) | LCC KZ6373 (ebook) | DDC 341.5/82—dc23

LC record available at https://lccn.loc.gov/2016020805

Series: Studies in International Law, volume 62

Typeset by Compuscript Ltd, Shannon
Printed and bound in Great Britain by
Lightning Source UK Ltd

Contents

List of Contributors

Rachel Barnes is a barrister at 3 Raymond Buildings, London.

Pierre-Emmanuel Dupont is the head of Public International Law at the London Centre of International Law Practice.

Paul Eden is a Lecturer in Law at the University of Sussex.

Clemens A Feinäugle is Coordinator of Scientific Research and a Senior Research Fellow at the Max Planck Institute for Procedural Law, Luxembourg.

Matthew Happold is Professor of Public International Law at the University of Luxembourg and a barrister at 3 Hare Court, London.

Penelope Nevill is a barrister at 20 Essex Street, London.

Alexander Orakhelashvili is a Senior Lecturer in Law at the University of Birmingham.

Luca Pantaleo is a Senior Researcher, International and EU Law, at the TMC Asser Institute, The Hague.

Antonios Tzanakopoulos is Associate Professor of Public International Law at the University of Oxford and a Fellow in Law at St Anne's College.

Table of Cases

European Court of First Instance

European Court of Human Rights

European Court of Justice

European General Court

International Court of Justice

International Criminal Tribunal for the former Yugoslavia

Other Courts and Arbitrations

Permanent Court of International Justice (PCIJ)

Table of Materials

Domestic Legislation

UK

US

1

Economic Sanctions and International Law: An Introduction

MATTHEW HAPPOLD

THE USE OF sanctions and embargoes as tools of foreign policy or (to put it more bluntly) of economic warfare[1] has rarely been more prevalent. At present, there are 17 United Nations sanctions regime and 37 European Union sanctions regimes in force, along with various others imposed by States acting unilaterally or under the umbrella of other international organisations. Yet, at the same time, such practices have rarely been more contested. Targeted or 'smart' sanctions against individuals and entities—in particular, asset freezes and travel bans—imposed by the UN Security Council and Member States acting under its authorisation have been subjected to sustained challenge: to begin with, because they reduced those subject to them to conditions of indigency; and, more generally, because they are based on undisclosed evidence and are not subject to judicial review. So-called unilateral or autonomous sanctions—that is, those imposed by States and international organisations without the Security Council's imprimatur—are criticised as being contrary to international law and in breach of the rights of the States targeted by such measures, including by the UN General Assembly and the Human Rights Council.

Sanctions, it can already be seen, take various forms. United Nations sanctions have traditionally had a special status, as they benefit from the combined effects of Charter Articles 25 (requiring Member States 'to accept and carry out the decisions of the Security Council') and 103 (providing that Member States' obligations under the Charter shall prevail in cases of conflict with any other of their treaty obligations). And although it is sometimes argued that the wording of Article 103 means that only

[1] See generally V Lowe and A Tzanakopoulos, 'Economic Warfare' in *Max Planck Encyclopedia of Public International Law* online edn (last updated March 2013), available at: http://0-opil.ouplaw.com.catalogue.ulrls.lon.ac.uk/view/10.1093/law:epil/9780199231690/law-9780199231690-e292?rskey=J2Nj55&result=1&prd=EPIL.

Member States' treaty obligations, and not their obligations under general international law, are trumped, application of the *lex specialis* principle would seem to argue the contrary, absent a customary rule having *jus cogens* status.[2] What this means is that discussions about whether the Security Council has acted lawfully in establishing particular sanctions regimes tend to focus on whether the Council has acted within its powers as set out in the Charter.[3]

Unilateral or autonomous sanctions, however, cannot rely on such support. Here, legal justifications differ.

— Some measures, such as embargoes on the export of arms and materiel are occasionally argued as necessary to prevent the State or States imposing them breaching their own legal obligations (under, eg, the law of neutrality)[4] or being complicit in another State's illegal conduct (under international human rights or humanitarian law or the Arms Trade Treaty).[5] If so, then properly speaking, they are not sanctions.

— Sanctions imposed by an international organisation on one of its Member States—such as those imposed by the African Union and threatened in the Organisation of American States in reaction to unconstitutional changes of Member States' governments[6]—can be justified on the basis of consent. The targeted Member State, as a member of the organisation, has agreed to be bound by its rules.

— Sanctions can also be justified as retorsion rather than reprisals (countermeasures), as they breach no obligation owed to the target State.

— Should any such obligation exist, however, then unilateral or autonomous sanctions can only be lawful if they are countermeasures,

[2] See International Law Commission (ILC), 'Report of the Study Group of the International Law Commission on Fragmentation of International Law: Difficulties Arising from the Diversification and Expansion of International Law' (13 April 2006) UN Doc A/CN.4/L.682 (13 April 2006) 175–78.

[3] See the critiques of the UN sanctions against Iran, esp UNSC Res 1083 (2008), made by A Orakhelashvili at ch 2, s V.

[4] This seems to be an aspect of Orakhelashvili's argument concerning the EU's abandonment of its arms embargo against Syria: seech 2, s V.C.

[5] Albeit that States' human rights obligations seem to have limited impact on arms exports: see *Tugar v Italy* App no 22869/93, Commission Decision on admissibility, DR no 83-B, at 2, but *cf Soering v UK*, ECtHR judgment of 7 July 1989, Series A no 161, at 33. See also Arms Trade Treaty (adopted 2 April 2013, entered into force 24 December 2014).

[6] See (as regards the AU) A Charron, 'Sanctions and Africa: United Nations and Regional Response' in J Boulden (ed), Responding to Conflict in Africa: The United Nations and Regional Organizations (2nd edn, Basingstoke, Palgrave Macmillan, 2013); M Eriksson, 'Supporting Democracy in Africa: The African Union's Use of Targeted Sanctions to Deal with Unconstitutional Changes of Government', FOL-R—3000—SE (Swedish Defence Research Agency, 2010); and (as regards the OAS) G Thompson and M Lacey, 'OAS Votes to Suspend Honduras over Coup' *New York Times*, 4 July 2009.

> meaning they are subjected to the stringent criteria codified in the ILC Articles on State Responsibility and its Draft Articles on the Responsibility of International Organisations.[7]

Indeed, this appears to be the crux of the dispute concerning the lawfulness of unilateral or autonomous sanctions. On one side, it is argued that a State's freedom includes the liberty to revise its relations with other States as it pleases providing no specific legal obligations are breached doing so, and that, as there are no customary obligations to maintain any particular economic relations with other States, this includes the restriction or interruption of trade relationships. On this reading, providing sanctions do not breach any applicable treaty (the GATT or other WTO-covered agreement; a regional free trade agreement; a treaty of friendship, commerce and navigation; or a bilateral investment treaty) or customary rules (such as those relating to the treatment of foreign nationals and their property present on the territory of the State), they are lawful. Certainly, this seems to have been the position taken by the International Court of Justice in the *Nicaragua* case,[8] when, discussing the legality of the trade embargo imposed by the USA on Nicaragua, the Court stated that '[a] State is not bound to continue particular trade relations longer than it sees fit to do so in the absence of a treaty commitment or other specific legal obligation'.[9]

On the other hand, however, it is argued that all 'coercive measures' are unlawful; that is, measures which are coercive in the sense of seeking to require the target State to change its policies on any matter within its domestic jurisdiction, in particular with regard to its political, economic and social system. It is a variant of this latter view that has lately been advanced by the UN Human Rights Council and the General Assembly, and (in this volume) by Alexander Orakhelashvili and Pierre-Emmanuel Dupont.[10] It appears to find its justification in the 1970 Friendly Relations Declaration[11] and, in particular, in Article 32 of the 1974 Charter of

[7] ILC, Articles on the Responsibility of States for Internationally Wrongful Acts, Annex, GA Res 56/83 (12 December 2001) (ASR); and ILC, Draft Articles on the Responsibility of International Organizations, 'Report on the Work of Its Sixty-Third Session' (26 April–3 June and 4 July–12 August 2011) Supp No 10, UN Doc A766/10. As A Tzanakopoulos points out in his contribution at ch 4, s III.A, however, not all of the procedural requirements set out in the ILC Articles may reflect customary international law.

[8] *Military and Paramilitary Activities in and against Nicaragua (Nicaragua v USA)* (Merits) [1986] ICJ Rep 14.

[9] Ibid para 276. As it happened, the USA was a party to a treaty of friendship, commerce and navigation with Nicaragua, which the Court found it had breached in imposing the embargo.

[10] See chs 1 and 2.

[11] Declaration on Principles of International Law concerning Friendly Relations and Co-operation among States in accordance with the Charter of the United Nations, UNGA Res 2625 (XXV): (24 October 1970). See also S Neff, 'Boycott and the Law of Nations: Economic Warfare and Modern International law in Historical Perspective' (1988) 59 *British Yearbook of International Law* 113.

Economic Rights and Duties of States,[12] which provides that: 'No State may use or encourage the use of economic, political or any other type of measures to coerce another State in order to obtain from it the subordination of the exercise of its sovereign rights'. In purported application of the rule contained in Article 32, beginning in 1983,[13] the General Assembly has adopted a long series of resolutions on 'human rights and unilateral coercive measures'. The most recent of such, Resolution 68/180, is clear; stating in its preamble the conviction that 'unilateral coercive measures and legislation are contrary to international law, international humanitarian law, the Charter of the United Nations and the norms and principles governing peaceful relations among States'. The resolution goes on to urge:

> all States to cease adopting or implementing any unilateral measures not in accordance with international law, international humanitarian law, the Charter of the United Nations and the norms and principles governing peaceful relations among States, in particular those of a coercive nature, with all their extraterritorial effects, which create obstacles to trade relations among States, thus impeding the full realization of the rights set forth in the Universal Declaration of Human Rights and other international human rights instruments, in particular the rights of individuals and peoples to development.

States are 'strongly' urged not to adopt or apply unilateral measures, in particular economic financial or trade measures, not in accordance with international law which might impede economic and social development. The inclusion of States in unilateral lists 'under false pretexts ... including false allegations of terrorism sponsorship' is condemned. Such measures' 'extraterritorial nature' are also said to threaten the sovereignty of States. Indeed, unilateral coercive measures are stated to be 'one of the major obstacles to the implementation of the Declaration on the Right to Development'. And the resolution condemns:

> the continuing unilateral application and enforcement by certain Powers of unilateral coercive measures, and rejects those measures with all their extraterritorial effects, as being tools for political or economic pressure against any country, in particular developing countries, adopted with a view to preventing those countries from exercising their right to decide, of their own free will, their own political, economic and social systems, and because of the negative effects of those measures on the realization of all the human rights of vast sectors of their populations, in particular children women, the elderly and persons with disabilities[.]

The Human Rights Council has also passed a series of similarly worded resolutions,[14] and in 2014 decided to appoint a Special Rapporteur on

[12] UNGA Res 3281 (XXXIX) (12 December 1974).
[13] UNGA Res 38/197 (20 December 1983).
[14] Beginning with UNHRC Res 6/7 (30 September 2007).

the negative impact of unilateral coercive measures on the enjoyment of human rights.[15]

It might be said, however, that such sweeping statements and blanket condemnations rest on uncertain foundations. The Charter of Economic Rights and Duties of States, despite its name, is nothing more than a General Assembly resolution and, although adopted by a large majority,[16] its customary status is doubtful given the number of developed States that abstained or voted against its adoption. The General Assembly and Human Rights Council's resolutions on human rights and unilateral coercive measures have been adopted by much less convincing majorities: General Assembly Resolution 69/180 received 134 votes for and 53 against, with one abstention. The most recent Human Rights Council resolution, Resolution 30/2,[17] was adopted by 33 to 14 votes with no abstentions. The least that can be said is that States are divided on the issue, with a substantial minority opposed to the view of the majority on the general illegality of unilateral economic sanctions.

In his chapter, Alexander Orakhelashvili argues that States possess rights under international law which other States are obliged to respect, with those rights being codified in the 1970 Friendly Relations Declaration, which provides, in particular, that:

> No State may use or encourage the use of economic political or any other type of measures to coerce another State in order to obtain from it the subordination of the exercise of its sovereign rights and to secure from it advantages of any kind.[18]

This seems a securer basis for arguing that unilateral or autonomous sanctions are generally illegal than the Charter of Economic Rights and Duties of States, given that the Friendly Relations Declaration was adopted by the General Assembly without a vote and is frequently considered to be an authoritative interpretation of the principles set out in Article 2 of the UN Charter. However, it might be recalled that the relevant provisions of the Friendly Relations Declaration fall within the section on '[t]he duty not to intervene in matters within the domestic jurisdiction of any State, in accordance with the Charter', and that the extent of a State's domestic jurisdiction at any one time is a relative question dependent on the development of international relations,[19] so that references in the Declaration to the illegality of measures taken against 'the personality of the

[15] UNHRC Res 27/21 (26 September 2014) para 22.

[16] It was adopted by 115 votes to 6, with 10 abstentions.

[17] UNHRC Res 30/2 (1 October 2015).

[18] Declaration on Principles of International Law concerning Friendly Relations and Co-operation among States in accordance with the Charter of the United Nations (n 11).

[19] See *Nationality Decrees Issued in Tunis and Morocco* (Advisory Opinion) (1923) PCIJ Series B no 4, at 24.

State', 'its political, economic and cultural elements' and 'its sovereign rights' need to be parsed carefully. Matters such as the degree to which a State respects the human rights of its nationals, which some decades ago might have been seen as wholly internal, are now seen as matters of international concern to which other States and international organisations may react.

It might also be questioned whether State practice comports with the high-minded statements of the General Assembly and the Human Rights Council. An obvious example is the Organisation of Arab Petroleum Exporting Countries' oil embargo in 1973–74 against Canada, Japan, the Netherlands, the UK and the USA in response to those States' support of Israel during the Six Days War. Ironically, the Arab States' use of their 'oil weapon' was at the time condemned by many Western scholars as unlawful coercion.[20] The point here, however, is not so much that the embargo sought to prevent those States targeted 'from exercising their right to decide, of their own free will, their own political, economic and social systems' but that it was expressly intended to be coercive and was justified on the basis either that the Arab States were not in breach of any treaty obligations owed towards the target States or because it was a countermeasure undertaken in the community interest.[21]

In addition, many treaties of an economic nature contain security exceptions permitting the interruption of commercial relations. One famous example is Article XXI of the GATT, which, inter alia, provides that:

> Nothing in this Agreement shall be construed
>
> ...
>
> (*b*) to prevent any contracting party from taking any action which it considers necessary for the protection of its essential security interests
>
> ...
>
> (iii) taken in time of war or other emergency in international relations;

It was Article XXI which the USA successfully relied upon when Nicaragua brought a complaint concerning its general embargo before a GATT panel.[22] And a similar provision of the 1955 USA-Iran Treaty of Amity, Economic Relations, and Consular Rights,[23] relied upon less successfully

[20] See J J Paust and A P Blaustein, 'Commentary: The Arab Oil Weapon—A Threat to International Peace' in J J Paust and A P Blaustein (eds), *The Arab Oil Weapon* (Dobbs Ferry, New York, Oceana, 1977).

[21] See I F Shihata, 'Destination Embargo of Arab Oil: Its Legality under International Law' in Paust and Blaustein, *The Arab Oil Weapon* (n 20).

[22] See Neff, 'Boycott and the Law of Nations' (n 11) 128.

[23] Art XX, which provided that: 'The present Treaty shall not preclude the application of measures: ... (d) ... necessary to protect its essential security interests'.

by the USA in the *Oil Platforms* case,[24] will also be recalled. For present purposes, however, what is important is not the precise ambit of such provisions (which, it might be thought, varies for treaty to treaty) nor even whether or not they are self-judging, but their existence. Were economic sanctions generally unlawful as a matter of customary international law then such provisions would be otiose. States' assumption when agreeing such provisions must have been that they would be effective. And their effectiveness can only have been premised on a further assumption that in the absence of the constraints imposed on them by the treaty the States parties enjoyed freedom of action regarding their economic relations.

Increasingly, of course, States do not enjoy such freedom of action, as their activities are constrained by ever-more-complex webs of treaty obligations. In such cases, sanctions can only be justified as countermeasures.[25] This introduction will not attempt to analyse the rules on countermeasures, which is done in a number of the contributions.[26] Suffice it to say, as Antonios Tzanakopoulos points out in his chapter,[27] that when enacting countermeasures a State does so at its peril; as if its assessments (in particular of the existence of prior wrongful conduct by the target State or of the proportionality of the measures undertaken against it as countermeasures) are incorrect, it acts illegally. Two issues have, however, taken on particular salience in recent years. The first concerns the legality of countermeasures taken in the community interest, that is, to enforce compliance with obligations owed by States *erga omnes* or (at least) *erga omnes partes*. Notoriously, the ILC Articles on State Responsibility avoided the issue.[28] Subsequent State practice, however, has increasingly been seen as arguing that such countermeasures are lawful.[29] And many of the sanctions regimes established by the European Union were established in response to patterns of human rights and humanitarian law violations.[30] Indeed, the EU's sanctions against Iran have been justified

[24] *Oil Platforms (Iran v USA)* (Judgment) [2003] ICJ Rep 161.

[25] See ASR (n 7) ch 3, pt II.

[26] See esp the chapters by A Orakhelashvili, at ch 2, s V.C, P-E Dupont, at ch 3, ss II.C and III and A Tzanakopoulos, at ch 4, s III.

[27] At ch 4, s III.A.

[28] ASR (n 7) Art 54 simply provides that: 'This chapter does not prejudice the right of any State, entitled under article 48, paragraph 1, to invoke the responsibility of another State, to take lawful measures against that State to ensure cessation of the breach and reparation in the interest of the injured State or of the beneficiaries of the obligation breached'. The term 'lawful measures' is, of course, entirely question-begging.

[29] See eg C Tams, *Enforcing Obligations Erga Omnes* (Cambridge, Cambridge University Press, 2010) and L-A Sicilianos, 'Countermeasures in Response to Grave Violations of Obligations Owed to the International Community' in J Crawford, A Pellet and S Olleson (eds), *The Law of International Responsibility* (Oxford, Oxford University Press, 2010).

[30] See European Commission, 'Restrictive Measures in Force' (TFEU, Art 215) available at: http://eeas.europa.eu/cfsp/sanctions/docs/measures_en.pdf.

on the basis that Iran has failed to comply with its obligations under the Non-Proliferation Treaty, which obligations are of an integral character, breach of which threatens the integrity of the treaty structure as a whole and therefore justifies a response by any of its parties.[31]

The second issue is the one that has received most publicity: the potential for sanctions to violate individuals' human rights. The argument that any sanctions amount to countermeasures cannot justify the application of sanctions which violate a State's obligations under international human rights law for two reasons: first, because countermeasures may not affect obligations for the protection of fundamental human rights;[32] and, secondly and more fundamentally, because a countermeasure 'concerns the legal relations between the injured State and the responsible State'.[33] A State's human rights obligations are owned not only to other States but also to individuals, in particular persons within its jurisdiction.[34]

In the last two decades, both the Security Council and States and international organisations acting of their own motion have moved away from comprehensive towards targeted sanctions directed at specific named persons and entities. Indeed, all current UN and EU sanctions have at least a targeted component, in particular through the imposition of asset freezes and travel bans. The reasons for this development are well known: comprehensive sanction were seen as both inefficient and indiscriminate, so that targeting sanctions specifically against those whose behaviour the sanctions sought to enjoin would be more effective and avoid collateral damage. Moreover, targeted sanctions can be directed not only at State organs and agents but against any persons or entities, including terrorist and other criminal groups which may not even have corporate personality under any legal system, being illegal organisations. Such problems are avoided because the measures are directed at the group's members, not at the group itself. Issues concerning sanctions and human rights are discussed in the contributions to this volume by Paul Eden and Clemens

[31] See N Jansen Calamita, 'Sanctions, Countermeasures, and the Iranian Nuclear Issue' (2009) 42 *Vanderbilt Journal of Transnational Law* 1393; and (more generally) M Happold, 'The "Injured State" in Case of Breach of a Non-Proliferation Treaty and the Legal Consequences of Such a Breach' and S Singh, 'Non-Proliferation Law and Countermeasures' both in D H Joyner and M Roscini (eds), *Non-Proliferation Law as a Special Regime: A Contribution to Fragmentation Theory in International Law* (Cambridge, Cambridge University Press 2012).

[32] ASR (n 7) Art 50(1)(b). Quite which human rights are 'fundamental human rights' is not wholly clear. The ILC Commentary suggests that it is those 'human rights which may not be derogated from even in time of war or other public emergency': ILC, 'Report on the Work of its Fifty-Third Session' (23 April–1 June and 2 July–10 August 2001), Official records of the General Assembly, Fifty-Sixth Session, Supp No 10, UN Doc A756/210, Commentary to draft Art 50, p 132.

[33] ILC Commentary, ibid, Commentary to draft Art 49, p 130.

[34] See eg European Convention on Human Rights, Art 1 and International Covenant on Civil and Political Rights, Art 2(1). Of course, what being within a State's jurisdiction requires remains hotly disputed.

Feinäugle (both of whom concentrate on UN sanctions), and by Matthew Happold (who ranges more widely to contrast the UN and EU regimes), as well as by Luca Pantaleo (in his examination of sanctions cases in the EU courts) and Rachel Barnes (who although concentrating on US sanctions, makes interesting comparisons between the approach of the US courts and those of the English and EU judiciaries).

Three things can be said about the effect of targeted sanctions on their targets' human rights. The first is that, in general, the substantive rights engaged are qualified rights (the right to property and to private and family life in particular), which means that restrictions on their exercise can be justified if they are proportionate and undertaken for an appropriate purpose. Secondly, sanctions regimes have in general evolved to provide for exemptions to take account of specific cases where the measures might have disproportionate effects or might breach absolute rights. Thus, asset freezes allow exceptions to permit the payment of listed persons' ordinary expenses, and travel bans allow them to return to their State of nationality. Thirdly, the real issue concerning targeted sanctions today is their compatibility with procedural rights: the right of access to a court, to a fair trial, and to a remedy when there has been a violation of their rights (ie if they have been wrongfully targeted). It is, one might say, a rule of law issue.[35] And, although as Luca Pantaleo shows, the Court of Justice of the European Union has gone a long way towards providing an effective system of judicial review for EU sanctions (and of UN sanctions implemented in the EU legal order), this is by no means the case at the UN level. With the exception of the Ombudsperson established to reviews requests from persons seeking removal of their names from the consolidated Al-Qaida Sanctions list,[36] there is nothing resembling judicial review of Security Council sanctions decisions, and the Ombudsperson herself suffers from a lack of objective independence.[37] Indeed, Clemens Feinäugle shows that problems with UN sanctions, from a rule of law perspective, go rather further than just the absence of judicial review, with different sanctions regimes taking inconsistent approaches and providing different levels of safeguards.[38]

[35] See C Feinäugle's chapter in this volume; J M Farrell, *United Nations Sanctions and the Rule of Law* (Cambridge, Cambridge University Press, 2009); F Stenhammar, 'United Nations Targeted Sanctions, the International Rule of Law and the European Court of Justice's Judgment in *Kadi and al-Barakaat*' (2010) 79 *Nordic Journal of International Law* 113; M Kanetake, 'The Interfaces between the National and the International Rule of Law: The Case of UN Targeted Sanctions' (2012) 9 *International Organizations Law Review* 267; and M Happold, 'United Nations Sanctions and the Rule of Law' in C A Feinäugle (ed), *The United Nations and the Rule of Law* (forthcoming, 2016).

[36] See UNSC Res 1904 (2009); UNSC Res 1989 (2011); UNSC res 2083 (2013); and UNSC Res 2161 (2014).

[37] See the chapters by M Happold and P Eden at ch 5, s V and ch 7, ss VII and IX.

[38] C Feinäugle's chapter at ch 6, s III.

More difficulties arise out of economic sanctions' effects on the population of countries targeted. This was the issue that discredited comprehensive sanctions in the 1990s, leading to the switch to targeted sanctions. However, the controversy surrounding targeted sanctions' human rights compatibility and, perhaps more importantly, the emergence of avenues permitting their judicial review, has had the perverse effect of reviving States' use of more generalised sanctions. Although such sanctions are not comprehensive, being directed against certain types of trade and transactions, they can have quite similar effects, especially when central banks and financial transactions are targeted.[39] Even if exceptions are provided for necessities (foodstuffs, medicaments and medical technology, etc), exporters may still be unwilling to trade, not considering the extra efforts worthwhile to access often quite small markets and concerned to avoid any risk of prosecution for violating sanctions.[40] So questions concerning sanctions' effects on the economic and social rights of the populations of targeted States have not gone away and seem to be moving up the agenda again,[41] as witnessed by the concerns expressed by the UN General Assembly and the Human Rights Council mentioned above;[42] and the appointment of a Special Rapporteur on the negative impact of the unilateral coercive measures on the enjoyment of human rights is likely to add to the issue's visibility.[43] The questions concerning sanctions' compatibility with economic and social rights are even more complex than those related to the human rights-compatibility of targeted sanctions. Although considerable work has recently been done seeking to demonstrate that States do have extraterritorial obligations in the area of economic and social rights,[44] it is less clear that all States agree. And to a very large extent fora do not exist to which affected individuals can bring claims that their rights have been violated.

[39] See P-E Dupont at ch 3, s I. In compliance with Council Regulation (EU) No 267/2012 of 23 March 2012 concerning restrictive measures against Iran and repealing Regulation (EU) No 961/2, OJ L 88/1, 24.3.12, SWIFT, the principal global provider of secure financial messaging services (which is incorporated in Belgium), disconnected all listed Iranian banks, including the Central Bank of Iran.

[40] See S Namazi, *Sanctions and Medical Supply Shortages in Iran*, Viewpoints No 20 (February 2013), Middle East Program, Woodrow Wilson International Center for Scholars.

[41] See M Happold at ch 5, s VI.

[42] Text to nn 13 to 15.

[43] The Special Rapporteur, Idriss Jazairy (Algeria), took office on 1 May 2015. He issued his first report in August 2015: Report of the Special Rapporteur on the negative impact of unilateral coercive measures on the enjoyment of human rights, Idriss Jazairy, UN Doc A/HRC/30/45 (10 August 2015).

[44] See the Maastricht Principles on the Extraterritorial Obligations of States in the Area of Economic, Social and Cultural Rights and their Commentary (2012) 34 *Human Rights Quarterly* 1084; and M Langford, W Vandenhole, M Scheinin and W van Genugten (eds), *Global Justice, State Duties: The Extra-Territorial Scope of Economic, Social and Cultural Rights in International Law* (Cambridge, Cambridge University Press, 2013).

This leads to a further issue: the extent to which the legality of sanctions can be contested. We have already seen how targeted sanctions, including those imposed by the UN Security Council, have been increasingly subject to judicial review before various national and international courts. As regards targeted States, however, matters are not so simple. Nicaragua's claims before the International Court of Justice and two GATT Panels are rare examples of a State challenging the unilateral imposition of sanctions through international adjudication,[45] whilst the International Court of Justice's decision on the indication of provisional measures in the *Lockerbie* cases revealed the Court's unwillingness to entertain challenges to Security Council sanctions regimes.[46] And problems can also arise when States consider that they are being asked to implement sanctions regimes which they consider to be unlawful. In his contribution, Antonios Tzanakopoulos rejects the idea that when the Security Council acts beyond its powers its decisions are legal nullities; ultra vires Council resolutions are, he argues, binding but disobedience can be justified as a countermeasure. Other commentators disagree, not least because of the apparent oddity of holding that a refusal to comply with an illegal act is a countermeasure to that act, as opposed to the simply holding that in such circumstances States do not have a legal obligation to comply.[47] In all cases, however, the lack of easy access to any form of adjudication means that States' responses to sanctions, whether imposed by the UN or by States acting unilaterally or autonomously, are played out at the political level—in diplomatic exchanges and before the political organs of the UN and other international fora—with legal arguments serving to bolster political positions rather than being decisive in themselves. This is, of course, the primary reason why the content of the applicable law on economic sanctions remains so contested.

While such high-level manoeuvrings continue, however, private parties continue to have to deal with the disruptions of commercial relationships that sanctions impose. Penelope Nevill's chapter on sanctions and commercial law examines how commercial operators have sought to mitigate the effects of sanctions on their contractual relationships (in particular through specific clauses in standard form contracts) and how the courts and the legislator have responded to such situations (such as through

[45] See Neff (n 11) and text to n 22.

[46] *Questions of Interpretation and Application of the 1971 Montreal Convention arising from the Aerial Incident at Lockerbie (Libya v UK)* (Provisional Measures, Order of 14 April 1992) [1992] ICJ Rep 3, 15; and *Questions of Interpretation and Application of the 1971 Montreal Convention arising from the Aerial Incident at Lockerbie (Libya v USA)* (Provisional Measures, Order of 14 April 1992) [1992] ICJ Rep 114, 126.

[47] Certainly this was the view of the ILC Study Group on the fragmentation of international law: see (n 2) 169.

development of the doctrine of frustration). What her chapter clearly shows is how far such attempts date back, as a result of the long history of States' use of economic warfare against their political adversaries; a history going back centuries before the adoption of the UN Charter. This also suggests that neither the UN Security Council, nor States and another international organisations acting autonomously, are likely to abandon such practices in the foreseeable future.

This introduction can only deal superficially with the myriad legal issues arising out of States' use of economic sanctions. For further elucidation readers are referred to the individual contributions. These, as might be expected, both deal with different aspects of the subject and do so from a variety of perspectives. The diversity of approaches and conclusions of the contributors, however, only serves to show how contested are the issues which they examine—and how current they are likely to remain.

******

This book has its origin in the 22nd Annual Society of Legal Scholars Subject Section on International Law and British Institute of International and Comparative Law conference on theory and international law, which was held at Charles Clore House on 29 April 2013. The editors, who at the time were the co-convenors of the SLS international law subject section, are grateful to BIICL and its director Professor Robert McCorquodale for their assistance in organising the event. Thanks are also due to our authors for their contributions; to Sinéad Moloney and Emily Braggins at Hart Publishing for bearing with us during the rather long gestation of the project; and to Johannes Hendrik Fahner, PhD candidate at the University of Luxembourg and Matthew Happold's assistant, for his help in editing the contributions.

One of the speakers at the 2013 conference was Professor Vera Gowlland-Debbas, who also kindly agreed to write the preface to this volume. Sadly, Vera passed away before its completion. Accordingly, the editors would like to dedicate the book to her memory.

2

Sanctions and Fundamental Rights of States: The Case of EU Sanctions Against Iran and Syria

ALEXANDER ORAKHELASHVILI

I. INTRODUCTION

THE WIDE-RANGING economic sanctions imposed on Iran and Syria by the UN and EU form part of one of the major legal and political controversies of our time. They also raise important issues of the relationship between general international law and universal and regional collective security mechanisms. Since 2006, both the UN and EU have adopted far-reaching sanctions programmes in relation to Iran, citing Iran's nuclear enrichment programme as a reason. In relation to Syria, where civil war between President Assad's government and rebels erupted in 2011, the UN Security Council has not adopted any resolution imposing sanctions on Syria, while the Council of the EU has imposed its own sanctions on that State.

While the magnitude of political will behind these sanctions cannot be overestimated, their legal foundations are less firm. The sanctions programmes are broad and intrusive in relation to the fundamental rights of the two target States as regards their political and economic development, and also inflict hardship on their populations. Both the legal authority behind, and the legal impact of, these sanctions require comprehensive analysis. Pursuant to this aim, section II of this chapter will focus on the development of the doctrine of the fundamental rights of States in international law, and its modern significance. Section III will describe sanctions imposed by the UN and EU on Iran and Syria. Section IV will discuss the relationship between the fundamental rights of States and the competence of collective security institutions, under Chapter VII of the UN Charter and beyond, and the positions taken on these matters by the UN, the International Atomic Energy Agency (IAEA), EU and Iran itself. Section V will address the legal basis of EU sanctions against Iran and Syria under Chapter VIII of the UN Charter, the EU constituent treaties and general international law. Section VI will then offer general conclusions.

II. THE ESSENCE OF THE FUNDAMENTAL RIGHTS DOCTRINE

A. Doctrinal Aspects

The discourse as to what fundamental rights States have goes back to the early stages of the classical theory of international law. In Vitoria's understanding, there are fundamental rights derived from natural reason that precede the existence of States. In the beginning of the world, when all things were held in common, everyone was allowed to visit and travel through any land, which intercourse was not intended to be suppressed by the establishment of the boundaries between States.[1] However, while the natural reason reinforcing those rights arguably precedes the existence of States, the discourse on these rights effectively draws on how far one State is bound to respect the territorial supremacy and sovereignty of another. Visiting, trading, exploring and travelling inevitably involves crossing national boundaries.

Subsequently the natural law approach embraced the conception of inherent fundamental rights of States derived directly from natural law. The discourse during the eighteenth and nineteenth centuries identified those natural rights as entitlements and prerogatives without which States could not viably exist.[2] The consolidation of the positivist doctrine from the eighteenth century onwards did not result in the denial of the natural law doctrine, but merely re-formulated it to serve the priority of securing the existence and independence of sovereign States and the patterns of their mutual interaction. Natural rights are no longer seen as pre-State, but as State-centred.

As Vattel observed, the State as a moral entity is obliged 'to preserve and perfect itself [which] is the sum of all duties to self', do anything to avoid its own destruction, and also to preserve and protect the lives of its citizens. 'The right to preservation carries with it the right to do whatever is necessary for that purpose, for natural law gives us the right to all those things without which we cannot satisfy our obligations'.[3]

[1] F de Vitoria, *De Indis* (first published 1532), as quoted in A Pagden and J Lawrence, *Francisco de Vitoria—Political Writings* (Cambridge, Cambridge University Press, 1991) 278.

[2] For the discussion of individual writers, see D Aland, *Anzilotti et le droit international public* (Paris, Pedone, 2012) 32.

[3] E de Vattel, *The Law of Nations or the Principles of Natural Law Applied to the Conduct and to the Affairs of Nations and of Sovereigns* in J Brown Scott (ed), *Classics of International Law* Vol 3 (The Carnegie Institute of Washington DC, 1916) 13–14.

In the nineteenth century, William Edward Hall suggested that '[t]he ultimate foundation of international law is an assumption that states possess rights and are subject to duties corresponding to the facts of their postulated nature'.[4] Thus:

> A state has a right to live its life in its own way, so long as it keeps itself rigidly to itself, and refrains from interfering with the equal right of other states to live their life in the manner which commends itself to them, either by its own action, or by lending the shelter of its independence to persons organising armed attack upon the political or social order elsewhere established.[5]

Hall's approach is similar to Vattel's and reflects even more the imperative of the co-existence of independent political communities that exercise territorial sovereignty within their boundaries and choose their own form of political organisation. On this version of the doctrine, fundamental rights give States legal certainty and serve the aim of securing the stability of their peaceful co-existence. Fundamental rights thus become more discursive and interaction-oriented, rather than being a matter for unilateral determination by a State as to what best serves its essential interests and survival.

Furthermore, the fundamental rights doctrine entails the freedom of States to determine their policy priorities in multiple areas, ranging from international economic relations to aspects of strategy and security. According to Hall, '[a] state is enabled to determine what kind and amount of intercourse it will maintain with other countries, … [and] it is permitted to form relations of alliance or of special friendship'.[6] Then,

> a state is free to adopt any commercial policy which it thinks most to its advantage; it may erect fortifications anywhere within its dominions; and it may maintain military or naval forces upon any scale, and organised in any way, that it likes. That the latter measures may invest it with a strategical position or a material strength which under certain contingencies may be a danger to other powers gives them in general no right to take umbrage or to endeavour to restrain its growth. In the absence of distinct menace the only precaution which can be taken is to arm with equal care. It is not an exception to this rule that it is legitimate to anticipate an attack which measures adopted by a state under colour, or in the exercise, of its right of self-development afford reasonable ground to expect. The same right to continued existence which confers the right of self-development confers also the right of self-preservation, and a point exists at which the latter of the two derivative rights takes precedence of the duty to respect the exercise of the former by another state.[7]

[4] W E Hall, *A Treatise on International Law* (Oxford, Clarendon Press, 1895) 45.
[5] Ibid 46.
[6] Ibid 50, 58.
[7] Ibid 46.

No one but the State in question could determine what it could do for the sake of its own self-preservation. Hall was more on the naturalist side of the scholarship,[8] and he captured the essence of the Vattelian foundational aspect of the fundamental rights doctrine. However, both with Vattel and Hall the fundamental rights doctrine was a matter of prioritising some values over others, rather than a consistent jurisprudential doctrine specifying particular rights and obligations. The values prioritised were State-centric, but their legal basis remained ambiguous.

The above uncertainty has been chiefly responsible for the scepticism with which the mainline positivist theory has subsequently approached the fundamental rights doctrine. Anzilotti considered that the doctrine of fundamental rights that precede the international legal order is deprived of a scientific value.[9] Oppenheim conceded that there were 'numerous real rights and duties are customarily recognised which are derived from the very membership of the Family of Nations', such as equality, territorial supremacy, self-preservation, intercourse and non-intervention. However, 'no unanimity exist[ed] with regard to the number, the names, and the contents of these alleged fundamental rights'.[10]

B. Development in Practice

The initial scepticism of the mainline positivist approach, led by Anzilotti and Oppenheim, was not misguided. In terms of the experience that the international legal system had accumulated by the early-twentieth century, the sources of positive law did not contain a clear indication as to the scope of fundamental rights. In the eighteenth and nineteenth centuries, the entire doctrine, and its application in practice, was about the essentially political process of balancing the competing values and interests through ad hoc decisions adopted by and within the European concerts and congresses that possessed a quasi-institutionalised status and authority, reinforced by the role of great powers to maintain the balance of power through interventions. They could be bound by the rights doctrine only on policy terms, but they would selectively apply them and at times override them. Thus, the independence of Switzerland and Belgium was guaranteed, yet Poland's partition was approved. In his a posteriori rationalisation of this process, Hedley Bull has claimed that this process of

[8] See, for detail regarding Hall and other 19th-century authors, A Orakhelashvili, 'The Relevance of Theory and History—The Essence and Origins of International Law' in A Orakhelashvili (ed), *Research Handbook on the Theory and History of International Law* (Cheltenham, Elgar, 2011) 3.

[9] Aland, *Anzilotti et le droit international public* (n 2) 34.

[10] L Oppenheim, *International Law*, Vol 1 (2nd edn, London, Longmans and Co 1912) 165–66.

political management embodied the primacy of the 'international order'—not directly international law—accorded to the survival of the State system over the survival of individual States.[11]

There were some attempts to enshrine the rights doctrine in legal terms. The Aix-La-Chapelle Declaration of the Five Cabinets (Great Britain, Austria, France, Prussia and Russia) of 15 November 1818 proclaimed that:

> The Sovereigns, in forming this august Union, have regarded as its fundamental basis their invariable resolution never to depart, either among themselves, or in their Relations with other States, from the strictest observation of the principles of the Right of Nations; principles, which, in their application to a state of permanent Peace, can alone effectually guarantee the Independence of each Government, and the stability of the general association.[12]

This was an early articulation of the connection of fundamental rights, as legal rights, to peace and security at the international level. However, the Declaration did not specify what those specific rights were; therefore, it showed no major or consistent deviation from the quasi-institutional selective approach that was otherwise prioritised during the eighteenth and nineteenth centuries.

All this illustrates the possibility of different conceptual-normative models. Under one model, fundamental rights are possessed by the system as well as by individual States; and some international agency would balance various rights against each other and decide whether the goals pursued by any particular intervention policy should outweigh the right of States to non-interference with their domestic affairs; or whether the imperatives of international trade and intercourse should prevail over the right of States to determine their foreign economic policies (in which the Opium War and the suppression of the Boxer Rebellion in the nineteenth century were cases in point). Under the alternative model, fundamental rights belong to States as legal rights which other States ought to respect, whether or not they consider their exercise in a particular manner to be desirable. The first model emphasises the community ownership of rights, while the second model emphasises their individual State ownership.

Developments subsequently have witnessed the crystallisation of fundamental rights as part of positive law, operable entirely within the jurisprudential dimension of rights and obligations of States, where the right of one State corresponds to the duties of other States to respect that right. The origins of the modern law on fundamental rights can be traced

[11] H Bull, *The Anarchical Society: A Study of Order in World Politics* (London, Macmillan, 1977) 104–05.

[12] Text in M Hurst (ed), *Key Treaties for the Great Powers 1814–1914* Vol 1 (New York, St Martin's Press, 1972) 147–49.

back to Article 3 of the 1933 Montevideo Convention on the Rights and Duties of States which provides, very much in Vattelian terms, that

> the state has the right to defend its integrity and independence, to provide for its conservation and prosperity, and consequently to organize itself as it sees fit, to legislate upon its interests, administer its services, and to define the jurisdiction and competence of its courts.

Further fundamental rights are the equality of States (Article 4), freedom from outside intervention in internal or external affairs (Article 8) and the inviolability of State territory (Article 11).

The well-known decision of the Permanent Court of International Justice (PCIJ) in the *Lotus* case provided the conceptual basis for grounding the fundamental rights doctrine in the context of that very independence of States which this doctrine seeks to safeguard. The Permanent Court observed that:

> International law governs relations between independent States. The rules of law binding upon States therefore emanate from their own free will as expressed in conventions or by usages generally accepted as expressing principles of law and established in order to regulate the relations between these co-existing independent communities or with a view to the achievement of common aims. Restrictions upon the independence of States cannot therefore be presumed.[13]

This approach enables us to see the fundamental rights of States as owned by their primary bearers. Therefore, international law allows of no prioritisation of values and interests but through agreement between States. Any restriction on States' fundamental rights can only derive from a particular source of international law.

A few years later, Article 3 of the Montevideo Convention seconded that: 'The exercise of these rights has no other limitation than the exercise of the rights of other states according to international law'.[14] In the case on *Nationality Decrees in Morocco*, the PCIJ also stated that: 'The question whether a certain matter is or is not solely within the [domestic] jurisdiction of a State is an essentially relative question; it depends upon the development of international relations', namely on 'the present state of international law'.[15] What this means in practice is that the domestic jurisdiction begins where the scope of validly assumed international obligations ends.

The same conception of fundamental rights was endorsed after the creation of the United Nations. In multiple instances, the position collectively taken by the international community of States has been to factor the doctrine of fundamental rights, as protected by positive international law, into any meaningful concept of peace and security. The UN General Assembly

[13] *The Case of the SS 'Lotus' (France v Turkey)* PCIJ Rep Series A No 10, 18.

[14] The Convention on Rights and Duties of States (adopted 26 December 1933, entered into force 26 December 1933) (Montevideo Convention) 165 LNTS 19.

[15] *Nationality Decrees Issued in Tunis and Morocco* (Advisory Opinion) PCIJ Rep Series B, No 4.

voiced the early position of the UN on this matter in its Resolution 290(IV) of 1 December 1949 on 'Essential of Peace'. According to this resolution, the UN Charter 'lays down basic principles necessary for an enduring peace; that disregard of these principles is primarily responsible for the continuance of international tension' (paragraph 1). States must refrain from threatening or using force contrary to the Charter, 'from any threats or acts, direct or indirect, aimed it impairing the freedom, independence or integrity of any State, or at fomenting civil strife and subverting the will of the people in any State', and 'carry out in good faith its international agreements' (paragraphs 2, 4, 6). Similarly, the 1962 General Assembly resolution on the Permanent Sovereignty over Natural Resources[16] affirms that every State has the right to use their natural resources for the benefit of their own population (paragraph 1), and that the 'Violation of the rights of peoples and nations to sovereignty over their natural wealth and resources is contrary to the spirit and principles of the Charter of the United Nations and hinders ... the maintenance of peace' (paragraph 7). This provides clarification that, despite some doctrinal claims to the contrary,[17] the United Nations system is not meant to prioritise politics over the law and peace over justice.

The 1970 General Assembly Resolution 2625(XXV) 'Declaration on Principles of International Law concerning Friendly Relations and Co-operation among States in accordance with the Charter of the United Nations' (the Friendly Relations Declaration) addresses the fundamental rights doctrine in the context of the sovereign equality of States:

> All States enjoy sovereign equality. They have equal rights and duties and are equal members of the international community, notwithstanding differences of an economic, social, political or other nature.
>
> In particular, sovereign equality includes the following elements:
>
> (a) States are juridically equal;
> (b) Each State enjoys the rights inherent in full sovereignty;
> (c) Each State has the duty to respect the personality of other States;
> (d) The territorial integrity and political independence of the State are inviolable;
> (e) Each State has the right freely to choose and develop its political, social, economic and cultural systems;
> (f) Each State has the duty to comply fully and in good faith with its international obligations and to live in peace with other States.

16 UNGA Res 1803 (1962) GAOR 17th Session Supp, 15.

17 See H Kelsen, 'Collective Security and Collective Self-Defence under the Charter of the United Nations' (1948) 41 *American Journal of International Law* 783, 788–89; T Franck, 'The United Nations as Guarantor of International Peace and Security: Past, Present and Future' in C Tomuschat (ed), *The United Nations at the Age of Fifty: A Legal Perspective* (The Hague, Kluwer, 1995) 25, 26.

Furthermore,

> No State or group of States has the right to intervene, directly or indirectly, for any reason whatever, in the internal or external affairs of any other State. Consequently, armed intervention and all other forms of interference or attempted threats against the personality of the State or against its political, economic and cultural elements, are in violation of international law.

As part of the principle of non-intervention, the Friendly Relations Declaration specifies that:

> No State may use or encourage the use of economic political or any other type of measures to coerce another State in order to obtain from it the subordination of the exercise of its sovereign rights and to secure from it advantages of any kind. Also, no State shall organize, assist, foment, finance, incite or tolerate subversive, terrorist or armed activities directed towards the violent overthrow of the regime of another State, or interfere in civil strife in another State.

The doctrine of fundamental rights thus shaped, including the duty of non-intervention, is part of customary international law, as the International Court of Justice confirmed in relation to US armed assistance to the *Contras* rebel group in Nicaragua.[18]

To sum up, the doctrine of fundamental rights can be conceptualised as a sum of specific fundamental rights; or as a residual freedom beyond the scope of international legal obligations that the State has voluntarily assumed. In either case, the duty to respect entitlements arising out of this doctrine binds States and international organisations as law. The doctrine of fundamental rights as part of positive law is about rights unconditionally owned by States individually, on equal terms; and its operation does not depend on any circumstantial consensus. As Cassese observed, even after the Cold War States are divided by their political and economic systems. The fundamental rights 'represent the fundamental set of standards on which [States] are not divided and which allow a modicum of relatively smooth international dealings'.[19]

III. THE SCOPE OF THE UN AND EU SANCTIONS AGAINST IRAN AND SYRIA

The Iranian nuclear enrichment issue was taken up by the UN Security Council in 2006, resulting in the imposition on Iran of targeted sanctions against individuals allegedly involved in the nuclear enrichment programme, and an arms embargo. In UNSC Resolution 1737 (2006),[20]

[18] *Military and Paramilitary Activities In and Against Nicaragua (Nicaragua v United States)* (Merits) [1986] ICJ Rep 14, 107–08.

[19] A Cassese, *International Law* (2nd edn, Oxford, Oxford University Press, 2005) 48.

[20] UNSC Res 1737 (23 December 2006) UN Doc S/RES/1737.

the Council, invoking Article 41, decided that all States had to take the necessary measures to prevent the supply, sale or transfer to Iran 'of all items, materials, equipment, goods and technology which could contribute to Iran's enrichment-related, reprocessing or heavy water-related activities, or to the development of nuclear weapon delivery systems' (paragraph 3).

UNSC Resolution 1803 (2008) introduced targeted sanctions obliging all States to prevent the entry into or transit through their territories of individuals directly associated with or providing support for Iran's proliferation-sensitive nuclear activities or for the development of nuclear weapon delivery systems (paragraph 5). UNSC Resolution 1929 (2010) prescribes that all States had to prevent the sale or transfer to Iran of 'battle tanks, armoured combat vehicles, large calibre artillery systems, combat aircraft, attack helicopters, warships, missiles or missile systems'.

Initially, the EU began operating on the premise of parallelism as between the UN and EU efforts. The EU Council's Common Position adopted in 2007 took the posture of following the sanctions policy embodied in Resolution 1737 (2007) and initiating EU coercive measures giving effect to it.[21] By a decision adopted on 26 July 2010, the EU Council again, by and large, attempted to follow the position taken by the UN Security Council, but has also introduced sanctions against Iran that went beyond those adopted within the UN system and began encompassing trade between EU members and Iran.[22] Article 17 of this Decision included a rather drastic requirement that:

> Member States, in accordance with their national legal authorities and legislation and consistent with international law, in particular relevant international civil aviation agreements, shall take the necessary measures to prevent access to the airports under their jurisdiction of all cargo flights operated by Iranian carriers or originating from Iran with the exception of mixed passenger and cargo flights.

By its decision adopted on 23 January 2012, the EU Council:

> Recall[ed] the potential connection between Iran's revenues derived from its energy sector and the funding of Iran's proliferation-sensitive nuclear activities and that chemical process equipment and materials required for the petrochemical industry have much in common with those required for certain sensitive nuclear fuel cycle activities, as underlined in UNSCR 1929 (2010), the sale, supply or transfer to Iran of further key equipment and technology which could be used in key sectors in the oil and natural gas industry or, in the petrochemical

[21] Council Common Position 2007/140/CFSP of 27 February 2007 concerning restrictive measures against Iran [2007] OJ L 61/49.

[22] Council Decision 2010/413/CFSP of 26 July 2010 concerning restrictive measures against Iran and repealing Common Position 2007/140/CFSP [2010] OJ L 195/39.

> industry, should be prohibited. Moreover, Member States should prohibit any new investment in the petrochemical sector in Iran.[23]

Under Article 1 of the same Decision,

> Member States shall not enter into any new short-, medium- or long-term commitments to provide financial support for trade with Iran, including the granting of export credits, guarantees or insurance, to their nationals or entities involved in such trade, nor shall Member States guarantee or reinsure such commitments.

This provision has amended a less stringent requirement under Article 8 of the EU Council Decision of 26 July 2010 that had earlier prohibited:

> new short term commitments for public and private provided financial support for trade with Iran, including the granting of export credits, guarantees or insurance, to their nationals or entities involved in such trade, with a view to reducing their outstanding amounts, in particular to avoid any financial support contributing to proliferation-sensitive nuclear activities, or to the development of nuclear weapon delivery systems. In addition, Member States shall not enter into new medium and long-term commitments for public and private provided financial support for trade with Iran.

It is thus obvious that trade restrictions against Iran have become more divorced from the original aim of stalling the nuclear enrichment effort and re-focused on the overall trade and economic relations between Iran and the EU.

Furthering such expansive spirit, the European Union has decreed that further, and qualitatively different, economic and financial sanctions should be applied against Iran, including the ban on financial transactions with the Central Bank, ship-building, maritime transport cooperation and trade in natural gas.[24] It was openly admitted, in the preambular paragraph 5 of the Decision 2012/635, that '[i]n view of Iran's failure to engage seriously in negotiations in order to address international concerns about its nuclear programme, the Council considers it necessary to adopt additional restrictive measures against Iran'. The new sanctions would also cover 'the sale, supply or transfer to Iran of graphite, and raw or semi-finished metals such as aluminium and steel';[25] and '[t]he sale, supply or transfer of key naval equipment and technology for ship-building, maintenance or refit to Iran…, shall be prohibited'.[26] If contrasted with the

[23] Council Decision 2012/35/CFSP of 23 January 2012 amending Decision 2010/413/CFSP concerning restrictive measures against Iran [2012] OJ L 19/22.

[24] Council Decision 2012/635/CFSP of 15 October 2012 amending Decision 2010/413/CFSP concerning restrictive measures against Iran [2012] OJ L 285/58; Council Regulation (EU) No 267/2012 of 23 March 2012 concerning restrictive measures against Iran and repealing Regulation (EU) No 961/2010 [2012] OJ L 88/1.

[25] Council Decision 2012/635/CFSP, Art 1 amending Council Decision 2010/413/CFSP, Art 4.

[26] Ibid Art 1 adding Art 4g to Council Decision 2010/413/CFSP.

scope of underlying UN Security Council resolutions, it is obvious that these trade and economic sanctions are products of the EU's own initiative, not a follow-up to implement the Security Council's decisions.

The European Union's sanctions against Syria began with the adoption of the Decision 2011/273/CFSP, which provides for an arms embargo, a ban on internal repression equipment, restrictions on the admission to the Union and the freezing of funds and economic resources, of certain persons and entities responsible for the violent repression against the civilian population in Syria.[27] Article 1(1) of this Council Decision states:

> The sale, supply, transfer or export of arms and related matériel of all types, including weapons and ammunition, military vehicles and equipment, paramilitary equipment and spare parts for the aforementioned, as well as equipment which might be used for internal repression, to Syria by nationals of Member States or from the territories of Member States or using their flag vessels or aircraft, shall be prohibited, whether originating or not in their territories.

Similar to the developments in relation to Iran, the subsequent Council Regulation (EU) 36/2012 expanded sanctions further.[28] Article 6 of this Council Regulation specifies that:

> It shall be prohibited:
>
> (a) to import crude oil or petroleum products into the Union if they:
> (i) originate in Syria; or
> (ii) have been exported from Syria;
>
> (b) to purchase crude oil or petroleum products which are located in or which originated in Syria;
>
> (c) to transport crude oil or petroleum products if they originate in Syria, or are being exported from Syria to any other country.

The EU measures against Syria have also included an arms embargo. The initial Council Decision, soon after the outbreak of civil war in Syria, provided that:

> The sale, supply, transfer or export of arms and related matériel of all types, including weapons and ammunition, military vehicles and equipment, paramilitary equipment and spare parts for the aforementioned, as well as equipment which might be used for internal repression, to Syria by nationals of Member States or from the territories of Member States or using their flag vessels or aircraft, shall be prohibited, whether originating or not in [the EU member-States'] territories.[29]

[27] Council Decision 2011/273/CFSP of 9 May 2011 concerning restrictive measures against Syria [2011] OJ L 121/11.

[28] Council Regulation (EU) No 36/2012 of 18 January 2012 concerning restrictive measures in view of the situation in Syria and repealing Regulation (EU) No 442/2011 [2012] OJ L 16/1.

[29] Council Decision 2011/273/CFSP of 9 May 2011 concerning restrictive measures against Syria [2011] OJ L 121/11, Art 1.

However at a later stage the EU declined to continue the arms embargo, as part of the political move to back the Syrian National Coalition for Opposition and Revolutionary Forces, which the EU has considered to be 'legitimate representatives of the Syrian people',[30] in their fight against President Assad's government. Accordingly, '[w]ith regard to the possible export of arms to Syria, the Council took note of the commitment by Member States to proceed in their national policies'; and that they 'shall assess the export licence applications on a case-by-case basis'; but 'Member States [would] not proceed at this stage with the delivery of the equipment'.[31]

IV. THE INTERACTION BETWEEN SANCTIONS, THEIR AUTHORITY AND THE FUNDAMENTAL RIGHTS OF STATES

As the law and evidence stands at this moment, the adverse impact of sanctions on Iran's and Syria's fundamental rights is shown through unwarranted and unsubstantiated interferences with their fundamental rights protected both under general international law (related to trade, intercourse and choice of economic policies, especially in relation to natural resources) that, in the absence of some clear legal restriction, both these States are fully entitled to exercise; as well as with Iran's fundamental right under Article IV of the NPT to pursue nuclear enrichment for peaceful purposes.

The conceptual and normative basis on which international institutions can interfere with the exercise of those fundamental rights is far from being doctrinally uncontested. To illustrate, Sir Arthur Watts has suggested that the Security Council manages international affairs in a way similar to the European concerts of great powers in the eighteenth and nineteenth centuries.[32] There are important differences, however. Great power concerts operated without delegated powers and, effectively, without positive law constraints, while modern international institutions possess no authority but one delegated to them by States parties to their constituent instruments.

The delegated nature of the competence of United Nations organs requires identifying a clear legal basis for any action that adversely affects the rights of States. The International Court in *Namibia*, while interpreting the Security Council's powers broadly, was careful to emphasise that

[30] Council Decision 2013/186/CFSP of 22 April 2013 amending Decision 2012/739/CFSP concerning restrictive measures against Syria [2013] OJ L 111/101, preambular para 3.

[31] Council Declaration on Syria, 3241st Foreign Affairs Council meeting, Brussels, 27 May 2013, para 2; see also press release regarding the 3241st Council meeting, PRESSE 211, PR CO 27, Brussels, 27–28 May 2013.

[32] Sir A Watts, 'The Importance of International Law' in M Byers (ed), *The Role of Law in International Politics* (Oxford, Oxford University Press, 2000) 5, 11.

the Council is subject to certain legal standards that prominently include fundamental rights of States forming part of the purposes and principles of the UN Charter.[33] Similarly, the ICTY Appeals Chamber in *Tadic* stated that the Council is not *legibus solutus* (unbound by law).[34]

It seems that, owing to its subjection to Articles 1 and 2 of the UN Charter, the Security Council is bound by all fundamental rights all the time and in all circumstances. There is only one exception to that position. The principle of non-intervention is one that serves as a legal limitation on the policies of States as well as of the principal organs of the UN, unless the Security Council takes action under Chapter VII, as Article 2(7) of the Charter specifies. However, the least that is required to achieve this effect is that the relevant exercise of the Chapter VII authority must otherwise be in accordance with the systemic and substantive requirements of the Charter.

Much as the Security Council possesses a wide margin of discretion under Chapter VII, it is still subjected to international legal limitations. Judge ad hoc Sir Robert Jennings clearly adopted such view in the *Lockerbie* case (Libya v US and UK) before the International Court of Justice, stating that:

> all discretionary powers of lawful decision-making are necessarily derived from the law, and are therefore governed and qualified by the law. This must be so if only because the sole authority of such decisions flows itself from the law. It is not logically possible to claim to represent the power and authority of the law and, at the same time, claim to be above the law.[35]

As Higgins also persuasively clarifies, the Security Council's political character does not place it above international law, but merely provides the room for its 'political operation *within* the law'.[36] This is sufficient to dispel the doctrinal and policy temptation to view the process of operation of the Security Council under Chapter VII as a purely political process of the exercise of discretion, divorced from its sole proper basis which is the treaty-based delegation of powers from the Member States.

Instead, Chapter VII is one single structural whole that requires a series of criteria to be satisfied before the validity of its use can be properly ascertained. Under Chapter VII, a necessary precondition for imposing

[33] *Legal Consequences for States of the Continued Presence of South Africa in Namibia (South West Africa) notwithstanding Security Council Resolution 276 (1970)* (Advisory Opinion) [1971] ICJ Rep 16, 50–52.

[34] *Prosecutor v Tadíc* (Decision on the Defence Motion for Interlocutory Appeal on Jurisdiction) ICTY-94-1, paras 20–28 (Appeals Chamber Decision, 2 October 1995).

[35] *Questions of Interpretation and Application of the 1971 Montreal Convention arising from the Aerial Incident at Lockerbie (Libyan Arab Jamahiriya v United Kingdom)* [1998] ICJ Rep 9, 110 (Jennings diss op).

[36] R Higgins, 'The Place of International Law in the Settlement of Disputes by the Security Council' (1970) 64 *American Journal of International Law* 1, 16 (emphasis in original).

sanctions on any State is that the Security Council identifies the existence of a 'threat to the peace' in the underlying conduct or situation as required by Article 39, and then proceeds to impose economic or other measures under Article 41 to restore international peace and security. The Council must transparently and intelligibly—that is expressly (to say the least)—demonstrate which facts, situations and circumstances on the ground involve a' threat' for the purposes of Article 39.

The analysis of the relevant Security Council resolutions compellingly evidences that this principal statutory requirement has not been met. The Security Council's handling of the Iranian nuclear issue is, as a whole, marked by a rather nebulous treatment of the issue of whether that situation involves a threat to the peace warranting application of Chapter VII measures. UNSC Resolution 1696 (2006) speaks of nuclear proliferation risks. The Security Council goes very near to the ambit of Article 39 but does not cross its boundaries by specifying that these risks constitute a 'threat'. The Security Council was thus conscious that this was not a valid case of the use of Article 39.

UNSC Resolution 1737 (2006), imposing sanctions on Iran to address its non-compliance with international demands to freeze its uranium enrichment programme, refers, in its preambular paragraphs, to the concerns expressed by the IAEA regarding Iran's nuclear programmes. The Council's entire reasoning is based on the concern not that Iran has actually been doing anything problematic, but that it failed to prove that it has not been so doing to the Council's satisfaction. The problems identified were that certain Iranian nuclear programmes '*could* have a military nuclear dimension' and that 'Iran has not established full and sustained suspension' of its presumed activities. That said, the resolution does not specify what Iranian conduct constitutes the 'threat to the peace'. The subsequent resolution 1803 (2008) does not identify a 'threat to the peace' either. It notes with concern that 'Iran has not established full and sustained suspension of all enrichment related and reprocessing activities and heavy water-related projects as set out in UNSC Resolutions 1696 (2006), 1737 (2006), and 1747 (2007)', is concerned 'by the proliferation risks presented by the Iranian nuclear programme,' and then moves straight to Article 41 of the Charter to impose further sanctions. Unfortunately, this resolution did not take the matter beyond the area of speculation and allegations either. The most recent Security Council Resolution 1929 (2010) likewise restates presumptive statements from previous resolutions and relies on the lack of Iran's 'cooperation with the IAEA under the Additional Protocol', and the presumptive need 'to exclude the possibility of military dimensions of Iran's nuclear programme'.

The principal cause of the Security Council's involvement with the Iranian nuclear enrichment issue is a divergence of views between Iran, the IAEA and the UN over the scope of Iran's obligations regarding the use of nuclear energy, more specifically Iran's decision in 2007 to revert to the old Code 3.1 of its Safeguards Agreement with the IAEA.[37] The new Agreement had been accepted by Iran in 2003, but not yet ratified by its parliament. The Agency's position was that Code 3.1 could not be modified unilaterally, and that: 'The Agency's right to verify design information provided to it is a continuing right, which is not dependent on the stage of construction of, or the presence of nuclear material at, a facility'.[38] The matter thus turned on two legal questions: whether Iran was already bound by the unratified agreement; and, if so, whether Iran could modify it unilaterally.

Security Council Resolution 1803 (2008) took a clear position on this matter. In its preamble, the Council noted 'with concern that Iran has taken issue with the IAEA's right to verify design information which had been provided by Iran pursuant to the modified Code 3.1', and then reiterated the IAEA's finding above.[39] The Council's entire approach is framed as a legal argument, which is then used to justify action under Chapter VII. However, while treating alleged violations of the NPT as a cause of action, it is not certain that the Council has used the proper standard of proof to ascertain the existence of a breach of that treaty, relying instead on presumptive concerns rather than established facts.

Iran's position is that 'international peace and security cannot be threatened by a peaceful and transparent nuclear program'.[40] Iran has pointed out the inconsistencies in position as between the IAEA and the Security Council as to whether Iran was in compliance with relevant legal requirements. In 2012, Iran alleged that the IAEA was seen to contradict

[37] Statement of the IAEA Legal Adviser to the Meeting of the Board of Governors, March 2009, para 1

[38] *Implementation of the NPT Safeguards Agreement and Relevant Provisions of Security Council Resolutions in the Islamic Republic of Iran*, GOV/2007/22, 23 May 2007, paras 12–14.

[39] For the Iran-IAEA Safeguards Agreement, see INFCIRC/214, 13 December 1974. The scope of Iran's pertinent obligations has been described in the IAEA Director General's report: 'The Subsidiary Arrangements General Part in force with Iran from 1976 to 26 February 2003 included what was, until 1992, standard text which called for provision to the Agency of design information on a new facility no later than 180 days before the introduction of nuclear material into the facility, and the provision of information on a new LOF [location outside facility] together with the report relating to the receipt of nuclear material at the LOF. With the acceptance by Iran on 26 February 2003 of the modifications to the Subsidiary Arrangements proposed by the Agency, the Subsidiary Arrangements General Part now requires Iran to inform the Agency of new nuclear facilities and modifications to existing facilities through the provision of preliminary design information as soon as the decision to construct, to authorize construction or to modify has been taken, and to provide the Agency with further design information as it is developed. Information is to be provided early in the project definition, preliminary design, construction and commissioning phases'. *Implementation of the NPT Safeguards agreement in the Islamic Republic of Iran*, GOV/2003/40, 6 June 2003, para 15.

[40] *Communication dated 22 March 2012 received from the Permanent Mission of the Islamic Republic of Iran to the Agency regarding the Report of the Director General on the Implementation of Safeguards in Iran*, INFCIRC/837, 30 March 2012, para 25(f).

its previous positions when it stated that it saw no dual-use materials at the relevant sites when these were visited, there were no indications of nuclear material being used and no unusual activities were observed.[41]

In its Explanatory Note presented to the IAEA Director-General, Iran expressly submitted that the relevant Security Council resolutions contradicted the basic principles of the UN Charter, and thus violated Iran's fundamental rights.[42] Any valid limitation on Iran's right to pursue its own development in economic and energy spheres could only be inferred from the rules of international law to which Iran has freely consented. The relevant international legal instruments are the 1968 Nuclear Non-Proliferation Treaty (NPT) and the Safeguards Agreement concluded between Iran and the IAEA.

Article 4 of the NPT confirms 'the inalienable right of all the Parties to the Treaty to develop research, production and use of nuclear energy for peaceful purposes'. However, in 2006, the IAEA demanded of Iran the 'full and sustained suspension of all enrichment-related and reprocessing activities, including research and development, to be verified by the Agency'.[43] The IAEA also demanded that Iran provide further transparency measures which it acknowledged 'extend beyond the formal requirements of the Safeguards Agreement and Additional Protocol'.[44] This demand was then supported by the Security Council in its Resolution 1737 (2007). The Security Council demanded, in blanket terms, that Iran suspend without delay:

> all enrichment-related and reprocessing activities, including research and development, to be verified by the IAEA; and work on all heavy water-related projects, including the construction of a research reactor moderated by heavy water, also to be verified by the IAEA.

According to Iran, requiring the suspension of peaceful nuclear activities breaches Iran's rights to development, to the use of its natural resources and self-determination, and broadly violates the principle of non-interference with States' domestic affairs.[45] On its face, it appears that the IAEA and Security Council take issue with Iran's Article 4 of the NPT right and seek to trump them through reliance on Article 103 of the UN Charter.[46] However, doubts arise as to whether their resolutions are intra vires (due to the lack of the Security Council's proper use of Article 39).

[41] Ibid 14–15.

[42] Ibid 7.

[43] *Implementation of the NPT Safeguards Agreement in the Islamic Republic of Iran Resolution adopted on 4 February 2006*, GOV/2006/14, 4 February 2006, operative para 1.

[44] Ibid.

[45] INFCIRC/837 (n 40) para 25(f).

[46] Under Art 103, 'In the event of a conflict between the obligations of the Members of the United Nations under the present Charter and their obligations under any other international agreement, their obligations under the present Charter shall prevail'.

Furthermore, Article 103 does not extend to the rights of States, but only to their obligations in conflict with the Charter[47] (and presumably with decisions validly premised on the Charter), and therefore the provision cannot be used to trump Iran's rights under Article IV of the NPT.

Iran's own position is that 'the [IAEA] should not [take] arbitrary step beyond its statutory and legal mandate in preparing its reports by failing to base its assessments and comments on concrete obligations of States', and that 'Iran's peaceful nuclear activities have unlawfully been put on the agenda of the UNSC'. The Security Council has adopted politically motivated resolutions and the IAEA's further requests stemming from those resolutions are illegitimate and unacceptable.[48]

As for the scope of its legal obligations, Iran's position is that it is fully implementing the relevant safeguards in accordance with the Safeguards Agreement. With regard to the Additional Protocol providing for more enhanced supervision, '[i]t is not acceptable that a voluntary instrument is turned into a legal obligation'.[49] Furthermore, and '[a]s the sovereignty right, Iran has not yet ratified the Additional Protocol and therefore is not obliged to implement it'.[50] Iran had not signed the Modified Code 3.1 of the Safeguards Agreement until 2003, and considers that it was not required to declare the site of Natanz Enrichment Plant before 2003, because the site received no nuclear material before 2003.[51] The Iranian Government's position is that:

> Iran was voluntarily implementing the modified code 3.1 of the Subsidiary Arrangements since 2003, but suspended its implementation pursuant to the illegal UNSC resolutions against Iran's peaceful nuclear activities. ... Iran is not obliged to implement modified code 3.1 and Iran has adhered to its obligations to provide design information in proper timing.[52]

All the above clearly demonstrates that sanctions against Iran operate near the thin red line that separates legal activities covered by the doctrine of fundamental rights by the Non-Proliferation Treaty from unlawful activities prohibited by the same Treaty. As the Security Council has from the outset treated this as a legal issue, the proper burden of proof had to be discharged before it can be ascertained whether sanctions target Iran's lawful activities or its violations of the NPT. Precise aspects of violations of international law suitable for a collective security action relate to whether the NPT and the Safeguards Agreement have been breached; and

[47] As was clearly articulated by the ECtHR in *Al-Jedda v UK* (GC) (2011) 53 EHRR 23, para 101.

[48] INFCIRC/837 (n 40) 4.

[49] Ibid 5–6.

[50] *Communication dated 12 September 2013 received from the Permanent Mission of the Islamic Republic of Iran to the Agency regarding the Report of the Director General on the Implementation of Safeguards in Iran*, INFCIRC/854, 26 September 2013, para 75.

[51] INFCIRC/837 (n 40) 15.

[52] INFCIRC/854 (n 50) para 85.

whether the shift in the burden of proof is a suitable and sufficient basis for a collective security action to follow.

The reality is that a 'threat to the peace' has never been properly identified, nor has a violation of Iran's international obligations that could properly sustain an Article 39 determination. At the least, this shows that a cause of action is lacking, and the sanctions are therefore ultra vires, both objectively and in terms of the Security Council's own awareness. Similarly, the prevailing opinion in State practice representing the view of the majority of States in the international community is that the Iranian nuclear enrichment issue should be handled through the IAEA, not through the Security Council.[53]

V. LEGAL BASIS OF EU SANCTIONS AND COLLECTIVE SECURITY FRAMEWORKS

A. Chapter VIII of the UN Charter

As is clear from the EU's relevant instruments, the cause of action on which the EU claims to premise its sanctions against Iran is one relating to Iranian nuclear enrichment and has already been identified as such, albeit inconsistently, by the UN Security Council. As for the Syria sanctions, the EU has itself identified the civil war in Syria as the basis for its own sanctions. A number of EU measures against Iran and Syria do not replicate pre-existing UN Security Council's decisions but constitute instances of the exercise of the EU's independent judgement as to what responses are adequate or necessary to the civil war in Syria or the nuclear enrichment programme in Iran. It is similarly, and plainly, obvious that the EU's handling of the issue of arms supply to Syria has been developed in response to its decision to take the rebels' side in the civil war, and is therefore premised on the violation of the principle of non-intervention without the Security Council having authorised any such interference pursuant to Articles 2(7) and 39 of the UN Charter.

[53] For views of most States as expressed through regional organisations such as the Organisation of Islamic Conference and the Non-Aligned Movement, see OIC/SUMMIT-11/2008/FC/Final, para 83; see also OIC Resolution No 9/11-P(IS), Dakar Summit, 13–14 March 2008, paras 3–4; Declaration of the 33rd Islamic Conference of Foreign Ministers, Baku, 19–21 June 2006, para 12; NAM Statement on the Islamic Republic of Iran's nuclear issue, Havana, 11–16 September 2006, para 2, S/2006/1018, para 3; Ministerial Meeting of the Coordinating Bureau of the Non-Aligned Movement, Final Document, Putrajaya, Malaysia, 27–30 May 2006, para 91; reaffirmed in identical terms in the NAM Statement on the Islamic Republic of Iran's Nuclear Issue, 15th Ministerial Conference, Tehran, 27–30 July 2008, paras 3, 8.

An additional problem is that the EU sanctions against Iran are qualitatively different from (that is, wider than) the UN-imposed sanctions and encompass a variety of economic relations between Iran and the international community, giving rise to significant adverse effects on the Iranian population. Thus, even if the UN sanctions as such were lawful, a separate legal problem arises as to whether the EU can supplement them by additional, and qualitatively different, sanctions of its own. The damage that sanctions cause to target States and their populations, directly or incidentally, can be very far-reaching and can only be justified to the extent that the legal framework of collective security allows for them.

Taking UN sanctions against Libya in 1990s as an example, the measures, which primarily consisted of an air embargo under Resolutions 748 (1992) and 883 (1993), caused the nearly crippling damage to the country's agricultural sector and of its medical sector. Farmers and agricultural cooperatives were unable to export their surplus production, which would usually have been shipped by air. Libya has asserted that financial losses amounted to $710,777,777. It was not possible to import fruit seedlings for planting out in conditions allowing for them to be protected against plant diseases. The country's plans and programmes for development of the animal health sector through the establishment of veterinary units and clinics in various areas were also crippled, since the supplies could no longer be shipped in by air freight.[54] Sanctions seriously disrupted the operation in Libya of the global child immunisation programme run by the WHO by making it difficult to obtain vaccines; reduced the effect of vaccines due to spoilage, as they were transported overland instead of by air; impeded the medical procurement programme; and prevented ambulance aircraft from being repaired and made serviceable.[55] The UN Fact-Finding Mission on sanctions against Libya further stated that:

> Although the air embargo did not apply to domestic air travel, the restrictions on the purchase of aircraft, spare parts, navigational and landing equipment and on training and certification of pilots and other crew had reduced the number of airworthy aircraft and curtailed domestic air travel. That had placed restrictions on the ability of Libyans to respond to humanitarian emergencies ... The most adverse impact of the air embargo had been on the health sector, for it had restricted emergency medical evacuation both within and outside the country.[56]

[54] *Sixth Comprehensive Report on Damage Caused by the Implementation of Security Council Resolutions 748 (1992) and 883 (1993) during the Period from 15 April 1992 to 31 December 1995*, S/1996/717, 4 September 1996, 5, 7–8.

[55] *Damage Caused by the Implementation of Security Council Resolutions 748 (1992) and 883 (1993) during the Period from 15 April 1992 to 5 April 1999*, S/2000/243.

[56] UNYB 1998, 157; see also text of the report in S/1998/201.

While limited sanctions can entail such wide-ranging effects, more comprehensive sanctions adopted by the EU against Syria and Iran, encompassing a multitude of economic, financial and trade relations, have an even greater potential adversely to affect the civilian population.

It is obvious that comprehensive economic sanctions in the cases of Iraq, Yugoslavia or Haiti did not bring the desired political or economic effects. The humanitarian disaster inflicted on Iraq in the 1990s was all too obvious. The Iraqi population was left without the means of subsistence and nutrition, and just as in Haiti, the black market flourished. Sanctions were effectively a collective punishment of the Iraqi people. Despite being aimed at inducing the populations of Iraq and Yugoslavia to put pressure on their governments, sanctions profoundly failed to bring about that result.[57]

An increasing acknowledgement of the futility of comprehensive economic sanctions led to a growing recognition that a better way of handling crises and conflicts would consist in adopting targeted sanctions aimed at relevant government officials, military commanders and other related persons, including members and affiliates of terrorist organisations, rather than at States and their populations as such. By and large, the initial UN sanctions against Iran under the above-discussed Security Council resolutions had such targeted character. What we have seen with the EU measures against Iran and Syria is a return to the practice of comprehensive economic sanctions, not, this time, posed by the UN but by the EU acting independently.

Article 53 of Chapter VIII of the UN Charter provides that the Security Council can utilise 'regional arrangements or agencies for enforcement action under its authority. But no enforcement action shall be taken under regional arrangements or by regional agencies without the authorisation of the Security Council'. Therefore, the EU can be used to give further effect to coercive measures that the UN Security Council has already adopted under Chapter VII. However, it is not allowed to resort, on its own initiative, to coercive measures that are qualitatively different from those adopted within the UN system. It is the Security Council only and exclusively which can judge the issues arising out of the operation of Articles 39 and 41 of the Charter. In relation to its economic sanctions

[57] M Bennouna, 'Les sanctions économiques des Nations Unies' (2002) 300 *Recueil des Cours* 9, 40–42. It is also pointed out that 'the "theory" behind economic sanctions is that economic pressure on civilians will translate into pressure on the Government for change. This "theory" is bankrupt both legally and practically, as more and more evidence testifies to the inefficacy of comprehensive economic sanctions as a coercive tool'; M Bossuyt, 'The Adverse Consequences of Economic Sanctions on the Enjoyment of Human Rights' Working paper, E/CN.4/Sub.2/2000/33, 9. The House of Lords Report adopts a similar approach: HL Select Committee on Economic Affairs, *The Impact of Economic Sanctions* (HL 2006–07, 96–I) para 130.

against Iran and Syria, the EU has certainly not been utilised by the UN Security Council under Article 53.

B. EU Treaties

The legal basis for the EU sanctions against Iran and Syria is not conclusively clear under the EU's own legal framework either, especially when the EU acts in defiance of the UN Charter. The above-mentioned EU instruments that introduce sanctions are unclear as to their legal basis under EU law, let alone under international law. The EU Treaty contains certain provisions to that effect, such as Article 215, which envisages the interruption of economic relations with third States:

> Where a decision, adopted in accordance with Chapter 2 of Title V of the Treaty on European Union, provides for the interruption or reduction, in part or completely, of economic and financial relations with one or more third countries, the Council, acting by a qualified majority on a joint proposal from the High Representative of the Union for Foreign Affairs and Security Policy and the Commission, shall adopt the necessary measures. It shall inform the European Parliament thereof.

Furthermore, Article 24 addresses the EU measures in furtherance of the Union's strategic interests:

> (1) Within the framework of the principles and objectives of its external action, the Union shall conduct, define and implement a common foreign and security policy, based on the development of mutual political solidarity among Member States, the identification of questions of general interest and the achievement of an ever-increasing degree of convergence of Member States' actions
>
> (2) The Member States shall support the Union's external and security policy actively and unreservedly in a spirit of loyalty and mutual solidarity and shall comply with the Union's action in this area.

However, it is not obvious whether the clauses reproduced above provide for the independent competence of the EU to decide what kind of coercive sanctions should be adopted in relation to a particular crisis. In the first place, the EU provisions have to be read in line with Article 53 of the UN Charter which, pursuant to Article 103 of the UN Charter, prevails over the obligations of EU Member States under the EU's constituent instruments. Under this approach, if measures adopted under the EU treaties are enforcement measures and are unsupported by the authorisation from the UN Security Council, the EU Member States—all of which are also parties to the UN Charter—are no longer meant to uphold those EU measures. The conclusion thus must follow that at this level the EU treaties do not provide a legal basis for the EU's economic, trade and financial measures against Iran and Syria.

C. Legal Basis Under General International Law

An alternative basis on which one might defend the EU measures against Iran is under the law governing countermeasures as part of State responsibility. The UN International Law Commission (ILC) has observed that countermeasures are:

> measures that would otherwise be contrary to the international obligations of an injured State *vis-à-vis* the responsible State, if they were not taken by the former in response to an internationally wrongful act by the latter in order to procure cessation and reparation. Countermeasures are a feature of a decentralized system by which injured States may seek to vindicate their rights and to restore the legal relationship with the responsible State which has been ruptured by the internationally wrongful act.[58]

As ILC's Article 49 on State responsibility suggests, '[c]ountermeasures shall, as far as possible, be taken in such a way as to permit the resumption of performance of the obligations in question'. This could arguably be seen as reflective of the EU's claim that it is seeking to persuade the Iranian Government to comply with its international obligations in the area of nuclear non-proliferation. However, this conclusion is nullified by the ILC's another observation that '[a] fundamental prerequisite for any lawful countermeasure is the existence of an internationally wrongful act which injured the State taking the countermeasure'.[59] The key requirement thus is to identify which international legal obligations Iran allegedly has breached in relation to the EU, that the latter's coercive measures seeks to vindicate.

However, it is unclear on what basis the EU could have any standing here, for it is difficult to identify the initial wrongful act committed by Iran against the EU. Iran's breach of the 1968 Non-Proliferation Treaty has not been plausibly established and neither the IAEA nor the Security Council have so far definitively pronounced on that issue. Nor can the EU be seen as an injured party in relation to Iran's breach of the Safeguards Agreement, because these are operative as between Iran and the IAEA. Thus, general international law provides no legitimating basis for the EU measures.

On a broader plane, Chapter VII sanctions adopted by the UN Security Council differ in their essence from countermeasures. Much as Chapter VII sanctions are often adopted against a State which has committed an internationally wrongful act that a 'threat to the peace' almost inevitably

[58] Report of the International Law Commission on the work of its Fifty-Third Session (23 April–1 June and 2 July–10 August 2001) UN Doc A/56/10 reproduced in (2001) II(2) *Ybk ILC* 128.

[59] Ibid 130.

involves, they do not necessarily involve a reciprocal violation of international obligations towards the target State. The area to which Chapter VII applies covers both inter-State relations deriving from legal obligations of States and those that could arise out of States' discretionary choices. The imposition of an arms embargo would not, in the absence of an arms supply treaty between the States concerned, involve a violation of international law towards the target State. The same applies to economic sanctions and boycotts, as under general international law no State is obliged to sell to or purchase any sort of goods from anyone. The impact of the Security Council's injunction against doing so is to transform a matter of national policy choice into that of a legal prohibition ultimately derivable from the Charter. Similarly, there is no inherent legal obstacle to the EU introducing an arms embargo against Syria; and, moreover, its introduction could be motivated by the desire to refrain from interfering with an internal armed conflict. However, the EU's subsequent failure to renew the embargo and its 'nationalisation' of the matter approves a policy permitting individual EU Member States to violate the principle of non-intervention at their discretion.

Article 103 confirms the above approach. If Chapter VII sanctions are simply countermeasures, their legality could be sustained by the law of State responsibility alone. The difference Article 103 is meant to make is to provide a justification to Member States implementing Chapter VII sanctions towards a target State even in violation of treaties in force, where the target State has not committed an internationally wrongful act towards the State implementing the Chapter VII measures. No need for such a safeguard arises as regards coercive measures that can be defended as countermeasures.

The purpose of Chapter VII sanctions is different from countermeasures under the law of State responsibility also in the sense that their purpose is to coordinate a collective response to matters of common concern as identified by the Security Council, not to avenge a previous breach in the interest of particular States. The necessity and proportionality of Chapter VII sanctions is, correspondingly, not the same as that of countermeasures; the calculus of necessity and proportionality should be determined by no one other than the Security Council.

It therefore appears that the measures adopted by the EU against Iran and Syria are generically and qualitatively different from countermeasures that international law permits a State to adopt in response to a previous internationally wrongful act and in the absence of a previous Security Council determination. Even under the law of countermeasures, one is tempted to observe that some discrepancies persist in the case of EU sanctions against Iran and Syria. As the International Law Commission observed, '[c]ountermeasures are more likely to satisfy the requirements of necessity and proportionality if they are taken in relation to the same or a closely related obligation'.[60] How proportionate sanctions targeting Iran's Central Bank, civil aviation and ship-building sectors, or the overall trade between Iran and EU States, or even sanctions in relation to oil and gas, could be in relation to nuclear non-proliferation is highly questionable.

The conclusion that compels itself is that by imposing comprehensive economic sanctions against Iran and Syria, and by its handling the Syria arms embargo issue, the EU has sought to arrogate to itself a competence available exclusively to the UN Security Council under Articles 39 and 41 of Chapter VII of the UN Charter. The imposition of sanctions other than those that can be justified as countermeasures is premised on the determination of a 'threat to the peace' under Article 39 of the UN Charter, and the subsequent calculation of the necessity and proportionality of the imposed measures under its Article 41, on which both issues the Security Council has the exclusive authority to decide. The Council of the European Union has no authority to make decisions on either of those matters. In addition, and unlike the Security Council's Chapter VII measures, the EU sanctions are not supported by Articles 25 and 103 of the UN Charter, which permit the overriding of contrary international obligations.

VI. CONCLUSION

The above analysis has demonstrated that both UN and EU sanctions against Iran and Syria constitute unwarranted interferences with the two States' fundamental rights under general international law and the United Nations Charter, such as their freedom from external intervention in their domestic affairs, and their freedom to conduct their economic policies, including the administration of their natural resources. In relation to Iran, the agenda pursued both by the Security Council and the EU also purports to override Iran's fundamental rights conferred to it under Article IV of the NPT. The act of lifting the arms embargo against Syria similarly constitutes a violation of the duty not to intervene in Syria's internal affairs by taking sides in the internal armed conflict in that country. Against this background, the sanctions imposed by the two organisations involve violations of legal standards that bind them both as conditions for their exercise of their delegated powers, and are therefore based on decisions that exceed the authority of both organisations (ultra vires). The lack of their lawfulness is obvious in the light of both their constituent instruments and of general international law.

[60] Ibid 128.

3

Unilateral European Sanctions as Countermeasures: The Case of the EU Measures Against Iran

PIERRE-EMMANUEL DUPONT

I. INTRODUCTION

THE PRESENT CHAPTER seeks to assess the lawfulness under international law of the economic measures targeting the Islamic Republic of Iran (Iran) agreed by EU Member States in early 2012.[1] It thus concerns measures enacted unilaterally by EU countries, albeit in the framework of a regional organisation (the EU) in a situation where the targeted country has already been the object of sanctions adopted by the UN Security Council pursuant to Chapter VII of the UN Charter.[2]

[1] At the time of editing, the situation is evolving swiftly and significantly as regards the various sanctions regimes in force against Iran. On 14 July 2015, following months of negotiations the group of E3/EU+3 (China, France, Germany, Russia, the United Kingdom and the United States, with assistance of the EU) and Iran reached agreement on a 'Joint Comprehensive Plan of Action' (JCPOA) designed to ensure that Iran's nuclear programme will be exclusively peaceful. The JCPOA provides for the 'comprehensive lifting of all UN Security Council sanctions as well as multilateral and national sanctions related to Iran's nuclear programme, including steps on access in areas of trade, technology, finance, and energy' (JCPOA, preamble), according to a timeline sequence specified in the JCPOA. Para 19 of the JCPOA provides that '[t]he EU will terminate all provisions of the EU Regulation, [...], implementing all nuclear-related economic and financial sanctions, [...], simultaneously with the IAEA-verified implementation of agreed nuclear-related measures by Iran [...] which cover all sanctions and restrictive measures in [inter alia] Import and transport of Iranian oil, petroleum products, gas and petrochemical products'. Assuming that both sides abide by their commitments under the JCPOA, the EU measures examined in this chapter shall now belong to history, which in no way affects the importance of the underlying legal questions as to the validity of such measures under international law.

[2] These UN Security Council Resolutions are Res 1696 (31 July 2006) UN Doc S/Res/1696; Res 1737 (23 December 2006) UN Doc S/Res/1737; Res 1747 (24 March 2007) UN Doc S/Res/1747; Res 1803 (3 March 2008) UN Doc S/Res/1803; Res 1835 (27 September 2008) UN Doc S/Res/1835; and Res 1929 (9 June 2010) UN Doc S/Res/1929. For a comprehensive analysis of Res 1737 and Res 1929, see eg D H Joyner, 'The Security Council as a Legal

In general, EU sanctions (the official term used by the EU institutions is 'restrictive measures') are adopted within the framework of the Common Foreign and Security Policy (CFSP),[3] and their stated purpose is 'to bring about a change in policy or activity by the target country, part of country, government, entities or individuals, in line with the objectives set out in the Common Position'.[4] On 23 January 2012, following intense negotiations between the EU Member States and their international partners, mainly the United States,[5] the European Council adopted a set of additional restrictive measures against Iran. The conclusions adopted by the Council provide that:

> [t]he Council has agreed additional restrictive measures in the energy sector, including a phased embargo of Iranian crude oil imports to the EU, in the financial sector, including against the Central Bank of Iran, in the transport sector as well as further export restrictions, notably on gold and on sensitive dual-use goods and technology, as well as additional designations of persons and entities, including several controlled by the Islamic Revolutionary Guards Corps (IRGC).[6]

As regards measures targeting Iran's oil or gas sector, the Council went into the following detail:

> The Council banned imports of Iranian crude oil and petroleum products. The prohibition concerns import, purchase and transport of such products as well as related finance and insurance. Already concluded contracts can still be executed until 1 July 2012. A review of the measures relating to oil and petroleum products will take place before 1 May 2012.

Hegemon' (2012) 43 *Georgetown Journal of International Law* 225, 238–48. For general background on the Iranian nuclear controversy, see eg S N Kile (ed), *Europe and Iran. Perspectives on Nonproliferation* (Oxford, Oxford University Press, 2005); S N Kile, 'Nuclear Arms Control and Non-proliferation' in *SIPRI Yearbook 2009. Armaments, Disarmament and International Security* (Oxford, Oxford University Press, 2009) 387 ff; S N Kile, 'Nuclear Arms Control and Non-proliferation' in *SIPRI Yearbook 2011. Armaments, Disarmament and International Security* (Oxford, Oxford University Press, 2011) 3811 ff; P-E Dupont, 'The EU-Iran Dialogue in the Context of the Nuclear Crisis' (2009) 3 *Central European Journal of International and Security Studies*, 97–112; N Jansen Calamita, 'Sanctions, Countermeasures, and the Iranian Nuclear Issue' (2009) 42 *Vanderbilt Journal of Transnational Law* 1393–42.

[3] For precedents in EU/EC practice, see L-A Sicilianos, 'Countermeasures in Response to Grave Violations of Obligations Owed to the International Community' in J Crawford, A Pellet and S Olleson (eds), *The Law of International Responsibility* (Oxford, Oxford University Press, 2010) 1137, 1141.

[4] Council of the EU, 'Guidelines on implementation and evaluation of restrictive measures (sanctions) in the framework of the EU Common Foreign and Security Policy', 2 December 2005, para 4.

[5] See eg 'EU Discussing Plan to Start Iran Oil Ban on July 1' *Reuters*, 17 January 2012; 'EU States Agree in Principle to Sanction Iran Central Bank' *Reuters*, 18 January 2012.

[6] Council of the EU, 'Council conclusions on Iran' (3142th Foreign Affairs Council meeting, Brussels, 23 January 2012) para 2.

In addition, the Council outlawed imports of petrochemical products from Iran into the EU as well as the export of key equipment and technology for this sector to Iran. New investment in petrochemical companies in Iran as well as joint ventures with such enterprises are also no more allowed.[7]

The measures took the form of a Council Decision 2012/35/CFSP of 23 January 2012, amending Decision 2010/413/CFSP concerning restrictive measures against Iran.[8] The central feature of the Decision is the prohibition on 'the purchase, import or transport from Iran of crude oil and petroleum products, as well as of petrochemical products'. Among the other significant measures contained in the Decision, the most important is the freezing of assets of the Central Bank of Iran, which is a consequence of its inclusion in the list in Annex I to the Decision.

On a technical level, the Decision has been followed by a Council Regulation of 23 March 2012, passed to implement certain of the additional measures.[9] It provides for some amendments to existing measures as well as clarifications as to the scope of the measures. Regarding the oil embargo, Article 11(1) of the Regulation provides that:

It shall be prohibited:

(a) to import crude oil or petroleum products into the Union if they:
  (i) originate in Iran; or
  (ii) have been exported from Iran;
(b) to purchase crude oil or petroleum products which are located in or which originated in Iran;
(c) to transport crude oil or petroleum products if they originate in Iran, or are being exported from Iran to any other country; and
(d) to provide, directly or indirectly, financing or financial assistance, including financial derivatives, as well as insurance and re-insurance related to the import, purchase or transport of crude oil and petroleum products of Iranian origin or that have been imported from Iran.

The assessment of the measures' lawfulness presupposes a determination of their legal nature in order to determine what the applicable legal framework is. Then, depending upon the conclusion reached as to the legal nature of the measures, their lawfulness is to be assessed with respect to the relevant rules governing their use. As regards the first step, the measures under consideration may prima facie qualify either as measures

[7] See Council of the EU, Press release 5457/12 of 23 January 2012, 'Iran: New EU sanctions target sources of finance for nuclear programme'.

[8] Council Regulation (EU) 56/2012 of 23 January 2012 amending Regulation (EU) No 961/2010 on restrictive measures against Iran [2012] OJ L19/10; Council Decision (EU) 2012/35/CFSP of 23 January 2012 amending Decision 2010/413/CFSP concerning restrictive measures against Iran [2012] OJ L19/22.

[9] Council Regulation (EU) 267/2012 of 23 March 2012 concerning restrictive measures against Iran and repealing Regulation (EU) No 961/2010 [2012] OJ L88/1.

of retorsion, as sanctions (whether mandated or authorised by the UN Security Council, or 'autonomous'), or as countermeasures. The present chapter examines what legal category adequately describes the EU measures considered (section II) and concludes with reasonable certainty that they display the general characteristics of countermeasures, as the term is used in the International Law Commission's (ILC) Articles on Responsibility of States for Internationally Wrongful Acts (ASR).[10] This finding entails the applicability of the law of State responsibility (as well as the law of responsibility of international organisations, the measures considered having been enacted at the EU level), which is relevant to assess the lawfulness of the measures, both from a procedural and a substantive perspective (section III).

II. THE LEGAL NATURE OF THE EU MEASURES

The Council of the EU has made clear that it views the measures taken against Iran in early 2012 as a response to, and as a consequence of, an internationally wrongful act attributed to Iran:

> Iran continues to refuse to comply with its international obligations and to fully co-operate with the IAEA to address the concerns on its nuclear programme, and instead continues to violate those obligations. In this context and in accordance with the Council conclusions of 1 December 2011, the Council has agreed additional restrictive measures.[11]

The present chapter will not deal with the issue of the identification of the internationally wrongful act(s) attributed to Iran, nor will it try to verify the existence of, and the materiality of, such acts.[12] It will focus instead

[10] Draft Articles on Responsibility of States for Internationally Wrongful Acts in (2001) II(2) *ILC Ybk* 26.

[11] 'Council conclusions on Iran' (n 6) para 2. Along the same line, a statement by the EU (unsigned and undated), posted in 2013 on the website of various EU embassies in Tehran (available at: www.mzv.cz/public/2f/9d/14/996135_923542_Common_messages_regarding_EU_sanctions_against_the_Iranian_nuclear_programme.doc) mentions that '[s]anctions are a response to Iran's violations of its international obligations', but fails to give a precise indication of exactly what obligations would have been breached. In fact, it is noteworthy that the statement limits itself to pointing to the violation by Iran 'of several resolutions of the United Nations Security Council and IAEA Board of Governors resolutions', and does not state explicitly that Iran would have breached either its Safeguards Agreement with the IAEA, or the NPT itself (which mandates in its Art III the implementation of such safeguards).

[12] For an assessment of the validity of such claims, see P-E Dupont, 'Compliance with Treaties in the Context of Nuclear Non-proliferation: Assessing Claims in the Case of Iran' (2014) 19 *Journal of Conflict and Security Law* 161–210.

on the characterisation of the response to such act(s), ie the nature of the EU measures. As ILC Rapporteur Arangio-Ruiz noted in his Third Report on State responsibility, there exists in international practice 'a variety of measures to which States resort in order to secure fulfilment of the obligations deriving from, or otherwise react to, the commission of an internationally wrongful act'.[13] It is necessary to determine, within the variety of such measures identified by the practice and legal writings (and collectively and generally termed in English 'unilateral remedies' and in French '*réactions décentralisées*'), to which category the present EU measures belong. The most widely used measures, Arangio-Ruiz observed, 'are self-defence (distinguished to a greater or lesser degree from the wider concept of self-help), sanctions, retorsion, reprisals, reciprocity, countermeasures, termination and suspension of treaties, *inadimplenti non est adimplendum*'.[14] Among these categories, those relevant prima facie to the measures under consideration are (1) retorsion, (2) sanctions (whether UN-mandated or 'autonomous') and (3) countermeasures. Each of these possibilities will be examined in turn.

A. Retorsion

The notion of retorsion, according to the ILC, refers to 'unfriendly' conduct 'which is not inconsistent with any international obligation of the State engaging in it even though it may be a response to an internationally wrongful act'.[15] In other words, retorsion 'embraces any retaliatory act by which a State responds, by an unfriendly act not amounting to a violation of international law, to either (a) a breach of international law or (b) an unfriendly act, by another State'.[16] Measures restricting or impeding trade relations (in general or in specific areas), such as an embargo,

[13] G Arangio-Ruiz, 'Third Report on State Responsibility' UN Doc A/CN.4/440 and Add 1, (1991) II(1) *ILC Ybk*, para 8.

[14] Ibid.

[15] 'Commentaries on the Draft Articles on Responsibility of States for Internationally Wrongful Acts' in (2001) (II)2 *ILC Ybk* 128. See also Arangio-Ruiz, 'Third Report on State Responsibility' (n 13) para 16, defining retorsion as 'hostile but lawful action in response to a prior internationally wrongful act'.

[16] A Cassese, *International Law* (Oxford, Oxford University Press, 2004) 310; see also M N Shaw, *International Law* (Cambridge, Cambridge University Press, 2008) 1128; see also P Daillier, M Forteau and A Pellet, *Droit international public* (Paris, LGDJ, 2009) 1055; O Schachter, *International Law in Theory and Practice* (Dordrecht, Martinus Nijhoff Publishers, 1991) 198, defining retorsion as 'counter-measures of a non-amicable character (short of use of force) that do not involve a breach of an international obligation by the State taking such measures. They are measures that an aggrieved State is legally free to take whether or not an offending State committed a breach on its part'.

are a typical example, often quoted, of retorsion.[17] Measures of retorsion, unlike countermeasures, are in principle within the discretion of the State concerned, and are not subject to procedural requirements. However, the legality of recourse to such measures supposes that the State considered does not, in implementing retorsion, violate international obligations vis-à-vis the target State. The intrinsic lawfulness of the measure serves thus to distinguish retorsion and countermeasures. As emphasised by the ILC,

> [w]hatever their motivation, so long as such acts are not incompatible with the international obligations of the States taking them towards the target State, they do not involve countermeasures and they fall outside the scope of the [ASR].[18]

Therein lies the difficulty in the instant case. As it has been rightly noted, the measures of the kind of those enacted by the EU in January 2012 'go beyond mere expressions of disapproval and involve the suspension of the performance of international legal obligations otherwise owed to Iran'.[19] Indeed, the EU measures actually imply suspension—or, more exactly, non-performance—of various international legal obligations owed to Iran, in particular of obligations contained in treaties in force between Iran and various EU Member States, in particular substantive standards of investment protection found in bilateral investment treaties, which are de facto disregarded by the oil embargo.[20] It might also be thought that the oil embargo, involving the mandatory termination of existing contracts related to import, purchase and transport of petrochemical products, raises prima facie an issue of compliance by the EU countries with customary standards of investment protection, and that it might be deemed to amount to some form of expropriation.

[17] See ILC, 'Commentaries' (n 15) 128: '[a]cts of retorsion may include the prohibition of or limitations upon normal diplomatic relations or other contacts, embargoes of various kinds or withdrawal of voluntary aid programmes'. Schachter, *International Law in Theory and Practice* (n 16) 198, mentions that '[t]ypical examples [of retorsion] include rupture of diplomatic relations, cessation of trade in general or in specific areas, non-recognition of acts of the offending government, denial of benefits otherwise available to the offending government, curtailment of migration from the offending government'. See also Daillier, Forteau and Pellet, *Droit international public* (n 16) 1057–58.

[18] ILC, 'Commentaries' (n 15) 128. See also D Alland, 'The Definition of Countermeasures' in Crawford, Pellet and Olleson (eds), *The Law of International Responsibility* (n 3) 1127, 1131–32.

[19] Calamita, 'Sanctions, Countermeasures, and the Iranian Nuclear Issue' (n 2) 1397.

[20] See eg Agreement on Reciprocal Promotion and Protection of Investments between the Government of the Republic of Austria and the Government of the Islamic Republic of Iran (signed 15 February 2001); Treaty between the Federal Republic of Germany and the Empire of Iran concerning the Promotion and Reciprocal Protection of Investments (signed 11 November 1965); Accord entre le Gouvernement de la République française et le Gouvernement de la République islamique d'Iran sur l'encouragement et la protection réciproques des investissements (signed 12 May 2003).

The fact that the measures have been adopted in the framework of the EU also has implications. The Treaty on the European Union provides that the EU is committed to 'the strict observance and the development of international law, including respect for the principles of the United Nations Charter'.[21] Applying this general commitment to the specific field of sanctions, the Council of the EU has stressed that:

> [t]he introduction and implementation of restrictive measures must always be in accordance with international law. They must respect human rights and fundamental freedoms, in particular due process and the right to an effective remedy. The measures imposed must always be proportionate to their objective.[22]

As a consequence of this commitment, it might be assumed that EU restrictive measures should comply with the EU's and its Member States' international commitments regarding international trade and investment. Under EU law, restrictive measures may be deemed legitimate only if they fit into the exceptions related to security (sometimes referred to as 'public order' or 'national security' exceptions) found in the free trade and/or investment protection provisions of international instruments entered into by the EU or its Member States,[23] or if they comply with the defence of necessity as recognised in customary international law. In the case of the EU embargo, it is prima facie dubious that such a 'public order' or 'national security' exception, or a state of necessity, allowing the EU or its Member States to take restrictive measures departing from their commitments relating to international trade and investment, exists. As regards measures of retorsion decided by the EU, considered *in abstracto*, an author has noted that:

> [i]n general terms, the Community can revoke any unilateral concession voluntarily granted in the area of free movement of capital to a third country as long as it does not violate any international obligation. In the latter case, the restrictive measure must fulfill the requirements of a countermeasure.[24]

It might also be observed that the European Court of Justice, in *Centro-Com*, a case dealing with EU measures adopted on the basis of a Security

[21] Treaty on the European Union, Art 3(5).

[22] Council of the EU, 'Guidelines on implementation and evaluation of restrictive measures (sanctions) in the framework of the EU Common Foreign and Security Policy' (2 December 2005) para 9.

[23] See OECD (Investment Division, Directorate for Financial and Enterprise Affairs), 'Security-related terms in International Investment Law and in National Security Strategies' (2009) available at: https://www.oecd.org/investment/investment-policy/42701587.pdf

[24] S Hindelang, *The Free Movement of Capital and Foreign Direct Investment* (Oxford, Oxford University Press, 2009) 317.

Council resolution, has ruled that Member States are allowed to take measures that would otherwise be contrary to EU law only to the strictest extent necessary to comply with Security Council mandatory resolutions.[25] In any case, they cannot invoke foreign or security policy objectives to justify the adoption of national measures contrary to the common commercial policy or the relevant regulations.[26] Such finding might be applied a fortiori to the measures under consideration, which have, as will be demonstrated below, been adopted independently of any Security Council resolution.

In addition, as regards the measures taken against the Iranian Central Bank, they might be deemed to conflict with the rules governing immunities and privileges of foreign States under international law, and in particular of the 2004 UN Convention on Jurisdictional Immunities of States and their Property, which is widely considered as reflecting customary international law,[27] and which provides for the immunity of the property of a central bank or other monetary authority from execution.[28] It might also be thought that this measure violates the rules of the IMF, in particular Article VIII(2)(a) of the IMF Agreement, which provides indeed that no IMF member 'shall, without the approval of the Fund, impose restrictions on the making of payments and transfers for current international transactions'.[29]

In conclusion, insofar as they imply the non-performance of international obligations owed to Iran, the EU measures cannot be characterised as retorsion. It is, however, to be noted that, even if it were assumed that the EU measures qualify as retorsion, they would nonetheless

[25] Case C-124/95, *R v HM Treasury and Bank of England, ex p Centro-Com Srl* [1997] ECR I-00081.

[26] See T Gazzini, 'The Normative Element Inherent in Economic Collective Enforcement Measures: United Nations and European Union Practice' in L-A Sicilianos and L Picchio Forlati, *Les sanctions économiques en droit international/Economic sanctions in international law* (Leiden, Nijhoff, 2004) 279, 307.

[27] See eg the statement by Lord Bingham in *Jones v Ministry of Interior of Saudi Arabia* [2006] UKHL 26, [2007] 1 AC 270, 26: 'Despite its embryonic status, this Convention is the most authoritative statement available on the current international understanding of the limits of state immunity in civil cases'. Lord Hoffmann (ibid 47) described the 2004 Convention as 'the result of many years work by the International Law Commission and codifies the law of state immunity'); see R Gardiner, 'UN Convention on State Immunity: Form and Function' (2006) 55 *International and Comparative Law Quarterly* 407.

[28] UN Convention on Jurisdictional Immunities of States and their Property, UNGA Res 59/38 (2 December 2004) UN Doc A/RES/59/38, Art 21(1)(c).

[29] Articles of Agreement of the International Monetary Fund, adopted at the United Nations Monetary and Financial Conference, Bretton Woods, New Hampshire, 22 July 1944, entered into force on 27 December 1945, as amended, 22 UNTS 2203. For an analysis of earlier controversies on the extent of obligations of IMF members in the context of the settlement of claims between Iran and the United States, see A Mouri, 'Treatment of the Rules of the International Law of Money by the Iran-U.S. Claims Tribunal' (1994) 3 *Asian Yearbook of International Law* 71–110.

be subject to legal limits, even if less stringent than those applicable to countermeasures. It has been observed that the general assumption that a State may freely adopt retorsion measures against a State that has violated its international obligations or even, short of that, has engaged in unfriendly conduct may be subject to question in some circumstances.[30] Professor Schachter, while noting that '[i]t would perhaps be going too far to suggest that legal acts of retorsion should be subject to requirements of necessity and proportionality',[31] expressed the view that per se legal measures of retorsion may become illegal when taken for an illegal objective.[32] He illustrates his view by the example of a State discontinuing trade with an offending country but imposing as a condition for resumption of such trade a change in the internal or foreign policy of the target State.[33] In that case, he argues:

> an otherwise discretionary act, the retorsion, is used as a means of coercing the object of that retorsion to give up its sovereign right, quite apart from the alleged violation of law that gave rise to the retorsion. There is good reason to consider such use of retorsion as illegal because of its improper objective.[34]

In that situation, the illegality of the act of retorsion might either flow from the characterisation of the conduct as an abuse of rights,[35] or as a violation of a primary rule precluding such coercion, as set out in the 1970 Declaration of Principles of International Law Concerning Friendly Relations adopted unanimously by the UN General Assembly, which provides that:

> No State may use or encourage the use of economic, political or any other type of measures to coerce another State in order to obtain from it the subordination

[30] See Daillier, Forteau and Pellet (n 16) 1056–57; also Schachter (n 16) 198.

[31] Schachter (n 16) 198.

[32] This position is discussed in Arangio-Ruiz (n 13) para 18.

[33] Schachter (n 16) 199. See also L Boisson de Chazournes, 'Other Non-derogable Obligations' in Crawford, Pellet and Olleson (eds) (n 3) 1205, 1209–11.

[34] Schachter (n 16) 199. He adds that '[t]he fact that retorsion is used when the target of its use has violated an international law obligation would not legally entitle the government using it to demand that the offending State give up its sovereign rights'.

[35] Here Schachter (n 16) 199 notes that 'some writers might consider the situation covered by the concept of abuse of rights since it involves use of a right "to inflict upon another State an injury which cannot be justified by a legitimate consideration of its own advantage"'; here he quotes Oppenheim, *International Law*, 8th edn (1955) Vol I, 345. He also observes that '[o]ne might wonder whether a requirement of proportionality can be applied to an act of retorsion that is generally within the discretion of the State. [...] To terminate diplomatic or commercial relations for a minor offence (say, the misconduct of a diplomat) may be so excessive a retaliation as to call into question the good faith of the State reacting in that way. It may be too difficult to formulate a legal principle to meet this kind of situation, but it would not be inappropriate to draw attention to an underlying ethic of reasonableness and good faith in the mutual relations of States. To use retorsion inappropriately and disproportionately to meet minor offences departs from that ethic and tends to debase the currency of international intercourse'.

> of the exercise of its sovereign rights and to secure from it advantages of any kind.[36]

Concerns over cases of 'improper' use of retorsion measures, particularly directed at developing countries, are regularly expressed in debates before the Second Committee of the UN General Assembly, as well as by the Non-Aligned Movement[37] and the Group of 77.[38] For instance, the General Assembly recently reaffirmed, in a resolution adopted on 22 December 2011, the 1970 Declaration on Friendly Relations, and urged the international community:

> to adopt urgent and effective measures to eliminate the use of unilateral coercive economic measures against developing countries that are not authorized by relevant organs of the United Nations or are inconsistent with the principles of international law as set forth in the Charter of the United Nations and that contravene the basic principles of the multilateral trading system.[39]

Similarly, the 'Doha Mandate' adopted at the recent UNCTAD Thirteenth Session held in Doha (Qatar) in April 2012 'strongly urged' States:

> to refrain from promulgating and applying any unilateral economic, financial, or trade measures not in accordance with international law and the Charter of the United Nations that impedes the full achievement of economic and social development, particularly in developing countries, and that affects commercial interests.[40]

[36] Res 2625 (XXV) (24 October 1970) UN Doc A/Res/25/2625, annex. See Daillier, Forteau and Pellet (n 16) 1057.

[37] See eg the 'Final Document of the XV Summit of Heads of State and Government of the Non-Aligned Movement' (11–16 July 2009) NAM2009/FD/Doc1, para 17.4 where the NAM 'reiterated the need to eliminate unilateral application of economic and trade measures by one State against another that affect the free flow of international trade. They urged States that have and continue to apply such laws and measures to refrain from promulgating and applying them in conformity with their obligations under the Charter of the United Nations and international law, which, inter alia, reaffirm the freedom of trade and navigation'.

[38] In their joint Position paper on the draft outcome document for the Thirteenth Session of the United Nations Conference on Trade and Development (UNCTAD-XIII) adopted on 14 October 2011, the Group of 77 and China called on UNCTAD to 'study the unilateral economic, financial or trade measures, contrary to international law and WTO rules, which hinder market access, investments, freedom of transit, and the welfare of the population of the affected countries. In this regard, UNCTAD XIII should strongly urge States to refrain from enacting and implementing unilateral economic, financial or trade measures that are not in accordance with international law or the Charter of the United Nations and that hamper the full achievement of economic and social development as well as trade, particularly in developing countries', UNCTAD, 'Group of 77 and China Position Paper' (14 October 2011) TD/445, para 45.

[39] Res 66/186, 'Unilateral economic measures as a means of political and economic coercion against developing countries' (22 December 2011) UN Doc A/Res/66/186, adopted by a vote of 122 in favour to 2 against (Israel, United States) and 53 abstentions.

[40] See UNCTAD, 'The Doha Mandate' (26 April 2012) UN Doc TD/L.427, para 25. The declaration emphasised that these actions 'hinder market access, investments and freedom of transit and the well-being of the population of affected countries'.

It might be argued with some credibility in the present case that the EU measures considered qualify as 'unilateral coercive economic measures', insofar as cumulatively they meet the three alternative characteristics of such measures, as set out in the Declaration on Friendly Relations: (1) they were not authorised by relevant organs of the United Nations, as will be demonstrated below; (2) they are not consistent with the principles of international law as set out in the Charter of the United Nations, and (3) they contravene the 'basic principles of the multilateral trading system'. In addition, the EU measures might be seen as a form of 'economic warfare'.[41] As such, and insofar as they are used in peacetime, they are governed by the UN Charter, which, as it has been noted, impacts on economic warfare in that 'it institutionalises it and attempts to place it within the framework of Chapter VII'.[42] The following discussion will be therefore devoted to the question whether the present measures belong to the realm of Chapter VII action.

B. Sanctions

Given that the EU measures cannot be properly qualified as retorsion, do they qualify as 'sanctions'? If the answer to the question is positive, a subsequent question arises: that of whether these measures qualify as 'enforcement' measures based on a UN Security Council resolution, or as 'independent' restrictive measures?

The first observation that may be made is that none of the UN Security Council resolutions adopted so far in the context of the Iranian nuclear program provide for a prohibition of oil imports from Iran.[43] In the latest to date, UNSC Resolution 1929 (2010), the Security Council merely noted:

> the potential connection between Iran's revenues derived from its energy sector and the funding of Iran's proliferation-sensitive nuclear activities, and … that chemical process equipment and materials required for the petrochemical

[41] See V Lowe and A Tzanakopoulos, 'Economic Warfare' in R Wolfrum (ed), *Max Planck Encyclopedia of Public International Law* (Oxford, Oxford University Press, 2012) also available at: http://papers.ssrn.com/sol3/papers.cfm?abstract_id=1701590. They describe economic warfare as 'conduct ranging from economic methods of warfare such as belligerent blockade and the strategic bombing of factory infrastructure, to decentralised economic (counter) measures in peacetime, such as trade embargoes or even boycotts voluntarily undertaken by the citizens of one State against the products of another, and to collective sanctions imposed by the UN Security Council'.

[42] Ibid.

[43] See the UNSC resolutions mentioned in (n 2).

industry have much in common with those required for certain sensitive nuclear fuel cycle activities.[44]

At the EU level, on 17 June 2010, the European Council, welcoming the adoption of Resolution 1929 (2010), invited the Council:

> to adopt measures implementing those contained in UNSCR 1929 (2010) as well as accompanying measures, with a view to supporting the resolution of all outstanding concerns regarding Iran's development of sensitive technologies in support of its nuclear and missile programmes, through negotiation. These should focus on the areas of trade, the financial sector, the Iranian transport sector, *key sectors in the oil and gas industry* and additional designations in particular for the Islamic Revolutionary Guards Corps (IRGC).[45]

Such measures targeting in a specific way 'key sectors' in Iran's oil and gas industry, allegedly 'implementing those contained in UNSCR 1929 (2010)', were enacted by the EU Council in its Decision of 26 July 2010, which provides that:

> [EU] Member States should prohibit the sale, supply or transfer to Iran of key equipment, and technology as well as related technical and financial assistance, which could be used in *key sectors in the oil and natural gas industries*. Moreover, Member States should prohibit any new investment in these sectors in Iran.[46]

Subsequent measures targeting Iran's oil and gas sector, enacted by EU Council Regulation of 25 October 2010, did not include an embargo on Iran's oil or gas.[47] On the contrary, the latter Regulation provided that '[t]he restrictive measures should not affect the import or export of oil or

[44] In the same resolution, the Security Council decided 'that all States shall require their nationals, persons subject to their jurisdiction and firms incorporated in their territory or subject to their jurisdiction to exercise vigilance when doing business with entities incorporated in Iran or subject to Iran's jurisdiction, including those of the IRGC and IRISL, and any individuals or entities acting on their behalf or at their direction, and entities owned or controlled by them, including through illicit means, if they have information that provides reasonable grounds to believe that such business could contribute to Iran's proliferation-sensitive nuclear activities or the development of nuclear weapon delivery systems or to violations of resolutions 1737 (2006), 1747 (2007), 1803 (2008) or this resolution', Res 1929 (9 June 2010) UN Doc S/Res/1929, para 22.

[45] As recalled in Council Decision (EU) 2010/413/CFSP concerning restrictive measures against Iran and repealing Common Position 2007/140/CFSP [2010] OJ L195/39) (emphasis added).

[46] Ibid (emphasis added).

[47] See Council Regulation (EU) 961/2010 on restrictive measures against Iran and repealing Regulation (EC) No 423/2007 [2010] OJ L281/1. This Regulation contains a prohibition on the sale, supply, transfer or export to Iran of 'certain key equipment or technology which could be used in the key sectors of the oil and natural gas industries', as well as restrictions on investment in the Iranian oil and gas sector, extending to the prohibition of 'joint ventures as well as other forms of associations and cooperation with Iran in the sector of the transmission of natural gas'.

gas to and from Iran, including the fulfilment of payment obligations in connection with such import or export'.

As mentioned above, the first EU measures targeting in a specific way 'key sectors' in Iran's oil and gas industry, enacted by the EU Council in its Decision of 26 July 2010, merely constituted—according to the EU—implementation measures of 'those contained in UNSCR 1929 (2010)'. In the same way, the subsequent EU Council Regulation of 25 October 2010 contended that the 'additional restrictive measures enacted on 26 July 2010 through Decision 2010/413/CFSP' were adopted 'in order to comply with UN Security Council Resolution 1929 (2010)'. These contentions were hardly convincing with respect of the previous sanctions on 'key sectors' in Iran's oil and gas industry; and they are even more difficult to maintain with respect to the comprehensive embargo on Iranian oil. Indeed, the mere *observation* made by the Security Council in the *preamble* of Resolution 1929 (2010) on the 'potential connection between Iran's revenues derived from its energy sector and the funding of Iran's proliferation-sensitive nuclear activities', can hardly be deemed to be a legal basis for sanctions on 'key sectors' in Iran's oil and gas industry, given the lack of any express provision to that effect in the *operative paragraphs* of the resolution.[48] A fortiori, it can hardly provide a legal basis for a comprehensive embargo on Iran's oil and gas. On the contrary, such interpretation of Resolution 1929 (2010) can be seen as instance of *misinterpretation*, in this case 'extensive interpretation' of the relevant Council resolutions. Such interpretation departs from the rules of interpretation found in Articles 31 and 32 of the 1969 Vienna Convention on the Law of Treaties, which apply *mutatis mutandis* to Security Council resolutions insofar as they are ultimately agreements between the Member States of the Council.[49] In that respect, Professor Sicilianos has questioned whether 'States can allocate to themselves the power to auto-interpret Security Council resolutions in order to take significant liberties regarding the content of the measures to be taken in execution of the sanctions'.[50] He asserts that:

> [t]he recognition of a large power of auto-interpretation on the part of States of mandatory decisions of the Security Council enacting sanctions under

[48] See eg M Wood, 'The Interpretation of Security Council Resolutions' (1998) 2 *Max Planck Yearbook of United Nations Law* 73, 86–87, who emphasises that the role of preambles to Security Council resolutions, as opposed to their operative paragraphs; is merely to 'assist in interpretation, by giving guidance as to their object and purpose'.

[49] See A Orakhelashvili, 'Unilateral Interpretation of Security Council Resolutions: UK Practice' (2010) 2 *Göttingen Journal of International Law* 823–42. On interpretation of SC Resolutions in general, see Wood, 'The Interpretation of Security Council Resolutions' (n 48).

[50] Sicilianos, 'Countermeasures in Response to Grave Violations of Obligations Owed to the International Community' (n 3) 1141. Reviewing the practice of the EC/EU in the

> Chapter VII does not find any support in the UN Charter and would risk distortion of Chapter VII.[51]

The fact that the interpretation of Resolution 1929 (2010), which purportedly finds in its provisions a legal basis for a comprehensive embargo on Iran's oil and gas, is an *incorrect* interpretation, is confirmed by the fact that, as already mentioned, subsequent EU measures targeting Iran's oil and gas sector, enacted by EU Council Regulation of 25 October 2010, which purported to 'implement' Resolution 1929 (2010), did not include an embargo on Iran's oil or gas, but on the contrary, provided that such restrictive measures 'should not affect the import or export of oil or gas to and from Iran, including the fulfilment of payment obligations in connection with such import or export'. It is difficult to understand the legal reason why, absent a subsequent UNSC resolution, such provision, adopted in the context of the implementation of Resolution 1929 (2010), would a posteriori have needed to be repealed, and a provision to the contrary effect (ie enacting an embargo) would be deemed adequately to implement the same Resolution 1929 (2010).

Regarding the EU measures considered, it may be noted that the lack of a legal basis in a UN Security Council resolution raises an issue with respect to Article 53(1) of the UN Charter, which provides that 'no enforcement action shall be taken under regional arrangements or by regional agencies without the authorization of the Security Council'. Do the measures taken by the EU qualify as 'enforcement action' in the meaning of this article? While it seems uncontroversial that the European Union qualifies as a 'regional arrangement' within the meaning of Article 53 of the Charter,[52] there has been doctrinal debate as to whether 'enforcement action' was to be equated with the powers conferred upon the Security Council under Chapter VII of the Charter, ie apart from measures involving the use of military force, economic sanctions or other measures short of the use of force.[53] This question remains unsettled to date. However,

implementation of UN sanctions, he observes instances of measures 'having no more than a remote connection or no connection at all with UN sanctions. Certainly, the grounds for Security Council resolutions were recalled to demonstrate that the measures adopted were situated "in the slipstream" of sanctions enacted by the UN. However, this has not concealed the fact that some sanctions have moved from the institutional regime to individual measures'.

[51] Ibid.

[52] See M Pugh and WP Singh Sidhuat, *The United Nations & Regional Security: Europe and Beyond* (Boulder, Lynne Rienner Publishers, 2003) 76 ff.

[53] See eg A Abass, *Regional Organisations and the Development of Collective Security: Beyond Chapter VIII of the UN Charter* (Oxford, Hart Publishing, 2004) 46–52, expressing the view that economic sanctions may constitute enforcement actions within the meaning of Art 53 of the Charter. But see *contra* U Villani, 'The Security Council's Authorization of Enforcement Action by Regional Organizations' (2002) 6 *Max Planck Yearbook of United Nations Law* 535, 538–40.

with respect to economic sanctions, an author has expressed an interesting view, according to which:

> Where economic or other peaceful sanctions are at stake the need for authorization in Article 53, paragraph 1, second sentence, must be interpreted in the context of what public international law permits in general. When the regional agency has a specific title to apply economic sanctions within its system against a Member State of the regional organization there is no need for formal Security Council authorization. As soon as the regional agency applies the economic sanctions to third States it will depend on whether a title under public international law exists. This may be the case where the right to take reprisals, particularly because of the violation of *erga omnes* obligations, can be the legal basis for the regional agency to act. Where no justification under public international law would otherwise exist the Security Council must authorize the enforcement action because the charter of the regional system cannot justify action vis-à-vis a third State.[54]

Following this line of reasoning, the question of the existence, in the instant case, of a justification under general international law which would allow the EU lawfully to enact countermeasures against Iran will be examined below.

C. Countermeasures

The EU measures, being characterised as countermeasures, are therefore governed by the law of State responsibility, more precisely by the provisions on countermeasures contained in the 2001 Articles on State Responsibility (ASR). However, insofar as these measures were enacted in the framework of the EU Common Foreign and Security Policy (CFSP), the 2011 Draft Articles on the Responsibility of International Organizations (DARIO) are also relevant.[55] As to the interaction between the two sets of rules set out in the ASR and DARIO (which are to a large extent similar),[56] it may be useful to recall some points of relevance in the present context.

[54] J A Frowein, 'Reactions by Not Directly Affected States to Breaches of Public International Law' (1994) 248 *Recueil des Cours* 345, 388–89.

[55] Draft Articles on the Responsibility of International Organizations (2011) II(2) *ILC Ybk*. On the responsibility of international organisations in general, see eg P Klein, 'The Attribution of Acts to International Organizations' in Crawford, Pellet and Olleson (eds) (n 3) 297–315.

[56] ILC, 'Commentaries' (n 15) 'General Commentary' para 4. The ILC however notes that the provisions of DARIO 'do not necessarily yet have the same authority as the corresponding provisions on State responsibility'; ibid para 5.

First, the EU is obviously an international organisation for the purposes of and within the meaning of DARIO,[57] even if it displays, in several respects, specific features which contrast with 'classic' international organisations.[58] Second, DARIO is not concerned with countermeasures taken by an international organisation against a State, but only with countermeasures taken by an international organisation against another international organisation.[59] The ILC commentary on DARIO, Article 22 emphasises that:

> [t]he present draft articles do not examine the conditions for countermeasures to be lawful when they are taken by an injured international organization against a responsible State. Thus paragraph 1, while it refers to articles 51 to 57 insofar as countermeasures are taken against another international organization, only refers to international law for the conditions concerning countermeasures taken against States. However, one may apply by analogy the conditions that are set out for countermeasures taken by a State against another State in articles 49 to 54 on the responsibility of States for internationally wrongful acts. It is to be noted that the conditions for lawful countermeasures in articles 51 to 57 of the present draft articles reproduce to a large extent the conditions in the articles on responsibility of States for internationally wrongful acts.[60]

Therefore, the legal framework applicable to the EU measures (taken by an international organisation) is the ASR (Articles 49 to 54), applied by analogy to countermeasures taken by an international organisation against a State.

[57] See DARIO (n 55) Art. 2(a), which provides that 'for the purposes of the present draft articles, "international organization" means an organization established by a treaty or other instrument governed by international law and possessing its own international legal personality'. This definition is consistent with that given in the 1969 Vienna Convention on the Law of Treaties and in the 1986 Vienna Convention on the Law of Treaties between States and International Organizations or between International Organizations. See O Corten and P Klein (eds), *The Vienna Conventions on the Law of Treaties* (Oxford, Oxford University Press, 2011) 52–53 (on the meaning of 'international organization' in Art 2 of the 1969 Convention) and 63–64 (on its meaning in Art 2 of the 1986 Convention). See also the commentary on DARIO, Art 2 in ILC, 'Commentaries' (n 15), and the comments of the European Commission on DARIO; ILC, 'Responsibility of International Organizations: Comments and Observations Received from International Organization' (25 June 2004) UN Doc A/CN.4/545 5; S Talmon, 'Responsibility of International Organizations: Does the European Community Require Special Treatment?' in M Ragazzi (ed), *International Responsibility Today. Essays in Memory of Oscar Schachter* (Leiden, Martinus Nijhoff Publishers, 2005) 405–21.

[58] See Talmon, 'Responsibility of International Organizations' (n 57).

[59] DARIO, Art 22(1) provides that:

> the wrongfulness of an act of an international organization not in conformity with an international obligation towards a State or another international organization is precluded if and to the extent that the act constitutes a countermeasure taken in accordance with the substantive and procedural conditions required by international law, including those set forth in Chapter II of Part Four for countermeasures taken against another international organization.

[60] ILC, 'Commentaries' (n 15).

As regards the enactment of countermeasures by the EU, and the responsibility which might be incurred by the EU in the event of the measures being considered unlawful, Article 17(1) of DARIO provides that:

> [a]n international organization incurs international responsibility if it circumvents one of its international obligations by adopting a decision binding member States or international organizations to commit an act that would be internationally wrongful if committed by the former organization.

The ILC's commentary on that provision refers inter alia to a statement of the legal counsel of the World Intellectual Property Organisation, according to whom:

> in the event a certain conduct, which a member State takes in compliance with a request on the part of an international organization, appears to be in breach of an international obligation both of that State and of that organization, then the organization should also be regarded as responsible under international law.[61]

This is consistent with an observation formulated by an author, according to which, through CFSP common positions, 'both the EU and its Member States may hit the otherwise legally protected interests of the target State, and therefore incur international responsibility'.[62] In the event of proven unlawfulness of the EU measures, this means that the international responsibility of both the EU as an international organisation and of the EU Member States could be simultaneously incurred.

III. EU SANCTIONS AND THE LEGAL REGIME OF COUNTERMEASURES

Recourse by States to countermeasures, given their 'exceptional character' and the fact that, as noted by the ILC, '[l]ike other forms of self-help, countermeasures are liable to abuse and this potential is exacerbated by the factual inequalities between States',[63] is subject to both procedural and substantial conditions. We will examine whether these two sets of conditions have been complied with as regards the EU's measures against Iran.

[61] ILC, 'Comments and Observations Received from Governments and International Organizations' (12 May 2005) UN Doc A/CN.4/556, N.5.

[62] See Gazzini, 'The Normative Element Inherent in Economic Collective Enforcement Measures' (n 26) 302.

[63] ILC, 'Commentaries' (n 15) 128.

A. Procedural Conditions

First of all, the taking of countermeasures involves certain procedural preconditions. These are of particular importance given the fact that, while the intrinsic wrongfulness of countermeasures is precluded only if the target State has committed an internationally wrongful act, the existence of such conduct and its wrongfulness will not, at the time when countermeasures are taken, have been objectively determined.[64]

The first precondition is that before resorting to countermeasures, an injured State (or an injured international organisation) shall call on the responsible State to fulfil its obligations.[65] Such requirement in the ASR reflects a well-established rule under customary international law, having been inter alia affirmed by the arbitral tribunal in the *Naulilaa* case (in the context of armed reprisals under the pre-UN Charter regime)[66] and by the ICJ in *Gabčíkovo-Nagymaros Project*, where the Court ruled that the requirement applied also to non-armed countermeasures under contemporary international law.[67] Secondly, the State or international organisation considering taking countermeasures shall notify the responsible State in advance of any decision to take countermeasures, and offer to negotiate with that State.[68]

If these rules are applied to the case considered, it should be admitted that the requirement of Article 52(1)(a) has been fulfilled, insofar as lengthy negotiations over the Iranian nuclear program have already taken place inter alia between Iranian and EU officials. However, it is less clear that the EU has complied with the requirement of Article 52(1)(b). In particular, we have no knowledge of the existence of any formal prior notification, which, according to authors, must contain 'detailed explanations of contemplated countermeasures',[69] sent by the EU to Iran before the oil embargo was enacted.

Another 'procedural' requirement, conditioning the lawfulness of recourse to countermeasures, which has long been controversial, is the requirement of prior exhaustion of means of dispute settlement.[70] Iran and several EU Member States are currently engaged in negotiations for the settlement of the Iranian nuclear programme, in the framework of the

[64] See Y Iwasawa and N Iwatsuki, 'Procedural Conditions' in Crawford, Pellet and Olleson (eds) (n 3) 1149, 1149.

[65] ASR (n 10) Art 52(1)(a).

[66] *Responsibility of Germany for Damage Caused in the Portuguese Colonies in the South of Africa (Portugal v Germany) ('Naulilaa')* 31 July 1928, 2 *RIAA* 1011, 1026.

[67] *Gabčíkovo-Nagymaros Project (Hungary v Slovakia)* [1997] ICJ Rep 7, 56 (para 84).

[68] ASR (n 10) Art 52(1)(b).

[69] See Iwasawa and Iwatsuki, 'Procedural Conditions' (n 64) 1152.

[70] Ibid 1152–54.

so-called 'P5+1'.[71] While it was held by the arbitral tribunal in the *Air Services Agreement* case that the fact that negotiations are underway does not entail as a matter of principle a prohibition from resorting to countermeasures,[72] it has nonetheless been observed that:

> [w]hen the target State is engaged in negotiations in good faith, there should be no need to resort to countermeasures, and thus countermeasures would not be permitted under the requirement of necessity. It is only when the target State refuses to cooperate in dispute settlement in good faith that countermeasures become necessary.[73]

Several difficulties are linked to this principle, namely the difficulty in practice of identifying the degree of non-cooperation (of the target State) that makes countermeasures necessary and justifiable, as well as the difficulty of assessing the good faith of the State contemplating the taking of countermeasures whilst engaged in negotiations. These difficulties are among the reasons why the submission of the dispute over Iran's (non-) compliance with its international obligations to an international court or tribunal would be desirable.

B. Substantial Conditions

As regards the substantial conditions for the recourse to countermeasures found in the ASR, as applied to the measures considered, it may be argued that: (1) the existence of the wrongful act, on which the lawfulness of the countermeasures ultimately rests, is dubious; (2) whether the EU qualifies as an 'injured' international organisation, entitled as such to take countermeasures, is also dubious; (3) the measures at issue do not prima facie comply with the requirement of proportionality, and (4) the availability of recourse by States (or regional organisations) to countermeasures in situations in which the Security Council has taken action under Chapter VII of the UN Charter, is a matter of controversy. Each of these arguments will be examined in turn.

[71] These negotiations have resulted in an interim agreement named 'Joint Plan of Action', signed in Geneva on 24 November 2013 between Iran and the P5+1 (United States, United Kingdom, Germany, France, Russia and China, facilitated by the European Union). It aims at a 'comprehensive solution' to the crisis, which according to the preamble 'would enable Iran to fully enjoy its right to nuclear energy for peaceful purposes under the relevant articles of the NPT in conformity with its obligations therein'. At the time of writing, it is unclear whether it will be implemented bona fide by both sides and result in a final settlement of the Iranian nuclear issue.

[72] *Case Concerning the Air Services Agreement of 27 March 1946 between the United States of American and France* (9 December 1978) 54 *ILR* 304, 339–40.

[73] See Iwasawa and Iwatsuki (n 64) 1153.

i. The Existence of the Wrongful Act

Article 49 of the ASR provides inter alia that:

> [a]n injured State may only take countermeasures against a State which is responsible for an internationally wrongful act in order to induce that State to comply with its obligations.

This provision raises first the question whether Iran is actually 'responsible for an internationally wrongful act'. It is uncontroversial that EU enforcement measures adopted independently from any mandatory or exhortatory Security Council resolution (as in the case considered) can be resorted to only as a reaction to an internationally wrongful act.[74] In other words, the lawfulness of EU enforcement measures adopted independently from any mandatory or exhortatory Security Council resolution rests upon the effective occurrence of a prior violation of international law by the targeted State.[75]

In this context, it has been noted that with respect to enforcement measures, whether qualifying as sanctions or as countermeasures, '[t]he lawfulness of the action on the international plane depends, in the first place, on the effective occurrence of the international wrongful act by the target State'.[76] Such a determination, as the same author asserts, 'may be made exclusively by an international tribunal'.[77] This raises the issue of the relevance of the involvement of an international court or tribunal in the adjudication of the dispute considered. In determining whether Iran is actually 'responsible for an internationally wrongful act', it is to be mentioned that the lawfulness of the EU measures, as well as of the various UN Security Council resolutions against Iran, including Resolution 1929 (2010), rests ultimately on the reality of the alleged violations by Iran of its Safeguards Agreement with the International Atomic Energy Agency (IAEA),[78] as well as of provisions of the Nuclear Non-proliferation Treaty (NPT)[79] which have been invoked by the Security Council and the Council of the EU as a cause of action. In that respect, it has been observed that 'it

[74] Gazzini (n 26) 302.

[75] Ibid.

[76] Ibid 280 (fn 5) and 302 (fn 95). See also Arangio-Ruiz (n 13) paras 37–38.

[77] Gazzini (n 26) 280 (fn 5) and 302 (fn 95). The author further observes that '[g]iven the inorganic structure of the international community and the non-existence of compulsory adjudication, however, the reacting State often remains *judex in re sua*, and its actions may trigger a chain of responses each State considers as lawful countermeasures', ibid 280 (fn 5).

[78] Agreement between Iran and the Agency for the application of safeguards in connection with the Treaty on the Non-Proliferation of Nuclear Weapons, IAEA Doc INFCIRC/214 (entered into force on 15 May 1974).

[79] Treaty on the Non-Proliferation of Nuclear Weapons (NPT), 729 UNTS 161; IAEA Doc INFCIRC/140.

is not certain that the [Security] Council adopted the proper standard of proof in ascertaining the existence of a breach of [the NPT], relying on presumptive concerns instead of established facts'.[80] Such criticism has been echoed by various authors, among whom one has questioned the reality of Iran's alleged breach of its obligations under Article III of the NPT.[81] Suffice it to say here that an authoritative determination of the existence of a breach by Iran of its Safeguards Agreement with the IAEA and/or of the NPT, which would imply inter alia an accurate interpretation of the relevant provisions of both instruments as well as an in-depth analysis of the practice of the IAEA in the implementation of safeguards on nuclear materials and activities,[82] which has never been made to date, is beyond the scope of the present chapter.

Even assuming that Iran has failed to comply with obligations under its Safeguards Agreement with the IAEA, the existence of specific provisions on the legal consequences of non-compliance in the instrument governing the relationship between Iran and the IAEA (Article XII(C) of the IAEA Statute, by reference of Article 19 of the Safeguards Agreement) should be noted. The IAEA Statute provides that non-compliance may trigger, in addition to a reporting of the non-compliance to other IAEA members and to the Security Council and the UN General Assembly, one or several of the following measures: curtailment or suspension of assistance by the IAEA to the country considered, call for the return of materials and equipment made available to the recipient member by the IAEA, or suspension of the State from 'the exercise of the privileges and rights of membership'.[83] The existence of these provisions regarding the consequences of non-compliance, as well as the mechanisms of dispute

[80] See A Orakhelashvili, *Collective Security* (Oxford, Oxford University Press, 2011) 24–25.

[81] See eg D H Joyner, *Interpreting the Nuclear Non-Proliferation Treaty* (Oxford, Oxford University Press, 2011) 126.

[82] On the IAEA practice in the implementation of safeguards, see eg P C Szasz, *The Law and Practices of the International Atomic Energy Agency* (Vienna, International Atomic Energy Agency, 1970); R H Rainer and P C Szasz, *The Law and Practices of the International Atomic Energy Agency 1970–1980. Supplement 1 to the 1970 edition of Legal Series No 7* (Vienna, International Atomic Energy Agency, 1993). The analysis of the annual Safeguards Statements issued by the IAEA is also relevant. The latest released to date is the 'Safeguards Statement for 2010', available at: www.iaea.org.

[83] Art XII(C) of the IAEA Statute provided in relevant part that:

> [t]he Board shall report the non-compliance to all members and to the Security Council and General Assembly of the United Nations. In the event of failure of the recipient State or States to take fully corrective action within a reasonable time, the Board may take one or both of the following measures: direct curtailment or suspension of assistance being provided by the Agency or by a member, and call for the return of materials and equipment made available to the recipient member or group of members. The Agency may also, in accordance with article XIX, suspend any non-complying member from the exercise of the privileges and rights of membership.

settlement provided for in Article XVII(A) of the IAEA Statute[84] and in the Safeguards Agreement, might be seen as characterising the non-proliferation regime established under the NPT, the IAEA Statute and the Safeguards Agreement as a 'self-contained regime',[85] and, as such, excluding the availability of countermeasures normally at the disposal of an injured State.[86]

The same consideration could be applied *mutatis mutandis* to Iranian non-compliance with the Security Council resolutions. Indeed, UN Security Council Resolution 1929 (2010) provides for a mechanism to deal with non-compliance on the part of Iran.[87]

ii. The 'Injured State' Issue

The reference in Article 49 of the ASR (applied by analogy to the corresponding provision of DARIO) to the 'injured State' raises another issue: whether the EU, in the case at issue, qualifies as an 'injured' international organisation. EU enforcement measures adopted independently from any mandatory or exhortatory Security Council resolution can be resorted to only if all EU Member States consider themselves as injured States, as it is the case for violations of *erga omnes* obligations.[88] It may be conceded

[84] Art XVII(A) of the IAEA Statute provides that:

> Any question or dispute concerning the interpretation or application of this Statute which is not settled by negotiation shall be referred to the International Court of Justice in conformity with the Statute of the Court, unless the parties concerned agree on another mode of settlement.

[85] ILC Special Rapporteur Arangio-Ruiz (n 13) 25 described self-contained regimes as 'those treaty-based systems or combinations of systems which tend to address, within their own contractual or special framework, the legal regime governing a considerable number of relationships among the State parties, including in particular the consequences of any breaches of the obligations of States parties under the system'. See Jansen Calamita (n 2) 1435–37, who argues against the characterisation of the non-proliferation regime as a 'self-contained' regime, due to the alleged 'absence of treaty-based enforcement of NPT obligations' (at 1435), and to the fact that (1) the IAEA Statute 'provides only minimal procedures for addressing non-compliance' (at 1436), and (2) the 'sanctions' provided for by Art XII of the IAEA Statute are 'very unlikely to deter a non-complying State' (at 1436, note 180). In our view, these arguments are both irrelevant and incorrect, and the author also fails to take account of the provisions on settlement of disputes contained in the IAEA Statute and in the Safeguards Agreement.

[86] Boisson de Chazournes, 'Other Non-derogable Obligations' (n 33) 1205. On self-contained regimes and their interaction with the general law of State responsibility, see also B Simma and D Pulkowski, '*Leges Speciales* and Self-Contained Regimes' in Crawford, Pellet and Olleson (eds) (n 3) 139–63.

[87] SC Res 1929 (2010), operative para 37 affirms that the Security Council 'shall, in the event that the report shows that Iran has not complied with resolutions 1737 (2006), 1747 (2007), 1803 (2008) and this resolution, adopt further appropriate measures under Article 41 of Chapter VII of the Charter of the United Nations to persuade Iran to comply with these resolutions and the requirements of the IAEA, and underlines that further decisions will be required should such additional measures be necessary'.

[88] Gazzini (n 26) 302.

that, under Article 48(1)(a) of the ASR, the invocation of responsibility 'by a State other than an injured State' is admissible (and accordingly the taking of countermeasures is admissible under Article 54 of the ASR) when 'the obligation breached is owed to a group of States including that State, and is established for the protection of a collective interest of the group'. Two observations can be formulated regarding the requirement of being 'injured'. First, the obligations that Iran is accused of having breached have been deemed by several analysts as being of a purely 'technical'—as opposed to 'substantive'—nature,[89] and probably do not fall within the category of *erga omnes* obligations.[90] Second, it is not at all certain, or at least unclear, that the combination of Articles 48(1)(a) and 54 of the ASR provide the EU with standing to invoke the responsibility of Iran. The interpretation of the two provisions, and particularly of the notion of 'collective interest of the group', has been a matter of debate,[91] to the extent that the question of countermeasures in response to violations of obligations representing a general interest 'number among the most controversial subjects in the field of State responsibility'.[92]

It is finally to be noted that an author, examining the standing to take countermeasures against Iran from the point of view of individual States (presumably directly 'injured'), has questioned, through an analysis which seems prima facie convincing, the relevance of Article 42(b)(ii) of the ASR, which provides that countermeasures may be taken in case of a 'breach of the obligation [...] of such a character as radically to change the position of all other States to which the obligation is owed with respect to the further performance of the obligation'.[93]

[89] See eg Joyner, *Interpreting the Nuclear Non-Proliferation Treaty* (n 81) 91–92.

[90] For a discussion on the concept of obligations *erga omnes*, see ILC, 'Commentaries' (n 15) 127.

[91] See eg M Craven, 'For the "Common Good": Rights and Interests in the Law of State Responsibility' in M Fitzmaurice and D Sarooshi (eds), *Issues of State Responsibility before International Judicial Institutions* (Portland, Hart Publishing, 2004) 105–27.

[92] Sicilianos (n 3) 1137.

[93] See S Singh, 'Iran, The Nuclear Issue & Countermeasures' (10 January 2012) available at: www.ejiltalk.org/iran-the-nuclear-issue-countermeasures/#more-4376. His core arguments are as follows: 'Two reasons emerge as to why these requirements of Article 42(b)(ii) cannot be met. First, not all other state parties to the NPT will have their further performance of this particular obligation compromised or affected, for the simple reason that not all other states are required to perform the obligation not the manufacture. The obligation not to "manufacture" only attaches to non-nuclear weapon states (NNWS), not to nuclear weapon states (NWS) such as the US, and is owed to all the NPT state parties. Second, as a direct consequence of the first point, the future non-performance of the same specific obligation is not necessarily at issue (as required by the core criteria of interdependent obligations). For NWS, potential non-performance would attach to different, but related, substantive obligations contained in Article I NPT. The apparent asymmetry between those obligations being breached and those obligations in danger of future non-performance, reveals a core problem as to which substantive non-proliferation obligations can be qualified as interdependent [...]. Turning to Iran's safeguard obligations under Article III(1), it should be clear that from a

iii. The Requirement of Proportionality

Article 51 of the ASR is concerned with the requirement of the proportionality of countermeasures.[94] It provides that:

> [c]ountermeasures must be commensurate with the injury suffered, taking into account the gravity of the internationally wrongful act and the rights in question.

In the EU context, enforcement measures adopted by the EU Council independently from any mandatory or exhortatory Security Council resolution are governed by international law and therefore subject to the limits set by the relevant conventional and customary norms, including respect for the principle of proportionality.[95] Proportionality is a well-established requirement for taking countermeasures, being widely recognised in State practice, doctrine and jurisprudence.[96] In the *Air Service Agreement* arbitration, the majority ruled that the measures taken by the United States 'do not appear to be clearly disproportionate when compared to those taken by France'.[97] In that case, the countermeasures taken were in the same field as the initial measures and concerned the same routes, even if they were rather more severe in terms of their economic effect than the initial French action.[98] If an international court or tribunal were to apply the *Air Service Agreement* test to the determination of conformity with the principle of proportionality in the instant case, it might well find significant disproportionality between the 'wrongful act' (the alleged, as yet unproven, non-compliance by Iran with some of its obligations under its Safeguards Agreement with the IAEA and/or the NPT) and the 'countermeasures' taken (the oil embargo and the freeze of assets of the Iranian Central Bank). The problem of (dis)proportionality of the countermeasures considered is to be linked to the prohibition of 'extreme

state responsibility and Art. 42(b)(ii) perspective, these cannot be considered as interdependent within the strict test. Yet, under a treaty law perspective it is my position that only a specific sub-set of safeguard obligations (namely those with a distinct and concrete link to substantive obligations) in only cases of a significant breach, can be qualified as interdependent. There are two sub-issues here; the type of verification obligation involved and the type of breach involved. First, one must differentiate those procedural safeguard obligations that have a distinct and direct connection to substantive obligations (e.g. the obligation to disclose and report and the existence of a facility utilizing WMDs for peaceful purposes) and those that do not (e.g. reporting within a specific timeframe). Second, one must consider that for the first type of obligation just submitted, the significance of the breach involved is critical. Should it be a case of technical non-compliance, which are manifest, of a safeguard obligation that is strongly linked to substantive ones, then this is hardly sufficient to enable standing for all state parties to that obligation to take countermeasures'.

[94] See R O'Keefe, 'Proportionality' in Crawford, Pellet and Olleson (eds) (n 3) 1157–68.

[95] Arangio-Ruiz (n 13) paras 63 ff. See also Gazzini (n 26) 302.

[96] See ILC, 'Commentaries' (n 15) 134.

[97] *Case Concerning the Air Services Agreement* (n 72).

[98] See ILC, 'Commentaries' (n 15) 134.

economic or political coercion', which was found in the version of the draft ASR adopted in 1995. This draft included a provision that an injured State cannot resort, by way of countermeasures, to 'extreme economic or political coercion designed to endanger the territorial integrity or political independence of the State which has committed an internationally wrongful act'.[99] While this provision did not find its way into Article 50 of the ASR as adopted in 2001, one commentator has expressed the view that 'economic and political countermeasures may be illegal if they are aimed at coercing a State to subordinate the exercise of its sovereign rights or its independence'.[100] Measures of 'extreme economic coercion' may in any case be covered by the prohibition of countermeasures involving use of force 'as embodied in the Charter of the United Nations', found in Article 50(1)(a) of the ASR.[101]

iv. The Availability of Countermeasures in Situations of Action Taken pursuant to Chapter VII by the UN Security Council

The question has also been raised whether recourse to countermeasures is available to States in situations where the Security Council has taken action under Chapter VII to compel compliance from the non-performing State.[102] Opposing views have been expressed on this issue. Some argue that:

> the limited scope of the Security Council's sanctions resolutions does not mean that additional reactive measures against Iran by states acting individually or in concert are foreclosed. Iran's noncompliance with its NPT obligations has its own effects under the law of state responsibility.[103]

Other authors have held, on the contrary, that recourse by the Security Council to the measures provided for in Chapter VII of the Charter is an instance of limitation on the unilateral use of countermeasures, or in other words that 'countermeasures could be applied only as long as sanctions had not been decided by a competent international body'.[104]

During the debates at the ILC on the role of countermeasures in the law of State responsibility, Alain Pellet took the view that:

> recourse to the measures provided for in Chapter VII of the Charter was the first essential limitation on the unilateral use of countermeasures. If the

[99] ARSIWA, draft Art 14(b) in (1995) II(2) *ILC Ybk* 66.

[100] Boisson de Chazournes (n 33) 1211.

[101] For a comprehensive summary of the opinions of States and authors on that point, see Arangio-Ruiz (n 13) paras 101 ff.

[102] See Calamita (n 2) 1398.

[103] Ibid 1418–19.

[104] See comments by Alain Pellet on the Fourth Report of the Special Rapporteur on State Responsibility (A/CN.4/444 and Add.1-3), (1992) I *ILC Ybk* 144.

> Security Council had decided on sanctions, in accordance with Articles 41 and 42 of the Charter, it was hardly likely that States would take no notice of them and continue to carry out measures of their own, just as individual or collective self-defence was allowed in the event of aggression only, according to Article 51, "until the Security Council has taken measures necessary to maintain international peace and security". If the Security Council had decided on measures within the meaning of Articles 41 and 42, States were no longer free to decide as they wished on countermeasures of their own.[105]

This view rests on the primacy of Security Council action in the system of collective security, which has been stressed by an author as follows:

> The UN Charter constitutes a collective security system with the Security Council as its focus. A collective security system can be defined in broad terms as a system where a collective measure is taken against a member of a community that has violated certain community defined values. An important feature of collective security is the maintenance of the *status quo* of the system. This relies, however, on the perception by States that their individual interest is best served by ensuring that the interests of the community of States—in Charter terms, international peace and security—is preserved. In the case of the Charter, it is the Security Council which has been given the authority to determine the content of the community value or interest in a particular case and consequently that its violation necessitates a collective security response.[106]

While the availability to individual States (or regional organisations) of countermeasures in situations in respect to which the UN Security Council has taken action pursuant to Chapter VII of the Charter is still controversial, it can be argued in general that the taking of countermeasures in such situations tends to undermine the coherence of the Charter-based collective security system. Countermeasures, even 'collective' ones (understood here as measures adopted by any State not individually injured in response to grave violations of *erga omnes* obligations, or of essential obligations for the protection of a collective interest, in the sense of Article 48 of the ASR), assume a 'subsidiary character in relation to the powers of the Security Council',[107] or, in other words, if the Security Council acts in the institutional framework of Chapter VII, the power to adopt countermeasures on an individual level disappears.[108] Professor Sicilianos has summarised the rationale underlying this argument, distinguishing the period

[105] Ibid.

[106] D Sarooshi, *The United Nations and the Development of Collective Security. The Delegation by the UN Security Council of its Chapter VII Powers* (Oxford, Oxford University Press, 1999) 5–6.

[107] Sicilianos (n 3) 1138.

[108] Ibid.

preceding Security Council Chapter VII action from the period following adoption of such measures:

> First, the problem of 'collective' countermeasures presents itself in the case of a failure of the Security Council, which manifests itself either because the Council does not judge itself competent to deal with a situation concerning a grave breach of a relevant rule of international law or because it cannot enact sanctions because of the use of the veto, or because it is slow to do so. Second, beginning from the moment when the Council occupies itself with the adoption of mandatory sanctions, Member States transform into agents for the execution of these sanctions, their duty being to implement them in good faith without undermining their effective application. For States not individually injured, this implies an obligation to suspend countermeasures already adopted at the individual level, if they are different or incompatible with the measures decided by the Security Council, or in any case, to modify them in order to harmonize them with the UN sanctions. A fortiori, the States in question should not adopt 'collective' countermeasures after the pronunciation of mandatory sanctions, but only measures which are necessary and sufficient for the execution of those mandatory sanctions. In short, unless the Security Council invites States to go further than its own measures—a rare event in practice—the triggering of Chapter VII ends the power of States not individually injured to react as they please at the individual level. This view is consistent with the spirit of the Charter as a 'constitutional' instrument of the international community, and it is also consistent with article 59 [ASR], which stipulates that the articles are 'without prejudice' to the Charter.[109]

In the context of measures adopted within the framework of the EU, it has also been observed that the Council of the EU, 'unlike the UN Security Council, has been granted no enforcement power in the field of international peace and security'.[110]

IV. CONCLUSION

This chapter has pointed out several difficulties generated by an analysis of the oil embargo and the freezing of assets of the Central Bank of Iran from the point of view of the law of international responsibility of States and of international organisations. It appears that these measures may be unlawful for several reasons, in particular because they disregard both

[109] Ibid 1142.

[110] Gazzini (n 26) 302. See also A Orakhelashvili, 'The Impact of Unilateral EU Economic Sanctions on the UN Collective Security Framework: The Cases of Iran and Syria' in A Z Marossi and M R Bassett (eds), *Economic Sanctions under International Law* (The Hague, TMC Asser Press, 2015) 4–21.

procedural and substantial preconditions for the enactment of countermeasures in international law.

Two final observations may be made in this respect. First, it might be thought that a desirable outcome to the crisis generated by the EU measures would be the referral of the dispute to the ICJ or to an arbitral tribunal. In this context, the provisions of Article 52(3) of the ASR, pursuant to which 'countermeasures may not be taken, and if already taken must be suspended without undue delay if … the dispute is pending before a court or tribunal which has the authority to make decisions binding on the parties' appear of particular relevance. On a more general level, one might legitimately take the view—which was expressed among others by Professor Bowett during the 1992 discussion of Professor Arangio-Ruiz's draft Article 12 of the ASR—that recourse to *any* method of peaceful dispute settlement, in the wide meaning of Article 33 of the UN Charter, including negotiation, would entail suspension of countermeasures already taken. In Professor Bowett's opinion, 'any right to take countermeasures must be suspended, first, when the breach has ceased, and, secondly, when the wrongdoing State has accepted and implemented bona fide a method for the peaceful settlement of disputes'.[111]

One might note that the application of Article 52(3) of the ASR is dependent upon the fact that 'the internationally wrongful act has ceased'; but the determination of this fact—whether or not there has actually been an 'internationally wrongful act' on the part of Iran, and whether or not such act 'has ceased'—would be the subject matter of the dispute on the merits on which the judicial or arbitral body concerned would be required to rule. This determination, being of an essentially technical character (verification of Iran's compliance with its safeguards obligations), falls, of course, within the competence of the IAEA.

If, on the contrary, no negotiated or judicial settlement of the case of Iran occurs, and if the practice of unilateral 'sanctions' is unchallenged by any actors in the international arena, it may be that the case of Iran will constitute a precedent for other instances of 'unilateral' coercive measures, of a species the prohibition of which has been assumed since the adoption of the ASR. The ILC's works on the legal regime of countermeasures raised expectations about an enhanced role for peaceful settlement procedures in the context of wrongful acts attributed to a State, and more precisely an expectation, formulated by several members of the ILC, that the taking of unilateral measures would be made subject (in one way or

[111] See Provisional summary record of the 2266th meeting, UN Doc A/CN.4/SR.2266 (1992) 16. For developments on that point, see eg B Simma, 'Counter-measures and Dispute Settlement: A Plea for a Different Balance' (1994) 5 *European Journal of International Law* 102–05.

another) to prior recourse to dispute settlement mechanisms.[112] Christian Tomuschat, among others, expressed the opinion that 'the international community would make a great step forward if it succeeded in bringing unilateral responses by States to encroachments upon their rights under stricter discipline'.[113] From this point of view, the behaviour of the EU, in enacting the latest 'sanctions' on Iran, can be seen as a significant step backward.

Second, in our opinion, the adoption of the countermeasures by the EU is likely to have a negative impact on the coherence of the collective security system. Indeed, it is quite paradoxical that, when a given situation has been referred to the Security Council, and when the Council has taken action pursuant to Chapter VII, States, either acting individually or in the framework of a regional organisation such as the EU, nonetheless retain the right to enact countermeasures going beyond the sanctions decided by the Security Council. In doing so, the States enacting countermeasures purport to retain for themselves de facto an authority which, in their capacity as Member States of the UN and the IAEA,[114] they have conferred upon the Security Council under the Charter. One might wonder whether such a practice can be reconciled with the requirement of the performance in good faith of treaty provisions, in this instance the UN Charter and the IAEA Statute.

[112] For a detailed account of this debate, see eg M E O'Connell, 'Controlling Countermeasures' in Ragazzi (ed), *International Responsibility Today* (n 57); also T Treves, 'The International Law Commission's Articles on State Responsibility and the Settlement of Disputes' in Ragazzi (ed), ibid 223–34.

[113] See C Tomuschat, 'Are Counter-Measures Subject to Prior Recourse to Dispute Settlement Procedures?' (1994) 5 *European Journal of International Law* 77, 78.

[114] It was the Member States of the IAEA who voted in favour of the transfer of the Iranian file to the Security Council through the IAEA Board of Governors.

4

State Reactions to Illegal Sanctions

ANTONIOS TZANAKOPOULOS

I. INTRODUCTION

THIS SHORT STUDY discusses the potential legal characterisations of State reactions to sanctions that are unlawful under international law. Two specific questions are to be dealt with in this respect: the first is whether 'sanctions', either unilateral or collective (ie imposed by the United Nations under Chapter VII of the UN Charter), may actually be unlawful, in other words whether their adoption and/or implementation may be in violation of international law. The second, related, question is what remedies are available to States targeted by such illegal sanctions. But before launching into these issues, some terminological clarifications are in order (section II). The following two sections will discuss State reactions to potentially illegal sanctions. The first such section focuses on reactions to 'unilateral' or 'decentralised' sanctions, otherwise known as 'countermeasures' (section III),[1] while the second relevant section deals with reactions to 'collective' or 'institutional' sanctions (section IV). Section V concludes.

II. ON VARIOUS 'SANCTIONS'

The title of this chapter refers to illegal 'sanctions'. But while the term may seem rather self-explanatory, it defies easy definition. What is a sanction in international law? Kelsen defined the term 'sanction' as a reaction to illegality.[2] It is the main consequence of illegal conduct. For this reason, no reference will be made to 'retorsion', ie unfriendly but perfectly legal

[1] See generally L-A Sicilianos, *Les réactions décentralisées à l'illicite: des contre-mesures à la légitime défense* (Paris, LGDJ, 1990).

[2] H Kelsen, *The Law of the United Nations: A Critical Analysis of its Fundamental Problems* (New York, Praeger, 1950) 706; and H Kelsen, *Allgemeine Theorie der Normen* (Vienna, Manz, 1979) 115.

acts which can be used by one State to put pressure on another.[3] Such acts may include for example the breaking off of diplomatic relations or the cessation of the provision of voluntary aid. Measures of retorsion can be taken at any time, and they need not be a reaction to unlawful conduct on the part of the targeted State. As such, they are not a reaction to illegality, and do not qualify as 'sanctions' according to the Kelsenian definition.

A multitude of adjectives have already been used to describe reactions to illegality, ie sanctions. They have been called, even in the course of these few sentences, 'unilateral', 'decentralised', 'collective' and 'institutional', and one could go on adding such adjectives. What about 'multilateral' for example? Or one could even go on throwing terms into the mix. How about 'countermeasures', 'reprisals' and so forth? Some delimitation of the scope of these various terms is required to avoid confusion.

The terms 'countermeasures', 'unilateral sanctions' and 'decentralised sanctions' or even 'decentralised reactions to illegality' presuppose the existence of an internationally wrongful act to which the State resorting to the relevant measures is reacting. They are taken by an injured State against the State responsible for the internationally wrongful act.[4] In the past, such measures were called 'reprisals', but the term 'countermeasures' is now preferred, following the ILC,[5] also because it is more neutral and does not invoke parallels with the practice of armed reprisals short of war so prevalent in earlier times. Even if multiple States are injured by the same internationally wrongful act and resort to countermeasures (even coordinated countermeasures) against the responsible State,[6] their reaction is not a 'collective' sanction, but rather a 'multilateral' response to illegality. A multilateral measure is one taken by a plurality of States, while the term 'collective' sanction should be reserved, again following the ILC,[7] for measures imposed by international organisations. Indeed, only such measures are truly collective,[8] and for this reason the terms 'collective' or

[3] See the 'ILC Commentary on the Articles on the Responsibility of States for Internationally Wrongful Acts' (ASR) in 'Report of the ILC on the Work of its Fifty-Third Session' (2001) II(2) *Ybk ILC* 137, para 3.

[4] See ASR, Art 49.

[5] See P Malanczuk, 'Countermeasures and Self-Defence as Circumstances Precluding Wrongfulness in the International Law Commission's Draft Articles on State Responsibility' (1983) 43 *Zeitschrift für ausländisches öffentliches Recht und Völkerrecht* 705, 724; and *cf* E Zoller, *Peacetime Unilateral Remedies: An Analysis of Countermeasures* (Dobbs Ferry, Transnational Publishers, 1984) xv–xvii.

[6] See ASR, Art 46.

[7] See the 'ILC Commentary' on Article 22 ASR (n 3) para 3. See also the 'Report of the ILC on the Work of its Thirty-First Session' (1979) II(2) *Ybk ILC* 121, para 21 of the commentary to draft Art 30 (countermeasures).

[8] See also D Alland, *Justice privée et ordre juridique internationale: étude théorique des contre-mesures en droit international public* (Paris, Pedone, 1994) 26.

'institutional' sanctions or reactions to illegality should only be used to denote the reaction of an international organisation to an internationally wrongful act. The following two sections take up reactions to illegal unilateral and collective sanctions in turn.

III. REACTIONS TO ILLEGAL UNILATERAL SANCTIONS

A. Countermeasures

A unilateral reaction to illegality, ie a countermeasure, may itself constitute an illegality. But this statement needs to be approached with the utmost care. A countermeasure is, by definition, an unlawful act in the first instance. It is an act by a State that is not in conformity with what is required of that State under an international obligation owed by that State to another State.[9] But the wrongfulness of that act is precluded if it constitutes a countermeasure taken by an injured State against a State that is responsible for a previous internationally wrongful act injuring that former State.[10] In order however for the act to be characterised properly as a countermeasure, and thus to preclude the wrongfulness of the reaction, it must itself comply with a number of conditions.[11] If not, then the wrongfulness is not precluded, and the unilateral reaction to illegality is itself unlawful. As such, it engages the reacting State's international responsibility, allowing the State targeted by the reaction to resort itself to countermeasures.[12]

The conditions for lawful resort to countermeasures are both substantive and procedural. The principal substantive conditions are two: the countermeasure must be a measure responding to an internationally wrongful act; and it must be a measure taken by an injured State against the responsible State.[13] There are, to be sure, further substantive conditions that need to be fulfilled for lawful resort to countermeasures. These include the obligation to respect the principle of proportionality in taking countermeasures,[14] as well as the obligation to respect the prohibition of resorting to measures that breach certain fundamental obligations, such as the prohibition of the use of force, obligations relating to the protection of human rights, the obligations of international humanitarian law prohibiting reprisals, as well as

[9] See ASR, Arts 22 and 49(2).
[10] Ibid Arts 22 and 49.
[11] Ibid Arts 49–53.
[12] See generally *Air Service Agreement of 27 March 1946 (United States v France)* (1978) 18 RIAA 417.
[13] ASR, Art 49.
[14] Ibid Art 51.

other obligations of *jus cogens* (ie peremptory norms of international law, in the preferred language of the ILC).[15]

A State purportedly reacting to the internationally wrongful act of another State may violate these substantive conditions for lawful resort to countermeasures. Consider for example that State A determines that the conduct of State B constitutes a breach of an obligation that State B owes to State A, but that, actually, the conduct of State B is not at all in breach of that (or any other) obligation. Since there is no compulsory jurisdiction in international law, ie there is no obligation to submit disputes for resolution to a court or tribunal with the power to make a binding decision, the power to make a determination as to whether State B violated its obligations towards State A rests with State A.[16] Except, of course, any such auto-determination by State A is made at State A's own risk; if State A is found to be wrong in its determination of State B's act's legality, then it has itself perpetrated an internationally wrongful act injuring State B. Countermeasures as a circumstance precluding wrongfulness is not available to State A in order to justify its act and avoid the resulting engagement of its international responsibility. State B then is entitled to resort to countermeasures against State A, on account of State A's internationally wrongful act.

This structure may obviously result in an escalation where the two States take turns resorting to countermeasures against each other; each resort to countermeasures may be claimed by the targeted State to have been unlawful, hence justifying further countermeasures. But in the final analysis this escalation of the conflict will have to end, in the sense that the two States are prohibited from resorting to force in order to resolve it.[17] If they choose to resolve the dispute (rather than live with the stalemate or let the dispute dissipate) they are obligated to do so peacefully,[18] so they will either have to negotiate some way out or they will have to submit the dispute to some international jurisdiction. The arbitration between the US and France in the *Air Service Agreement* case demonstrates such an escalation by consecutive employment of countermeasures and its resolution by resort to an international tribunal.[19]

[15] Ibid Art 50.

[16] See *Affaire du Lac Lanoux (Espagne c France)* (1957) 12 RIAA 281, 310, para 16: 'il appartient à chaque État d'apprécier, raisonnablement et de bonne foi, les situations et les règles qui le mettent en cause' ['it is for each state to appreciate for itself, reasonably and in good fairth, those factual situations and rules which relate to it' (author's translation)].

[17] See UN Charter, Art 2(4).

[18] Ibid Arts 2(3) and 33.

[19] See *Air Service Agreement of 27 March 1946 (United States v France)* (n 12) 454.

Lawful resort to countermeasures is also subject to compliance with a number of procedural requirements. These include, notably, an obligation of notification of resort to countermeasures and an obligation to offer to negotiate with the responsible State.[20] The violation of these procedural conditions has the same consequences as the violation of any substantive conditions: the reaction to illegality can no longer be qualified as a countermeasure, and thus its wrongfulness will not be precluded but will engage the responsibility of the reacting State. As such, the targeted State may respond by taking its own countermeasures, resulting in escalation of the conflict. However, these procedural conditions are in reality not as important as the substantive conditions, or at least not in every case. The substantive conditions are not subject to circumvention, but the procedural ones may be circumvented by resort to 'urgent' countermeasures, which do not require compliance with any procedural niceties such as notification and negotiation.[21] What is more, the relevant provision of the ILC Articles on State Responsibility seems to leave it to the reacting State to decide definitively whether such 'urgent' countermeasures are in order.[22] Finally, it is questionable to what extent the procedural conditions required by the ILC for lawful resort to countermeasures actually reflect customary international law—they seem to constitute progressive development,[23] and of a rather soft kind for that matter (given the almost self-judging power of a reacting State to circumvent them).

Multilateral countermeasures, ie countermeasures taken against the responsible State by a plurality of injured States, pose similar problems. Here multiple States auto-determine the existence of a breach and the concomitant engagement of responsibility of the allegedly responsible State. This may attenuate the subjectivity of the determination, but it makes it more difficult for the multilateral countermeasures to be in conformity with the requirement of proportionality (unless they are very carefully coordinated). In any event, these multilateral countermeasures are rather rare. What is of more interest is the employment of 'countermeasures in the general interest', ie the reaction of States 'other than the injured State', and it is to this issue that the next subsection now turns.

[20] See ASR, Art 52(1).

[21] Ibid Art 52(2).

[22] Ibid.

[23] See L-A Sicilianos, 'La codification des contre-mesures par la Commission du droit international' (2005) 38 *Revue belge de droit international* 447, 479; and *cf* C Laly-Chevalier, *La violation du traité* (Bruxelles, Bruylant, 2005) 561.

B. 'Lawful' Measures by States 'Other than the Injured State': Countermeasures in the General Interest

Countermeasures in the general interest,[24] or in the 'collective' interest,[25] or 'third-party' countermeasures,[26] are *not* reactions by a plurality of injured States. They are rather a reaction by States that have not been individually injured by the breach to which they react. These States, peculiarly called by the ILC 'States other than the injured State',[27] are probably better characterised as 'indirectly' injured.[28] They are 'indirectly' injured by the breach of an obligation *erga omnes partes*, ie owed collectively to a particular group of States to which they belong, or *erga omnes*, ie owed to the international community as a whole.[29]

The ILC Articles on State Responsibility do not take a position as to the legality of such countermeasures in the general or collective interest:[30] Article 54 clearly avoids the issue by providing that 'States other than the injured State' under Article 48 may still take 'lawful measures'. The provision could be seen as a denial of a right to take countermeasures in the general interest: only lawful measures are allowed, and countermeasures are inherently unlawful measures whose wrongfulness is merely precluded. On the other hand, there would be no need for a provision that States can take 'lawful' measures. That they can do in any event, and such an interpretation would make the provision redundant. Still, the provision is worded as a 'no prejudice' clause and thus does not provide any useful guidance on the issue.[31]

Doctrine is divided as to the permissibility of countermeasures in the general interest,[32] even though the stronger position seems to be the

[24] See generally D Alland, 'Countermeasures of General Interest' (2002) 13 *European Journal of International Law* 1221.

[25] See eg H P Aust, *Complicity and the Law of State Responsibility* (Cambridge, Cambridge University Press, 2011) 365–72.

[26] M Dawidowicz, 'Public Law Enforcement without Public Law Safeguards? An Analysis of State Practice on Third-party Countermeasures and Their Relationship to the UN Security Council' (2006) 77 *British Year Book of International Law* 333.

[27] ASR, Arts 48 and 54.

[28] See generally L-A Sicilianos, 'The Classification of Obligations and the Multilateral Dimension of the Relations of International Responsibility' (2002) 13 *European Journal of International Law* 1127.

[29] See ASR, Art 48.

[30] Dawidowicz, 'Public Law Enforcement without Public Law Safeguards?' (n 26) 347, speaks of an 'agnostic' provision; C Tams, *Enforcing Obligations* Erga Omnes *in International Law* (Cambridge, Cambridge University Press, 2005) 200, considers that the ILC 'decided not to decide'. See also Sicilianos, 'The Classification of Obligations and the Multilateral Dimension of the Relations of International Responsibility' (n 28) 1142, for a similar assessment.

[31] ASR Commentary (n 3) 139, para 7 of the commentary to Art 54.

[32] The ILC considers that the relevant practice is 'limited and rather embryonic': see ASR Commentary (n 3) 137, para 3 of the commentary to Art 54. However, many authors cite

one accepting that practice supports the taking of such measures. In any event, this is not a question that could be resolved in this short study. But the heated discussion of the issue highlights the importance and the necessity of some reaction against illegality in the collective or general interest.[33] The United Nations possesses, according to its Charter, such a power of reacting in the name of the 'international community', whatever that term may mean.[34] This must lead to a discussion of collective or 'institutionalised' sanctions imposed by the United Nations, and it is the subject of the next—and last—substantive section.

IV. REACTIONS TO ILLEGAL COLLECTIVE SANCTIONS

Roberto Ago, sometime Special Rapporteur on State Responsibility, wrote in his Eighth Report on the issue that 'it is understandable' that the international community, in progressively institutionalising:

> reserves to international institutions, rather than to States, the task of determining the existence of a breach of an international obligation which is of fundamental importance for the international community as a whole, and, accordingly, the task of deciding on the measures to be taken and on their implementation.[35]

The United Nations Security Council is undeniably the most important such international institution. The Charter of the United Nations, that is to say, in the final analysis, the States, has endowed the Security Council with the power to react to threats to the peace through the imposition of measures not including the use of armed force under Article 41.[36] These latter measures are, quite interestingly, commonly referred to as

to considerable relevant practice: see eg Dawidowicz (n 26), Sicilianos (n 28) and Tams, *Enforcing Obligations* (n 30). See further on this, P-E Dupont, 'Countermeasures and Collective Security: The Case of EU Sanctions Against Iran' (2012) 17 *Journal of Conflict and Security Law* 301; C Hillgruber, 'The Right of Third States to Take Countermeasures' in C Tomuschat and J-M Thouvenin (eds), *The Fundamental Rules of the International Legal Order:* Jus Cogens *and Obligations* Erga Omnes (Leiden, Martinus Nijhoff Publishers, 2006) 265; J Frowein, 'Reactions By Not Directly Affected States to Breaches of Public International Law' (1994) 248 *Recueil des cours de l'Académie de droit international de La Haye* 345; K Hailbronner, 'Sanctions and Third Parties and the Concept of International Public Order' (1992) 30 *Archiv des Völkerrechts* 2; T Stein, 'International Measures Against Terrorism and the Sanctions By and Against Third States' (1992) 30 *Archiv des Völkerrechts* 38; and M Akehurst, 'Reprisals by Third States' (1970) 44 *British Year Book of International Law* 1.

[33] I have elsewhere made the argument that 'collective' and 'general' interest are not one and the same thing, but the terms are used here interchangeably to denote the fact that they are variously so used in the literature. For that first position, see A Tzanakopoulos, 'The Permanent Court of International Justice and the "International Community"' in C Tams and M Fitzmaurice (eds), *Legacies of the Permanent Court of International Justice* (Leiden, Martinus Nijhoff Publishers, 2013) 347–51.

[34] See generally ibid.

[35] R Ago, 'Eighth Report on State Responsibility' (1979) II(1) *Ybk ILC* 43, para 91.

[36] UN Charter, Art 39.

'sanctions', even though the Charter does not use this term in the relevant provisions (or anywhere else for that matter). However, the former Special Rapporteur considered, along with many other jurists, that the Security Council does not actually adopt 'sanctions' in the strict sense when it acts under Article 41 of the Charter.[37] Accordingly, the argument goes, Security Council sanctions are not truly reactions to illegality, that is responses to internationally wrongful acts.

Still, it is worth noting that the Council may only adopt Article 41 measures after having determined the existence of a threat to the peace, a breach of the peace, or an act of aggression, in accordance with Article 39 of the Charter. As broad a discretion as the Council may have in making that determination, such discretion may only exist within the law;[38] so, in particular, the Council may only exercise that discretion within the outer limits of the concept of 'threat to the peace' as prescribed by law.[39] The characterisation of a situation as a threat to the peace has then certain legal consequences, here the capacity to adopt sanctions against the entity responsible for constituting or posing a threat to the peace. This means that the determination of the existence of a threat to the peace is a *legal* determination. In other words, in determining the existence of a threat to the peace, the Council is concretising the general obligation (under the Charter) not to constitute such a threat to the peace, and is holding responsible the entity against which it prescribes sanctions in accordance with Article 41. As the practice of the Security Council confirms,[40] measures taken under Article 41 of the Charter are actually proper sanctions. But is it possible that these sanctions are themselves unlawful?

A. Unlawful Sanctions

The United Nations, like any entity with a measure of international legal personality, has the capacity to violate international law. To the extent indeed that the United Nations has 'a large measure of international legal

[37] Ago, 'Eighth Report on State Responsibility' (n 35) para 92. See also G Arangio-Ruiz, 'Seventh Report on State Responsibility' (1995) II(1) *Ybk ILC* 22, paras 97–98; V Gowlland-Debbas, 'Responsibility and the United Nations Charter' in J Crawford, A Pellet and S Olleson (eds), *The Law of International Responsibility* (Oxford, Oxford University Press, 2010) 125–27.

[38] I Brownlie, 'The Decisions of Political Organs of the United Nations and the Rule of Law' in R St J Macdonald (ed), *Essays in Honour of Wang Tieya* (Dordrecht, Martinus Nijhoff Publishers, 1994) 95.

[39] It must stay within the 'interpretative radius' of the provision of Art 39: see E Hexner, 'Teleological Interpretation of Basic Instruments of Public International Organisations' in S Engel (ed), *Law, State, and International Legal Order: Essays in Honour of Hans Kelsen* (Knoxville, University of Tennessee Press, 1964) 123.

[40] Gowlland-Debbas, 'Responsibility and the United Nations Charter' (n 37) 128–33.

personality', and thus the capacity to have rights under international law,[41] it also has the capacity to assume international obligations. When the Organisation breaches these obligations, it engages its international responsibility. This is both evident from practice, and confirmed by the ILC in its Articles on the Responsibility of International Organisations ('DARIO').[42]

For the UN to engage its international responsibility with respect to sanctions imposed by the Security Council under Article 41, it must be demonstrated that conduct which is attributable to the UN is not in conformity with what is required of the Organisation under an international obligation incumbent upon it.[43] Establishing these two elements of the internationally wrongful act, attribution of conduct and breach of an international obligation, is no easy feat, to be sure. However, in the briefest terms it is possible to argue that, the Council being an organ—and a principal organ, at that—of the Organisation, its conduct is directly and automatically attributable to the UN.[44] Since the Security Council does not have any self-standing operational capacity, such conduct will be almost exclusively normative conduct, ie limited in the promulgation of decisions. However, even conduct undertaken by Member States in implementation of such decisions may be attributable to the United Nations if the Security Council (ie the UN) effectively controls that conduct. Such effective control need not be factual effective control on the ground along *Nicaragua* lines: it may also be normative effective control, in the sense of the adoption of a binding decision which leaves States no room for discretion in its implementation.[45] The power to adopt such binding decisions which unilaterally create international obligations for other subjects of international law is a particular characteristic of international organisations, to which the following paragraphs will return. For now, suffice it say that if such conduct attributable to the UN is also in breach of UN obligations, the Organisation's responsibility will be engaged, if there is no circumstance which can preclude the wrongfulness of the relevant act.

And there are many obligations incumbent on the UN. These may stem, in the first instance, from its own Charter, its constitutive instrument. Indeed the Charter, in delineating the competence and powers of the Organisation and its various organs, imposes international obligations on

[41] See *Reparation for Injuries Suffered in the Service of the United Nations* (Advisory Opinion) [1949] ICJ Rep 179.

[42] Draft Articles on the Responsibility of International Organisations and Commentary, in 'Report of the International Law Commission on the Work of its Sixty-Third Session' (2011) UN Doc A/66/10, 54, para 87, commentary on Art 1 at 71–72, para 4. See also DARIO, Art 3 and commentary, ibid 80–81.

[43] DARIO, Art 4.

[44] Ibid Art 6(1).

[45] For this argument, see in detail A Tzanakopoulos, *Disobeying the Security Council: Countermeasures against Wrongful Sanctions* (Oxford, Oxford University Press, 2011) ch 2.

the Organisation.[46] These include, for present purposes, the obligation to determine the existence of a threat to the peace before adopting sanctions, or the obligation to respect the principle of proportionality when adopting such sanctions.[47] But international obligations may also be incumbent on the UN under general international law, including obligations under peremptory norms of international law, or obligations to respect human rights.[48]

In certain cases, it is possible to conceptualise or understand the responsibility of an international organisation in a manner identical to that of a State. This is the case, for example, where the international organisation breaches an obligation incumbent upon it by virtue of a bilateral treaty. However, as briefly mentioned above, certain international organisations have the exceptional characteristic of being able to unilaterally obligate States through their normative conduct (the adoption of binding decisions). This is a crucial difference between international organisations and States (who do not have the power to unilaterally impose obligations on other subjects of international law), and it has certain repercussions when it comes to attribution of conduct (it allows the attribution of State conduct to the international organisation, when that State conduct is effectively normatively controlled by the organisation by means of a strict binding decision, as noted above). In particular, the Security Council has the power to adopt measures which are binding on UN Member States by virtue of Chapter VII of the Charter. Such measures may be, at one and the same time, both normative acts that impose international obligations on States, and internationally wrongful acts (illegal acts) that engage the responsibility of the United Nations.

There are numerous examples of Security Council sanctions that may possess this double 'quality'. One may mention here the demarcation of the Iraq-Kuwait boundary by means of Resolution 687 (1991), which was considered by some as being in violation of general international law;[49] the sanctions against Libya in connection with the Lockerbie incident between 1992 and 1998, which the Member States of the (then) Organisation of African Unity (OAU)[50] and the (then) Organisation of the Islamic Conference (OIC)[51] found to be in breach of the freedom of religion and the obligation to determine the existence of an actual threat to the peace;[52] the Resolutions proscribing the prosecution of peacekeepers

[46] See DARIO, Art 2(b) and commentary.
[47] Tzanakopoulos, *Disobeying the Security Council* (n 45) ch 3.
[48] Ibid.
[49] I Brownlie, 'International Law at the Fiftieth Anniversary of the United Nations' (1995) 255 *Recueil des cours de l'Académie de droit international de La Haye* 220.
[50] Now the African Union.
[51] Now the Organisation of Islamic Cooperation.
[52] See OUA Doc CM/Res.1566 (LXI) (1995); OUA Doc AHG/Decl.2 (XXXIII) (1997); OUA Doc AHG/Dec.127 (XXXIV) (1998); UN Doc S/PV.3864 (1998).

before the International Criminal Court in 2002 and 2003, which did not respond, according to some, to any actual threat to the peace;[53] the sanctions against the former Yugoslavia during the 1990s, which the OIC considered to be in violation of the inherent right of self-defence (as far as it concerned Bosnia and Herzegovina);[54] and of course the anti-terrorist sanctions established by Resolution 1267 (1999), which are still in force today (though the sanctions regime has been split in two by Resolutions 1988 and 1989 (2011)) and which can be seen as violating the rights of access to a court and to an effective remedy,[55] among others.

Turning now to the consequences of such potentially internationally wrongful sanctions of the United Nations, the usual response in the literature is to consider the relevant decisions imposing them as null and void or invalid. This assessment rests on a questionable interpretation of Article 25 of the UN Charter, which is seen as implying that Member States of the UN are only under an obligation to accept and carry out decisions of the Security Council which are 'in accordance with' the Charter. This is understood as meaning that ultra vires decisions of the Council are not 'in accordance with' the Charter and are thus devoid of binding force.[56]

[53] See eg UN Doc S/PV.4568 (2002). See further A Zimmermann, '"Acting Under Chapter VII (...)": Resolution 1422 and Possible Limits of the Powers of the Security Council' in J Frowein et al (eds), *Verhandeln für den Frieden:* Liber Amicorum *Tono Eitel* (Berlin, Springer, 2003) 262–66.

[54] Res No 6/22-P (10–12 December 1994) para 7; *cf* Res No 7/21-P (25–29 April 1993) 12th preamb; Res No 6/23-P (9–12 December 1995) paras 12–15. See also the Declaration of Heads of State and Government of the OIC on Bosnia and Herzegovina at their Seventh Conference (13, 15 December 1994) para 4.

[55] See generally A Tzanakopoulos, 'Domestic Court Reactions to UN Security Council Sanctions' in A Reinisch (ed), *Challenging Acts of International Organisations before National Courts* (Oxford, Oxford University Press, 2010) 54.

[56] See eg D Akande, 'The International Court of Justice and the Security Council: Is there Room for Judicial Control of Decisions of the Political Organs of the United Nations?' (1997) 46 *International and Comparative Law Quarterly* 333–35; E de Wet, 'The Role of Human Rights in Limiting the Enforcement Power of the Security Council: A Principled View' in E de Wet and A Nollkaemper (eds), *Review of the Security Council by Member States* (Antwerp, Intersentia, 2003) 25–27; M Happold, 'Reviewing the Security Council: The Role of Other International Organisations' University of Luxembourg Law Working Paper No 2011-4; D Joyner, 'Non-Proliferation Law and the United Nations System: Resolution 1540 and the Limits of the Power of the Security Council' (2007) 20 *Leiden Journal of International Law* 512–15; T Schilling, 'Die "neue Weltordnung" und die Souveränität der Mitglieder der Vereinte Nationen' (1995) 33 *Archiv des Völkerrechts* 96; K Parameswaran, 'Der Rechtsstatus des Kosovo im Lichte der aktuellen Entwicklungen' (2008) 46 *Archiv des Völkerrechts* 187–89. For other interpretations of Art 25 of the Charter, see eg N Angelet, 'Protest Against Security Council Decisions' in K Wellens (ed), *International Law: Theory and Practice: Essays in Honour of Eric Suy* (The Hague, Martinus Nijhoff Publishers, 1998) 278; J Alvarez, 'The Security Council's War on Terrorism: Problems and Policy Options' in De Wet and Nollkaemper, this footnote, 124–25. For my own interpretation, see Tzanakopoulos (n 45) 164–66 and the new introduction to the paperback edition of that work (2013) xxxvii–xxxviii.

However, if accepted, such a position would eliminate the normal legal consequences entailed by international responsibility for an internationally wrongful act, and would replace them with a rather novel concept of 'invalidity' or 'non-existence' of the offending (internationally wrongful) act. That is, instead of dealing with an international wrong, we are to pretend that the international wrong simply did not happen, in the sense that it does not produce its intended legal effects. At the heart of this position may be a misplaced double analogy. This analogy is either to internationally wrongful acts of States, which are sometimes said to be 'nullities' and not to produce their intended legal effects, or to the domestic legal orders of States, which have crucially different characteristics from the international legal order in this respect.

An analogy to internationally wrongful acts of States which are sometimes called 'nullities' is misplaced, because these internationally wrongful acts still bring about the normal consequences of international responsibility, even if they are unable to bring about their intended change in the international legal order. For example, the invasion, occupation and annexation by one State of the territory of another may be called 'null and void', but this merely means that no transfer of sovereignty takes place, due to the prohibition of acquisition of territory by force. However, there is still a secondary obligation of the responsible State not only to cease the wrongful act and to offer restitution by withdrawing from the territory, and compensation for the damage caused, but also to offer juridical restitution by withdrawing the normative acts purporting to annex the territory and to compensate for any taking of property on the basis of these or other relevant normative acts. By contrast, considering a Security Council decision a nullity would mean that no international obligation for the Member States arises, and that there is in fact no act which can be considered internationally wrongful; unlike domestic normative acts (which produce effects both domestically and potentially internationally, and whose international invalidity or nullity cannot affect their domestic existence),[57] international normative acts only produce effects internationally (and impose obligations of domestic implementation). If they do not produce such international effects, there are correspondingly no obligations of domestic implementation. As such, there is no internationally wrongful act to cease, and nothing for which to offer reparation. The analogy is misplaced as a result of the peculiar power of international organisations to unilaterally create obligations for their Member States, discussed above: while States cannot unilaterally impose international obligations on other States, international organisations do exceptionally have this power.

[57] See *Arrest Warrant of 11 April 2000 (Democratic Republic of the Congo v Belgium)* [2002] ICJ Rep 32, para 76.

This fundamental difference between States and international organisations cannot be ignored and speaks against any analogies between the normative acts of States and those of international organisations.

An analogy to domestic legal orders of States is equally misplaced. There is compulsory jurisdiction in domestic legal orders, which is conspicuously absent at the international level. Any coherent theory of nullity or invalidity (of which there is none in international law)[58] and thus also any relevant analogy, would require the existence of compulsory jurisdiction which could finally decide the issue, either declaring the act's invalidity, or invalidating the act. The absence of such compulsory jurisdiction in general international law eliminates the possibility of drawing an analogy between the two systems. By contrast, such a theory of nullity is possible in certain partial international legal systems or orders, sometimes called 'integral',[59] such as that established by the EU treaties. There, the existence of compulsory jurisdiction allows for the elaboration and operation of a theory of nullity. The Courts of the EU have indeed the power to invalidate the acts of other organs of the Union.[60]

It is important to stress at this point that, in the theory of law, nullity or invalidity is merely one of the possible consequences of illegality.[61] There are other potential consequences, responsibility being one such 'direct, if not always immediate' consequence.[62]

[58] P Weil, 'Le droit international en quête de son identité: cours général de droit international public' (1992) 237 *Recueil des cours de l'Académie de droit international de La Haye* 319: 'le système international est allergique [...] à l'idée de ne pas faire crédit aux actes juridiques et à mettre en doute leur validité' ['the international system is allergic to the idea of not giving credit to juridical acts and to putting their validity in doubt'] (author's translation); see also ibid 320; E Osieke, '*Ultra Vires* Acts of International Organisations: The Experience of the International Labour Organisation' (1976–77) 48 *British Year Book of International Law* 262; R Bernhardt, '*Ultra vires* Activities of International Organisations' in J Makarczyk (ed), *Theory of International Law at the Threshold of the 21st Century: Essays in Honour of Krzysztof Skubiszewski* (The Hague, Kluwer, 1996) 599; *cf* E Lauterpacht, 'The Legal Effects of Illegal Acts of International Organisations' in *Cambridge Essays in International Law: Essays in Honour of Lord McNair* (London, Stevens & Sons, 1965) 115 specifically on a theory of nullity in the UN Charter.

[59] See P-M Dupuy, 'Responsabilité et légalité' in Société française pour le droit international (ed), *La responsabilité dans le système international* (Paris, Pedone, 1991) 274: 'le contentieux de légalité [...] a seulement pour objet de constater et de dénoncer la violation du droit par une conduite donnée (avec, *dans le cadre de certains systèmes juridiques intégrés*, la possibilité corrélative d'annuler l'acte s'il présente un caractère normatif)' (emphasis added) ['a legal challenge has solely the objective of determining and of denouncing the violation of the law by a given conduct (accompanied, in certain integrated legal systems, by the correlative possibility of annuling the act, if the latter has normative character)'] (author's translation).

[60] And indeed excluding any such power of the Member States. See eg Case 44/79, *Hauer v Land Rheinland Pfalz* [1979] ECR 3727.

[61] See H Kelsen, *Introduction to the Problems of Legal Theory* (Oxford, Clarendon Press, 1994) 118–19. *Cf* Ian Brownlie, *System of the Law of Nations: State Responsibility—Part I* (London, Clarendon Press, 1983) 87: responsibility and invalidity are pertinent forms of illegality. Illegality is thus the *genus* and invalidity one *species* of that *genus*.

[62] See Dupuy, 'Responsabilité et légalité' (n 59) 263.

Bearing in mind the presumption of the validity of UN acts,[63] and in the absence of an organ with competence to finally and definitively determine the invalidity or nullity of acts of the Security Council, the premise must be that Security Council acts are always to be considered as valid, and thus as producing their intended legal effects. Sanctions resolutions then are always valid, but they may also be unlawful, thus constituting internationally wrongful acts that engage the international responsibility of the United Nations.

B. Reaction: Disobedience as a Countermeasure

The United Nations may have engaged its international responsibility through the internationally wrongful act perpetrated by the Security Council—and yet, this does not answer the question what the potential reaction of the States might be. How might they react to the illegality and seek to implement the Organisation's responsibility, that is to induce the UN to comply with its secondary obligations, notably those of cessation and reparation?

The answer, it is submitted, is the same as in general international law: the reaction to an unlawful sanction can only be a sanction, and in this case a decentralised sanction—a countermeasure. Indeed, in the decentralised international legal order, the norm is the decentralised implementation of international responsibility, that is to say its implementation without necessary prior recourse to any judicial or executive organ. And the primary means for such decentralised implementation is resort to countermeasures. But could it really be that States can take countermeasures against the United Nations and its Security Council?

There is no provision in the UN Charter excluding resort to countermeasures against the Organisation. This is not necessarily the case for other international organisations: for example, the Court of Justice of the European Union has determined that EU Member States may not take countermeasures against the Union for violations of EU law.[64] This

[63] *Certain Expenses of the United Nations* (Advisory Opinion) [1962] ICJ Rep 168; *cf Legal Consequences for States of the Continued Presence of South Africa in Namibia (South West Africa) Notwithstanding Security Council Resolution 276 (1970)* (Advisory Opinion) [1971] ICJ Rep 22, para 20.

[64] See Joined Cases 90/63 and 91/63, *Commission v Luxembourg and Belgium* [1964] ECR 1232: 'except where otherwise expressly provided, the basic concept of the treaty requires that the Member States shall not take the law into their own hands. Therefore, the fact that the Council failed to carry out its obligations cannot relieve the defendants from carrying out theirs'. For the prohibition of countermeasures between EU Member States for violation of EU law see Case C-5/94, *Hedley Lomas* [1996] ECR I-2553, paras 17–21.

proscription of countermeasures, however, is based precisely on the fact that the States, in establishing the EU, put in place a judicial organ and vested it with compulsory jurisdiction, as well as with the power to invalidate normative acts of other Union organs.[65] By doing this, they effectively denounced their own power to undertake any auto-determination of the legality of Union acts by transferring it to the judicial organ that they established.[66] No such transfer has taken place in the context of the UN, whose principal judicial organ cannot pronounce on the legality of UN acts with binding force on Member States.[67]

The International Law Commission has recognised the possibility of countermeasures being taken against an international organisation for the purposes of responding to an international wrongful act by that organisation and of implementing its responsibility.[68] However, the Commission reversed its position between the first and second reading of the DARIO in 2009 and 2011 respectively, and has now suggested a distinction between two types of countermeasures against international organisations. The first type comprises countermeasures taken in response to a violation of general international law by the organisation. Such countermeasures are admitted unless the rules of the organisation prohibit them.[69] The second type refers to countermeasures adopted in response to a violation of the 'internal' law of the organisation. These are admitted only if the rules of the organisation expressly allow them.[70] This approach has no basis in positive law and is not supported by practice.[71] Even the commentary to the provisions introducing the distinction is laconic at best, offering no explanation as to why exactly such a distinction is required or even desired.[72] In any event, the Commission does not explain why an international organisation should be allowed to violate its 'internal' law

[65] See also DARIO, Art 52 and commentary (n 42) 152–53, para 7.

[66] On conferrals of powers to international organisations and their various forms, see generally D Sarooshi, *International Organisations and their Exercise of Sovereign Powers* (Oxford, Oxford University Press, 2005).

[67] See generally Tzanakopoulos (n 45) chs 4 and 5.

[68] DARIO, Art 51(1).

[69] Ibid Art 52(1)(b), which provides specifically that countermeasures may not be 'inconsistent with the rules of the organisation'.

[70] See DARIO 2011, Art 52(2), which provides that countermeasures may not be taken 'unless [they] are provided for by [the] rules of the organisation', and *cf* DARIO 2009 (first reading), Art 51 which includes no such proviso.

[71] The relevant provisions were criticised by States and the UN Legal Counsel in the Sixth Committee of the General Assembly. See eg UN Docs A/C.6/66/SR.18 (2011) 6, para 28 (Legal Counsel); A/C.6/66/SR.19 (2011) 6, para 33 (Greece); A/C.6/66/SR.20 (2011) 8, para 38 (Belarus). *Contra* UN Doc A/C.6/66/SR.19 (2011) 8, para 42 (India).

[72] See the Commission's commentary to DARIO, Art 52 (n 42) 153, para 8. The only reason given for the provision in the 5-line commentary is 'the special ties existing between an international organisation and its members'.

(which in the final analysis is still international law, as the Commission itself has conceded)[73] with impunity, or why the Member States should be rendered powerless in responding to such a violation. This is exactly what this novel and curious distinction achieves, and it cannot be accepted. The better position is that countermeasures can be taken against any breach of international obligations of the international organisation with a view to implementing the secondary obligations of cessation and reparation, unless the constitutive act of the organisation clearly rules them out (and introduces some other form of control of legality)—which the Charter does not.[74]

The principal countermeasure that UN Member States may employ in the case of unlawful Security Council sanctions is to disobey the Security Council.[75] In refusing to comply with the Council's binding decision, a Member State breaches its obligation under Article 25 of the Charter. If this temporary non-execution of an international obligation owed to the internationally responsible organisation is a measure adopted by an injured State against that organisation, it can be regarded as a countermeasure.[76] This is because the measure taken (disobedience) is a measure 'limited to the non-performance for the time being of international obligations of the State [...] taking the measures towards the responsible international organisation'.[77]

That the Organisation has become responsible was demonstrated above. However, there are further conditions for disobedience being admitted as a lawful countermeasure. The Member State reacting to the Security Council's decision by disobeying it (or by not performing some other obligation it owes the responsible organisation) must be an 'injured' State. Whether in fact the reacting Member States qualifies as an injured State depends on the type of obligation the UN has breached. If it is an obligation stemming from general international law (such as certain human rights obligations), the traditional classification of obligations reflected in Articles 42 and 48 ASR, and Articles 43 and 49 DARIO applies and will determine whether the reacting State is in fact an 'injured' State.[78] If the obligation breached is one stemming from the Charter (such as the obligation to determine the existence of a threat to the peace or to

[73] See DARIO, Art 10(2).

[74] See the example of the EU, above.

[75] See generally Tzanakopoulos (n 45) ch 7.

[76] For a detailed analysis of all the conditions for the characterisation of disobedience as a countermeasure, see Tzanakopoulos (n 45) 177–89.

[77] DARIO, Art 51(2).

[78] See generally Sicilianos (n 28) 1127; Sicilianos, 'La codification des contre-mesures par la Commission du droit international' (n 23) 447.

take measures proportionate to the threat), all UN Member States can be considered as injured States, because the obligations stemming from the Charter (the constitutive act of the UN) are owed to a group of States, ie the members of the Organisation. Furthermore, the violation by the UN of these obligations 'is of such a character as radically to change the position of all States to which the obligation is owed with respect to further performance of the obligation':[79] a violation of the Charter, if unprotested by Member States, may bring about a modification of the Charter, and thus may radically change the position of members as to further performance of their obligations.[80] Obvious examples of Charter modifications through (questionable) practice that went unprotested are the establishment of the *contra legem* interpretation of Article 27(3) of the Charter,[81] and the expansion of the notion of 'threat to the peace' under Article 39. As such, all Member States can be considered injured in the event that the UN violates its constitutive instrument.

There are some examples of reactions against wrongful sanctions decisions that can be characterised as countermeasures. The disobedience of the OAU (as it then was) Member States in 1998 of the sanctions imposed by the Council against Libya is one such obvious example.[82] Another could be the open call of the OIC Member States on UN Member States to disobey the arms embargo imposed by the Security Council against the former Yugoslavia, to the extent that this referred to Bosnia and Herzegovina.[83]

However, even the disobedience imposed on UN Member States by their own domestic courts in the case of anti-terrorist sanctions under the regime established by Security Council Resolution 1267 (1999) can be qualified as a countermeasure. In a number of cases before national (and regional international, which in the present circumstances may be equated with national) courts, such as *Ahmed* before the UK Supreme Court,[84]

[79] ASR, Art 42(b)(ii); and DARIO, Art 43(b)(ii).

[80] I Brownlie, 'The United Nations as a Form of Government' in J E S Fawcett and R Higgins (eds), *International Organisation: Law in Movement—Essays in Honour of John McMahon* (London, Oxford University Press, 1974) 429: 'It is well known that changes in political facts may be reflected in constitutional amendments, the process of interpretation, and the generation of conventions of the constitution'.

[81] See *Namibia* (n 63) 20, paras 21–22.

[82] See generally T Kalala, 'La décision de l'O.U.A. de ne plus respecter les sanctions décrétées par l'O.N.U. contre la Libye: Désobéissance civile des États africains à l'égard de l'O.N.U.' (1999) 32 *Revue belge de droit international* 545.

[83] See (n 54); some UN Member States did ostensibly heed that call: see L F Damrosch, 'Enforcing International Law through Non-Forcible Measures' (1997) 269 *Recueil des cours de l'Académie de droit international de La Haye* 125.

[84] *HM Treasury v Mohammed Jabar Ahmed and others (FC); HM Treasury v Mohammed al-Ghabra (FC); R (on the application of Hani El Sayed Sabaei Youssef) v HM Treasury* [2010] UKSC 2.

Abdelrazik before the Canadian Federal Court,[85] *Kadi* before the EU Courts,[86] and *Nada* before the European Court of Human Rights,[87] these courts struck down domestic implementing measures of Security Council binding resolutions and forced their States to disobey the Council.

A relevant objection might be that court decisions cannot of themselves qualify as countermeasures.[88] In the cases above, however, it can be argued that the domestic courts demanding that States disobey the Council, also furnish the States with a relevant justification for that disobedience (the violation of human rights obligations on the part of the Security Council). While these violations may have been determined by reference to domestic constitutional law and the relevant protection it affords to human rights, the content of human rights obligations in the instance is very similar to that under general international law. As such, the argument is easily translatable into international legal argument on the part of the government—which, in the final analysis retains the (not particularly viable) option of disobeying its own court rather than the Security Council.

Indeed, it should be noted that executives have resolved to disobey Security Council sanctions, in following in part their courts and in responding to popular pressure. On 22 March 2010, for example, the Swiss Permanent Representative to the UN sent a letter to the Chair of the Security Council 1267 Sanctions Committee, notifying the Committee that the Swiss Federal Council had decided to disobey certain sanctions against individuals included in the 1267 Consolidated List.[89]

Finally, any countermeasure of disobedience would seem to comply with the requirements of the principle of proportionality, as substantive condition for the lawfulness of countermeasures, as discussed above. It is easily reversible and truly constitutes an *ultima ratio*, ie a measure resorted to only once every other possibility of negotiation or recourse has been exhausted. In the Libyan example, the OAU had tried for many years to mediate between Libya and the Security Council, and then to negotiate with the Council, to no avail.[90] In August 1998, no less, the Organisation

[85] Case T- 727/08, *Abdelrazik v Minister of Foreign Affairs and Attorney General of Canada* (2009) FC 580. See for commentary, A Tzanakopoulos, 'United Nations Sanctions in Domestic Courts: From Interpretation to Defiance in *Abdelrazik v Canada*' (2010) 8 *Journal of International Criminal Justice* 249.

[86] Cases C-402/05 P, *Kadi and Al Barakaat International Foundation v Council and Commission* [2008] ECR I-6351; T-85/09, *Kadi v Commission* [2010] ECR II-5177; C-584/10 P, C-593/10 P and C-595/10 P, *Council and Commission v Kadi*, Judgment of 18 July 2013, reported in OJ C 260, 7 September 2013, 2–3. For brief commentary on the last case, see A Tzanakopoulos, '*Kadi* Showdown: Substantive Review of (UN) Sanctions by the ECJ' [2013] EJIL: Talk! (19 July) available at: www.ejiltalk.org/kadi-showdown.

[87] *Nada v Switzerland* (2013) 56 EHRR 18.

[88] But see further Tzanakopoulos (n 45) 194–97.

[89] Letter copied in COE AS/Jur/Inf (2010) 05, 7 December 2010, 6.

[90] See the documents cited in (n 52).

notified to the Council its decision no longer to comply with what it considered to be illegal sanctions against Libya.[91] Almost within days the Council had decided to accept the solution negotiated with Libya by the OAU, and suspended the sanctions.[92]

In the case of the 1267 regime of anti-terrorist sanctions, on the other hand, the many cases where domestic courts had come close or had threatened to force disobedience of Council sanctions upon their States led to slow but palpable improvements in the procedure for listing and delisting of individuals, and, finally, after disobedience had been adopted as a countermeasure, even to the establishment of a continuously improving procedure for delisting by recourse to an independent and impartial Ombudsperson.[93] What is more, the constant threat of disobedience issued by the domestic courts over the years can be considered as having served as a notification of the intention to disobey the relevant sanctions.

V. CONCLUSION

Reactions to illegality, whether decentralised (countermeasures) or centralised/institutionalised (sanctions) may themselves be illegal and thus engage the responsibility of the entity resorting to them. The State targeted or affected by such unlawful sanctions (that is, any State specially affected by the breach or any State even 'indirectly' injured by it) may then resort to its own countermeasures against the responsible State or international organisation. In the case of the predominant institutionalised sanctions under international law, namely the sanctions imposed by the UN through its Security Council, the principal such countermeasure is disobedience.

Characterising disobedience of Security Council binding decisions as a lawful countermeasure may seem inherently dangerous. Such disobedience may threaten to weaken or destabilise the system of collective security under the UN Charter, and finally even the whole architecture of the contemporary international legal order. But at the same time it must be admitted that the Security Council possesses enormous coercive power that is only marginally (and at that only politically) controlled. International law does provide for decentralised control of legality, precisely to make up for such shortcomings. And since there is nothing to exclude the application of general international law in this instance, disobedience remains the last resort of Member States, and is allowed by international

[91] Ibid.

[92] See Res 1192 (1998) para 8.

[93] See eg the changes in the 1267 regime brought about by Res 1904 (2009) and Res 1989 (2011).

law, subject to complying with the conditions for taking countermeasures. The only other option is for further reform and integration of the system of UN sanctions, and even of the operation of the Security Council in general, in order to ensure the compliance of Council action with international law. In that, international law is unique in being a legal system that sanctions disobedience. After all, '[i]t is through disobedience that progress has been made, through disobedience and through rebellion'.[94]

[94] O Wilde, *The Soul of Man and Prison Writings* (Oxford, Oxford University Press, 1990) 4.

5

Targeted Sanctions and Human Rights

MATTHEW HAPPOLD

I. INTRODUCTION

THIS CHAPTER EXAMINES the compatibility of targeted sanctions—that is, sanctions directed against specific named persons—with the human rights of those who they target. It will address both sanctions imposed by the United Nations Security Council and other international organisations, in particular the European Union, and individual States. And it will do so by looking at the compatibility of such sanctions with procedural and substantive human rights.

The main legal distinction, when considering whether targeted sanctions breach human rights, is said to be that Security Council resolutions imposing sanctions benefit from the effects of Articles 25 and 103 of the United Nations Charter, so that UN Member States' obligations to comply with such decisions 'trump' their obligations under other treaties to which they are party, including international human rights treaties. Such a view, however, ignores the possibility that the UN may itself be bound to comply with human rights norms,[1] and that Article 103 may not apply to rules of customary international law or, at the least, to norms of *jus cogens*.[2] In practice, moreover, adjudicators have found various ways around the distinction. The issue will be revisited later but, in the meantime, the compatibility of targeted sanctions with human rights standards will be

[1] See, among many others, F Mégret and F Hoffmann, 'The UN as a Human Rights Violator? Some Reflections on the United Nations' Changing Human Rights Responsibilities' (2003) 25 *Human Rights Quarterly* 314; G Verdirame, *The UN and Human Rights: Who Guards the Guardians?* (Cambridge, Cambridge University Press, 2011); and E de Wet, 'Human Rights and the Rule of Law as Applicable to the UNSC: Implications for the Right to a Fair Hearing' in C Feinäugle (ed), *The Rule of Law and its Application to the United Nations* (forthcoming, 2016).

[2] See E de Wet, *The Chapter VII Powers of the United Nations Security Council* (Oxford, Hart Publishing, 2004) 187–91; A Orakhelashvili, 'The Impact of Peremptory Norms on Interpretation and Application of the UN Security Council Resolutions' (2005) 16 *European Journal of International Law* 59; and Case T-315/01, *Kadi v Council and Commission* ECLI:EU:T:2005:332, paras 226–30.

assumed to be an issue of real, not just theoretical, concern, even in the case of Security Council sanctions.

II. THE DEVELOPMENT OF TARGETED SANCTIONS

The United Nations Security Council's use of sanctions has evolved considerably in recent decades.[3] Newly liberated from Cold War deadlock, no sooner did the Security Council become more active in exercising its Chapter VII powers than it began to be criticised for doing so. Consideration of the human rights impact of sanctions first emerged as an issue at the international level in the aftermath of the 1991 Gulf War as a result of the consequences of the comprehensive sanctions then imposed against Iraq.[4] Those sanctions, combined with the destruction of much of the Iraqi infrastructure during the conflict, caused widespread suffering. Indeed, up to 100,000 Iraqi children may have died as a result.[5] This gave rise to widespread criticism of the United Nations' actions, which criticisms, in turn, gave rise to considerable debate about how sanctions might best be imposed, with a series of projects and workshops undertaken seeking to find new ways of addressing the issue.[6] The principal solution devised was targeted (or, as they are sometimes called, smart) sanctions.[7]

There were two ideas behind targeted sanctions, which sought to tackle different failings in comprehensive sanctions. The first was that targeted rather than comprehensive sanctions should be imposed for the sake of humanity. Because the sanctions were targeted, they would avoid collateral damage and avoid harming innocent bystanders. On the other hand, however, there was a belief (also taken from the Iraqi example) that comprehensive sanctions were not particularly effective. They caused the innocent to suffer but allowed those responsible for the conduct against which the sanctions were directed to escape scot-free, as by virtue of their leadership positions they were able to avoid the effects of such regimes. So, the idea behind targeted sanctions was twofold: to avoid collateral damage but also to be more effective through striking hard at those whose behaviour was responsible for the situation which the sanctions sought

[3] See J M Farrall, *United Nations Sanctions and the Rule of Law* (Cambridge, Cambridge University Press, 2009) 58–70.

[4] See eg 'Symposium: The Impact on International Law of a Decade of Measures against Iraq' (2002) 13 *European Journal of International Law* 1; and V Gowlland-Debbas (ed), *United Nations Sanctions and International Law* (The Hague, Kluwer, 2001).

[5] See M M Ali and I H Shah, 'Sanctions and Childhood Mortality in Iraq' (2000) 335(9218) *The Lancet* 1851.

[6] For a summary, see J Gordon, 'Smart Sanctions Revisited' (2011) 25 *Ethics and International Affairs* 315, 317–18.

[7] Ibid 318–20.

to address. In addition—and this was an advantage that became increasingly important—targeted sanctions could also be used against non-State actors which had not assumed State-like attributes (eg because they do not control territory) and might even be banned under national law (that is, criminal associations) because they were directed at individual members of the organisation, not at the group itself.

Targeted sanctions began to be imposed by the United Nations from the mid-1990s. The first example of individuals being targeted was in 1994, when the Council imposed travel bans on persons connected with the regime of General Raoul Cedras in Haiti.[8] Their first use against members of a non-State group was in connection to the situation in Angola in 1997, where persons associated with the rebel group UNITA were targeted.[9] In addition, from Council Resolution 1267 (1999) onwards,[10] targeted sanctions have been used against persons associated with Al-Qaida and other terrorist groups. Indeed, it is the targeted sanctions pursuant to Resolutions 1267 and 1373[11] and successive resolutions building upon and developing them that have been most controversial.

It is important, however, to distinguish between different forms of non-comprehensive sanctions, as the terms 'targeted' or 'smart' sanctions are not always used consistently. As here so far, the terms have largely been used to refer to sanctions which target specific persons, particularly through asset freezes and travel bans, but they have also been used to refer to measures imposing so-called 'sectoral sanctions' imposing embargoes prohibiting particular forms of imports or exports. Asset freezes require the freezing of all funds and other assets of a targeted person, so as to prevent them from having access to financial resources. Travel bans oblige States to prevent such persons from entering into or exiting from their national territories, thus preventing them from travelling internationally. Sectoral sanctions, by contrast, seek to prevent the flow of resources to the actors whose behaviour the sanctions regime seeks to constrain: most

[8] UNSC Res 917 (1994). The persons targeted were all officers of the Haitian military, including the police, and their immediate families; the major participants in the 1999 coup d'état and in the illegal governments since the coup and their immediate families; and those employed by or acting on behalf of the Haitian military and their immediate families. The resolution also authorised States to impose an assets freeze on the same persons.

[9] UNSC Res 1127 (1997).

[10] Although Resolution 1267 referred to the Taliban and Al-Qaida and established a sanctions committee, it originally only targeted Taliban leaders, not Al-Qaida members. Al-Qaida members and supporters were first targeted pursuant to UNSC Res 1333 (2000).

[11] Resolution 1373 is anomalous in that it does permit the Council to impose sanctions but instead requires the Member States to freeze the financial assets of 'persons who commit, or attempt to commit, terrorist acts or participate in or facilitate the commission of terrorist acts, or entities owned or controlled directly or indirectly by such persons; and of persons or entities acting on behalf of, or at the direction of such persons or entities'. It is for the individual Member States to decide who to designate, not the Council: see eg *Ahmed v HM Treasury (No 2)* [2010] UKSC 5.

obviously, money, through export bans of valuable commodities; and arms and military materiel, through import bans. Arms embargoes are the best-known form of import ban,[12] as well as being the oldest type of sanctions imposed by the United Nations.[13] But in recent years the United Nations has also imposed a number of export bans in relation to conflicts in Africa, such as prohibitions of the export of timber and diamonds,[14] and the most prominent contemporary example of such an embargo is that imposed by the USA and the European Union on the import of Iranian oil.[15]

This chapter will primarily discuss the first type of sanctions; that is, sanctions targeted at particular persons. At present, although sectoral sanctions (in the form of import and export bans) continue to be used, all current UN sanctions regimes have as a component measures targeted at particular persons; not only natural persons (individuals) but also legal persons (corporations and other collective entities). With renewed use of sectoral sanctions, however, consideration of their potential humanitarian impact cannot be avoided. Indeed, it will be argued that by concentrating on the human rights compatibility of individually-targeted sanctions, other issues have been forgotten or ignored.

III. TARGETED SANCTIONS TODAY

In general, sanctions seem increasingly to be used as a foreign policy tool, not only by the United Nations but also at the regional level and by individual States. All current United Nations and European Union sanctions regimes are, or at least claim to be, targeted. There are presently 17 UN sanctions committees charged with administering targeted sanctions,[16] although some of them are moribund or, to say the least, inactive.[17] In addition, as of September 2015, 37 restrictive measures regimes imposed by the EU under Article 215 TFEU (Treaty on the Functioning of the

[12] Albeit that such forms of sanctions seem often to be ineffective: see A Vines, 'The Effectiveness of UN and EU Sanctions: Lessons for the Twenty-first Century' (2012) 88 *International Affairs* 867, 871–72.

[13] UNSC Res 232 (1966) (Rhodesia) and UNSC Res 418 (1977) (South Africa).

[14] See UNSC Res 1343 (2001) (diamonds) and UNSC Res 1478 (2003) (timber), both against Liberia.

[15] See the US Comprehensive Iran Sanctions, Accountability, and Divestment Act of 2010 (Pub L 111–195) and Council Decision 2012/35/CFSP of 23 January 2012 amending Decision 2010/413/CFSP concerning restrictive measures against Iran and Council Regulation (EU) No 264/2012 of 23 March 2012 amending Regulation (EU) No 359/2011 concerning restrictive measures directed against certain persons, entities and bodies in view of the situation in Iran.

[16] A list can be found at: www.un.org/sc/suborg/en/sanctions/information.

[17] There is still one covering Iraq established pursuant to UNSC Res 1518 (2003) as the successor body to the committee established pursuant to UNSC Res 661 (1990) concerning Iraq and Kuwait.

European Union) were in force.[18] Whilst 17 of them seek to implement Security Council sanctions in the EU legal order (albeit that in some cases the EU goes rather further than has the Council),[19] the other 20 are autonomous regimes, imposed for the EU's own purposes.

The discussions during the 1990s saw little consideration of how targeted sanctions might affect their targets' human rights. Given the persons targeted at the time—who included such luminaries as Slobodan Milosevic in the former Yugoslavia and Mullah Omar in Afghanistan—this becomes less surprising. They were not a particularly sympathetic group (albeit that even rogues have rights). Targeted sanctions were, moreover, if not more selective, at least less frequently utilised; they targeted fewer people, and those targeted tended to hold leadership roles, either in State governments or opposition factions, rather than being private persons alleged to be supporting such regimes or groups. In consequence, in many cases asset freezes only really amounted to a freeze on targeted persons' external assets, as their leadership position protected their assets within their own territories. It also had the consequence that targeted persons did not seek judicially to challenge their listing.

But things changed after 9/11. This chapter will not focus in any detail on the first *Kadi* decision of the European Court of Justice.[20] Much has been written about it already.[21] However, it was the listing of individuals as Al-Qaida associates under Security Council Resolution 1267[22] or as involved in the commission of terrorist acts pursuant to Council

[18] European Commission, 'Restrictive Measures in Force' (TFEU, Art 215) available at: http://eeas.europa.eu/cfsp/sanctions/docs/measures_en.pdf. Somewhat surprisingly, the USA is included on the list (under Council Regulation (EC) No 2271/1996 of 22 November 1996 on protection against certain effects of sanctions imposed by the USA, OJ L 309, p 1 (since amended)) but this is only as regards EU responses to sanctions undertaken by the US; that is, it provides for blocking measures.

[19] Iran being the obvious example, although the EU and Iran having adopted the Joint Comprehensive Plan of Action related to the Iranian nuclear programme on 18 October 2015, the nuclear-related measures seem likely rapidly to be lifted: see European External Action Service, 'Iran Nuclear Deal: Another Step towards Implementation', 18 October 2015, available at: www.eeas.europa.eu/top_stories/2015/181015_federica_mogherini_iran_deal_adoption_en.htm.

[20] Case C-402/05 P and C-415/05 P, *Kadi and Al Barakaat International Foundation v Council* [2008] ECR I-635.

[21] See, to give only a selection: E Cannizzaro, 'Security Council Resolutions and EC Fundamental Rights: Some Remarks on the ECJ Decision in the *Kadi* Case' (2010) 28 *Yearbook of European Law* 593; A Gattini, 'Yassin Abdullah Kadi v Council and Commission' (2009) 46 *Common Market Law Review* 213; L van den Herik and N Schrijver, 'Eroding the Primacy of the UN System of Collective Security: The Judgment of the European Court of Justice in the Case of Kadi and Al Barakaat' (2008) 5 *International Organizations Law Review* 329; L M Hinojosa-Martinez, 'Bad Law for Good Reasons: the Contradictions of the *Kadi* Judgment' (2008) 5 *International Organizations Law Review* 339; and T Tridimas, 'Terrorism and the ECJ: Empowerment and Democracy in the EC Legal Order' (2009) 34 *European Law Review* 103.

[22] To be accurate, targeted sanctions were imposed on 'Usama bin Laden and individuals and entities associated with him' pursuant to UNSC Res 133 (2000), albeit by the Sanctions Committee established under UNSC Res 1267 (1999).

Resolution 1373,[23] and the very draconian consequences that listing had on those individuals—leaving them unable to travel and impecunious (at least in those countries that actually imposed sanctions upon them)—that led to the controversies concerning the human rights impact of targeted sanctions that we now see today. And it is the decisions of the Court of Justice of the European Union (CJEU) in the counter-terrorism context that forms the basis of the jurisprudence that that court has developed as regards targeted sanctions generally.

In *Kadi I*, as is well known, the European Court of Justice took the view that whatever their origin and purpose (in that case, the transposition of a decision of the UN Security Council into the EU legal order), restrictive measures were imposed by decisions of EU institutions and therefore were subject to the same standards of review as any other decision taken by those institutions. Although this meant that formally the Court was reviewing not the Security Council resolution listing Kadi but the Council regulation implementing the resolution within the EU legal order, the result was the same. For that reason, the judgment spurred developments not only within the EU but at the UN. And there have been various other decisions of other national and international courts, with similar results and implications.[24]

However, not only the UN and the EU impose sanctions. Sanctions are imposed by States unilaterally (such as the USA) and by other regional organisations. The African Union, for example, now has a line of practice of imposing sanctions in response to extra-constitutional changes of government within its Member States.[25] These developments will not, however, be discussed here because, at least as yet, the developments regarding judicial or quasi-judicial control over the imposition of sanctions have come largely from within the UN and the EU.

IV. TARGETED SANCTIONS AND SUBSTANTIVE HUMAN RIGHTS

Neither asset freezes nor travel bans—the two main forms of targeted sanctions—can be said, in general, to infringe substantive human rights,

[23] UNSC Res 1373 (2001). To an extent this resolution was anomalous. No sanctions committee was established under the resolution: rather, UN Member States were required to freeze the assets of persons and entities involved in the commission of terrorist acts. A number did so with alacrity.

[24] As regards decisions of national courts, see A Tzanakopoulos, 'Domestic Court Reactions to UN Security Council Sanctions' in A Reinisch (ed), *Challenging Acts of International Organisations before National Courts* (Oxford, Oxford University Press, 2010).

[25] See A Charron, 'Sanctions and Africa: United Nations and Regional Response' in J Boulden (ed), *Responding to Conflict in Africa: The United Nationals and Regional Organizations* (New York, Palgrave Macmillan, 2013); and M Eriksson, 'Supporting Democracy in Africa: The African Union's Use of Targeted Sanctions to Deal with Unconstitutional Changes of Government', FOL: Swedish Defence Research Agency, 2010.

at least when targeted at persons who actually fit the criteria established for the measures' imposition and provided the criteria themselves are not too widely drawn. Herein, however, as we shall see, lies the rub.

As regards the freezing of a person's assets, it will be recalled that the UK House of Lords held that a refusal of financial support to certain asylum seekers, coupled with a prohibition on their seeking employment, amounted to ill-treatment prohibited under Article 3 of the European Convention on Human Rights.[26] Lord Bingham stated that:

> Treatment is inhuman or degrading if, to a seriously detrimental extent, it denies the most basic needs of any human being. As in all article 3 cases, the treatment to be proscribed, must achieve a minimum standard of severity, and I would accept that in a context such as this one, not involving the deliberate infliction or pain or suffering, the threshold is a high one ... But I have no doubt that the threshold may be crossed if a late applicant [for asylum] with no means and no alternate sources of support, unable to support himself, is, by the deliberate action of the state, denied shelter, food or the most basic necessities of life.[27]

Current sanctions regimes, however, permit exceptions to asset freezes to allow those targeted access to the necessities of life. Indeed, this has been the case for some time. Already, Resolution 1267 permitted exemptions to be made 'on the grounds of humanitarian need'.[28] The problem was instead one of process: such exemptions had to be authorised on a case-by-case basis by the 1267 Sanctions Committee,[29] which did not always respond to requests expeditiously. In 2002, however, Council Resolution 1452 provided that funds or financial assets or other economic resources necessary for basic expenses should not be frozen; with 'basic expenses' being defined as including 'payments for foodstuffs, rent or mortgage, medicines and medical treatment, taxes, insurance premiums, and public utility charges', as well as legal fees and service charges for the holding of frozen assets.[30] Rather than exemptions having to be sought from the 1267 Sanctions Committee, they were to be determined by the relevant State and notified in advance to the Committee, which had only 48 hours to block their adoption.[31]

The same procedure has been adopted subsequently by the Security Council when establishing other sanctions regimes.[32] So, for example Resolution 2134 (2013) on the situation in the Central African Republic

[26] *R (Adam) v Secretary of State for the Home Department* [2005] UKHL 66, [2006] 1 AC 396.
[27] Ibid 7.
[28] UNSC Res 1267 (1999) para 4(b).
[29] Ibid.
[30] UNSC Res 1452 (2002) para 1.
[31] Ibid. States could also authorise the use of assets for 'extraordinary expenses', albeit such decisions had to be notified and approved by the Sanctions Committee.
[32] For full analysis of the Council's practice on targeted sanctions, see C A Feinäugle's chapter in this volume.

requires Member States to freeze the assets of, and prevent the provision of economic support to, any person designated by the CAR Sanctions Committee. However, it goes on to provide exemptions for both basic and extraordinary expenses. Access to assets for the former, which is stated to include 'payment for foodstuffs, rent or mortgage, medicines and medical treatment, taxes, insurance premiums, and public utility charges', is authorised by the relevant Member State and is permitted providing that, on notification by that State, the Sanctions Committee does not, within five days of such notification, take a contrary decision. Access to assets to pay extraordinary expenses (which are not specified in the resolution except by contrast to those falling within the description of basic expenses) is also authorised, in the first instance, by the relevant Member State but must, in addition, be approved by the Sanctions Committee.

Consequently, in the first (and in most cases the last) instance, whether assets should be released to fund 'ordinary expenses' is a question now left to the UN Member States, on whose shoulders the burden falls of ensuring that decisions are made swiftly and correctly. Problems might thus remain at the procedural level, but they are now the responsibility of the Member States, not the Security Council; and, importantly, States can no longer shelter behind the excuse that they are acting to enforce the orders of the Council so that their duties under international human rights law (or, indeed, national constitutional standards) are trumped by their Charter obligations. Similar provisions permitting exceptions to asset freezes also appear in EU sanctions regimes. And although EU Member States have a discretion whether to release funds when requested, the discretion is not absolute, must be exercised taking account of the human rights standards applicable in the EU legal order and is subject to judicial supervision, including by the CJEU under the preliminary reference procedure.[33]

Indeed, in many cases asset freezes only really amount to a freeze on targeted persons' external assets, as their leadership position protects their assets within their own countries, so questions of impecuniosity do not arise. It might also be argued that an asset freeze is a restriction on the

[33] See Case C-314/13, Uzsieno reikalu ministerija & Ors v Vladimir Peftiev & Ors, judgment of 12 June 2014. On an application by lawyers instructed by an individual to challenge his listing in Regulation No 765/2006 of 18 May 2006 concerning restrictive measures in respect of Belarus for the release of frozen funds to pay their professional fees, the competent Lithuanian authorities refused to do so 'having regard to all legal and political circumstances'. Following a request for a preliminary ruling from the Lithuanian Court, the CJEU held that national authorities do not have an absolute discretion when they are deciding whether to release frozen funds for legal expenses but that they must exercise their powers compatibly with the EU Charter of Fundamental Rights. The same would seem to apply, *mutatis mutandis*, to Member States' consideration of requests for the release of frozen funds to satisfy basic needs, such as payments for foodstuffs, rent or mortgage, medicines and medical treatment, taxes, insurance premiums and public utility charges.

targeted person's property rights. However, the right to property is not an absolute right.[34] Although an asset freeze is a restriction on the targeted person's property rights, it is not an absolute deprivation (as it is not necessarily permanent), and it will, in most cases, be a proportionate restriction given the other interests at stake: the maintenance or restoration of international peace and security, suppressing terrorist activity, preventing the proliferation of weapons of mass destruction and so on. Certainly, this is the view that has consistently been taken by the CJEU with regard to targeted sanctions imposed by the Council of the EU. As the Court of First Instance stated in *Bank Melli v Council*:

> the applicant's freedom to carry on economic activity and its right to property are restricted to a considerable degree, on account of the adoption of the contested decision, for it may not, in particular, dispose of its funds situated within the territory of the Community or held by Community nationals, except by virtue of special authorisation ... However, given the primary importance of maintaining international peace and security, the disadvantages caused are not inordinate in relation to the ends sought, especially because, first, those restrictions concern only part of the applicant's assets and, secondly, Articles 9 and 10 of Regulation No 423/2007 provide for certain exceptions allowing the entities affected by fund-freezing measures to meet essential expenditure.[35]

In *Bank Melli*, the impugned restrictive measures had been imposed by the Council of its own initiative[36] but the reasons advanced by the Court would seem to apply, with even greater force, to decisions of the Security Council. European Union restrictive measures merely seek to advance the foreign policy aims of the EU and its 28 Member States, whereas the Security Council is the organ of the United Nations with principal responsibility for international peace and security and Articles 25 and 103 of the Charter at the least argue for compliance with its edicts where possible.

An exception might be as regards targeted sanctions which seek to strip designated persons of assets held in their names: an example being Security Council Resolution 2161 (2004), which permitted the freezing and transfer of the financial assets of those targeted ('Saddam Hussein or other senior officials of the former Iraqi regime and their immediate family members') to another person (the Development Fund for Iraq).[37] The reason for the Council's decision was straightforward. It considered that those persons had enriched themselves at the expense of the Iraqi people, to whom restitution should be made. If such an assertion is

[34] Indeed, the customary status of the right can be questioned, given, in particular, that it does not appear in the International Covenant on Civil and Political Rights. But *cf* Case T-315/01, *Kadi v Council and Commission* [2005] ECR II-03649, paras 241–42.

[35] Case C-390/08, [2009] ECR II-3967, para 71.

[36] The Security Council, in Res 1803 (2008) para 9, had simply called on UN Member States 'to exercise vigilance over the activities' of, inter alia, the applicant.

[37] UNSC Res 1483 (2003) para 23.

correct, there cannot, of course, be any breach of the right to property but an opportunity to contest the decision before a properly-constituted court or tribunal would be required, and access to judicial review in such a case would only be effective if it allowed the question of ownership of the property to be determined, thus settling the substantive issue. In purporting to make a final determination of the issue, the Council deprived the affected persons of due process. This latter issue was avoided in the European Court of Human Rights judgment in *Al-Dulimi v Switzerland*,[38] which found only a violation of the right of access to a court under Article 6(1) of the European Convention on Human Rights. The case has, however, been appealed to the Grand Chamber.[39]

As regards travel bans matters are much the same. International human rights law only tangentially affects States' right to decide who to admit into their territories.[40] Some travel bans might prevent family reunification and an inability to travel might disrupt aspects of a person's private affairs to such an extent as to interfere with a targeted person's right to private life (although such cases would appear exceptional). However, given that the right to private and family life is a qualified right and the other interests at stake, in most cases the restriction imposed would seem proportionate. *Nada v Switzerland*[41] shows this will not always be the case, but the facts of that case were quite exceptional. Mr Nada (a dual Egyptian/Italian national) was confined to the 1.6 km^2 Italian enclave of Campione d'Italia for some seven years because he was unable to obtain passage to the rest of Italy through Switzerland, which entirely surrounds the enclave. Mr Nada was 70 years old at the time he was listed by the 1267 (Al-Qaida) Sanctions Committee and 72 when Switzerland revoked his border-crossing permit, and in poor health. It took eight years, proceedings before the Swiss courts and applications to the Security Council Focal Point for delisting, to have his name removed from the 1267 Sanctions Committee's list. It was in the light of these factors that the Grand Chamber of the European Court of Human Rights held that the applicant's right to respect for family and private life had been breached, the Court stating that:

> the Swiss authorities did not sufficiently take into account the realities of the case, especially the unique geographical situation of Campione d'Italia, the

[38] *Al-Dulimi and Montana Management Inc v Switzerland* App no 5809/08 (ECtHR, 26 November 2013).

[39] Registrar of the European Court of Human Rights, press release, 'Cases Referred to the Grand Chamber', ECHR 105 (2014) 16 April 2014; and Registrar of the European Court of Human Rights, press release, 'Grand Chamber hearing concerning the freezing of assets in Switzerland following the general embargo on Iraq in 1990', ECHR 368 (2014) 10 December 2014.

[40] In particular by application of the principle of non-discrimination: see *Abdulaziz, Cabales and Balkandali v United Kingdom* (1985) Series A, No 94.

[41] *Nada v Switzerland* [2012] ECHR 1691.

considerable duration of the measures imposed or the applicant's nationality, age and health.[42]

One exception to the rule that States have a discretion as to who they admit onto their national territory is that States do not generally have the right to refuse entry to their own nationals. The Universal Declaration on Human Rights proclaims that: 'Everyone has the right to leave any country, including his own, and to return to his country';[43] whilst the International Covenant on Civil and Political Rights states that: 'No one shall be arbitrarily deprived of the right to enter his own country'.[44] Given that Article 12(c) of the International Covenant does allow restrictions on the right of return, albeit they must not be 'arbitrary', a question arises as to the extent to which it can be limited. One might think the bar should be placed higher than for the restriction of property rights. However, in the case of Security Council sanctions the issue must be seen as moot, as they make exception for persons seeking to return to their own country. Council Resolution 1526, which imposed a travel ban on persons listed by the 1267 Sanctions Committee, also provided that: 'nothing in this paragraph shall oblige any State to deny entry or require the departure from its territories of its own nationals'.[45] In *Abdulrazik v Canada (Minister for Foreign Affairs)*,[46] the respondents argued that they could not act to repatriate the applicant to Canada from Sudan because in doing so they would be breaching the travel ban through the applicant's transit through other Member States' airspace. Zinn J, sitting in the Federal Court of Canada, rejected this submission, stating that such an interpretation of the travel ban would lead to a 'nonsensical result'[47] and was contrary to the Sanctions Committee's own views: 'In fact, the 1267 Committee seems to have wisely recognized that if it is to permit a citizen to return home, it cannot require countries to prevent his transit through their territory'.[48] Other UN sanctions regimes have similar exemptions and, given this, would appear to comply with the right of return enshrined in international law, whatever its extent might be. Whether the right is, in practice, breached thus, once again, devolves to the Member States charged with deciding whether the exception applies. Similarly, EU sanctions regimes, when they impose travel bans on listed persons, provide that they do not oblige Member

[42] Ibid para 195.

[43] UDHR, Art 13(2); UNGA Res 217 A (III) (10 December 1948).

[44] ICCPR, Art 12(c).

[45] UNSC Res 1526 (2004) para 1(b).

[46] FC 580 [2010] 1 FCR 267.

[47] Ibid para 127: because, on such a reading, the resolution would permit 'a citizen to enter Canada if and only if he happens to be standing at the Canadian border crossing, but … prevents that same citizen from reaching that border crossing as he cannot transit over land or through air to reach it'.

[48] Ibid para 128.

States to refuse their nationals entrance into their territories. Indeed, it appears that they are not even obliged to inform the EU Council when they apply such provisions.[49]

International human rights law, however, does require States to allow persons to leave their territories.[50] It might be thought that a right to exit a country is of little practical importance absent an ability subsequently to enter somewhere else. However, conceptually the two aspects are distinct and in *Sayadi and Vinck v Belgium*[51] the Human Rights Committee was willing to find the respondent State in violation of Article 12(2) of the International Covenant on Civil and Political Rights for that reason. The principal justification for that decision, however, was that (to begin with) the applicants had been listed by the 1267 Sanctions Committee at the initiative of Belgium and that (subsequently) the Belgian Government had on two occasions requested their removal from the sanctions list. It was this latter ground, in particular, the Committee stated, that meant the respondent could not justify the interference with the applicants' rights as being necessary to protect national security or public order. Again, however, provided targeted persons are given proper opportunity to challenge their listing, such a restriction on their rights would appear prima facie to be proportionate.

The imposition of targeted sanctions, because of its stigmatising effect, could also be argued to amount to a violation of the person's private life because it so besmirches his or her reputation and honour. This was the view of the Human Rights Committee in *Sayadi and Vinck*, with the Committee stating that: 'the dissemination of personal information about the authors constitutes an attack on their honour and reputation, in view of the negative association that some persons could make between the authors' names and the title of the sanctions list'[52] in violation of Article 17 of the International Covenant on Civil and Political Rights. The applicants had, however, been listed on the Al-Qaida sanctions list for some five years, whilst Belgium, the State which had proposed their inclusion, had subsequently (unsuccessfully) sought their removal. Again, given the qualified nature of the right, listing and the negative publicity that flows

[49] See Joined Cases T-307/12 and T-408/13, *Adib Mayaleh v Council*, judgment of the General Court (Ninth Chamber, extended composition) of 5 November 2014, para 188.

[50] See International Covenant on Civil and Political Rights, Art 12(2), which provides that: 'Everyone shall be free to leave any country, including his own'. Art 12(2), however, provides that restrictions on the right may be imposed 'which are provided by law, are necessary to protect national security, public order (ordre public), public health or morals or the rights and freedoms of others, and are consistent with the other rights recognized in the present Covenant'.

[51] *Sayadi and Vinck v Belgium*, Human Rights Committee, Views, 22 October 2008, Communication No. 1472/2006, UN Doc CCPR/C/94/D/1472/2006 (29 December 2008).

[52] Ibid para 10.12.

from it would only appear to be a violation if a listed person is unable to judicially review, within a reasonable time, the decision to target them.

The primary issue with targeted sanctions has thus been their compatibility with procedural rights: the right of access to a court, to a fair trial and to a remedy.[53] The question of their compatibility with substantive rights has almost always been subsidiary, as the substantive rights at issue are qualified rights. This is because whether there has been a breach (as opposed simply to an interference) with the targeted person's rights depends largely on the existence of proper factual and legal bases for their targeting, which is something which, in case of dispute, needs to be determined through the judicial process. Such a conclusion does, however, leave one issue outstanding: the question of how widely the net can be drawn. Asset freezes and travel bans might seem a proportionate response when directed against participants in the conduct which the Council seeks to enjoin, but is this the case when they target relatives or associates whose activities do not directly facilitate such conduct? The question is thus not whether a person falls within the class of persons targeted by the Council but whether listing itself violated their human rights because it cannot be justified as a proportionate response. This is an issue that has appeared at the European level[54] but not yet at that of the United Nations. However, it should be recalled that the UN Declaration on the Rule of Law specifically stated that Security Council sanctions should be 'carefully targeted, in support of clear objectives and designed carefully so as to minimize possible adverse consequences'.[55] The stance of the CJEU not to engage in a full proportionality exercise is thus open to criticism,[56] in particular what seems to be a tendency by the EU Council to adopt ever-wider criteria for listing.[57]

V. TARGETED SANCTIONS AND PROCEDURAL HUMAN RIGHTS

In the cases so far discussed, the principal issue and basis for the tribunal's decision was a failure to accord the applicant due process. In *Kadi I*, when reviewing the Council's actions for conformity with fundamental rights,

[53] European Convention on Human Rights, Arts 6 and 13; International Covenant on Civil and Political Rights, Arts 2(3) and 14; and EU Charter of Fundamental Rights, Art 47.

[54] See Case C-376/10 P, *Tay Za v Council* [2010] ECR II-1965, in which the son of a businessman associated with the Burmese regime had his listing annulled.

[55] Declaration of the High-Level Meeting of the General Assembly on the rule of law at the national and international levels, UNGA Res 67/1 (24 September 2012) UN Doc A/RES/67/1, para 29.

[56] See inter alia Case T161/13, *First Islamic Investment Bank Ltd v Council*, judgment of the General Court of 22 September 2015, paras 98–99.

[57] See Case T-578/12, *National Iranian Oil Company v Council*, judgment of the General Court (Seventh Chamber) of 16 July 2014; and Case T-563/12, *Central Bank of Iran v Council*, judgment of the General Court (First Chamber) 25 March 2015.

the European Court of Justice held that the applicants' rights of defence, in particular the right to be heard, and of effective judicial protection, had been breached because the Council had not provided them with the evidence relied upon to justify their listing, nor permitted them to make representations concerning it.[58] And it was only in the context of these failures that the Court held that the asset freeze imposed had breached Mr Kadi's right to property, because '[t]he contested regulation ... was adopted without furnishing any guarantee enabling him to put his case to the competent authorities'.[59] In *Kadi II*, Advocate General Bot argued that the listing and delisting procedures within the Sanctions Committee (particularly the creation of the Office of the Ombudsperson) provided sufficient procedural guarantees for the Court of Justice to presume that the Committee's decisions were justified.[60] However, the Court of Justice considered that:

> despite the improvements added ... the procedure for delisting and *ex officio* re-examination at UN level do not provide to the person whose name is listed on the Sanctions Committee Consolidated List ... the guarantee of effective judicial protection.[61]

Accordingly, the Court considered that full judicial review by the European judiciary of an applicant's listing was required, including ensuring that the decision to list was taken on a sufficiently solid factual basis.[62] Similarly, in *Nada* (to which the CJEU in *Kadi II* made express reference)[63] the Grand Chamber of the European Court of Human Rights' finding of a violation of Article 8 of the European Convention was to a large extent based on the delay occasioned by Swiss authorities' failures to act to alleviate the applicant's situation.[64] Indeed, the Court also found a violation of Article 13 of the European Convention (the right to an effective remedy) in conjunction with Article 8 on the basis that the Swiss Federal Court had considered itself unable to act to lift the sanctions imposed on the applicant because to do so would breach Switzerland's obligations under the UN Charter, despite its acknowledgement that the 1267 Sanctions Committee's delisting procedures could not be regarded as affording an effective remedy.[65]

[58] Joined Cases, C-402/05 P and C-415/05 P, *Kadi and Al Barakaat International Foundation v Council and Commission* [2008] ECR I-6351, paras 332–53.
[59] Ibid para 369.
[60] Joined Cases C-584/10 P, C-593/10 P and C-595/10 P, *Commission and Council v Kadi*, Opinion of AG Bot of 19 March 2013, paras 81–84.
[61] Joined Cases C-584/10 P, C-593/10 P and C-595/10 P, *Commission and Council v Kadi*, judgment of the CJEU (Grand Chamber) of 18 July 2013, para 133.
[62] Ibid para 119.
[63] Ibid para 133.
[64] *Nada v Switzerland* (n 41) para 195.
[65] Ibid paras 210–11.

At first sight, the process of listing persons as subject to Security Council sanctions appears to conform to due process criteria. It is not generally disputed that the Security Council has the power, under the UN Charter, to impose targeted sanctions. Article 41 of the UN Charter permits the Council, once it has determined the existence of a threat to the peace, breach of the peace or act of aggression, to order 'measures not involving the use of armed force' to maintain or restore international peace and security; Article 25 of the UN Charter requires UN Member States to accept and carry out the Council's decisions, and Article 103 of the UN Charter provides that in the event of conflicts between Member States' obligations under the UN Charter and their obligations under other international agreements, their obligations under the Charter shall prevail. Security Council resolutions imposing targeted sanctions set out criteria for listing, establish a Council Sanctions Committee and mandate that committee to decide which persons satisfy the criteria and should be listed. Recent resolutions go into considerable detail about who qualifies for listing, what listing entails and the exceptions or possible exceptions to the measures imposed on listed persons.[66]

One might point out that the meetings of the various sanctions committees take place in private, that their agendas are not published and that persons are not given notice that their inclusion on a sanctions list has been proposed. On the other hand, it might be thought that given that the criteria for listing and the consequences of being listed are known, there exists the necessary predictability and accessibility.[67] Any additional notice requirements would prevent sanctions having a surprise effect, on which much of their efficacy is said to rest. Certainly, this is the view that has been taken, as regards sanctions imposed by the EU Council, by the European Court of Justice.[68] The same cannot, however, be said as regards listed persons' opportunities to seek review of sanctions imposed on them. Here, as with the content of sanctions regimes, there have been improvements, but they cannot be said to go far enough to comply completely with rule of law principles. Although listing of persons as subject to targeted measures takes place as a result of decisions of Security Council sanctions committees, it generally takes place following a proposal by one or more Council members, and the discussions leading up to listing—and, in most cases, the evidence and information on which such decisions are made—are confidential. Only the result (a person's designation) is made

[66] See (as regards the situation in the Central African Republic) UNSC Res 2127 (2013) paras 54, 57 and 58, and UNSC Res 2134 (28 January 2014) paras 30–42; (as regards the situation in Yemen) UNSC Res 2140 (2014) paras 11–23; and (as regards the situation in South Sudan) UNSC Res 2206 (2015) paras 6–20.

[67] See the UN Declaration on the Rule of Law (n 55) para 2, where specific reference is made to the importance of predictability.

[68] See *Kadi I* (n 58) paras 338–40.

public. At least until recently, the specific reasons and the evidential basis on which persons are listed have been entirely unknown to them.

Advances have been made. Indeed, as regards Resolution 1267 sanctions, the Al-Qaida Sanctions Committee is now required both to publish a narrative summary of reasons for listing and, on request, to provide the statement of case by the designating Member States (although the State can require that parts of the statement are kept confidential).[69] Listings must be published immediately and notified to the State of the person's location and (for individuals) nationality, who are themselves, in turn, required to notify the listed person of their listing and its consequences, and of the possibility of submitting petitions to the Ombudsperson and requests for available exemptions.[70] However, different sanctions regimes have different procedures and each sanctions committee is, largely, a law unto itself.

It is, however, the issue of access to a judicial forum before which a person can challenge their designation which remains most controversial. Originally, a person seeking to be delisted could only approach the Security Council through his or her State of citizenship or residence, which might have been the very State which had requested that that person be listed. Two institutions have now been created by the Council to which individuals can themselves go. Both, however, suffer from defects when assessed using human rights standards.

The Focal Point for delisting was established by Security Council Resolution 1730 (2006). It covers all Security Council sanction regimes[71] and is precisely what its name states: a unit established within the UN Secretariat to which a person can apply if they consider that their targeting is unjustified. Applications thus no longer have to be made by a person's State of citizenship or residence.[72] However, the Focal Point has no power to make any decision on an application itself, except to confirm it is a not a repetitious application (or, at least, that it seeks to rely on new evidence).[73] Instead, the application is subject to a consultation process between the designating State (ie the States which originally proposed that the person be listed) and the petitioner's State(s) of citizenship and residence.[74] Should any of those States recommend delisting, the matter is put on the agenda of the relevant sanctions committee for it to make a decision

[69] UNSC Res 2161 (2014) paras 32–33 and 36.

[70] Ibid paras 38–39.

[71] Originally, persons whose names are inscribed on the Al-Qaida Sanctions List were excluded from using the Focal Point procedure. However, in UNSC Res 2083 (2012) para 37, the Security Council authorised the Focal Point, subject to certain conditions, to receive travel ban and assets freeze exemption requests in relation to persons on that list.

[72] UNSC Res 1730 (2006), Annex: De-listing procedure, para 1.

[73] Ibid paras 2–3.

[74] Ibid para 5.

whether the person should be delisted or not.[75] The petitioner is simply informed of the result.[76]

Although an improvement on the original situation, it is difficult to see the Focal Point procedure as providing an effective remedy for applicants, not least because it is avowedly not a form of judicial review. Listed persons continue to be unable to know the full reasons for their listing, and consequently to respond to them when drafting their applications. During the process, petitioners cannot respond to new points raised by designating (or other) States, as they are not party to the proceedings. And there is no obligation on sanctions committees to give reasoned decisions; so that the bases for their conclusions remain opaque. It was these failures that led Advocate General Poiares Maduro to state in *Kadi I* that:

> The existence of a de-listing procedure at the level of the United Nations offers no consolation in that regard. That procedure allows petitioners to submit a request to the Sanctions Committee or to their government for removal from the list. Yet, the processing of that request is purely a matter of intergovernmental consultation. There is no obligation on the Sanctions Committee actually to take the views of the petitioner into account. Moreover, the de-listing procedure does not provide even minimal access to the information on which the decision was based to include the petitioner in the list. In fact, access to such information is denied regardless of any substantiated claim as to the need to protect its confidentiality.[77]

In *Al-Dulimi v Switzerland*, the respondent State did not even attempt to argue that the Focal Point procedure provided protection equivalent to that guaranteed under the European Court of Human Rights. And the Court agreed, stating that:

> the respondent Government themselves admit that the system in place, even in its improved form since Resolution 1730 (2006), enabling the applicants to apply to a 'Focal Point' for the deletion of their names from the Security Council lists, does not provide a level of protection that is equivalent to that required by the Convention [reference omitted]. The Court shares that view.[78]

An attempt to address these criticisms was made with the appointment of the Al-Qaida Sanctions Ombudsperson. The Office of the Ombudsperson was established by Security Council Resolution 1904 (2009), and its mandate has subsequently been extended, most importantly in Resolution 1989 (2011). The procedure only applies as regards listing on the consolidated Al-Qaida sanctions list first established by Resolution 1267. Persons seeking to have their name removed from the list can address a request

[75] Ibid para 6.

[76] Ibid para 8.

[77] Case C-402/05 P, *Kadi v Council and Commission*, Opinion of AG Poiares Maduro, 16 January 2008, para 51.

[78] *Al-Dulimi and Montana Management Inc v Switzerland* (n 38) para 118.

to the Ombudsperson, who investigates (including by interviewing, if at all possible, the petitioner and seeking information from the designating State).[79] At the end of her investigation, the Ombudsperson addresses recommendations to the Al-Qaida Sanctions Committee, including a recommendation (if she thinks it appropriate) that the person be delisted.[80] Originally, it was then for the Committee to decide on whether to do so. Since Resolution 1989, however, it is now the case that unless the Committee, within 60 days and acting by consensus (ie in the absence of any expressed disagreement), rejects a recommendation by the Ombudsperson to delist a listed person, that person will be delisted.[81] A State which disagrees with a recommendation but cannot achieve consensus at committee level can take the matter to the Security Council itself for decision.[82] This has not as yet, however, happened.

Taken in combination with the requirement, also set out in Council Resolution 1904, that a 'narrative' should be adopted setting out the reasons why a person has been added the Consolidated List and petitioners' ability to obtain designating States' statements of case (or, at least, the non-confidential parts), the Ombudsperson's procedures do give listed persons a greater opportunity to know and to respond to the allegations against them, and to challenge their designation.[83] However, listed persons remain unable to access the evidence alleged to justify their listing, albeit that the extent to which evidence justifying a person's listing, or even the gist of the allegations made against him or her, must be disclosed, remains disputed.[84] The Ombudsperson has been able to reach agreement with some States over access to confidential material.[85] However, it has

[79] See UNSC Res 1904 (2009) para 20 and Annex II; UNSC Res 1989 (2011) para 21 and Annex II; UNSC Res 2083 (2012) para 19 and Annex II; and UNSC Res 2161 (2014) para 41 and Annex II.

[80] UNSC Res 1989 (2011) para 21; UNSC Res 2083 (2012) para 19; and UNSC Res 2161 (2014) para 41.

[81] UNSC Res 1989 (2011) para 23; UNSC Res 2083 (2012) para 121; and UNSC Res 2161 (2014) para 43.

[82] Ibid.

[83] According to the Ombudsperson, she does not engage in judicial review of the decision to designation. Rather, in the light of all the information currently available to her, she determines whether or not the petitioner's listing is justifiable: Chatham House, 'International Law Summary: UN Sanctions, Human Rights and the Ombudsperson', 17 May 2013, 5. The standard applied by the Ombudsperson is set out in Second Report of the Office of the Ombudsperson pursuant to UNSC Res 2161 (2011) Annex III.

[84] For the view of the ECtHR, see *A and others v UK* ECHR 2009-II 137, paras 218–20.

[85] 15 in total, according to the Ombudsperson's most recent report: Ninth Report of the Office of the Ombudsperson pursuant to UNSC Res 2161 (2014) UN Doc S/2015/80 (2 February 2015) para 49. Details can also be found on the website of the Office of the Ombudsperson at: https://www.un.org/sc/suborg/en/ombudsperson/classified_information, which lists one 'agreement' and 15 'arrangements', as well as stating that another State (the USA) 'has expressed willingness, and demonstrated an ability, to share confidential information on an ad hoc basis'.

been on the basis that any information provided is as a matter of grace not of obligation, and that is not shared either with the petitioner or the Sanctions Committee.

The Ombudsperson has argued that her procedures are effective and that they provide substantive justice, as in practice the Committee has always adopted her recommendations and there have as yet been no referrals to the Council.[86] It was for these reasons that Advocate General Bot, in *Kadi II*, suggested that the European Court of Justice apply a doctrine of 'equivalent protection' to the review of sanctions listing by the Ombudsperson.[87] However, petitioners remain unable to see all the evidence against them, and decisions of the Ombudsperson are not formally binding. It was perhaps for these reasons that the Court of Justice did not adopt the Advocate General's suggestion.[88] And the UN Special Rapporteur on the promotion of human rights and fundamental freedoms while countering terrorism stated in 2012, following the Resolution 1989 reforms, that:

> [A]s regards an (objective) appearance of independence, the structural flaws remain the same… The 'very existence' of an executive power to overturn the decision of a quasi-judicial body is sufficient to deprive that body of the necessary 'appearance' of independence however infrequently the power is exercised and irrespective of whether its exercise was, or even could have been, at issue in any particular case.
>
> It follows that, despite the significant improvements brought about by resolution 1989 (2011), the mandate of the Ombudsperson does not meet the structural due process requirement of objective independence from the [Al-Qaida sanctions] Committee.[89]

To this, one might add a certain precarity concerning the Ombudsperson's position. Not only is the Ombudsperson's mandate subject to regular renewals but, it has been argued, the administrative structures relied on to support the mandate lack autonomy and independence.[90] In practice, there is no separate Office of the Ombudsperson. Indeed, when the mandate of Judge Prost was coming to an end, the Security Council waited until 13 July 2015, one day before its termination, to appoint her successor;

[86] For a summary of the Ombudsperson's position, see (n 83), which summarises an on-the-record meeting with Judge Kimberly Prost. Statistics concerning the Ombudsperson's work can be found in the Ombudsperson's Ninth Report, ibid, paras 2–7 and Annex II.

[87] Joined Cases C-584/10 P, C-593/10 P and C-595/10 P, *Commission and Council v Kadi*, Opinion of AG Bot (n 60).

[88] *Kadi II* (n 61). The ECtHR in *Al-Dulimi* (n 38) para 119 also took the view, albeit obiter, that the Ombudsperson procedure fell short of 'international minimum standards' of due process.

[89] 2nd Annual Report of the United Nations Special Rapporteur on the promotion and protection of human rights and fundamental freedoms while countering terrorism, UN Doc A/67/396 (26 September 2012) paras 34–35, quoted in *Al-Dulimi* (n 38) para 63.

[90] See Letter from the Permanent Representative of Argentina to the United Nations Secretary-General, UN Doc S/2014/725 (8 October 2014) 5.

and the new Ombudsperson, Catherine Marchi-Uhel, did not take up her appointment until 27 July 2015, some two weeks later.[91]

By contrast and as has already been averted to, the CJEU requires 'full review' of Council decisions.[92] A person who is listed as subject to restrictive measures benefits from the guarantees contained in the EU Charter of Fundamental Rights. In addition to the right to property and the principle of proportionality (which have already been examined), this means they benefit from the rights of the defence and the right to effective judicial protection.[93] As a corollary of the principle of the right to respect for the rights of the defence, the Council is under an obligation to provide the listed person with both the legal basis and the actual and specific reasons for its decision so as to enable that person to determine whether its listing is well-founded or can be legally challenged, and to permit the EU judiciary to review the legality of the decision.[94] And the Council must also, on request, disclose the evidence it relied on when coming to its decision, on the ground that:

> The effectiveness of the judicial review guaranteed by Article 47 of the Charter [the right to an effective remedy and to a fair trial] also requires that, as part of the review of the lawfulness of the grounds which are the basis of the decision to list or to maintain the listing of a given person…, the Courts of the European Union are to ensure that that decision, which affects that person individually, is taken on a sufficiently solid factual basis. That entails a verification of the factual allegations in the summary of reasons underpinning that decision, with the consequence that judicial review cannot be restricted to an assessment of the cogency in the abstract of the reasons relied on, but must concern whether those reasons, or, at the very least, one of those reasons, deemed sufficient in itself to support that decision, is substantiated.[95]

This chapter will not go into further detail about the jurisprudence of the CJEU, which is fully covered in Luca Pantaleo's contribution to this volume. Disclosure by the Council of the evidence justifying a person's listing has, however, proved a particularly problematic issue. In response to numerous requests, the Council has simply provided redacted versions of the agendas and minutes of the relevant meetings, which say nothing more than that a proposal was made (although not by whom) and accepted for the reasons appearing in the relevant Council Decision and Regulation. Beyond that, the Council has stated that it holds no additional information; the reason for this being that although the Council decides, it does

[91] Letter dated 13 July 2015 from the Secretary-General addressed to the President of the Security Council, UN Doc S/2015/534 (13 July 2015); and un.org/en/sc/ombudsperson.

[92] See *Kadi II* (n 61) para 97.

[93] Charter of Fundamental Rights of the European Union, Arts 41(2) and 47.

[94] See Case T-228/02, *Organisation des Modjahedines du peuple d'Iran v Council* [2006] ECR II-4665, paras 140–46; and Case C-417/11 P, *Council v Bamba* ECLI:EU:C:2012:718, paras 49–52.

[95] *Kadi II* (n 61) para 119 (citations omitted).

not propose. Designations are made on the request of Member States, who hold the evidence themselves, albeit it may be circulated at the meeting. The argument of the Council has been that the Member State must consent to the release of such evidence. Member States have, however, been unwilling so to do, on the grounds that it is secret, ie the information was obtained via intelligence or confidential sources which disclosure would jeopardise. This is, of course, an issue not unique to the EU Courts. However, the distinction between the Council and the Member States complicates matters, as does the CJEU's identity as a supranational institution.

The Court of Justice considered the situation where listing is based on confidential material in *Fulmen and Mahmoudian v Council*.[96] The Court admitted that certain reasons, including the security of the European Union or its Member States or the conduct of their international relations, might preclude disclosure of information or evidence to a listed person and/or their lawyers. However, the existence of such reasons could not justify failure to disclose to the EU Courts, as it fell to them to decide whether such grounds are well-founded and, if so, what measures should be taken:

> [T]o strike an appropriate balance between the requirements attached to the right to effective judicial protection... and those flowing from the security of the European Union or its member States or the conduct of their international relations.[97]

Failure to disclose such material to the Court, however, requires it to base its decision solely on the material disclosed to it, and numerous applicants have thus had their listings annulled on the basis that the EU Council failed to discharge the burden of proof placed on it by Article 47 of the Charter of Fundamental Rights.[98]

The Court's jurisprudence on the subject has had two consequences. The first is that the Council has increasingly relied on 'open source material', that is, material already in the public domain, to justify its listing decisions. This must be seen as a positive development. The second development, however, is more problematic. The EU General Court has recently amended its Rules of Procedure[99] to include a new provision on 'the treatment of information or material pertaining to the security of the EU or that of one or more of its Member States or to the conduct of their international relations'. Article 105 of the new Rules provides that when 'a main party' (ie in restrictive measures cases, the Council) wishes to rely on information or material whose communication, it is argued, would

[96] Case C-280/12 P, Judgment of 28 November 2013, ECLI:EU:C:2013:775 paras 70–78.
[97] Ibid para 73.
[98] See *Kadi II* (n 61) para 57.
[99] OJ L 105/1 (in force from 1 July 2015).

harm the security of the EU or its Member States or the conduct of their international relations, such material should be produced to the Court alone together with the reasons relied upon as justifying its remaining confidential. It will then be for the Court to decide whether such information or material is relevant and whether it should be disclosed to the other main party (ie the designated person). If the Court decides the information or material is relevant and not confidential, the party seeking to rely on it has the option either to permit its disclosure to the other party, or to have it returned and not taken into account by the Court in determining the case. If the Court decides the information or material is relevant and confidential (that is, that there exist 'overriding reasons ... strictly required by the exigencies of the situation' justifying its confidentiality), then the Court:

> shall weigh the requirements linked to the right to effective judicial protection, particularly observance of the adversarial system, against the requirements flowing from the security of the Union or one or more of its Member States or the conduct of their international relations.[100]

This second exercise has as its objective a decision as to what procedures might be adopted to accommodate the two requirements, including by requiring the production by the party concerned of 'a non-confidential version or a non-confidential summary of the information or material' and its communication to the other main party.[101] Where the General Court, however, concludes that confidential information or material the gist of which cannot be communicated to the other main party is essential for it to rule on the case, it may base its judgment upon such information or material.[102]

The resemblance between this procedure and 'closed material proceedings' in the English courts[103] is clear. Indeed, the inspiration has been implicitly acknowledged.[104] The judgment of the Court of Justice in *ZZ*[105] was specifically concerned with the compatibility with Article 47 of the Charter of Fundamental Rights of the closed material procedures of the

[100] Ibid Art 105(5). Quite how this balancing relates to the previous inquiry as concerning the confidential nature of the information or material is unclear.

[101] Ibid Art 105(6).

[102] Ibid Art 105(8). One might consider the use of the term 'may' inappropriate, as if the information or material is 'necessary' for the Court to rule on the case, it cannot be ignored.

[103] See esp Special Immigration Appeals Commission Act 1997, ss 5 and 6; Special Immigration Appeals Commission (Procedure) Rules 2003, pt 7; and Justice and Security Act 2013, pt 2.

[104] Draft Rules of Procedure of the General Court, 14 March 2014, EU Council doc 7795/14 (17 March 2014) 103.

[105] Case C-300/11, *ZZ v Secretary of State for the Home Department* [2013] QB 1136; [2013] 3 CMLR 46.

UK Special Immigration Appeals Commission (SIAC). In distinction from the UK procedures, however, the General Court's includes no provision for the appointment of a 'special advocate' to permit independent scrutiny of the undisclosed material by an advocate appointed to represent the interests of the other party to the proceedings.[106] Certainly, the European Court of Human Rights seems to have thought the special advocate fulfilled an important role. In *A and others v United Kingdom*,[107] considering the compatibility of 'control order' proceedings before SIAC with Article 5(4) of the European Convention on Human Rights,[108] the Court's Grand Chamber stated that:

> The Court considers that SIAC, which was a fully independent court ... and which could examine all the relevant evidence, both closed and open, was best placed to ensure that no material was unnecessarily withheld from the detainee. In this connection, the special advocate could provide an important, additional safeguard through questioning the State's witnesses on the need for secrecy and through making submissions to the judge regarding the case for additional disclosure...
>
> The Court further considers that the special advocate could perform an important role in counterbalancing the lack of full disclosure and the lack of a full, open, adversarial hearing by testing the evidence and putting arguments on behalf of the detainee during the closed hearings.[109]

Given this emphasis on the role of the special advocate in ensuring procedural fairness, the absence of such an institution in the General Court's procedures puts into question the latter's compliance with principles of due process, including those set out in the Charter of Fundamental Rights.

VI. CONCLUSION

What the European Union experience shows is that once judicial review of sanctions is provided, attention largely shifts from issues of substantive

[106] Albeit that a special advocate cannot take instructions from the party whose interests they are representing or their ordinary legal representatives once they have had sight of the undisclosed material, and cannot disclose that material to the party or its ordinary legal representatives.

[107] App no 3455/05 (ECtHR, 19 February 2009).

[108] Art 5(4) provides that. 'Everyone who is deprived of his liberty by arrest or detention shall be entitled to take proceedings by which the lawfulness of his detention shall be decided speedily by a court and his release ordered if the detention is not lawful'. Having examined the applicants' complaints under Art 5(4), the Court did not consider it necessary to consider them under Art 6(1) of the Convention (the right to a fair trial). Ibid para 233.

[109] Ibid paras 219–20 (citations and paragraph numbers omitted).

rights protection to matters of fact and questions of procedure.[110] Although the recent amendments to the EU General Court's Rules of Procedure raise concerns, how the General Court will interpret the new provisions remains to be seen. As for the United Nations, the robust stance taken by the European Court of Justice and by various other courts, national and international, has had an effect. Security Council practice in the sanctions area has changed, and changed in ways that have moved its practice more into compliance with human rights principles, both as regards the content of targeted sanctions and how such measures, once imposed, can be reviewed. Recent developments regarding the Ombudsperson, however, are concerning, and serve to support criticisms that the Office is too dependent on the Security Council. And one might also recall that the Ombudsperson's mandate, as yet, encompasses only one of the Security Council sanctions regimes. Suggestions have been made for its comprehensive extension but they have met with stiff resistance and been, as yet, unsuccessful.[111] Persons challenging their designation by all other Council sanctions committees remain restricted to applying to the Focal Point, which entirely fails to satisfy due process standards. So although targeted sanctions can be seen generally to comply with substantive human rights, much progress remains to be made as regards their compatibility with procedural rights.

Looking back at the 1990s, however, very little was then said about procedural rights or judicial review. Instead, the focus was on protecting economic and social rights. Comprehensive sanctions were seen as contrary to the right to food, the right to health, even the right to life, in the effects they had on the populations of the countries targeted. And the proposals that were being made at the time as to how sanctions regimes should be reformed focused not on *post facto* but on *ex ante* review; that is, on the need for advanced examination of the possible human rights impact of proposed sanctions, albeit that it was also recognised that, once a regime was in place, continued monitoring of those impacts was required.

As we have seen, control now takes place *post facto* and concentrates on guaranteeing civil and political rights. One might ask, however, whether this is altogether an improvement. In many respects, the answer is yes. The human rights impact of targeted sanctions is firmly on the agenda. But it might be asked whether that improvement has not had a negative effect in that it has blinded us to other issues. It has already been mentioned that targeted and sectoral sanctions have become broader and broader in their

[110] Although attention may now be shifting back to the Council's use of its powers to subject very broad classes of person to restrictive measures: see the cases cited at (n 57).

[111] See (n 90) 3 and 5; and Statement on behalf of the group of Liked-Minded States on targeted sanctions delivered by HM Ambassador Geir O Pederson, Permanent Representative, Norway, on 23 October 2014.

scope. The sanctions imposed by the Security Council, the EU and the USA against Iran provide a good example, in particular because of their targeting of financial transactions. And the result has been the development of a crisis as regards access to medicaments in Iran.[112]

Although there are exceptions to the sanctions as regards the import of medicaments into Iran, the hurdles imposed to take advantage of those exceptions dissuade pharmaceutical companies from dealing with Iran; they simply see it as too much trouble. Problems also arise as regards financial transactions and convertibility. And the result has been developing shortages of particular medicaments in Iran, such as chemotherapy and anti-haemophilia drugs.[113] The argument can of course be made that any adverse effects of such shortages (ie the death of a number of sick Iranians) would be a result of the intransigence of the Iranian Government, not of those countries imposing the sanctions. But this was the very same argument made in the 1990s as regards sanctions against Iraq and it does not gain by repetition.

The development of judicial control of targeted sanctions is a positive development. But the number of individuals who are targeted by targeted sanctions in the world today is at most a few thousand. And examination of the identities of the persons who appeal to the CJEU shows that those who do so are generally rich and well-connected. Plainly they, as anyone else, should be able to vindicate their human rights. But their success in doing so, may be having the effect that sanctions regimes are becoming less targeted and, as a result, less amenable to judicial challenge.

[112] J Borger and S Kamali Dehghan, 'How Life-saving Drugs are Caught up in Iranian Sanctions' *The Guardian* 13 January 2013; S Namazi, *Sanctions and Medical Supply Shortages in Iran*, Viewpoints No 20 (February 2013), Middle East Program, Woodrow Wilson International Center for Scholars.

[113] This chapter was completed prior to the lifting of nuclear proliferation-related sanctions against Iran.

6

UN Smart Sanctions and the UN Declaration on the Rule of Law

CLEMENS A FEINÄUGLE

I. INTRODUCTION

THE MOVE FROM comprehensive sanctions to smart sanctions in the 1990s was intended to bring about justice and a more appropriate targeting of those responsible for threats to international peace and security.[1] While smart sanctions, therefore, were first expected to be a tailor-made solution, the fact that they directly address individuals with harsh sanctions without at the same time granting the opportunity of effective defence or review has triggered concerns by UN Member States and those affected by the sanctions with regard to due process, legal protection and proportionality.[2] Sanctions regimes were seen as lacking the necessary legitimacy which led to reluctance among UN Member States to implement such sanctions and thus to problems concerning the proper functioning of UN sanctions regimes.[3]

The legitimacy of smart sanctions necessary for their acceptance and implementation by UN Member States could derive from the application of the rule of law to UN action. The discussion of the rule of law

[1] See on this and on the development from global to smart sanctions, A Pellet and A Miron, 'Sanctions' in R Wolfrum (ed), *The Max Planck Encyclopedia of Public International Law* (Oxford, Oxford University Press, 2012) Vol IX, 1, 6–7, para 29 ff 34; G Verdirame, *The UN and Human Rights, Who Guards the Guardians?* (New York et al, Cambridge University Press, 2011) 311 ff 319.

[2] On these and other criticisms expressed, see J M Farrall, *United Nations Sanctions and the Rule of Law* (Cambridge, Cambridge University Press, 2007) 185 ff; specifically on due process, B Fassbender, 'Targeted Sanctions Imposed by the UN Security Council and Due Process Rights' (2006) 3 *International Organizations Law Review* 437 ff.

[3] States were unwilling to conform to rule of law ideals as long as the UN itself did not obey such principles; see R Peerenboom, M Zürn and A Nollkaemper, 'Conclusion' in M Zürn, A Nollkaemper and R Peerenboom (eds), *Rule of Law Dynamics: In an Era of International and Transnational Governance* (New York et al, Cambridge University Press, 2012) 305, 309.

for the international law and for the UN is not new. This topic has been addressed more than once by both scholars[4] and the UN governing bodies themselves[5] during the last decade. What is new is, however, that a recent UN document has put the topic back on the agenda: The 'Declaration of the high-level meeting of the General Assembly on the rule of law at the national and international levels' adopted as a resolution by the UN General Assembly on 24 September 2012 ('the UN Declaration') declares the rule of law applicable to the UN itself and to its principle organs.[6] This chapter addresses, first, the extent to which the UN Declaration reflects the crystallising principles which have so far been discussed by scholars in relation to the role for the rule of law in international law and, secondly, what the rule of law as provided for in the UN Declaration means for the various UN smart sanctions regimes.

The first part of this chapter takes a short look at the debate on the concept within the UN and then turns to the question of the content of the rule of law. In the second part, the chapter analyses different smart sanctions regimes to investigate whether individual regimes follow the rule of law taken individually (an intra-regime perspective) and when compared to each other (an inter-regime perspective).

II. THE RULE OF LAW WITHIN THE UNITED NATIONS

Globalisation has increasingly led to a transfer of competences to institutions on the international level. As a consequence, today international institutions are ever-more frequently exercising public authority.[7] This development has triggered concerns about the legitimacy of the activities of these institutions as they take binding decisions on matters traditionally seen as within States' jurisdiction, eg sanctions that directly address

[4] See eg Farrall, *United Nations Sanctions and the Rule of Law* (n 2); S Chesterman, 'The Security Council and the Rule of Law' (7 May 2008) United Nations General Assembly Security Council, UN Doc A/63/69-S/2008/270; Société Française pour le Droit International, *L'état de droit en droit international* (Paris, Pedone, 2009); R McCorquodale (ed), *The Rule of Law in International and Comparative Context* (London, British Institute of International and Comparative Law, 2010); Zürn, Nollkaemper and Peerenboom, *Rule of Law Dynamics* (n 3).

[5] See eg the agenda items of the Security Council 'Strengthening international law: rule of law and maintenance of international peace and security' (see UNSC, Statement by the President of the Security Council (22 June 2006) UN Doc S/PRST/2006/28). The UN General Assembly has eg adopted a resolution on 'The rule of law at the national and international levels' (18 December 2006) UN Doc A/RES/61/39, and further resolutions under the same title in the following years, eg UN Doc A/RES/62/70 (8 January 2008).

[6] See UNGA, 'Declaration of the high-level meeting of the General Assembly on the rule of law at the national and international levels' A/RES/67/1 (30 November 2012) para 2.

[7] See eg the comprehensive work on the topic by A von Bogdandy, R Wolfrum, J von Bernstorff, P Dann and M Goldmann (eds), *The Exercise of Public Authority by International Institutions* (Heidelberg, Springer, 2010).

individuals.[8] The debate on the rule of law over the last few years reflects these concerns.

A. Debate over the Concept of the Rule of Law within the UN

Whereas a Declaration on the rule of law adopted by a prominent high-level meeting of the UN General Assembly might come as a surprise to some, the topic of the rule of law had been on the agenda of the Assembly and other UN bodies for several years. It is worthwhile having a short look at the debate and views leading to the genesis of the UN Declaration in order to find out what the considerations behind the adoption of the Declaration were. This helps to understand better the background and the meaning of the rule of law in the UN.

At a high-level meeting in 2000, the Security Council discussed the need to ensure an effective role for the Council in the maintenance of international peace and security, and adopted a Declaration which underlined in a general way 'the need for respect for human rights and the rule of law'[9] although without further elaboration. In 2003, the Council discussed the topic 'Justice and the rule of law: the United Nations' role' and stressed the

> vital importance of these issues, recalling the repeated emphasis given to them in the work of the Council, for example in the context of the protection of civilians in armed conflict, in relation to peacekeeping operations and in connection with international criminal justice.[10]

This was a little more precise than the general reference made at the high-level meeting of 2000 but still did not explain how the rule of law should apply in the named fields of UN activity.

In 2004, the Secretary-General delivered a report requested by the Security Council with the title 'The Rule of Law and Transitional Justice in Conflict and Post-conflict Societies'[11] which was seen as providing for

[8] T Gemkow and M Zürn, 'Constraining International Authority through the Rule of Law: Legitimatory Potential and Political Dynamics' in Zürn, Nollkaemper and Peerenboom (n 3) 68, 69, 72.

[9] UNSC Resolution 1318 (7 September 2000) UN Doc S/RES/1318(2000) Annex, para I; the contributions of the participants during the meeting had been more explicit, UNSC S/PV4833 (24 September 2003). See also UNGA, United Nations Millennium Declaration (18 September 2000) UN Doc A/RES/55/2, para 9: 'respect for the rule of law in international as in national affairs and, in particular, to ensure compliance by Member States with the decisions of the International Court of Justice'.

[10] See the Statement by the President of the Security Council (24 September 2003) S/PRST/2003/15.

[11] UNSG, 'The Rule of Law and Transitional Justice in Conflict and Post-conflict Societies' Report of the Secretary-General (23 August 2004) UN Doc S/2004/616.

the first time a common concept of the rule of law.[12] The Secretary-General stressed the need for the rule of law, since peace in post-conflict situations could not 'be achieved unless the population is confident that redress for grievances can be obtained through legitimate structures for the peaceful settlement of disputes and the fair administration of justice'.[13] While the statement seems to refer to the rule of law as it has to be implemented on the national level, the report later also addressed the UN by setting out minimum standards of behaviour expected of all UN personnel in peacekeeping operations.[14] The Secretary-General repeated that point in a later report:

> Since the rule of law is an essential element of lasting peace, United Nations peacekeepers and peacebuilders have a solemn responsibility to respect the law themselves, and especially to respect the rights of the people whom it is their mission to help.[15]

Cases of alleged sexual abuse by UN staff had led to protests and thus triggered legitimacy concerns regarding UN activities, so the Secretary-General called for better safeguards to ensure that interventions designed to protect women and children did not result in their even further victimisation.[16] To address these concerns, a legal framework was established that the Secretary-General assigned to the rule of law, and which included minimum standards of behaviour, accountability and the rule that no one is above the law.[17]

The topic of the rule of law took a more prominent position in the World Summit Outcome document of the General Assembly in 2005.[18] The resolution identified 'human rights and the rule of law' as one of four problematic areas in which multilateral solutions should be provided.[19] The general spirit of the outcome document, however, was to recognise the need for UN Member States to adhere to the rule of law at the national and international levels, calling them, for example, to become parties to international treaties or to consider accepting the jurisdiction of the International Court of Justice,[20] rather than addressing the UN itself, let alone specifying precise obligations the UN would have to follow under the rule of law.

[12] See T Fitschen, Inventing the Rule of Law for the United Nations in A von Bogdandy and R Wolfrum (eds), *Max Planck Yearbook of United Nations Law*, Vol 12 (2008) 347, 350.

[13] UNSG, 'The Rule of Law and Transitional Justice in Conflict and Post-conflict Societies' (n 11) para 2.

[14] Ibid.

[15] UNSG, 'In Larger Freedom: towards Development, Security and Human Rights for All' Report of the Secretary-General (21 March 2005) UN Doc A/59/2005, para 113.

[16] UNSG, 'The Rule of Law and Transitional Justice in Conflict and Post-conflict Societies' (n 11) para 33.

[17] Ibid.

[18] UNGA, '2005 World Summit Outcome' (24 October 2005) A/RES/60/1.

[19] Ibid para 16.

[20] Ibid para 134.

Following the World Summit, in a debate of the Security Council in 2006 on the item 'Strengthening international law: rule of law and maintenance of international peace and security' the Secretary-General set out his views on minimum standards for listing and delisting procedures in sanctions regimes, which included: (1) a right to be informed with a statement of the case and information on options of review and exemptions; (2) a right to be heard and direct access to the decision-making body, as well as the right to be assisted or represented by counsel and time-limits for the consideration of the case; (3) a right to review by an effective review mechanism able to provide an effective remedy, including the lifting of the measure and/or compensation; and (4) periodical review of the sanctions in order to mitigate the risk of violating the right to property and related human rights.[21]

In 2008, the Secretary-General said in a report that' [t]he Organization has little credibility if it fails to apply the rule of law to itself. ... Appropriate rules of international law apply mutatis mutandis to the Organization as they do to States'.[22] He continued:

> [D]ue process concerns are critical in relation to Security Council sanctions regimes. A focal point to receive requests for de-listing has been established, reflecting the widely shared perception that action was needed. I consider further advances to be necessary, not only to protect individual rights, but also to maintain the effectiveness of sanctions.[23]

In the sanctions regimes, there was, on the one hand, a lack of human rights protection (due process) and, on the other, a concern that the current status of the sanctions regime was detrimental to the effectiveness of the sanctions, which can be read as meaning a threat to UN Member States' willingness to implement them. Indeed, in the debate during the high-level meeting at which the UN Declaration was adopted in 2012, the argument was reiterated that the rule of law had to apply to the UN itself for reasons of credibility: 'Only an organization that upholds the highest standards itself can be credible in promoting those standards elsewhere'.[24]

As we can see, the debate on the rule of law in the UN was marked by concerns of legitimacy, credibility and effectiveness of UN activity in different fields. Respect for the law, accountability, peaceful settlement of disputes, due process, transparency, proportionality and human rights protection were suggested as remedies.

[21] UNSC, 5474th meeting, UN Doc S/PV.5474 (22 June 2006) 5.

[22] UNSG, 'Strengthening and Coordinating United Nations Rule of Law Activities' Report of the Secretary-General (6 August 2008) UN Doc A/63/226, para 27.

[23] Ibid para 28.

[24] Swiss Confederation in United Nations, General Assembly, 67th session, 4th plenary meeting, Official Records, UN Doc A/67/PV.4 (24 September 2012), p 2 and Luxembourg, p 7.

B. Identifying the Content of the Rule of Law at the International Level

As already mentioned, the rule of law on the international level as applicable to the UN has been discussed by scholars and also institutions for some time. It is worthwhile looking first at some of the views which appear particularly relevant in order to get an idea of what the rule of law on the international level could mean.[25] This will then help to identify and concretise the content of the rule of law as laid down in the UN Declaration.

i. The Discussion on the Contents of the Rule of Law

Lord Bingham counted among his eight sub-rules or principles of the rule of law that: (1) the law must be accessible and so far as possible, be intelligible, clear and predictable; (2) questions of legal right and liability should ordinarily be resolved by application of the law and not by the exercise of discretion; (3) the law should apply equally to all, except to the extent that objective differences justify differentiation; (4) the law must afford adequate protection of human rights; (5) means must be provided for resolving, without prohibitive cost or inordinate delay, bona fide civil disputes which the parties themselves are unable to resolve; (6) ministers and public officers at all levels must exercise the powers conferred on them reasonably, in good faith, for the purpose for which the powers were conferred and without exceeding the limits of such powers; (7) the adjudicative procedures provided by the State should be fair; and (8) there must be compliance by the State with its international law obligations, the law which, whether deriving from treaty or international custom and practice, governs the conduct of nations.[26] While these principles were developed for application at the national level, it has been argued that the rule of law principles could also be applied in the international legal system.[27]

With regard specifically to UN and UN sanctions, Farrall identified five basic rule of law principles:[28] (1) the principle of transparency, requiring that in the exercise of political power, decision-making should be as open and transparent as possible, with reasons for applying and modifying

[25] For an in-depth recent discussion of a definition of the rule of law, see C May, *The Rule of Law, The Common Sense of Global Politics* (Cheltenham, Edward Elgar, 2014) 33 ff.

[26] T Bingham, 'The Rule of Law' (2007) 66 *Cambridge Law Journal* 67, 69–84; R McCorquodale, 'Business, the International Rule of Law and Human Rights' in McCorquodale (ed), *The Rule of Law in International and Comparative Context* (n 4) 21, 22 ff.

[27] R McCorquodale, 'The Rule of Law Internationally: Lord Bingham and the British Institute of International and Comparative Law' in M Andenas and D Fairgrieve (eds), *Tom Bingham and the Transformation of the Law* (Oxford, Oxford University Press, 2009) 137, 145; T Bingham, *The Rule of Law* (London, Penguin, 2011) 111.

[28] Farrall (n 2) 40.

sanctions clearly expressed;[29] (2) the principle of consistency, requiring that decisions are made in a predictable rather than arbitrary manner and that UN practice is consistent from one sanctions regime to another;[30] (3) the principle of equality, according to which all parties exposed to political power should be considered equal before that power and any decisions affecting their rights should be made in an impartial manner;[31] (4) the principle of due process, calling for a fair hearing of the affected individual and the opportunity to express his or her point of view regarding the potential decision, as well as the presumption of innocence;[32] and (5) in the context of sanctions, the principle of proportionality, which requires that the coercive consequences of the application of sanctions are proportionate to the harm caused by the target against which sanctions are imposed and are consistent with the objectives for which sanctions are employed.[33]

One year after the suggestions made by Farrall, the Final Report and Recommendations of the Austrian Initiative suggested that 'fair and clear procedures' to protect individuals affected by smart sanctions should include, as a minimum, the right to be informed of measures taken by the Council and to know the case against one, including a statement of the case and information as to how requests for review and exemptions can be made; the right to be heard (via submissions in writing) within a reasonable time by the relevant decision-making body, with assistance or representation by counsel, and the right to review by an effective, impartial and independent mechanism with the ability to provide a remedy, such as the lifting of the measure or compensation.[34]

The Council of Europe, in a resolution on UN Security Council blacklists, stated that the minimum procedural standards under the rule of law included: the right for everyone (1) to be notified promptly and fully informed of the charges against them, and of the decision taken and the reasons for that decision; (2) to enjoy the fundamental right to be heard and to be able to defend oneself; (3) to be able to have the decision affecting one's rights speedily reviewed by an independent, impartial body with a view to modifying or annulling it; and (4) to be compensated for any violation of one's rights.[35] The Council added that the blacklisting procedure should be limited in time and that a clear definition of grounds

[29] Ibid 40–41.
[30] Ibid 41.
[31] Ibid.
[32] Ibid.
[33] Ibid 41–42.
[34] See Chesterman, 'The Security Council and the Rule of Law' (n 4) recommendation 15, p 27; *cf* UNSC (n 21) 5.
[35] Council of Europe, Parliamentary Assembly, Resolution 1597 (23 January 2008), 'United Nations Security Council and European Union blacklists', para 5.1.

for the imposition of sanctions and relevant evidence was required to support those grounds.[36]

Out of these four attempts at a definition—three of them focusing specifically on the meaning of the rule of law in the UN—several principles inherent in the rule of law can be discerned: (1) consistency and predictability of the exercise of power in the sense of non-arbitrariness; (2) the law should apply equally to all; (3) transparency in the sense of open and transparent decision-making processes;[37] (4) the principle of due process, including the right to be informed of a measure and the right to be heard as well as review by an independent, impartial body; and (5) the principle of proportionality.

After this short analysis the question arises to what extent the UN Declaration reflects these concrete principles.

ii. The Rule of Law Applicable to the UN as Provided in the Declaration

A first reading of the UN Declaration shows that there is no clear-cut definition of the rule of law; that it has different meanings at the national and the international level, and that one must be careful not to mix up the different audiences (the UN and its Member States) addressed by the Declaration.

The Secretary-General repeated in his report the definition of the rule of law given in his earlier[38] report:

> The United Nations defines the rule of law as a principle of governance in which all persons, institutions and entities, public and private, including the State itself, are accountable to laws that are publicly promulgated, equally enforced and independently adjudicated, and which are consistent with international human rights norms and standards. It requires, as well, measures to ensure adherence to the principles of supremacy of law, equality before the law, accountability to the law, fairness in the application of the law, separation of powers, participation in decision-making, legal certainty, avoidance of arbitrariness and procedural and legal transparency.[39]

This definition was not referred to in the Declaration and the high-level meeting only took note of the report of the Secretary-General[40] which

[36] Ibid paras 5.2 and 5.3.

[37] For more transparency in the context of UN sanctions regimes, see also D Hovell, 'The Deliberative Deficit: Transparency, Access to Information and UN Sanctions' in J Farrall and K Rubenstein (eds), *Sanctions, Accountability and Governance in a Globalized World* (Cambridge, Cambridge University Press, 2009) 92, 113.

[38] UNSG, 'The Rule of Law and Transitional Justice in Conflict and Post-conflict Societies' (n 11) para 6.

[39] UNSG, 'Delivering Justice: Programme of Action to Strengthen the Rule of Law at the National and International Levels' Report of the Secretary-General (16 March 2012) UN Doc A/66/749, para 2.

[40] UNGA, 'Declaration of the high-level meeting of the General Assembly on the rule of law at the national and international levels' (n 6) para 39.

means that it did not confer on that text any authoritative legitimacy.[41] This was certainly because the definition only addressed the rule of law at the domestic level in conflict and post-conflict societies.[42] Also, the program of action to strengthen the rule of law which was proposed in this report[43] and which made detailed suggestions with regard, for example, to the delivery of public services, was not adopted by the General Assembly.[44]

In the UN Declaration itself, only parts of the just-cited broad definition of the rule of law can be found:

> [A]ll persons, institutions and entities, public and private, including the State itself, are accountable to just, fair and equitable laws and are entitled without any discrimination to equal protection of the law.[45]

In this sentence, some elements of the rule of law can be recognised but not a detailed definition. A further difficulty with regard to the determination of the contents of the rule of law becomes apparent from the title of the Declaration: The Declaration deals with the 'rule of law at the national and international levels' at the same time. The Declaration also addresses UN Member States[46] and the UN itself.[47] This means that the rule of law at the national level and the rule of law at the international level could address both UN Member States and the UN itself.

Since the concrete design of the rule of law in the national constitutional order of a UN Member State is a matter of the internal affairs of that State,[48] the reference in the Declaration to the rule of law at the national level can only entail general encouragement for UN Member States, such as accountability to just, fair and equitable laws[49] without prescribing too many details.[50] In contrast to that, for UN Member States the rule of law at

[41] See C Tomuschat, 'United Nations, General Assembly' in R Wolfrum (ed), *The Max Planck Encyclopedia of Public International Law* (Oxford, Oxford University Press, 2012) Vol X, 371, 377, para 22.

[42] *Cf* J Crawford, 'Chance, Order, Change: the Course of International Law' (2013) *RdC* 365 (2013) 13, 262; P Bodeau-Livinec and S Villalpando, 'La promotion de l'"Etat de droit" dans la pratique des Nations Unies' in Société Française pour le Droit International, *L'état de droit en droit international* (n 4) 81, 93.

[43] UNSG, 'Delivering Justice: Programme of Action to Strengthen the Rule of Law at the National and International Levels' (n 39).

[44] UNGA, 'Declaration of the high-level meeting of the General Assembly on the rule of law at the national and international levels' (n 6) para 39.

[45] Ibid para 2.

[46] See eg Ibid paras 2–4.

[47] Ibid paras 2, 27 ff.

[48] S Besson, 'Sovereignty' in R Wolfrum (ed), *The Max Planck Encyclopedia of Public International Law* (Oxford, Oxford University Press, 2012) Vol IX, 366, 383, para 121. See also UNSG, 'Delivering Justice: Programme of Action to Strengthen the Rule of Law at the National and International Levels' (n 39) para 48: 'The rule of law is at the heart of State sovereignty'.

[49] UNGA, 'Declaration of the high-level meeting of the General Assembly on the rule of law at the national and international levels' (n 6) para 2.

[50] On the international expectations concerning the rule of law at the national level, see HP Aust and G Nolte, 'International Law and the Rule of Law at the National Level' in Zürn, Nollkaemper and Peerenboom (n 3) 48 ff.

the international level means first and foremost that they have to respect their obligations under international law, for example, to respect the sovereign equality of all States and their territorial integrity and political independence, refrain from the threat or use of force if inconsistent with the purposes and principles of the United Nations, etc.[51]

As far as the Declaration applies the rule of law to the UN, the rule of law at the national level could mean, for example, that UN peacekeeping operations when supporting capacity building have to be run in accordance with their mandates.[52] The international rule of law, on the one hand, obliges the UN to act (eg to assist countries in conflict and post-conflict situations)[53] and, on the other hand, to conduct itself in a specific manner when taking action (eg to target sanctions carefully).[54]

Despite these difficulties, we can take a closer look at the contents of the rule of law in the UN Declaration. For the topic of this chapter, this means analysing what kind of prescriptions the international rule of law provides for smart sanctions.

Paragraph 2 of the UN Declaration states that the rule of law also applies to 'the United Nations and its principal organs, and that respect for and promotion of the rule of law and justice should guide all of their activities and accord predictability and legitimacy to their actions'. This clarifies, on the one hand, the applicability of the rule of law to the UN and its principal organs, including the Security Council. On the other hand, there is the general formulation that the rule of law should guide all activities and accord predictability and legitimacy to them. Thus, though not explicitly mentioned there but following a broad interpretation of this section, consistency and predictability in the exercise of power in the sense of its non-arbitrary exercise, as discussed in the literature, could be argued to be covered by the UN Declaration.

In addition, paragraph 2 of the UN Declaration says that all persons and institutions should be accountable to just, fair and equitable laws, and are entitled without any discrimination to equal protection of the law. As far as this sentence can be seen as also referring to the UN, it would pick up the rule of law principle according to which the law should apply equally to all.

This passage at the beginning of the Declaration is reminiscent of the regulation of a State objective in a national constitution. Thus, rather than providing a clear-cut list of precise rule of law principles, this link to predictability and legitimacy speaks about the result: about what observation of the rule of law should achieve. This general phrasing could be

[51] See eg UNGA, 'Declaration of the high-level meeting of the General Assembly on the rule of law at the national and international levels' (n 6) paras 3, 4, 20.

[52] Ibid para 19.

[53] Ibid para 18.

[54] Ibid para 29.

justified since the rule of law should apply to the three pillars of the UN, as the preamble says; ie to international peace and security, human rights and development. Since these are quite diverse contexts, the rule of law might apply differently depending on which pillar is concerned in any particular case.[55]

Part II of the Declaration starts by addressing the major organs of the UN but stresses their contribution to the rule of law through their work[56] rather than talking about the application of rule of law requirements to their own activities. However, in paragraph 29 the Security Council is encouraged 'to ensure that sanctions are carefully targeted, in support of clear objectives and designed carefully so as to minimise possible adverse consequences, and that fair and clear procedures are maintained and further developed'. 'Fair and clear procedures' can be understood as referring to the principle of due process, including—as also suggested by the Secretary-General[57]—the right to be informed of a measure and the right to be heard, as well as review by an independent, impartial body.[58] It can also be associated with transparency[59] in the sense of open and transparent decision-making procedures.

Moreover, paragraph 29 can be divided into three elements: (1) 'carefully targeted, in support of clear objectives', (2) 'designed carefully so as to minimise possible adverse consequences' and (3) 'fair and clear procedures'. This means that there must be a clear objective for the adoption of sanctions, the sanctions must be suitable to attain this objective and the sanctions must be designed in a way that there are as little adverse consequences as possible. This is reminiscent of the elements of a proportionality test as seen, for example, in international human rights law.[60] Thus, the principle of proportionality[61] can also be identified in the UN Declaration.

The first result of the analysis of the UN Declaration is that the reading of the document may cause some confusion and the document does not give a precise definition of the rule of law. However, it can be said

[55] See the remarks by C Feinäugle in 'The 2012 UN Declaration on the Rule of Law and Its Projections' (2013) 107 *ASIL Proceedings*, 467 ff.

[56] See UNGA, 'Declaration of the high-level meeting of the General Assembly on the rule of law at the national and international levels' (n 6) paras 27–28.

[57] See UNSC, 5474th meeting (n 21) 5.

[58] *Cf* Chesterman (n 4) recommendation 15, p 18.

[59] The Secretary-General had also addressed transparency when he suggested clear criteria for listing in the interest of an adequate statement of case, see UNSC, 5474th meeting (n 21) 5.

[60] See eg ECtHR, *Handyside v UK* (1976) 1 EHRR 737, para 49. For the elements of proportionality in public international law, see E Crawford, 'Proportionality' in R Wolfrum (ed), *The Max Planck Encyclopedia of Public International Law* (Oxford, Oxford University Press, 2012) Vol VIII, 533, 534, para 2.

[61] The Secretary-General had also addressed proportionality when he suggested periodic review of the sanctions in order to mitigate human rights violations; see UNSC, 5474th meeting (n 21) 5.

that the UN Declaration reflects some of the crystallising principles which have been discussed by scholars before for the rule of law in international law. Thus, several rule of law elements may be identified: the principles of proportionality, transparency and due process, including the right to be informed of a measure and the right to be heard as well as review by an independent and impartial body, can be identified with some certainty while consistency and predictability, non-arbitrary exercise of power and equal application of the law to all might be inferred from a broad interpretation of the more generally phrased paragraph 2 of the Declaration. These principles will now be applied to contemporary UN smart sanctions regimes in order to explore to what extent these sanctions regimes follow the rule of law.

The legal basis for the rule of law in the UN is not totally clear from the UN Declaration. According to the UN Declaration, the rule of law belongs to the principles of the United Nations and the Secretary-General adds that the UN Charter was the foundation of the rule of law at the international level. It could thus be based on the argument that since measures taken to maintain international peace and security must be effective if the UN wants to fulfil its purpose (UN Charter, Article 1(1)), the UN is bound by the rule of law insofar as 'effective' measures require that related legitimacy concerns are addressed by rule of law safeguards.

III. UN SMART SANCTIONS AND THE RULE OF LAW

Targeted sanctions adopted by the UN Security Council are directed against individuals whose behaviour is deemed a threat to international peace and security. These individuals are listed by UN sanctions committees, which are subsidiary bodies of the Security Council. As a consequence, the listed persons are subject to sanctions like the freezing of their assets, a travel ban or an arms embargo.[62] The fact that the sanctions directly affect individuals with harsh effects has triggered concerns on behalf of UN Member States and those affected by the sanctions with regard to due process and formal review,[63] ie aspects of the rule of law. Many of the guidelines of the sanctions regimes have been amended over the last few years in order to dissipate these concerns.

The question addressed here is whether the procedural designs of the different UN smart sanctions regimes now meet the rule of law

[62] See generally on UN sanctions, Farrall (n 2) 43 ff, 79 ff.

[63] See M Kanetake, 'The Interfaces between the National and International Rule of Law: The Case of UN Targeted Sanctions' (2012) 9 *International Organizations Law Review* 267, 283, 305 ff, with further detailed references; S Chesterman, '"I'll Take Manhattan": the International Rule of Law and the United Nations Security Council' (2009) 1 *Hague Journal on the Rule of Law* 67, 70.

requirements foreseen in the UN Declaration. There are currently 16 sanctions committees in place which maintain lists of targeted individuals or entities.[64] The following analysis addresses the extent to which the realisation of the rule of law principles of the UN Declaration can be shown in these smart sanctions regimes taken individually (intra-regime perspective) and then comparatively (inter-regime perspective).

A. Intra-regime Perspective

Among the UN smart sanctions regimes currently in force, one can differentiate with regard to the degree to which rule of law requirements mentioned are achieved. In this respect, advanced, medium- and less-developed sanctions regimes can be identified.

i. Advanced Smart Sanctions Regimes

Undoubtedly, with a view to the rule of law achievements, the most advanced smart sanctions regime is the one pursuant to Resolutions 1267 (1999) and 1989 (2011) concerning Al-Qaida and associated individuals and entities. The rules and guidelines of this sanctions regime have seen quite extensive amendments over the last few years, which were adopted to accommodate rule of law concerns by States and targeted individuals: in 2002, exceptions for the release of funds for the payment of foodstuffs, medical treatment etc were introduced.[65] This amendment tried to find a balance between the fight against terrorism and human rights protection, thereby following the principle of proportionality (UN Declaration, para 29). In 2005, the 'associated with' standard was adopted[66] to clarify the

[64] The underlying sanctions regimes are in a chronological order: the sanctions regime pursuant to Resolutions 751 (1992) and 1907 (2009) concerning Somalia and Eritrea; the sanctions regime pursuant to Resolutions 1267 (1999) and 1989 (2011) concerning Al-Qaida and associated individuals and entities; the sanctions regime pursuant to Resolution 1518 (2003) concerning Iraq and Kuwait; the sanctions regime pursuant to Resolution 1521 (2003) concerning Liberia; the sanctions regime pursuant to Resolution 1533 (2004) concerning the Democratic Republic of the Congo; the sanctions regime pursuant to Resolution 1572 (2004) concerning Côte d'Ivoire; the sanctions regime pursuant to Resolution 1591 (2005) concerning the Sudan; the sanctions regime pursuant to Resolution 1636 (2005) on Lebanon; the sanctions regime pursuant to Resolution 1718 (2006) relating to the Democratic People's Republic of Korea; the sanctions regime pursuant to Resolution 1737 (2006) relating to the Islamic Republic of Iran; the sanctions regime pursuant to Resolution 1970 (2011) concerning Libya; the sanctions regime pursuant to Resolution 1988 (2011) relating to the Taliban; the sanctions regime pursuant to Security Council Resolution 2048 (2012) concerning Guinea-Bissau; the sanctions regime pursuant to Resolution 2127 (2013) concerning the Central African Republic; the sanctions regime pursuant to Resolution 2140 (2014) relating to Yemen; the sanctions regime pursuant to Resolution 2206 (2015) concerning South Sudan.

[65] See UNSC Resolution 1452 (20 December 2002) paras 1 and 2.

[66] See UNSC Resolution 1617 (29 July 2005) paras 2.

criteria according to which individuals, groups, undertakings and entities were to be listed.[67] This change was urgently needed in the interest of fair and clear procedures (UN Declaration, para 29), and consistency and predictability (UN Declaration, para 2) in the sanctions regime in order to avoid any arbitrary listings. In 2006, the 'Focal Point' to receive delisting requests was established.[68] Thus, the cumbersome procedure of diplomatic protection[69] could be avoided. This was an improvement of the procedure according to the principle of due process (UN Declaration, para 29). Also in 2006, with the cover sheet for listings[70] more transparency and a better basis for the listings came to the sanctions regime. This facilitates that sanctions are '*carefully targeted*' in the sense of paragraph 29 of the UN Declaration. In 2008, the obligation to publish a 'narrative summary of reasons' for the listing was introduced[71] which serves due process purposes, ie the right to be informed and thus the fair procedure (UN Declaration, para 29), and which increases transparency concerning the reasons for listings. Due process and transparency are also provided by the information the targeted person receives about their listing and which includes the information on reasons for listing available on the Sanctions Committee's website, the narrative summary of reasons, the description of the effects of the designation, the procedure for delisting and the provisions for available exemptions.[72] Also since 2008, there is regular review of the entries on the list. The Sanctions Committee conducts an annual review of all names on the al-Qaida sanctions list that have not been reviewed in three or more years.[73] The review does not lead to an automatic delisting—if no decision is taken by the Committee to remove a name under review, the listing of that name shall be confirmed to 'remain appropriate'.[74] Nevertheless, such a periodic review can be considered an element of the rule of law improving 'fair and clear procedures'[75] and being

[67] Ibid, preambular para 6.

[68] See UNSC Resolution 1730 (19 December 2006) para 1.

[69] See for the disadvantages of this procedure, J Dugard, 'Diplomatic Protection' in R Wolfrum (ed), *The Max Planck Encyclopedia of Public International Law* (Oxford, Oxford University Press, 2012) Vol III, 114, 128, para 68: discretionary power of the State, political decision.

[70] See UNSC Resolution 1735 (22 December 2006) para 7 and Annex I.

[71] See UNSC Resolution 1822 (30 June 2008) para 1. A standard form is also used in the Sanctions Committee under Resolution 1988 (2011), see Security Council Committee established pursuant to Resolution 1988 (2011), 'Guidelines of the Committee for the Conduct of its Work' (29 July 2013) www.un.org/sc/suborg/sites/www.un.org.sc.suborg/files/1988_committee_guidelines_0.pdf, para 7(h).

[72] See Security Council Committee pursuant to Resolutions 1267 (1999) and 1989 (2011) concerning Al-Qaida and associated individuals and entities, 'Guidelines of the Committee for the Conduct of its Work' (15 April 2013) www.un.org/sc/suborg/sites/www.un.org.sc.suborg/files/1267_guidelines_1.pdf, paras 6(v) and (u).

[73] See UNSC Resolution 1822 (n 71) paras 25–26.

[74] See 'Guidelines' (n 72) para 10(f)(ix).

[75] *Cf* Chesterman (n 4) recommendation 16, p 18.

proportionate[76] to the consequences the listed person suffers (UN Declaration, para 29: 'minimise possible adverse consequences'). In 2009, the cover sheet for listings was replaced by the 'standard form for listing'[77] which collects in one official form the identifying information for the listing, the basis for the listing and—in addition to what the cover sheet contained—the statement of case.[78] The same year, the Office of the Ombudsperson, which receives delisting requests and prepares an independent report for the Sanctions Committee, was established.[79] Since 2014, the sanctions list has to be published in all official languages of the UN.[80] Also in the meantime, individuals can directly apply through the Focal Point for exemptions to the sanctions imposed[81] or claim that they have been subject to the sanctions as a result of mistaken identification.[82] These are elements to provide 'fair and clear procedures' in the sense of paragraph 29 of the UN Declaration as well as transparency.[83]

Thus, as far as the 1267 sanctions regime is concerned, the UN Declaration in many respects only describes what has already been achieved in that sanctions regime. However, since the Ombudsperson is not an independent judge and does not have the power to deliver binding decisions on delisting requests, the question remains whether the rule of law requires the provision of judicial review for targeted individuals in the 1267 sanctions regime.

It is politically hardly feasible to establish such a court or quasi-judicial review.[84] The UN Declaration only speaks of 'fair and clear procedures' without explicitly mentioning any review of listings. In addition to that, the delisting procedure in place provides a quite advanced procedural design which tries to strike a balance between the maintenance of international peace and security and individual human rights protection: there is direct access for the individual to the UN level which enables them to submit a delisting request directly, a careful preparation of the case as well as the report and recommendation to the Sanctions Committee by the independent and impartial Ombudsperson. In case the Ombudsperson recommends delisting, the delisting will automatically take effect within a specific period of time—even if some members of the Sanctions Committee object—unless *all* members of the Committee object

[76] *Cf* Ibid, recommendation 16, p 18.

[77] See UNSC Resolution 1904 (17 December 2009) para 13.

[78] See Consolidated List: Standard Form for Member State Submissions to the Committee for Listing of Individuals, available at:www.un.org/sc/committees/1267/pdf/sfl_ind_basic.pdf.

[79] See UNSC Resolution 1904 (17 December 2009) para 20.

[80] See UNSC Resolution 2161 (17 June 2014) para 39.

[81] See UNSC Resolution 2083 (17 December 2012) para 37.

[82] See UNSC Resolution 2161 (n 80) para 63(b).

[83] See UNSC Resolution 1989 (17 June 2011) preambular para 13.

[84] See Chesterman (n 4) 17–18.

(reverse consensus procedure)[85] to the delisting proposal before the end of a 60-day period or a member of the Committee requests to submit the case to the Security Council.[86] These are quite effective procedural safeguards in the interest of the targeted individual and one might argue that this meets the legitimacy requirement under the UN Declaration.

It is true that the Sanctions Committee is still a *iudex in causa sua* and that the delisting procedure does not provide judicial review, at least not in the sense of the European Union law[87] and the European Convention of Human Rights[88] which could lead Member States to deem the procedure not legitimate. One detail should not be overlooked, however: the UN Sanctions Committee might still itself consider and reject delisting requests but if it does so it has to convey an updated narrative summary of reasons for listing.[89] There is still a difference between this procedure and proper judicial review with a subsequent new listing as only in the latter case does an independent body conduct the review and take a decision which is final and binding. The result, however, is very similar: there is an independent body, the Ombudsperson, who gives a recommendation, and the Sanctions Committee is then subject to quite strict procedural safeguards and has to defend its decision to keep the petitioner on the list in a way that could also justify a new listing. Although not being judicial review, taking into consideration the political realities and thus the low probability of judicial review, this might be seen as quite an effective review even from a rule of law perspective. This last point demonstrates that the rule of law is still a work in progress and future practice will show whether in the sanctions regime only listings for which a judicial review is available will be accepted and seen as legitimate.

ii. Medium-developed Sanctions Regimes

Other sanctions regimes are less advanced as regards the realisation of the rule of law. With reference to the listing procedure, the guidelines of

[85] The reverse consensus procedure is best known from the WTO; see K Kaiser, 'Article 2 DSU' in R Wolfrum, P-T Stoll and K Kaiser (eds), *WTO—Institutions and Dispute Settlement* (Leiden, Nijhoff, 2006) para 2.

[86] See UNSC Resolution 2161 (n 80) para 43 and Annex II, para 15; 'Guidelines' (n 72) para 7(z) (ee) to (ii); for the suggestion of this procedural arrangement, see C Feinäugle, *Hoheitsgewalt im Völkerrecht (The Exercise of Public Authority in International Law)* (Heidelberg, Springer, 2011) 244 and 379.

[87] This was criticised by the CJEU in its *Kadi II* case, Joined Cases C-584/10 P, C-593/10 P and C-595/10 P, *Commission, Council and UK v Kadi* ECLI:EU:C:2013:518, paras 133–34. A rule of law for the UN must, of course, not be defined by a few States only and, rather, it should reflect the interest of the entire international community, as B Tamanaha, *On the Rule of Law* (Cambridge et al, Cambridge University Press, 2004) 136, rightly points out.

[88] See *Nada v Switzerland* (2013) 56 EHRR 18, paras 211–13.

[89] See UNSC Resolution 2161 (n 80) Annex II, para 16.

a number of sanctions committees[90] only provide for the use of a statement of case in support of the proposed listing that forms the basis or justification for the listing in accordance with the relevant listing criteria. The requirement to provide in written form the facts that are meant to be sufficient evidence of a behaviour that fulfils the criteria for a listing are a decisive tool to ensure that sanctions are 'carefully targeted' in the sense of paragraph 29 of the UN Declaration. This avoids arbitrariness in listings and supports transparency and due process as aspects of the rule of law since the information in the statement of case is also used in the narrative summary of reasons for the listing which is later published on the website of the sanctions committees and provides the listed persons with the information on which they may base a delisting request. While the requirement of a statement of case thus serves rule of law purposes, it is still quite far from the 'standard form' used in the 1267[91] sanctions regime which collects the identifying information, the basis for the listing and the statement of case in one official form.[92] The advantage of one single document covering all information is that no information gets lost or is forgotten. This serves better the rule of law standard of due process described in the UN Declaration as 'fair and clear procedures'.[93]

None of these 'medium-developed' sanctions regimes grants listed individuals access to an Ombudsperson. While the so-called Focal Point is there to serve for all smart sanctions regimes,[94] the Ombudsperson is only responsible for delisting requests under the 1267 sanctions regime. Through direct access to the Focal Point, in these sanctions regimes as in the 1267 sanctions regime the use of diplomatic protection[95] can be avoided, which improves 'fair and clear procedures' (UN Declaration, para 29) of

[90] See eg Security Council Committee pursuant to Resolutions 751 (1992) and 1907 (2009) concerning Somalia and Eritrea, 'Guidelines of the Committee for the Conduct of its Work' (25 March 2014) www.un.org/sc/suborg/sites/www.un.org.sc.suborg/files/sc_751_and_1907_committee_guidelines_25_march_14.pdf, para 6(d); Security Council Committee established pursuant to Resolution 1521 (2003) concerning Liberia, 'Guidelines of the Committee for the Conduct of its Work' (30 March 2010) www.un.org/sc/suborg/sites/www.un.org.sc.suborg/files/revised_guidelines_30_mar_10_final.pdf, para 6(c); Security Council Committee established pursuant to Resolution 2048 (2012) concerning the Guinea-Bissau, 'Guidelines of the Committee for the Conduct of its Work' (19 July 2012) www.un.org/sc/suborg/sites/www.un.org.sc.suborg/files/2048_guidelines_1.pdf, para 5(c).

[91] The most recent sanctions regime concerning South Sudan also provides for the use of a standard form, see Security Council Committee established pursuant to Resolution 2206 (2015) concerning South Sudan, 'Guidelines of the Committee for the Conduct of its Work' (20 April 2015) www.un.org/sc/suborg/sites/www.un.org.sc.suborg/files/2206_guidelines_en_1.pdf, para 6(e), but did not establish an office of an Ombudsperson.

[92] See Consolidated List: Standard Form for Member State Submissions to the Committee for Listing of Individuals, available at: www.un.org/sc/suborg/sites/www.un.org.sc.suborg/files/standard_form_-_individuals_e.pdf.

[93] See UNGA, 'Declaration of the high-level meeting of the General Assembly on the rule of law at the national and international levels' (n 6) para 29.

[94] See UNSC Resolution 1730 (n 68) paras 1 and 2.

[95] See Dugard, 'Diplomatic Protection' (n 69) para 82.

delisting. At the same time, the Focal Point was merely established to receive delisting requests directly from the listed person and to forward the requests to specific governments and the sanctions committee.[96] Compared to that, the Ombudsperson offers much more to the petitioner as she deals with the case itself as an independent and impartial person and submits a recommendation for listing or delisting to the Sanctions Committee, with the Sanctions Committee being subject to strict time periods and a reverse consensus vote if it wants to keep someone on the list. Thus, while not providing for independent judicial review, the Ombudsperson would also in these sanctions regimes be a considerable improvement with regard to due process and fair and clear procedures.

Only some of the 'medium-developed' sanctions committees regularly review the entries on their sanctions lists.[97] Others provide for review but not on an established, regular basis.[98] While it is to be welcomed that there is review at all, a fixed date for review would be better placed to avoid any arbitrary handling of the listings and to remind the sanctions committees that adopted listings are not meant to automatically remain permanently. An additional option which is not even available in the 1267 sanctions regimes would be a 'sunset provision', according to which a listing automatically ends after a specific period of time if the sanctions committee does not take action to keep the person on the list. The introduction of such a provision is under discussion[99] and would improve the sanctions procedure according to the rule of law.[100]

iii. Less-developed Sanctions Regimes

There are several sanctions regimes that observe the rule of law only to a small extent.[101] One major deficiency in those regimes is that there is no detailed statement of case required for listings, let alone a standard form as in the 1267 sanctions regime. Instead, the guidelines of some sanctions

[96] See UNSC Resolution 1730 (n 68) Annex, paras 1–6.

[97] See Security Council Committee pursuant to Resolutions 751 (1992) and 1907 (2009) concerning Somalia and Eritrea, 'Guidelines of the Committee for the Conduct of its Work' (n 90) para 9: 'annual review'; Security Council Committee established pursuant to Resolution 2206 (2015) concerning South Sudan, 'Guidelines of the Committee for the Conduct of its Work' (n 91) para 9: 'annual review'.

[98] See Security Council Committee established pursuant to Resolution 1718 (2006), 'Guidelines of the Committee for the Conduct of its Work' (31 December 2014) www.un.org/sc/suborg/sites/www.un.org.sc.suborg/files/dprk_guidelines.pdf, para 7(b): 'continuous review'.

[99] See Security Council Report No 3 (28 October 2011) 41, 45.

[100] Council of Europe, Parliamentary Assembly, Resolution 1597, 'United Nations Security Council and European Union blacklists' (23 January 2008) para 5.3: 'The "blacklisting" procedure should be limited in time. It is unacceptable that persons remain on the blacklist for years'.

[101] The sanctions regime pursuant to Resolution 1518 (2003) concerning Iraq and Kuwait; the sanctions regime pursuant to Resolution 1636 (2005) on Lebanon.

committees still only require that the listing proposal should be accompanied by a narrative description of the information that justifies that the person fulfils the criteria for being listed.[102] Given the severe consequences of a listing, evidence related to the listing criteria must be convincing and must be thoroughly checked before a listing decision is taken. Thus, this quite lax handling of the evidence that brings a person onto the list is unacceptable from a rule of law point of view. With a new listing, there is no summary of reasons for it and while the updated list is promptly communicated to all UN Member States, they are not asked to inform the targeted person of the listing.[103] In the interest of due process and fair and clear procedures, the person listed has to be informed of the listing and the possibilities of a delisting procedure.

With regard to the delisting procedure, the less-developed sanctions regimes do not provide for an Ombudsperson nor are the sanctions committees subject to strict time periods or a reverse consensus vote if they want to keep someone on their list. With regard to these two points, these sanctions regimes suffer from the same deficiencies as the 'medium-developed' sanctions regimes. Some sanctions regimes do not have a review of the entries on their lists at all.[104]

These last points on delisting and the regular review of the entries which are both missing in the less-developed sanctions regimes, clearly go against rule of law principles of due process and proportionality and should be addressed by reforming the relevant sanctions regimes.

B. Inter-regime Perspective

The analysis of the different smart sanctions regimes reveals that there are considerable differences between the rule of law design in advanced, medium-developed and less-developed sanctions regimes. The availability or absence of the Ombudsperson mechanism is probably the most prominent example in that regard. Paragraph 2 of the UN Declaration

[102] Security Council Committee established pursuant to Resolution 1518 (2003) concerning Iraq and Kuwait, 'Guidelines for the Application of paragraphs 19 and 23 of Resolution 1483 (2003)', www.un.org.sc.suborg/files/1483guide.pdf, para 1(b); similarly Security Council Committee established pursuant to Resolution 1636 (2005), 'Guidelines of the Committee established pursuant to Resolution 1636 (2005) (8 March 2006) www.un.org.sc.suborg/files/committeeguidelines.pdf, para 2(c).

[103] Security Council Committee established pursuant to Resolution 1518 (2003) concerning Iraq and Kuwait, 'Guidelines for the Application of paragraphs 19 and 23 of Resolution 1483 (2003)' (n 102) para 1(e); Security Council Committee established pursuant to Resolution 1636 (2005), 'Guidelines of the Committee for the Conduct of its Work' (n 102).

[104] See the sanctions regime pursuant to Resolution 1518 (2003) concerning Iraq and Kuwait and the sanctions regime pursuant to Resolution 1636 (2005) on Lebanon.

states that all persons and institutions are accountable to just, fair and equitable laws and are entitled without any discrimination to equal protection of the law. This could mean that the rule of law requires that 'fair and clear procedures' should be the same or similar in all smart sanctions regimes so that advanced achievements like the Ombudsperson should also be established for other smart sanctions regimes.[105] Certainly, it cannot be ignored that different smart sanctions regimes deal with different subject matters and target different groups of individuals. In that regard, the novelty of the 1267 sanctions regime was that it was completely de-territorialised and the link between the sanctions' target and a given State was broken.[106] It was argued that all other sanctions regimes except for the 1267 regime provided for country-specific sanctions and aimed at political goals and that therefore due process rights were less relevant there.[107] One can admit that the targets 'Saddam Hussein or other senior officials of the former Iraqi regime and their immediate family members'[108] are, obviously, much more precisely defined than 'any individual, group, undertaking or entity either owned or controlled, directly or indirectly, by, or otherwise supporting, any individual, group, undertaking or entity associated with Al-Qaida'.[109] In case objective differences justify differentiation,[110] different sanctions regimes could, of course, be allowed to be designed differently with regard to the procedure for the conduct of their work. However 'fair and clear procedures' must be provided in all sanctions regimes[111] and include review by an independent, impartial body according to the rule of law principle of due process, as seen above. The idea of a similar design of the different smart sanctions regimes was already adopted by the Security Council with regard to some procedural improvements that are to be applied in nearly all smart sanctions regimes.[112]

From an inter-regime perspective, this leads to the conclusion that the rule of law principle that the law applies to all equally requires that there is the same or at least a similar design, inspired by the rule of law, for all smart sanctions regimes.

[105] See Security Council Report 2011 No 3 (n 99) 43.

[106] See Pellet and Miron, 'Sanctions' (n 1) para 36.

[107] See Security Council Report, 2011 No 3 (n 99) 43, citing voices of some States.

[108] See UNSC Resolution 1483 (22 May 2003) para 23 together with Resolution 1546 (2004) para 29.

[109] See UNSC Resolution 2161 (n 80) para 4.

[110] Bingham, 'The Rule of Law' (n 26) 69.

[111] See the wording of UNGA, 'Declaration of the high-level meeting of the General Assembly on the rule of law at the national and international levels' (n 6) para 29.

[112] The delisting procedure in UNSC Resolution 1730 (19 December 2006) para 1 and Annex, applies, eg, also to the sanctions regime pursuant to Resolution 1591 (2005) concerning the Sudan, see Security Council Committee established pursuant to Resolution 1591 (2005), 'Guidelines of the Committee for the Conduct of its Work' (23 December 2013), www.un.org/sc/suborg/sites/www.un.org.sc.suborg/files/sudan_guide_e.pdf, para 7(c) and (g).

IV. CONCLUSION

As international organisations and especially the UN increasingly exercise public authority, they have to justify their acts if these acts are to be accepted by their addressees. The UN Declaration on the rule of law which provides that the rule of law applies to the UN and should guide all its activities suggests that the UN should achieve legitimacy of its act through procedures that follow the rule of law.

With regard to UN sanctions, the application of rule of law principles, such as proportionality and due process, is not only advocated in literature but also reflected in the UN Declaration. The analysis of different smart sanctions regimes with a view to assessing the extent to which such rule of law elements have already been achieved shows that, indeed, the establishment of procedures that follow the rule of law can improve the legitimacy of UN sanctions. In this respect, the smart sanctions regime initially established under UNSC Resolution 1267 serves as a good example. Although there is still no judicial protection available for the listed individual, the improvements of the procedure over the years have to some extent led to less protest and more acceptance of the sanctions regime:[113] while the CJEU did not accept the delisting procedure on the UN level as sufficient in its *Kadi II* judgment because of the lack of judicial protection, it admitted that improvements had been achieved.[114] Indeed, the Advocate General had suggested an only limited review of cases involving UN sanctions stating that '[t]he improvements to the procedure within the United Nations allow, in particular, the presumption to be made that the reasons cited in support of listing are based on sufficient evidence and information'.[115]

Taking into consideration the political realities in the Security Council, it can thus be argued that means of procedural design, like time-limits for the sanctions committee for taking decisions, the fiction of a delisting if the committee remains inactive in connection with the establishment of an independent Ombudsperson, might serve as a useful tool to find solutions that can help substitute for judicial protection, which is presently not a politically viable option in the Security Council.

Compared to the 1267 sanctions regime, all other UN smart sanctions regimes are less developed with regard to the achievement of the rule of law. The requirements for the evidence based on which a person is listed are less strict, only some of these other sanctions committees regularly

[113] See eg Security Council Report, 2011 No 3 (n 99) 41.

[114] Joined Cases C-584/10 P, C-593/10 P and C-595/10 P, *Commission, Council and UK v Kadi* ECLI:EU:C:2013:518, para 133.

[115] Joined Cases C-584/10 P, C-593/10 P and C-595/10 P, *Commission, Council and UK v Kadi*, ECLI:EU:C:2013:176, Opinion of AG Bot, para 87.

review the entries on their sanctions lists and none of them provides access to the Ombudsperson. Insofar, considerable improvements can still be made in these sanctions regimes and especially the equal application of the law as one aspect of the rule of law would ask for making available the Ombudsperson's services also in these other sanctions regimes.

All in all, procedural design presents itself as a clever way to introduce improvements concerning the rule of law in UN sanctions regimes. It might be used in the future to enhance, for example, due process by providing the Ombudsperson with access to sensitive information or by introducing sunset provisions for listings.[116] More broadly, the rule of law—fluid as it still may be on the international level—could provide a solid basis for a consistent and predictable administration not only in the context of UN sanctions but for all UN activities.

[116] This was raised as a problem by UN Member States; see Security Council Report, 2011 No 3 (n 99) 44–45.

7

United Nations Targeted Sanctions, Human Rights and the Office of the Ombudsperson

PAUL EDEN

I. INTRODUCTION

ACTING UNDER CHAPTER VII of the UN Charter, the Security Council is empowered to employ measures not involving the use of armed force to give effect to its decisions taken to maintain or restore international peace and security. Article 41 of the UN Charter states that measures not involving the use of armed force 'may include complete or partial interruption of economic relations'.[1] Although economic sanctions were initially envisaged as being targeted against States, the humanitarian impact of comprehensive sanctions became the source of increasing concern in the 1990s[2] and these concerns led to the UN Security Council developing a more refined approach to the design, application and implementation of economic sanctions with the objective of making sanctions regimes more effective by targeting them more precisely on their political objectives.[3] The first examples of so-called 'smart sanctions' were the travel and financial restrictions against the União Nacional para

[1] The Charter of the United Nations (adopted 26 June 1945, entered into force 24 October 1945) 1 UNTS 16, Art 41 (UN Charter).

[2] See generally L F Damrosch, 'The Civilian Impact of Economic Sanctions' in L F Damrosch (ed), *Enforcing Restraint: Collective Intervention in Internal Conflicts* (New York, Council on Foreign Relations, 1993) 274–315; T G Weiss et al (eds), *Political Gain and Civilian Gain: Humanitarian Impacts of Economic Sanctions* (Lanham, Maryland, Rowman & Littlefield Publishers Inc, 1997); and E Hoskins, *A Study of Sanctions: A Study of UNICEF's Perspective* (UNICEF Office of Emergency Programmes, New York, 1998). See also M Bessler et al, *Sanctions Assessment Handbook: Assessing the Humanitarian Implications of Sanctions* (New York, United Nations Inter-Agency Standing Committee, 2004).

[3] See 'Security Council Subsidiary Bodies: An Overview' available at: www.un.org/sc/suborg.

a Independência Total de Angola (UNITA) in 1997 and 1998,[4] although in UNITA's case there was no State against which it would have been possible to target sanctions in any event other than by targeting those countries, organisations and individuals allegedly involved in trading with UNITA.[5]

II. TARGETED SANCTIONS AGAINST THE TALIBAN AND AL-QAIDA

The targeting of sanctions against specific individuals associated with named entities was extended to the Taliban in UNSC Resolution 1267 (1999)[6] and Osama bin Laden and his associates, including those in the Al-Qaida organization, in UNSC Resolution 1333 (2000).[7] As Lord Hope noted in *Ahmed v HM Treasury*:

> Although previous practice did not go that far, it has not been suggested that it lay outside the powers of the Security Council under article 41 to direct the taking of collective measures at an international level against individuals. The drafting history indicates the contrary.[8]

Paragraph 4(b) of UNSC Resolution 1267 specifically required States to

> Freeze funds and other financial resources, including funds derived or generated from property owned or controlled directly or indirectly by the Taliban, or by any undertaking owned or controlled by the Taliban.

Paragraph 6 of UNSC Resolution 1267 created a committee of the Security Council to effectively oversee implementation of the measures imposed by paragraph 4 by obtaining information from States and recommending appropriate measures in response to this information. This committee, which until December 2015 called itself 'the Al-Qaida Sanctions Committee',[9] was originally known as the 1267 Committee and changed its name to reflect the fact that the sanctions regime established in UNSC

[4] UNSC Res 1127 (28 August 1997) UN Doc S/RES/1127 (1997); UNSC Res 1173 (12 June 1998) UN Doc S/RES/1173(1998); and UNSC Res 1176 (24 June 1998) UN Doc S/RES/1176 (1998). Terminated by UNSC Res 1448 (9 December 2002) UN Doc S/RES/1448 (2002).

[5] See generally *The Final Report of the Panel of Experts on Violations of Security Council Sanctions Against UNITA* ('The Fowler Report') (10 March 2000) UN Doc S/2000/203.

[6] UNSC Res 1267 (15 October 1999); UN Doc S/RES/1267 (1999).

[7] UNSC Res 1333 (19 December 2000); UN Doc S/RES/1333 (2000) para 8(c).

[8] *Ahmed v HM Treasury* [2010] UKSC 2, [2010] 2 AC 534 at para 18 citing B Simma et al (eds), *The Charter of the United Nations: A Commentary* (2nd edn, Oxford, Oxford University Press, 2002) 737.

[9] It was also called 'the Al-Qaida and Taliban Sanctions Committee' but UNSC Resolutions 1988 and 1989 adopted on 17 June 2011 split the functions of the original 1267 Committee and created a new 1988 Committee to deal with sanctions relating to the Taliban. See UNSC Res 1988 (17 June 2011) UN Doc S/RES/1988 (2011) and UNSC Res 1989 (17 June 2011) UN Doc S/RES/1989 (2011).

Resolution 1267 has been modified by numerous subsequent UNSC resolutions and the extension of its mandate to cover individuals associated with Al-Qaida occurred in UNSC Resolution 1333.

III. THE EFFECT OF 9/11 ON TARGETED SANCTIONS

The tragic events of 11 September 2001 led the UN Security Council to adopt UNSC Resolution 1373 on 28 September 2001,[10] unanimously and without any debate.[11] Paragraph 1(c) of UNSC Resolution 1373 obliges all States to:

> Freeze without delay funds and other financial assets or economic resources of persons who commit, or attempt to commit, terrorist acts or participate in or facilitate the commission of terrorist acts; of entities owned or controlled directly or indirectly by such persons; and of persons and entities acting on behalf of, or at the direction of such persons and entities, including funds derived or generated from property owned or controlled directly or indirectly by such persons and associated persons and entities;

Paragraphs 2 and 3 of UNSC Resolution 1373 placed further obligations on States to adopt a post 9/11 anti-terrorist agenda that included an obligation to exchange information with other States and to provide assistance in obtaining evidence to support criminal investigations into the financing of terrorist acts. Paragraph 6 of UNSC Resolution 1373 established a committee of the Security Council, consisting of all the members of the Council, to monitor implementation of UNSC Resolution 1373 and called upon all States to report to the committee—no later than 90 days from the date of adoption of the resolution (and periodically thereafter according to a timetable to be proposed by the committee)—on the steps they had taken to implement UNSC Resolution 1373.

Although UNSC Resolution 1373 did not embody a new targeted sanctions regime, it had a twofold effect. First, it gave States *carte blanche* to target the assets of individuals that they unilaterally designated to be terrorists. Secondly, it turbo-charged the existing targeted sanctions regime initially created by UNSC Resolution 1267. Furthermore, UNSC Resolution 1390 adopted on 28 January 2002, that imposed additional sanctions

[10] UNSC Res 1373 (28 September 2001) UN Doc S/RES/1373 (2001).

[11] See UNSC Verbatim Record (28 September 2001) UN Doc S/PV.4385. The meeting was called to order at 9:55 pm. There was no objection to the President's proposal to put the draft resolution to an immediate vote. A vote was taken by a show of hands and the meeting rose at 10:00 pm. For an explanation of the lack of debate, see A Aust, 'The Role of Human Rights in Limiting the Enforcement Powers of the Security Council: A Practitioner's View' in E de Wet and A Nollkaemper (eds), *Review of the Security Council by Member States* (Antwerp, Intersentia, 2003) 31.

on Osama bin Laden, Al-Qaida and the Taliban omitted any requirement of a territorial connection.[12]

162 individuals and seven entities were subject to asset freezing under the first Consolidated List of persons and entities published by the Sanctions Committee on 8 March 2001 but, after 9/11, the list of persons and entities subject to asset freezing grew rapidly and by 30 July 2010 it included 443 names (including 311 associated with Al-Qaida and 132 associated with the Taliban).[13] The most recent Consolidated List (updated on 10 December 2015) consists of 621 individuals and 398 entities and other groups.[14]

IV. CRITICISM OF THE UNITED NATIONS ASSET FREEZING REGIME

The rapid expansion of the UNSC asset freezing regime after 9/11 led to criticism from both NGOs[15] and governments, most notably in the 2005 World Summit Outcome Resolution where the Heads of State and Government drew attention to the accountability gap in the designation process and the lack of fair and clear procedures for placing individuals and entities on sanctions lists and removing them, as well as a procedure for granting humanitarian exemptions.[16]

It is entirely possible that the UN Security Council would have been willing to bear the opprobrium of NGOs and Heads of State and Government with equanimity (or indifference) but the targeting of the financial assets of individuals and entities required the asset freezing to be conducted through mechanisms rooted in domestic legal systems and a number of legal challenges were brought against the UN Security Council

[12] UNSC Res 1390 (28 January 2002) UN Doc S/RES/1390 (2002).

[13] See 'Security Council Al-Qaida and Taliban Sanctions Committee Concludes Review of Its Consolidated List, Pursuant to Resolution 1822 (2008)' UN Security Council Press Release dated 2 August 2010 UN Doc Sc/9999, available at: www.un.org/press/en/2010/sc9999.doc.htm. See also G Sullivan and B Hayes, *Blacklisted: Targeted Sanctions, Pre-emptive Security and Fundamental Rights* (European Center for Constitutional and Human Rights, 2010) 12–13.

[14] See www.un.org/sc/suborg/en/sanctions/un-sc-consolidated-list.

[15] See eg The ICJ Declaration on Upholding Human Rights and the Rule of Law in Combating Terrorism (The Berlin Declaration) adopted 28 August 2004 reprinted in International Commission of Jurists, *Assessing Damage, Urging Action: Report of the Eminent Jurists Panel on Terrorism, Counter-terrorism and Human Rights* (2009) Annex 1.

[16] 2005 World Summit Outcome, UNGA Res 60/1 (24 October 2005) UN Doc A/RES/60/1 (2005) para 109. See also B Fassbender, *Targeted Sanctions and Due Process: The Responsibility of the UN Security Council to Ensure that Fair and Clear Procedures are Made Available to Individuals and Entities Targeted with Sanctions under Chapter VII of the UN Charter* A Study commissioned by the United Nations Office of Legal Affairs, 20 March 2006, available at: www.un.org/law/counsel/Fassbender_study.pdf.

asset freezing processes before both domestic courts[17] and international tribunals.[18] This chapter focuses on the *Kadi* case as this protracted legal challenge to the UN Security Council asset freezing processes demonstrates iterative interaction between the European Court of Justice (now Court of Justice of the European Union (CJEU)) and the UN Security Council not least because of the status of the CJEU within the Treaties of the European Union[19] and the Court's assertion of its role in a community based on the rule of law as the guardian 'of a constitutional guarantee stemming from the EC Treaty as an autonomous legal system which is not to be prejudiced by an international agreement'.[20]

V. THE *KADI I* CASE

A. Introduction

On 19 October 2001, the Sanctions Committee added the name 'Al-Qadi, Yasin (A.K.A. Kadi, Shaykh Yassin Abdullah; A.K.A. Kahdi, Yasin), Jeddah, Saudi Arabia' to the list first published by the Sanctions Committee on 8 March 2001. By Regulation (EC) No 2062/2001 of 19 October 2001, Mr Kadi's name was added to the list of persons subject to asset freezing within the European Union. On 18 December 2001, Mr Kadi brought an action against both the Council and the Commission seeking the annulment of the relevant EU Regulations in so far as they related to him. Mr Kadi alleged that the asset freezing breached his fundamental rights on three grounds; first, breach of the right to a fair hearing, secondly, breach of the right to respect for property and of the principle of proportionality and, thirdly, breach of the right to effective judicial review.

B. The 2005 Court of First Instance Judgment (*Kadi I* (CFI))

On 21 September 2005, having first rejected the argument that the contested regulations were ultra vires, the Court of First Instance of the

[17] See eg *Ahmed* (n 8) and *Abdelrazik v Canada (Minister of Foreign Affairs)* 2009 FC 580, [2010] 1 FCR 267 (Canadian Federal Court). See also *Kindhearts for Charitable Humanitarian Development Inc v Geithner* 647 F Supp 2d 857 (2009) but note that this decision is entirely based on US domestic asset freezing legislation and its failure to respect US constitutional due process guarantees.

[18] See eg *Sayadi and Vinck v Belgium*, Merits, UN Doc CCPR/C/94/D/1472/2006 (29 December 2008) (UN Human Rights Committee); *Nada v Switzerland* (2013) 56 EHRR 18; and *Al-Dulimi and Montana Management Inc v Switzerland* App no 5809/08 (ECtHR, 26 November 2013).

[19] Consolidated Version of the Treaty on European Union [2008] OJ C115/13, Art 19.

[20] Joined Cases C-402/05P and C-415/05P, *Yassin Abdullah Kadi and Al Barakaat International Foundation v Council of the European Union and Commission of the European Communities* [2008] ECR I-06351, para 316.

European Court of Justice (now renamed General Court of the European Union) declined to annul the relevant EU Regulations that gave effect to the asset freezing obligations contained in the relevant UNSC resolutions against persons named in the Consolidated List of persons and entities published by the Sanctions Committee.[21] Relying on Article 103 of the UN Charter and Article 307 EC, the Court of First Instance held that:

> It must therefore be considered that the resolutions of the Security Council at issue fall, in principle, outside the ambit of the Court's judicial review and that the Court has no authority to call in question, even indirectly, their lawfulness in the light of Community law. On the contrary, the Court is bound, so far as possible, to interpret and apply that law in a manner compatible with the obligations of the Member States under the Charter of the United Nations.[22]

The Court of First Instance did acknowledge that it had the power to check the lawfulness of UNSC resolutions indirectly by reference to *jus cogens*[23] but that, on the facts, this was not a case 'measured by the standard of universal protection of the fundamental rights of the human person covered by *jus cogens*'[24] because the contested regulation provided for exemptions relating to the funds necessary to cover basic expenses, including payments for foodstuffs, rent, medicines and medical treatment, taxes or public utility charges and thus:

> The express provision of possible exemptions and derogations thus attaching to the freezing of the funds of the persons in the Sanctions Committee's list clearly shows that it is neither the purpose nor the effect of that measure to submit those persons to inhuman or degrading treatment.[25]

The Court of First Instance did acknowledge that, in so far as respect for the right to property must be regarded as forming part of the mandatory rules of general international law, an arbitrary deprivation of that right through an asset freeze might be regarded as contrary to *jus cogens* but the deprivation under consideration was non-arbitrary.[26] In support of its conclusions, the Court of First Instance stressed the importance of the campaign against international terrorism,[27] the temporary and precautionary nature of the freezing of funds,[28] the existence of a means of reviewing the overall system of sanctions within the latter UNSC resolutions on the

[21] Case T-315/01, *Yassin Abdullah Kadi v Council of the European Union* [2005] ECR II-3649 ('*Kadi I* (CFI)').
[22] Ibid para 225.
[23] Ibid para 226.
[24] Ibid para 238.
[25] Ibid para 240.
[26] Ibid para 243 ff.
[27] Ibid para 245.
[28] Ibid para 248.

matter[29] and, finally, the fact that 'the legislation at issue settles a procedure enabling the persons concerned to present their case at any time to the Sanctions Committee for review, through the Member State of their nationality or that of their residence'.[30]

With regard to the claim that the UN Security Council's asset freezing regime denied Mr Kadi the opportunity to challenge the evidence that led to his assets being frozen ex post facto, the Court of First Instance held that the obligation to transpose the resolutions of the UN Security Council and decisions of the Sanctions Committee into the Community legal order meant that

> the Community institutions had no power of investigation, no opportunity to check the matters taken to be facts by the Security Council and the Sanctions Committee, no discretion with regard to those matters and no discretion either as to whether it was appropriate to adopt sanctions vis-à-vis the applicants. The principle of Community law relating to the right to be heard cannot apply in such circumstances, where to hear the person concerned could not in any case lead the institution to review its position.[31]

The Court of First Instance concluded that the Council was not obliged to give Mr Kadi the opportunity to challenge his inclusion in the list of persons and entities affected by the sanctions, in the context of the adoption and implementation of the contested regulation.[32] The Court of First Instance acknowledged that the relevant UNSC resolutions did not provide Mr Kadi with a right to be heard by the Sanctions Committee in connection with his inclusion in the list of persons whose funds must be frozen but asserted that the re-examination procedure first adopted in November 2002 by the Sanctions Committee in its Guidelines whereby an affected person could 'petition the government of residence and/or citizenship to request review of the case' discharged any obligations relating to the right to be heard.[33]

> Admittedly, the procedure... confers no right directly on the persons concerned themselves to be heard by the Sanctions Committee, the only authority competent to give a decision, on a State's petition, on the re-examination of their case. Those persons are thus dependent, essentially, on the diplomatic protection afforded by the States to their nationals.[34]

[29] Ibid para 249. The CFI refers to UNSC Res 1526 (30 January 2004) UN Doc S/RES/1526 (2004) but para 18 of this resolution merely 'strongly encourages all States to inform, to the extent possible, individuals and entities included in the Committee's list of the measures imposed on them, and of the Committee's guidelines and resolution 1452 (2002)'.

[30] Ibid para 250.

[31] Ibid para 258.

[32] Ibid para 259.

[33] Ibid para 265.

[34] Ibid para 267.

The Court of First Instance conceded that Mr Kadi had provided evidence that he had attempted to contact Saudi Arabia's permanent representative to the United Nations in order to assert his rights before the Sanctions Committee on 1 March 2002 and that his letter had been ignored but asserted that 'those circumstances have nothing to do with the Community and are therefore foreign to this dispute'.[35] Although the Court of First Instance was prepared to acknowledge the existence of an accountability gap, it concluded that

> there is no judicial remedy available to the applicant, the Security Council not having thought it advisable to establish an independent international court responsible for ruling, in law and on the facts, in actions brought against individual decisions taken by the Sanctions Committee.[36]

Mr Kadi appealed.

C. The 2008 Grand Chamber Judgment (*Kadi I*)

Mr Kadi's appeal was heard together with an appeal from a Court of First Instance judgment against the Al Barakaat International Foundation.[37] Both parties sought to set aside the respective judgments of the Court of First Instance and have the contested regulation declared null and void. The United Kingdom (supported by France) brought a cross-appeal contending that the Court should 'set aside that part of the judgments under appeal which deal with the question of *jus cogens*'.

The Grand Chamber upheld the Court of First Instance's conclusion that that the Council was competent to adopt that regulation albeit on other legal grounds to those invoked by the Court of First Instance.[38] However in relation to Mr Kadi's claim that the contested regulation freezing his assets breached his fundamental rights, the Grand Chamber adopted a radically different approach from the Court of First Instance. The Grand Chamber's foundational premise was that

> the Community is based on the rule of law, inasmuch as neither its Member States nor its institutions can avoid review of the conformity of their acts with the basic constitutional charter, the EC Treaty, which established a complete system of legal remedies and procedures designed to enable the Court of Justice to review the legality of acts of the institutions.[39]

[35] Ibid para 272.
[36] Ibid para 285.
[37] Joined Cases C-402/05P and C-415/05P, *Yassin Abdullah Kadi and Al Barakaat International Foundation v Council of the European Union and Commission of the European Communities* [2008] ECR I-06351 ('*Kadi I*').
[38] Ibid paras 121–236.
[39] Ibid para 281.

The Grand Chamber rejected the argument that an international agreement could impinge on the autonomy of the Community legal order or the exclusive jurisdiction conferred on the Court by Article 220 EC. Noting that fundamental rights (derived in part from international instruments for the protection of human rights) formed an integral part of the general principles of EU law whose observance the Court was tasked to ensure, the Grand Chamber concluded that respect for human rights was a precondition of the lawfulness of Community acts and that measures incompatible with respect for human rights were not acceptable in the Community.[40]

The Grand Chamber did not assert that it had jurisdiction to review the lawfulness of UN Security Council resolution (even if that review was limited to examination of the compatibility of the resolution with *jus cogens*) but did assert that annulling a Community measure giving effect to such a resolution 'would not entail any challenge to the primacy of that resolution in international law'.[41] The Grand Chamber also asserted that

> it is not a consequence of the principles governing the international legal order under the United Nations that any judicial review of the internal lawfulness of the contested regulation in the light of fundamental freedoms is excluded by virtue of the fact that that measure is intended to give effect to a resolution of the Security Council adopted under Chapter VII of the Charter of the United Nations.[42]

The Grand Chamber's judgment acknowledged the improvements to the re-examination procedure before the Sanctions Committee that had been implemented after the judgment of the Court of First Instance but stated, first, that in principle the amendments made after the contested regulation had been adopted could not be taken into consideration, and, secondly, that the existence of the re-examination procedure could not give rise to a generalised immunity from the Court's jurisdiction particularly given that the re-examination procedure did not offer the guarantees of judicial protection.[43] Specifically, the Grand Chamber observed that

> the procedure before that Committee is still in essence diplomatic and intergovernmental, the persons or entities concerned having no real opportunity of asserting their rights and that committee taking its decisions by consensus, each of its members having a right of veto.[44]

The Grand Chamber also noted that under the 2007 Guidelines of the Sanctions Committee, applicants were unable to assert their rights personally or through a nominated representative but were wholly reliant

[40] Ibid paras 282–84.
[41] Ibid para 288.
[42] Ibid para 299.
[43] Ibid paras 320–22.
[44] Ibid para 323.

on the government of their State of residence or citizenship to submit observations on his or her behalf. The Grand Chamber also expressed concern about the failure of the Guidelines to require the Sanctions Committee to provide an applicant with the reasons and evidence justifying his or her appearance on the list and the fact that 'if that Committee rejects the request for removal from the list, it is under no obligation to give reasons'.[45]

Having concluded that the powers granted to the Court by the EC Treaty entailed the full review of all Community acts (in the light of the fundamental rights that formed an integral part of the general principles of EU law), the Grand Chamber set aside the aspects of the judgment of the Court of First Instance that held that a regulation designed to give effect to a resolution adopted by the Security Council under Chapter VII of the Charter of the United Nations enjoyed immunity from the jurisdiction of the Court regarding lawfulness save a determination of its compatibility with the norms of *jus cogens*.

Although the Grand Chamber confirmed that the effectiveness of the freezing of funds and resources precluded prior communication, it held that:

> Because the Council neither communicated to the appellants the evidence used against them to justify the restrictive measures imposed on them nor afforded them the right to be informed of that evidence within a reasonable period after those measures were enacted, the appellants were not in a position to make their point of view in that respect known to advantage. Therefore, the appellants' rights of defence, in particular the right to be heard, were not respected.[46]

The Grand Chamber further held that the failure to inform the appellants of the evidence against them infringed their right to an effective legal remedy.[47]

The Grand Chamber also examined Mr Kadi's pleas relating to the infringement of his property rights. The Court acknowledged that the right to property, although not absolute, was one of the general principles of EU law.

> Consequently, the exercise of the right to property may be restricted, provided that those restrictions in fact correspond to objectives of public interest pursued by the Community and do not constitute, in relation to the aim pursued, a disproportionate and intolerable interference, impairing the very substance of the right so guaranteed.[48]

[45] Ibid para 325.
[46] Ibid para 348.
[47] Ibid paras 349–53.
[48] Ibid para 355. The Court also observed that '[i]n order to assess the extent of the fundamental right to respect for property, a general principle of Community law, account is to be taken of, in particular, Article 1 of the First Additional Protocol to the ECHR, which enshrines that right'; para 356.

Referring specifically to the derogations and exemptions relating to funds necessary to cover basic expenses, including payments for foodstuffs, rent, medicines and medical treatment, taxes or public utility charges as well as the mechanism, for the periodic re-examination by means of a direct request to the Sanctions Committee via the Focal Point for De-Listing, the Grand Chamber acknowledged that the restrictive measures imposed by the contested regulation might, in principle, be justified. Unfortunately for the Commission, the failure to afford Mr Kadi a meaningful opportunity of putting his case to the competent authorities (which constituted a procedural requirement inherent in Article 1 of Protocol No 1 to the ECHR),[49] meant that the asset freezing constituted an unjustified restriction of Mr Kadi's right to property and it followed that the contested regulation, in so far as it concerned the appellants, had to be annulled.[50]

The Grand Chamber acknowledged that annulling the contested regulation with immediate effect would potentially irreversibly prejudice the effectiveness of the restrictive measures which the Community was obliged to implement and thus the Grand Chamber ruled that the effects of the contested regulation could be maintained for a period of three months to allow the Council to remedy the defects.

VI. THE EVOLUTION OF THE OFFICE OF THE OMBUDSPERSON

A. Introduction

Initially the United Nations targeted sanctions regime under UNSC Resolution 1267 (1999) made no concessions to either international human rights or humanitarian law. Indeed, the UN Security Council resolution providing for exemptions to the financial sanctions for basic humanitarian expenses was only passed in December 2002.[51] Beginning in 2003, UN Security Council resolutions relating to combating terrorism began to contain boilerplate statements that 'States must ensure that any measure taken to combat terrorism comply with all their obligations under international law, and should adopt such measures in accordance with international law, in particular international human rights, refugee, and humanitarian law'.[52]

[49] Protocol to the Convention for the Protection of Human Rights and Fundamental Freedoms (adopted 20 March 1952, entered into force 18 April 1954) 213 UNTS 221 (ECHR, Protocol 1).

[50] *Kadi I* (n 37) paras 364–72.

[51] UNSC Res 1452 (20 December 2002) UN Doc S/RES/1452 (2002).

[52] UNSC Res 1456 (20 January 2003) UN Doc S/RES/1456 (2003) para 6. See also the Statement by the President of the Security Council (22 June 2006) UN Doc S/PRST/2006/28: 'The Council is committed to ensuring that fair and clear procedures exist for placing individuals and entities on sanctions lists and for removing them, as well as for granting humanitarian exemptions'.

B. The Focal Point for De-Listing and Related Developments

UNSC Resolution 1730[53] (adopted in December 2006) established, within the Secretariat (Security Council Subsidiary Organs Branch), a focal point to receive delisting requests. It is tempting to see this development as a response to the criticisms of the Court of First Instance about the failure of diplomatic representation by Saudi Arabia in the *Kadi I* case itself. Remarkably during the debate on UNSC Resolution 1730, the then President of the UN Security Council (speaking in his capacity as the representative of Qatar) criticised the resolution's improvements to the delisting procedures calling them 'very modest and weak' on the grounds that the proposed focal point lacked independence, neutrality and standards or controls for delisting and hence 'this point of contact does not at all constitute an effective means of fairness'.[54]

Although the Focal Point for De-Listing was largely superseded by the creation of the Office of the Ombudsperson in 2009 with regard to the individuals and entities included on the Al-Qaida Sanctions List, it remains the primary source of due process rights for individuals, groups, undertakings and/or entities inscribed on the sanctions list of all of the other UN Security Council sanctions committees.[55]

UNSC Resolution 1735 (adopted three days after UNSC Resolution 1730) strengthened the obligations of States to provide a statement of case indicating the basis(es) for proposed listings and laid down the procedures for providing those listed with a copy of the publicly releasable portions of the statement of case.[56] Paragraphs 13 and 14 UNSC Resolution 1735 also strengthened the delisting role of the Committee established pursuant to UNSC Resolution 1267 (1999) (now known as the Al-Qaida Sanctions Committee) by deciding that, in determining whether to remove names from the Consolidated List, the Committee should consider (1) whether the individual or entity was placed on the Consolidated List due to a mistake of identity; (2) whether the individual or entity no longer meets the criteria set out in relevant resolutions; and (3) whether the individual is

[53] UNSC Res 1730 (19 December 2006) UN Doc S/RES/1730 (2006).

[54] UNSC Verbatim Record (19 December 2006) UN Doc S/PV.5599, p 4.

[55] The relevant UN Security Council Committees are: 751 (1992) and 1907 (2009) concerning Somalia and Eritrea; 1518 (2003) concerning Iraq; 1521 (2003) concerning Liberia; 1533 (2004) concerning the Democratic Republic of the Congo; 1572 (2004) concerning Côte d'Ivoire; 1591 (2005) concerning the Sudan; 1636 (2005) concerning Lebanon and Syria; 1718 (2006) concerning the Democratic Republic of North Korea; 1737 (2006) concerning Iran; 1970 (2011) concerning Libya; 1988 (2011) concerning the Taliban; 2048 (2012) concerning Guinea-Bissau; 2127 (2013) concerning the Central African Republic; and 2140 (2014) concerning Yemen.

[56] UNSC Res 1735 (22 December 2006) UN Doc S/RES/1735 (2006) para 5. Annex I to this resolution contained a coversheet to be used by States proposing names for listing 'in order to ensure clarity and consistency in requests for listing' (para 6 of UNSC Res 1735 (2006)).

deceased, or whether the individual or entity has severed all association with Al-Qaida, Osama bin Laden, the Taliban and their supporters.

On 30 June 2008, the UN Security Council adopted UNSC Resolution 1822 which confirmed the obligations of Member States, when proposing names to the Committee established pursuant to UNSC Resolution 1267 (1999) (referred to in the resolution as 'the Committee') for inclusion on the Consolidated List, to provide a detailed statement of case and further decided that

> for each such proposal Member States shall identify those parts of the statement of case that may be publicly released, including for use by the Committee for development of the summary [to be placed on the Committee's website] or for the purpose of notifying or informing the listed individual or entity, and those parts which may be released upon request to interested States[57]

Paragraph 13 of UNSC Resolution 1822 also directed the Committee to publish a narrative summary of the reasons for listing on the Committee's website and indicated that this obligation also applied to the entries on the Consolidated List before the adoption of UNSC Resolution 1822. Paragraph 16 of the resolution underlined the need for the prompt updating of the Consolidated List on the Committee's website.

UNSC Resolution 1822 also addressed the obligations of Member States to provide individuals and entities located in their countries (as well as a separate obligation on the State of nationality of individuals where applicable) with a copy of the narrative summary of the reasons for listing, a description of the effects of designation, the possible exemptions and the Committee's procedures for considering delisting requests. Paragraphs 19–23 of UNSC Resolution 1822 reaffirmed the importance of delisting and the role of the Focal Point, paragraph 25 provided for a review of all the names on the date of the adoption of UNSC Resolution 1822 within two years and paragraph 26 directed the Committee, once the paragraph 25 review had been completed, 'to conduct an annual review of all names on the Consolidated List that have not been reviewed in three or more years'.

The establishment of the Focal Point and the related developments, particularly UNSC Resolution 1822, occurred during the period when the *Kadi I* case was being considered by the Grand Chamber of the European Court of Justice and most of the shortcomings noted by the Court of First Instance in the *Kadi I* case are addressed in these changes to the targeted sanctions regime. However the judgment of the Grand Chamber, delivered on 3 September 2008, expressly declined to consider the amendments made to the system of restrictive measures set up by the United Nations made after the contested regulation had been adopted in 2001.[58]

[57] UNSC Res 1822 (30 June 2008) UN Doc S/RES/1822 (2008) para 12.
[58] *Kadi I* (n 37) para 320.

The Grand Chamber's judgment contains some obiter comments on the re-examination procedure in general and on the Focal Point in particular. With regard to the former, the Grand Chamber stated:

> In any event, the existence, within that United Nations system, of the re-examination procedure before the Sanctions Committee, even having regard to the amendments recently made to it, cannot give rise to generalised immunity from jurisdiction within the internal legal order of the Community.[59]

With regard to Focal Point, the Grand Chamber's 2008 judgment makes it clear that an essentially diplomatic right of redress without any obligation to give reasons for a rejection of a delisting request (and where each of the members of the Sanctions Committee had a right of veto with regard to a delisting request) was inadequate.[60]

VII. THE OFFICE OF THE OMBUDSPERSON

A. Introduction

The Office of the Ombudsperson was created by UN Security Council Resolution 1904 (2009) adopted by the Security Council at its 6247th meeting on 17 December 2009.[61] The preamble to this resolution took note 'of challenges, both legal and otherwise, to the measures implemented by Member States' under previous UNSC resolutions directed at freezing the assets of individuals associated with Al-Qaida, Osama bin Laden and the Taliban. The resolution's preamble also welcomed the improvements to the Committee's procedures and the quality of the Consolidated List and expressed its intent to continue efforts to ensure that procedures were fair and clear.

After the vote adopting UNSC Resolution 1904 unanimously, the Austrian representative spoke in support of the resolution. He noted that, in his capacity as the Chairman of the Al Qaida and Taliban Sanctions Committee, he had witnessed some of the shortcomings of the pre-existing delisting system. He indicated that he was also aware of the growing number of cases filed by listed individuals and entities before national and regional courts in various parts of the world and opined that the resolution very substantially improved the sanctions regime procedures in terms of due process. The Austrian representative further asserted that he believed that the resolution represented 'a significant step forward in improving the fairness and transparency of the sanctions regime under resolution 1267, thus enhancing both its effectiveness and its legitimacy'.[62]

[59] Ibid para 321.
[60] Ibid paras 323–26.
[61] UNSC Res 1904 (17 December 2009) UN Doc S/RES/1904 (2009).
[62] UNSC Verbatim Record (17 December 2009) UN Doc S/PV.6247, p 2.

The Austrian representative praised the independent and impartial characteristics of the Ombudsperson process but the Costa Rican representative spoke of his country's disappointment that the resolution did not authorise the Ombudsperson to issue recommendations as opposed to comments. The Costa Rican representative expressed the hope that 'in the future we will achieve a sufficient consensus to incorporate new improvements into the sanctions regime established by this resolution'.[63]

Both the Austrian and Costa Rican representatives drew attention to the work of the informal Group of Like-Minded Countries[64] in the creation of the Office of the Ombudsperson and the Costa Rican representative stated that:

> The Group acknowledges that the improvements in the legal procedures serve as an acknowledgement of the concerns expressed by national and regional courts regarding the fundamental rights of sanctioned people and institutions, and that the new procedures adopted strengthen the sanctions regime.[65]

The Office of the Ombudsperson, created to assist the Al Qaida and Taliban Sanctions Committee in considering delisting requests, was initially established for a period of 18 months and its creation entailed the removal of the Al Qaida and Taliban Sanctions Consolidated List from the Focal Point mechanism.[66] Annex II of UNSC Resolution 1904 (2009) laid down the tasks that the Ombudsperson is required to perform.

The primary tasks the Ombudsperson is authorised to carry out upon receipt of a delisting request submitted by, or on behalf of, an individual, group undertaking or entity on the Consolidated List (referred to as 'the petitioner' in Annex II) are divided into three main groups:

1. Information gathering (two months—extendable to four months)
2. Dialogue (two months—extendable to four months)
3. Committee discussion and decision (two months).

The key weakness of the initial procedure were the fact that the Ombudsperson was only able draft a Comprehensive Report that, '[b]ased on an analysis of all the information available to the Ombudsperson and the Ombudsperson's observations, [laid] out for the Committee the principal arguments concerning the delisting request'.[67] Although the

[63] Ibid p 3.

[64] Ibid. The Costa Rican representative listed the Like-Minded Countries: Belgium, Costa Rica, Denmark, Finland, Germany, Liechtenstein, Netherlands, Norway, Sweden and Switzerland. Austria subsequently joined the informal Group of Like-Minded Countries in January 2011. See the 1st Report of the Office of the Ombudsperson pursuant to Security Council resolution 1904 (2009) (24 January 2011) UN Doc S/2011/29, p 4 fn 2.

[65] Ibid.

[66] UNSC Res 1904 (n 61) paras 20–21.

[67] Ibid Annex II, para 7(c).

Ombudsperson was empowered to present the Comprehensive Report in person and answer Al-Qaida and Taliban Sanctions Committee members' questions regarding the delisting request, the decision to approve or reject the delisting request was subject to the Committee's normal decision-making procedures. As the Al-Qaida Sanctions and Taliban Committee's procedure was to take all its decisions by consensus, this in effect gave every member of the Committee a veto power over a delisting request. In *Ahmed v HM Treasury*, Lord Rodger, making specific reference to the veto power of Committee members, expressed concern that:

> There is an obvious danger that States will use listing as a convenient means of crippling political opponents whose links with, say, Al-Qaida may be tenuous at best.[68]

Paragraph 20 of UNSC Resolution 1904 (2009) mandated the UN Secretary General, in close consultation with the Al-Qaida and Taliban Sanctions Committee, to appoint

> an eminent individual of high moral character, impartiality and integrity with high qualifications and experience in relevant fields, such as legal, human rights, counter-terrorism and sanctions, to be Ombudsperson

The UN Secretary General Ban Ki-moon appointed the Canadian Kimberly Prost (then serving as an *ad litem* judge of the International Criminal Tribunal for the former Yugoslavia) as the Ombudsperson on 3 June 2010[69] and she formally commenced her functions on 14 July 2010.

In addition to her delisting responsibilities, the Ombudsperson was tasked with (1) distributing publicly releasable information about Al-Qaida and Taliban Sanctions Committee procedures to anyone who requested such information; (2) notifying individuals or entities about the status of their listing where their address was known; and (3) submitting biannual reports summarising her activities to the UN Security Council.[70] These biannual reports show that the Ombudsperson demonstrated both her independence and integrity to become part of the iterative process.

B. The Road to UNSC Resolutions 1988 and 1989 (2011)

In her First Report (distributed in January 2011), the Ombudsperson summarised her initial work developing the Office of the Ombudsperson to carry out the mandate of the UN Security Council effectively. With regard

68 *Ahmed* (n 8) para 181.

69 Letter dated 3 June 2010 from the Secretary-General addressed to the President of the Security Council (4 June 2010) UN Doc S/2010/282.

70 UNSC Res 1904 (n 61) Annex II, para 15.

to the elements of fairness and due process, the Ombudsperson reported that:

> In an effort to better define relevant international standards and to access pertinent experience, the Ombudsperson also met with judges in national, regional and international courts, skilled in areas such as counter-terrorism sanctions implementation, domestic listing regimes and the handling of confidential information.[71]

The Ombudsperson also made reference to meeting with the Special Rapporteur on the promotion and protection of human rights and fundamental freedoms while countering terrorism, Martin Scheinin, who had criticised the listing procedure which, in his view, infringed a number of human rights.[72]

In his report issued in August 2010, the Special Rapporteur (Martin Scheinin) had welcomed the adoption of UNSC Resolution 1904 (2009) which established the Office of the Ombudsperson but he expressed concern that the revised procedures for delisting did not meet the standards required to ensure a fair and public hearing by a competent, independent and impartial tribunal established by law. His criticisms were that the Ombudsperson did not have the decision-making power to overturn the listing decision of the Committee. He also criticised the inability of the Ombudsperson to make recommendations as well as the fact that delisting decisions were confidential and 'by consensus of a political body (the Security Council Committee established pursuant to resolution 1267 (1999)), as opposed to being the result of judicial or quasi-judicial examination of evidence'.[73]

> Further, access to information by the Ombudsperson continues to depend on the willingness of States to disclose information, as States may choose to withhold information in order to safeguard their security or other interests. The system continues to lack transparency since there is no obligation for the Committee to publish in full the Ombudsperson's report or to fully disclose information to the petitioner. Without decision-making powers, the Ombudsperson cannot be regarded as a tribunal within the meaning of article 14 of the International Covenant on Civil and Political Rights.[74]

The Ombudsperson took advantage of her outreach role to respond to the criticisms of the due process aspects of the UN Security Council targeted

[71] 1st Report (n 64) para 5.

[72] See Report of the Special Rapporteur on the promotion and protection of human rights and fundamental freedoms while encountering terrorism (16 August 2006) UN Doc A/61/267 para 31 and Report of the Special Rapporteur on the promotion and protection of human rights and fundamental freedoms while encountering terrorism (6 August 2008) UN Doc A/63/223 para 16.

[73] Report of the Special Rapporteur on the promotion and protection of human rights and fundamental freedoms while encountering terrorism (6 August 2010) UN Doc A/65/258 para 56.

[74] Ibid.

sanctions regime. In a briefing to the annual informal meeting of Legal Advisers of the Ministries of Foreign Affairs of United Nations Member States in October 2010, the Ombudsperson noted that the criticisms of both the European Court of Justice in the *Kadi I* case and the United Kingdom's Supreme Court in *Ahmed v HM Treasury* occurred before her office was operational. The Ombudsperson's briefing also posed several questions.

> If we all accept that the Security Council is a unique body, exercising distinctive sanctions powers, is it not the case that the international due process regime for it can also be unique? And the follow up question is, if it is possible to have a special due process regime in this context, what are the contours of it and does my office meet them?[75]

In a presentation delivered to the 41st meeting of the Council of Europe Committee of Legal Advisors on Public International Law (CAHDI) in March 2011, the Ombudsperson responded to the criticism that she did not have the power to make recommendations by noting that:

> I have always said I will tell the Committee what I think about the sufficiency of the information, as it stands today, with reference to the listing. In my view, though it is not a conventional approach to review, I believe that it may be adequate to meet this aspect of due process.[76]

Fortunately, in April 2011, the Group of Like-Minded States, seeking to respond to the challenges to the implementation of the UN targeted sanctions regime by the decisions of national and regional courts, proposed a series of changes to listing, delisting and the Ombudsperson to address the due process concerns.[77] These suggestions were to bear fruit in the passing of UNSC Resolution 1989 (2011).

C. UNSC Resolutions 1988 and 1989 (2011)

i. Introduction

UNSC Resolutions 1988 and 1989 were adopted by the Security Council at its 6557th meeting on 17 June 2011. UNSC Resolution 1988 (2011) removed listed Taliban individuals and entities from the Consolidated List of the

[75] Remarks of Kimberly Prost, Ombudsperson, 1267 Al Qaida/Taliban Sanctions Committee delivered to the informal meeting of Legal Advisors, 25 October 2010, p 6, available at: www.un.org/sc/suborg/sites/www.un.org.sc.suborg/files/2010.10.25_e.pdf.

[76] Speaking Notes for Presentation by Kimberly Prost, Ombudsperson, 1267 Al Qaida/Taliban Sanctions Committee delivered to the 41st meeting of the Council of Europe Committee of Legal Advisors on Public International Law (CAHDI) (Strasbourg, 18 March 2011) available at: www.un.org/sc/suborg/sites/www.un.org.sc.suborg/files/cahdi_remarks_18.03.2011_e.pdf.

[77] 'Improving fair and clear procedures for a more effective UN sanctions system', document submitted to the Security Council by Switzerland and the Like-Minded States in April 2011, available at: www.news.admin.ch/NSBSubscriber/message/attachments/22759.pdf.

Committee established pursuant to Resolutions 1267 (1999) and 1333 (2000) and placed them on a separate list.[78] This new list was placed under the jurisdiction of a new sanctions committee with responsibility for considering listing and delisting requests. With regard to delisting requests, paragraph 20 of UNSC Resolution 1988 (2011) provides that 'individuals and entities seeking removal from the List without the sponsorship of a Member State are eligible to submit such requests to the Focal Point mechanism established in resolution 1730 (2006)'.

ii. UNSC Resolution 1989 (2011)

UNSC Resolution 1989 (2011) confirmed the transfer of all listing submissions and delisting requests associated with the Taliban to the Committee established pursuant to UNSC Resolution 1988 (2011) and the renaming of the remaining names on the Consolidated List as the Al-Qaida Sanctions List.[79] The other key developments contained in UNSC Resolution 1989 (2011) were: first, the extension of the mandate of the Office of the Ombudsperson by a further 18 months (from the date of adoption of the resolution); secondly, providing the Ombudsperson with a power to make a recommendation to retain the listing or a recommendation that the Committee consider delisting; and, thirdly, in the event of a delisting recommendation from the Ombudsperson, requiring a decision by consensus to maintain a listing (ie the support of a single member of the Committee would entail the enforcement of the Ombudsperson's recommendation subject to a possible referral to the UN Security Council for its decision).[80] The reverse consensus approach was also adopted in relation to delisting requests from the designating State.[81]

Paragraph 26 of UNSC Resolution 1989 (2011) expressly requested

> Member States and relevant international organizations and bodies encourage individuals and entities that are considering challenging or are already in the process of challenging their listing through national and regional courts to seek removal from the Al-Qaida Sanctions List by submitting delisting petitions to the Office of the Ombudsperson.

The sensitivity of the UN Security Council to external judicial challenge is also reflected in paragraph 17 of UNSC Resolution 1989 (2011) which intriguingly

> *Encourages* Member States and relevant international organizations and bodies to inform the Committee of any relevant court decisions and proceedings so that

[78] UNSC Res 1988 (17 June 2011) UN Doc S/RES/1988 (2011) para 1.

[79] UNSC Res 1989 (17 June 2011) UN Doc S/RES/1989 (2011) paras 1–3.

[80] Ibid paras 21–23.

[81] Ibid para 27. Where there are multiple designating States, para 28 of UNSC Res 1989 (n 79) requires consensus between or among all designating States for the purposes of para 27.

> the Committee can consider them when it reviews a corresponding listing or updates a narrative summary of reasons for listing.

Annex II of UNSC Resolution 1989 (2011) contains an updated list of tasks that the Ombudsperson is authorised to carry out upon receipt of a delisting request. The information gathering stage was extended to four months in the first instance (extendable to six months). The dialogue stage remained at two months (extendable to four months) and the Committee discussion and consideration was reduced to 30 days with a time-limit of a further 60 days for implementation of a delisting recommendation (subject to the reverse consensus procedure and possible referral to the UN Security Council).

D. Assessing UNSC Resolutions 1988 and 1989 (2011)

Speaking immediately after the vote to adopt UNSC Resolutions 1988 and 1989 (2011), various members of the UN Security Council reiterated the importance of the targeted sanctions regime as a counter-terrorism tool and expressed satisfaction at the enhanced powers of the Ombudsperson. In the view of the French representative:

> Les améliorations et les garanties apportées au régime de sanctions contre Al-Qaida nous permettent de répondre aux critiques qui lui ont été adressées, notamment par le pouvoir judiciaire, en Europe et ailleurs.[82]

The Portuguese representative, while welcoming the positive development of strengthening the role of the Ombudsperson, expressed concern that the UN Security Council had not gone further with respect to some specific issues in particular regarding time-limits or a sunset clause.[83]

All the UN Security Council members who spoke, stressed the importance of creating a new and separate regime for the Taliban. The United Kingdom's representative noted that UNSC Resolution 1988 (2011)

> introduces broader listing criteria and a greater role for the Afghan Government in consultation on listing and de-listing decisions. It also explicitly links de-listing individuals with the Kabul communiqué's reconciliation conditions of renouncing violence, cutting ties with Al-Qaida and accepting the framework of the Afghan Constitution.

Although the separation of the two regimes sought to facilitate the peace process in Afghanistan, one negative consequence was that it removed the

[82] UNSC Verbatim Record (17 June 2011) UN Doc S/PV.6557, p 5: 'The improvements made to and the guarantees included in the sanctions regime against Al-Qaida allow us to respond to the criticisms that have been made, including by judicial authorities in Europe and elsewhere'. (Official translation.)

[83] Ibid.

newly created Taliban sanctions regime from the oversight of the Office of the Ombudsperson. This retrograde development runs counter to the United Nations' stated commitment to promoting the rule of law at both the national and international level.[84]

In a press conference held on 15 July 2010 to present the Ombudsperson of the UN Security Council's 1267 Committee, the then chair of the 1267 Committee (Thomas Mayr-Harting (Austria)) in response to a question about why the Office of the Ombudsperson had been created only for the 1267 Committee and not other sanctions bodies, stated that the 1267 Committee was 'the mother regime of all sanctions regimes', in which the lack of due process was most criticised in court. In Mr Mayr-Harting's view, if the Office of the Ombudsperson proved effective in strengthening due process and the rule of law, it should serve as a model for others in the United Nations.[85]

In her Second Report submitted in July 2011, the Ombudsperson noted the significant changes to the delisting process, particularly the decision phase, but observed that 'any overall evaluation of the process will need to await implementation of and experience with those amendments'.[86] In her Third Report submitted in January 2012, the Ombudsperson, noting that although there had been limited practice with respect to the new procedures established under UNSC Resolution 1989 (2011), stated that it was clear that the revised process encouraged cooperation on the part of States and served to enhance the fairness and transparency of the decision-making process.[87] One issue that the Ombudsperson returned to in subsequent reports was the cooperation of States, in particular the non-response from some States.[88] Her Fourth Report also mentioned meeting with the Special Rapporteur on the promotion and protection of human rights and fundamental freedoms while countering terrorism in the context of the preparation and presentation of his 2012 report to the United Nations General Assembly.[89]

In September 2012, the Special Rapporteur on the promotion and protection of human rights and fundamental freedoms while countering

[84] See esp UNSG, 'Strengthening and Co-ordinating United Nations Rule of Law Activities' Report of the Secretary General (20 August 2010) UN Doc A/65/318 para 93: 'The Council should consider extending the mandate of the Ombudsperson to all the sanctions lists'. See also more generally: www.un.org/en/ruleoflaw/.

[85] See www.un.org/press/en/2010/100715_1267.doc.htm.

[86] Report of the Office of the Ombudsperson pursuant to Security Council resolution 1989 (2011) (22 July 2011) UN Doc S/2011/447 para 38 (2nd Report).

[87] Report of the Office of the Ombudsperson pursuant to Security Council resolution 1989 (2011) (20 January 2012) UN Doc S/2012/49 para 45 (3rd Report).

[88] See Report of the Office of the Ombudsperson pursuant to Security Council resolution 1989 (2011) (30 July 2012) UN Doc S/2012/590 para 33 (4th Report).

[89] Ibid para 17.

terrorism (Ben Emmerson, who replaced Martin Scheinin in 2011), while noting the significant improvements brought about by UNSC Resolution 1989 (2011), concluded that the Al-Qaida sanctions regime continued to fall short of international minimum standards of due process. One particular concern noted by the Special Rapporteur was that lawyers acting for petitioners had satisfied him that intelligence derived from torture had been used to justify the designation of individuals.[90] The Special Rapporteur also criticised the absence of a mechanism for funding legal representation in delisting cases.[91] The key recommendation made by the Special Rapporteur was re-designating the Office of the Ombudsperson as the Office of the Independent Designations Adjudicator with the power to ensure a full and fair review of all delisting requests.[92] The European Court of Human Rights expressed its agreement with the Special Rapporteur's conclusion that the Office of the Ombudsperson fell short of the international minimum due process standards in *Al-Dulimi and Montana Management Inc v Switzerland*.[93]

VIII. THE *KADI II* CASE

A. Introduction

Following the September 2008 Grand Chamber judgment annulling the contested regulation that froze Mr Kadi's assets within the European Union, the Permanent Representative of France to the United Nations (acting on behalf of the European Union) requested the Sanctions Committee, as a matter of urgency, to make available on its website, in accordance with paragraph 13 of UNSC Resolution 1822 (2008), the summary of reasons for Mr Kadi's inclusion on that committee's list. The Chairman of the Sanctions Committee communicated a summary of the reasons in October 2008 and this summary was sent to Mr Kadi to give him an opportunity to comment before the European Commission took its final decision to maintain his listing or not within the three-month grace period granted by the Grand Chamber in its September 2008 judgment to remedy the defects they had found in Mr Kadi's listing.

Mr Kadi submitted his comments in early November 2008 attempting to refute the allegations made in the summary of reasons but he also

[90] Report of the Special Rapporteur on the promotion and protection of human rights and fundamental freedoms while encountering terrorism (26 September 2012) UN Doc A/67/396 para 47.

[91] Ibid para 52.

[92] Ibid para 59.

[93] *Al-Dulimi* (n 18) para 119. This case was referred to the Grand Chamber on 14 March 2014.

requested disclosure of the evidence supporting the summary of reasons and an opportunity to make representations on that evidence once disclosed. On 28 November 2008, the Commission adopted Regulation (EC) No 1190/2008 amending Regulation No 881/2002[94] ('the contested regulation') that maintained Mr Kadi's listing. On 26 February 2009, Mr Kadi brought an action against the European Commission. The Council of the European Union, France and the United Kingdom sought, and were granted, leave to intervene in support of the European Commission.

B. The 2010 General Court's Judgment (*Kadi II* (GC))

On 30 September 2010, the General Court of the European Union delivered its judgment.[95] Although the General Court noted that it was not bound by the points of law decided by the Grand Chamber in its 2008 *Kadi I* judgment,[96] and the judgment devotes a great deal of space to criticisms of the Grand Chamber's 2008 judgment,[97] the General Court recognised that with regard to a measure adopted by the European Commission in response to an annulment by the Grand Chamber of an earlier measure a degree of judicial deference was entirely appropriate.[98]

The General Court concluded that, in the light of paragraphs 326 and 327 of the Grand Chamber's *Kadi I* judgment, it was obliged to ensure a full review in principle of the lawfulness of the contested regulation in the light of fundamental rights without affording the regulation any immunity from jurisdiction on the ground that it gave effect to UN Security Council resolutions adopted under Chapter VII of the UN Charter.[99] The General Court acknowledged the creation of the Office of the Ombudsperson but noted that removal of a person from the Sanctions Committee's list required consensus within the Committee and that the evidence which may be disclosed to the person concerned continued to be a matter entirely at the discretion of the State which proposed that he be included on the Sanctions Committee's list. Owing to these factors the General Court concluded that 'the creation of the focal point and the Office of the Ombudsperson cannot be equated with the provision of an effective judicial procedure for review of decisions of the Sanctions Committee'.[100]

Noting that nearly 10 years had passed since Mr Kadi's funds were originally frozen, the General Court questioned the classification of the

[94] [2008] OJ L 322/25.
[95] Case T-85/09, *Kadi v European Commission* [2010] ECR II-5177 ('*Kadi II* (GC)').
[96] Ibid para 112.
[97] Ibid paras 113–20 and 122.
[98] Ibid para 121.
[99] Ibid para 126.
[100] Ibid para 128.

freezing of funds as a temporary precautionary measure and the assertion in numerous UN Security Council resolutions that the freezing measures were 'preventative in nature and are not reliant upon criminal standards set out under national law'.[101] The General Court also stated that, in the context of a judicial review which was in principle a full review of the lawfulness of the contested regulation,

> the applicant's rights of defence have been 'observed' only in the most formal and superficial sense, as the Commission in actual fact considered itself strictly bound by the Sanctions Committee's findings and therefore at no time envisaged calling those findings into question in the light of the applicant's observations.[102]

The General Court, noting the Commission's failure to grant Mr Kadi even minimal access to the evidence against him and Mr Kadi's inability to challenge the imprecise allegations contained in the summary of reasons, concluded that the contested regulation was adopted in breach of Mr Kadi's rights of defence.[103]

> Moreover, the fact that the applicant had an opportunity to be heard by the Sanctions Committee in the re-examination procedure with a view to him being removed from its list clearly does not remedy that breach of his rights of defence.[104]

The General Court also stated that the fundamental position adopted by the Commission and supported by the Council and the intervening governments that no information or evidence may be the subject of investigation by the Community judicature entailed that the infringement of the right of defence could not be remedied in the course of the action.[105] The General Court did not rule out the possibility that the right of defence could be provided by an appropriate remedy at the level of the procedure before the Sanctions Committee[106] but asserted that 'the Security Council has still not deemed it appropriate to establish an independent and impartial body responsible for hearing and determining, as regards matters of law and fact, actions against individual decisions taken by the Sanctions Committee'.[107] The General Court annulled the contested regulation and the European Commission, the Council of the European Union and the United Kingdom appealed to the Court of Justice.

[101] Ibid para 150.
[102] Ibid para 171.
[103] Ibid para 179.
[104] Ibid para 180.
[105] Ibid para 182.
[106] Ibid para 187.
[107] Ibid para 128.

C. The 2013 Grand Chamber's Judgment (*Kadi II*)

The Commission, the Council and the United Kingdom raised three grounds of appeal. First, the Council alleged that the contested regulation enjoyed immunity from jurisdiction. Secondly, all three appellants challenged the level of intensity of judicial review appropriate to the contested regulation. Thirdly, all three appellants challenged the findings in relation to Mr Kadi's pleas in respect of the infringement of his rights of defence and his right to effective judicial protection.

The Grand Chamber delivered its judgment on 18 July 2013.[108] With regard to the claim that the contested regulation enjoyed immunity from jurisdiction, the Grand Chamber reaffirmed the position that it took in *Kadi I*.[109] The Grand Chamber examined the second and third grounds of appeal together.

With regard to respect for the rights of the defence and the right to effective judicial protection, the Grand Chamber held that the obligation to ensure the review, in principle the full review, of the lawfulness of Union acts in the light of the fundamental rights forming an integral part of the European Union legal order was expressly laid down in the second paragraph of Article 275 of the Treaty on the Functioning of the European Union and this included the review of measures designed to give effect to resolutions adopted by the UN Security Council acting under Chapter VII of the UN Charter.[110] The first of those fundamental rights, which was affirmed in Article 41(2) of the Charter of Fundamental Rights of the European Union ('the Charter'), included the right to be heard and the right to have access to the file, subject to legitimate interests in maintaining confidentiality. The second of those fundamental rights, affirmed in Article 47 of the Charter, was that the person affected must be able to ascertain the reasons upon which the decision was based.[111] The Grand Chamber acknowledged that Article 52(1) of the Charter allowed limitations on the exercise of the rights enshrined in the Charter, subject to the conditions that the limitation concerned respects the essence of the fundamental right in question and subject to the principle of proportionality.[112]

The Grand Chamber acknowledged that the question whether there had been an infringement of the rights of the defence and of the right to effective judicial protection must be examined in the circumstances of each

[108] C-584/10, P *European Commission and Others v Kadi* [2014] 1 CMLR 24 ('*Kadi II*').
[109] Ibid paras 65–69.
[110] Ibid para 97.
[111] Ibid paras 98–100.
[112] Ibid para 101.

particular case.[113] The Grand Chamber held that in order for the restrictive measures at issue to be lawful

> the Courts of the European Union consider that, at the very least, one of the reasons mentioned in the summary provided by the Sanctions Committee is sufficiently detailed and specific, that it is substantiated and that it constitutes in itself sufficient basis to support that decision, the fact that the same cannot be said of other such reasons cannot justify the annulment of that decision. In the absence of one such reason, the Courts of the European Union will annul the contested decision.[114]

The Grand Chamber held that the failure of the competent European Union authority to make information or evidence which was in the sole possession of the Sanctions Committee available to the person concerned (and subsequently the Courts of the European Union) could not, by itself, justify a finding that fundamental rights had been infringed.[115] However, if it was impossible for the Courts of the European Union to find that the reasons given to the person concerned were well-founded, those reasons could not be relied upon as the basis of the contested listing decision.[116]

The Grand Chamber reviewed the statement of reasons and, contrary to the findings of the General Court, accepted that four of the five reasons given were sufficiently detailed and specific but that the information and evidence produced to substantiate the adoption of restrictive measures against Mr Kadi (in the light of the detailed rebuttals by Mr Kadi) was insufficient.[117] The Grand Chamber concluded that although errors of law vitiated the General Court's judgment, these errors did not affect the validity of the operative part of the judgment, namely the annulment of the contested regulation in so far as it concerned Mr Kadi.[118]

D. Conclusion

Much has been made of the failure of the Grand Chamber's judgment to deal in any depth with the effect of the creation of the Office of the Ombudsperson (and particularly the reforms contained in UNSC Resolution 1989 (2011)) on Mr Kadi's due process rights. However this omission is explicable on a number of grounds. First, consistent with the Grand Chamber's judgment in *Kadi I*, amendments to the delisting process made

[113] Ibid para 102.
[114] Ibid para 130.
[115] Ibid para 139.
[116] Ibid para 137.
[117] Ibid paras 138–63.
[118] Ibid para 164.

after the contested regulation was adopted in November 2008 could not be taken into consideration and the creation of the Office of the Ombudsperson only occurred in December 2009. Secondly, any critical comments about the effectiveness of the Office of the Ombudsperson (such as those made by the General Court in its judgment in *Kadi II*) would risk appearing churlish given Mr Kadi's delisting on 5 October 2012 following his delisting request made through the Office of the Ombudsperson.[119] Thirdly, as the Special Rapporteur's second annual report issued in September 2012 makes clear,[120] the due process improvements to the Al-Qaida regime were a work in progress that were likely to be subject of further amendment and, thus, any obiter comments had as much potential to impede desired improvements as to impel desired improvements.

IX. THE OFFICE OF THE OMBUDSPERSON POST *KADI II*

A. UNSC Resolution 2083 (2012)

The UN Security Council revisited the issue of the mandate of the Office of the Ombudsperson in December 2012 when it adopted UNSC Resolution 2083 (2012).[121] Aspects of this resolution are clearly directed at the criticisms contained in the Special Rapporteur's second annual report issued in September 2012. The Special Rapporteur (Ben Emmerson) had recommended that, irrespective of any decision to re-designate the Office of the Ombudsperson as the Office of the Independent Designations Adjudicator with the power to ensure a full and fair review of all delisting requests, the mandate of the Ombudsperson should be renewed for a term of no less than three years.[122] Paragraph 19 of the resolution extended the mandate of the Office of the Ombudsperson for a period of 30 months from the date of the resolution's adoption.

Paragraph 12 of UNSC Resolution 2083 (2012) changed the position relating to the revelation of a Member State's status as a designating

[119] See www.un.org/press/en/2012/sc10785.doc.htm. See also Report of the Office of the Ombudsperson pursuant to Security Council resolution 2083 (2012) (31 January 2013) UN Doc S/2013/71 para 45 (5th Report) and 'Office of the Ombudsperson of the Security Council's 1267 Committee—Status of Cases' website, available at:www.un.org/sc/suborg/en/sc/ombudsperson/status-of-cases, Case 19 Yassin Abdullah Kadi (formerly listed as Yasin Abdullah Ezzedine Qadi (QI.Q.22.01)). One curious feature of Mr Kadi's delisting is that, although the decision to delist was taken in October 2012, the reasons for the delisting were only communicated to the Ombudsperson and Mr Kadi in August 2014.

[120] Report of the Special Rapporteur on the promotion and protection of human rights and fundamental freedoms while encountering terrorism (n 90) para 59.

[121] UNSC Res 2083 (17 December 2012) UN Doc S/RES/2083 (2012).

[122] Report of the Special Rapporteur on the promotion and protection of human rights and fundamental freedoms while encountering terrorism (n 90) para 59(b)(i).

State from *strongly encouraging* permitting the release of this information if requested to do so (as contained in paragraph 13 of UNSC Resolution 1989 (2011)) to a presumption that this information would be made known unless the designating State expressly objected to the release of this information. Paragraph 23 of UNSC Resolution 2083 (2012) strongly urged Member States to provide all relevant information in a timely manner and paragraph 36 of the resolution provided for the possibility of an exemption from travel restrictions to enable the Ombudsperson to interview petitioners somewhere other than their State of residence. The other key development in the improvement of due process rights in UNSC Resolution 2083 (2012) relates to the Committee's obligation to provide reasons for all decisions taken whether in favour of or against delisting.

The Ombudsperson's Fifth Report warmly welcomed these positive developments as well as the increased cooperation of States but noted:

> The most significant shortcoming with regard to cooperation, and one of the most pressing challenges to the effectiveness of the whole process, remains the lack of specificity in the material submitted by States with respect to individual cases. Of particular concern are States' responses that provide only broad assertions as to purported support activity on the part of petitioners and limited, and in some instances, no substantiating information or detail.[123]

Notwithstanding the positive developments, the Ombudsperson's Fifth Report was very critical of the fact that UNSC Resolution 2083 (2012) made only 'marginal progress' to enhance the transparency of the Ombudsperson process.[124] The Ombudsperson's Fifth Report also expressed disappointment at the lack of progress 'on the serious issue of continued restrictions once individuals and entities have been delisted'.[125] The Ombudsperson noted that she lacked a mandate to investigate possible post-delisting restrictions and she expressed the view that

> These situations, if verified to be correct, represent a general problem in terms of the implementation of the Committee's decisions and have the potential to impede the credibility and effectiveness of the Al-Qaida sanctions

[123] Office of the Ombudsman, 5th Report (n 119).

[124] Ibid para 41–45.

[125] Ibid para 46. See eg the case of Ali Ahmed Jumale (aka Ji'male) who was removed from Al-Qaida Sanctions List and immediately placed on the Somalia/Eritrea Sanctions Committee List: www.un.org/press/en/2012/sc10549.doc.htm. See also the discussion of this delisting in H Duffy, *The 'War on Terror' and the Framework of International Law* (2nd edn, Cambridge, Cambridge University Press, 2015) 621; and S Eckert and T Biersteker, *Due Process and Targeted Sanctions: An Update of the 'Watson Report'* (Watson Institute for International Studies, December 2012) 19.

regime. ... [C]onsideration should be given to mandating the Office of the Ombudsperson to follow up on claims of continued application of sanctions measures despite delisting.[126]

The Ombudsperson's Fifth Report also includes a detailed commentary on the recommendations contained in the Special Rapporteur's second annual report issued in September 2012.[127]

The Ombudsperson's Sixth Report drew attention to the problems with the lack of transparency and credibility due to the fact that, although UNSC Resolution 2083 (2012) allowed the Ombudsperson to communicate her recommendations to States that are not members of the Committee, her comprehensive reports remained confidential to the Committee.[128] The Ombudsperson's Sixth Report also highlighted the effect that delays in the production of reasons for all Committee decisions taken for or against delisting were having on the effectiveness of the practice in demonstrating the transparency and reasonableness of the Ombudsperson process.[129]

The Ombudsperson also expressed concern at the relisting of a petitioner immediately after the Committee decided to delist him on the basis of new information regarding the petitioner's alleged recent support to Al-Qaida. The Ombudsperson recognised that relisting on the basis of new information did 'not constitute an unfair procedure absent any other circumstances indicating to the contrary'.[130] The Ombudsperson reiterated these concerns in her Seventh Report[131] where she also expressed the view that time constraints should be imposed on the delivery of reasons.[132] The Ombudsperson's Seventh Report further noted that:

During the reporting period, reasons for the Committee's decision were communicated to petitioners in three cases. As at the time of writing the present report, however, reasons had not been provided in 14 cases. Several of the cases were decided months ago; in one instance, the decision was taken more than a year ago. While delayed delivery and limited content remains preferable to no

[126] Ibid para 49.

[127] Ibid paras 52–59.

[128] Report of the Office of the Ombudsperson pursuant to Security Council resolution 2083 (2012) (31 July 2013) UN Doc S/2013/452 para 50 (6th Report). See also Report of the Office of the Ombudsperson pursuant to Security Council resolution 2083 (2012) (31 January 2014) UN Doc S/2014/73 (7th Report) para 56: 'Provided that there are protections in place for confidential material, it is difficult to rationalize why interested States that are not members of the Committee (in particular designating States or States of residence) are not given access to the comprehensive report'.

[129] 6th Report, ibid para 38.

[130] Ibid para 36. See also www.un.org/press/en/2014/sc11241.doc.htm.

[131] 7th Report (n 128) paras 32–37.

[132] Ibid para 44.

reasons, the meaningfulness of communicating reasons in terms of the fairness of the process, especially in the perception of the petitioner, is reduced markedly by the passage of time.[133]

B. UNSC Resolution 2161 (2014)

UNSC Resolution 2161 (2014) was adopted by the Security Council on 17 June 2014. It extended the mandate of the Office of the Ombudsperson for a period of 30 months from the date of expiration of the Office of the Ombudsperson's then mandate in June 2015.[134] With regard to the issue of the timely communication of reasons, UNSC Resolution 2161 (2014) imposes a 60-day deadline for the transmittal of reasons by the Committee to the Ombudsperson and this time-limit was made applicable to existing cases and took effect from the date of the adoption of the resolution.[135]

The Ombudsperson welcomed this development in her Eighth Report but noted that although the language of the relevant paragraphs of Annex II to UNSC Resolution 2161 (2014) had been amended

> to better reflect the Ombudsperson procedure by providing for the Committee to convey to the Ombudsperson, at the end of the process, whether the sanction measures are to be retained or terminated, rather than communicating a decision. This amendment makes it even more clear that in a case of retention, the listing is maintained on the basis of the recommendation of the Ombudsperson, which has arisen from the analysis contained in the comprehensive report.[136]

The Ombudsperson also recommended that the procedure for the provision of reasons could be made fully consistent with the Ombudsperson process generally

> by according the responsibility for reasons to the Ombudsperson, in both delisting and retention cases, with appropriate safeguards regarding the release of confidential material. The only exception would be in the case of a Committee reversal or a Security Council decision, where responsibility for reasons would be left to the Committee and the Council respectively. Such a structure would be properly reflective of the process as a whole and would significantly enhance its fairness, transparency and efficiency.[137]

[133] Ibid para 40.
[134] UNSC Res 2161 (17 June 2014) UN Doc S/RES/2161 (2014) para 41.
[135] Ibid para 16.
[136] Report of the Office of the Ombudsperson pursuant to Security Council resolution 2161 (2014) (31 July 2014) UN Doc S/2014/553 para 40 (8th Report).
[137] Ibid para 42.

The Ombudsperson welcomed the change in UNSC Resolution 2161 (2014) with respect to the disclosure of information to interested States that are not members of the Security Council.[138] This change 'codified' a practice already in place but it is clear that the Ombudsperson would have liked UNSC Resolution 2161 (2014) to have gone further to allow her to release the comprehensive report which detailed the reasoning.[139]

One particularly thorny issue that the Ombudsperson had highlighted in her previous reports, the problem of post-delisting restrictions, did receive attention in UNSC Resolution 2161 (2014). Paragraph 63 of UNSC Resolution 2161 (2014) states that

> the Focal Point may receive, and transmit to the Committee for its consideration, communications from:
> (a) individuals who have been removed from the Al-Qaida Sanctions List;
> (b) individuals claiming to have been subjected to [asset freezes, travel bans and arms embargoes] as a result of false or mistaken identification or confusion with individuals included on the Al-Qaida Sanctions List;

Paragraph 64 of UNSC Resolution 2161 (2014) directs the Committee (with the assistance of the Monitoring Team and in consultation with relevant States) to respond to such communications, through the Focal Point within 60 days. The Ombudsperson welcomed this development but expressed concern that 'the limited experience to date with humanitarian exemption requests assigned to the Focal Point under resolution 2083 (2012) suggests that practical challenges can arise from the introduction of separate mechanisms for different types of requests under one sanctions regime'.[140]

C. The Independence of the Office of the Ombudsperson

One of the key concerns that the Ombudsperson has highlighted in her more recent reports is the issue of the independence of her office. In

[138] UNSC Res 2161 (n 134) Annex II, para 13.

[139] 8th Report (n 136) para 45: 'Unfortunately, resolution 2161 (2014) does not address disclosure by the Ombudsperson, and an obvious deficiency in transparency therefore remains. This is particularly perplexing given that the petitioner is free to disseminate the reasons—in whole or in part—while the Ombudsperson must continue to keep the information confidential. The benefits of, or reasons for, this non-disclosure requirement are opaque'.

[140] 8th Report (n 136) para 48. See also Report of the Office of the Ombudsperson pursuant to Security Council resolution 2161 (2014) (2 February 2015) UN Doc S/2015/80 para 50 (9th Report): 'interaction with petitioners during this reporting period supports the statement that the process of having a different authority and procedures to deal with a request related to the same listing is very confusing and does not generate confidence in either procedure. To date, it has only served to deter individuals from pursuing what may be well motivated and justified requests for humanitarian exemptions'.

her Eighth Report the Ombudsperson expressed dissatisfaction at the contractual, administrative and staffing arrangement through which her mandate had been implemented. In the Ombudsperson's view

> success in safeguarding the independence of the Ombudsperson and her Office has been due to the personal efforts of the Ombudsperson, relevant officials within the Department of Political Affairs and the staff members assigned to the Office. While achieved in practice, in principle, no separate office has been established and the applicable administrative arrangements, particularly for budget, staffing, staff management and resource utilization, lack the critical features of autonomy. Further, the contractual arrangements for the Ombudsperson are not consistent with the mandate accorded by the Security Council and contain insufficient safeguards for independence.[141]

The Ombudsperson returned to the issue of the independence of the Office of the Ombudsperson in her Ninth Report noting that the tensions caused by the nature of the consultancy contract which had been utilised raised the potential for interference with the performance of her mandate.[142] The Ombudsperson also expressed concern that the fragile basis for ensuring the independence of the Office of the Ombudsperson would be particularly vulnerable during a transition to a subsequent Ombudsperson.[143]

In her letter to the UN Secretary General on her last day in office as Ombudsperson for the UN Security Council Al-Qaida Sanctions Committee dated 13 July 2015,[144] Kimberly Prost noted that:

> The Ombudsperson mechanism stands as a unique and important achievement of the Security Council and the United Nations. Through it, individuals and entities have a recourse for consideration of their delisting requests at the international level, which provides a fair process and makes available an effective remedy.

However Kimberly Prost also drew attention to her concerns regarding the lack of full implementation of the Security Council mandate for an independent Office of the Ombudsperson. The concerns noted in Kimberly Prost's letter to the UN Secretary General dated 13 July 2015, namely, 'contractual status and the placement of the mechanism within

[141] Ibid para 50.

[142] The consultancy contract subjected the Ombudsperson to evaluation by the administering office (ie the Security Council Affairs Division—the very body from which the Ombudsperson was required to be independent in order to fulfil her mandate) as a precondition for remuneration.

[143] 9th Report (n 140) para 51.

[144] A copy of the letter appears with the permission of Kimberley Prost at the conclusion of this chapter on p 170.

the organization in terms of administrative oversight' are outlined in her final report to the UN Security Council.

The key concerns, as outlined in her Tenth Report,[145] were, first, the failure to establish an independent Office of the Ombudsperson within the structure of the United Nations as called for in UNSC Resolution 1904 (2009).[146] The importance of the independence requirement was also reiterated in UNSC Resolution 2161 (2014).[147] It is noteworthy that Kimberly Prost appears to have been forced out of her role as Ombudsperson by the fact that the guidelines, developed for the experts serving on panels, imposed a five-year contractual limitation which were retroactively applied to her.[148]

D. The Reform Proposals of the Like-Minded States

The failure of the contractual arrangements to fully implement relevant UN Security Council resolutions was also highlighted in an input paper transmitted to the UN Security Council by the Group of Like-Minded States on Targeted Sanctions on 17 April 2014.[149] The Group of Like-Minded States input paper drew attention to the fact that serious due process concerns had led to successful legal challenges in national and regional courts including both the European Court of Human Rights and the Court of Justice of the European Union (CJEU). In the view of the Group:

> As long as national and regional courts consider United Nations sanctions to fall short of the minimum standards of due process, national authorities may find themselves legally unable to fully implement them at the national level. This situation threatens the uniform and universal application of United Nations sanctions and needs to be addressed.[150]

Although some of their proposals were influential in the drafting of UNSC Resolution 2161 (2014), their proposals to make the Office of the Ombudsperson permanent and to extend the mandate of the Ombudsperson to other sanctions regimes were not adopted. In November 2015, the

[145] Report of the Office of the Ombudsperson pursuant to Security Council Resolution 2161 (2014) (13 July 2015) UN Doc S/2015/533, paras 55–93 (10th Report).

[146] UNSC Res 1904 (n 61) para 20.

[147] UNSC Res 2161 (n 134) para 26.

[148] 10th Report (n 145) para 73.

[149] Letter dated 17 April 2014 from the Permanent Representatives of Austria, Belgium, Costa Rica, Denmark, Finland, Germany, Liechtenstein, the Netherlands, Norway, Sweden and Switzerland to the United Nations addressed to the President of the Security Council (21 April 2014) UN Doc S/2014/286.

[150] Ibid 4.

Like-Minded States again reiterated the need for further improvements to the due process aspects of the various targeted sanctions regimes through the forthcoming update to UNSC Resolution 2161 (2014).[151]

X. CONCLUSION

The timeline of the challenges to the United Nations targeted sanctions regime and the improvements in the due process rights of those affected indicates a measure of iterative interaction between the various parties. The decisions of the Court of Justice of the European Union in the *Kadi* case indicate that deference to an appropriate remedy at the United Nations level is possible but it is doubtful that the remedy presently afforded by the Office of the Ombudsperson would meet the required standard without the implementation of the reforms recommended by the outgoing Ombudsperson Kimberly Prost and endorsed by the Group of Like-Minded States.

Given the fact that the most recent Consolidated List (updated on 10 December 2015) consists of 621 individuals and 398 entities and other groups[152] and the likelihood that the United Nations targeted sanctions regime originally established under UN Security Council Resolution 1267 (1999) will soon be extended to so-called Islamic State (formerly known as Islamic State in Iraq and the Levant (ISIL)), the need to ensure that this targeted sanctions regime meets the due process obligations of the States required to implement such measures remains vital.

XI. POSTSCRIPT

On 17 December 2015, the UN Security Council unanimously adopted UNSC Resolution 2253 (2015) at its 7587th meeting to expand its targeted sanctions framework to include Islamic State in Iraq and the Levant (ISIL/Da'esh).[153] Acting under Chapter VII of the UN Charter, the UN Security Council decided that the 1267/1989 Al-Qaida Sanctions Committee would be known as the '1267/1989/2253 ISIL (Da'esh) and Al-Qaida Sanctions Committee', while the Al-Qaida Sanctions List should be known as the 'ISIL (Da'esh) and Al-Qaida Sanctions List'. UNSC Resolution 2253 (2015)

[151] Proposal to the United Nations Security Council by the Group of Like-Minded States on targeted sanctions (Austria, Belgium, Costa Rica, Denmark, Finland, Germany, Liechtenstein, the Netherlands, Norway, Sweden and Switzerland), 'Fair and clear procedures for a more effective UN sanctions system' (12 November 2015).

[152] See www.un.org/sc/suborg/en/sanctions/un-sc-consolidated-list.

[153] UNSC Res 2253 (17 December 2015) UN Doc S/RES/2253 (2015).

also extended the mandate of the Office of the Ombudsperson established by UNSC Resolution 1904 (2009) for 24 months from the expiration of its mandate in December 2017.

Given the lack of debate when UNSC Resolution 1373 was adopted in September 2001, one remarkable aspect of the adoption of UNSC Resolution 2253 (2015) was the presence of a number of Finance Ministers from Member States who spoke in the debate about the importance of destroying ISIL through financial means. Also at the 7587th meeting was the President of the Financial Action Task Force who briefed the members of the UN Security Council on the financial structure of ISIL and the activities of the Financial Action Task Force before the adoption of the resolution.

Speaking after the adoption of UNSC Resolution 2253 (2015), the Spanish representative made reference to paragraph 59 of the resolution and expressed the hope that, on the basis of the new paragraph calling upon the Secretary-General to take all necessary measures to ensure the independence and effectiveness of the Office of the Ombudsperson 'we will make progress towards the full institutionalization of the Office of the Ombudsperson'.[154] It is difficult to read the statement in paragraph 59 of UNSC Resolution 2253 (2015) requesting the Secretary-General to make the necessary arrangements to ensure that the Office of the Ombudsperson is able to carry out its mandate in an independent, effective and timely manner as a copper-bottomed obligation to institutionalise that Office.

[154] UNSC Verbatim Record (17 December 2015) UN Doc S/PV.7587, p 13.

UNITED NATIONS

NATIONS UNIES

POSTAL ADDRESS-ADRESSE POSTALE: UNITED NATIONS, N.Y. 10017
CABLE ADDRESS -ADRESSE TELEGRAPHIQUE: UNATIONS NEWYORK

13 July 2015

Secretary-General,

Today marks my last day in office as Ombudsperson for the Security Council Al-Qaida Sanctions Committee after a five year term. I wish to thank you for the opportunity to serve as the first Ombudsperson. The Ombudsperson mechanism stands as a unique and important achievement of the Security Council and the United Nations. Through it, individuals and entities have a recourse for consideration of their delisting requests at the international level, which provides a fair process and makes available an effective remedy. It is in accord with the principles for effective independent review as envisaged by Secretary-General Annan and advocated for by you.

I note with appreciation the administrative support which the Department of Political Affairs has provided to the Ombudsperson over the five years. I would also like to thank the staff of the Office of the Ombudsperson Eric Butcher, the administrative assistant, and Natacha Wexels-Riser, the legal officer, for their excellent work for, and unwavering commitment to, the Office of the Ombudsperson.

However, I have today submitted my final report to the Security Council (S/2015/533). In it, as in preceding reports, I have noted with concern the lack of full implementation of the Security Council mandate for an independent office of the Ombudsperson. In particular, I have highlighted the shortcomings of the contractual, administrative and organizational arrangements in place, which threaten the independence and sustainability of the mechanism.

As outlined in the report, I would encourage you to consider a fundamental restructuring of those arrangements, especially with respect to contractual status and the placement of the mechanism within the organization in terms of administrative oversight. Most fundamentally there is a need to ensure that an independent Office of the Ombudsperson exists within the organizational structure and that its core feature of autonomy has institutional safeguards. This entrenchment of the Office of the Ombudsperson within the architecture of the organization would represent yet another important contribution stemming from the Secretary-General. It would reflect a significant further enhancement for fair process and adherence to the rule of law in the work of the Security Council and the United Nations, in accordance with the vision of the United Nations Charter.

It has been an honor to serve in this position during its initial phase and I wish the new Ombudsperson much success in carrying forward the work of this important fair process mechanism.

Kimberly Prost
Ombudsperson

BAN Ki-Moon
Secretary-General
United Nations
New York

8

Sanctions Cases in the European Courts

LUCA PANTALEO

I. INTRODUCTION

THE EUROPEAN UNION (EU) has a large number of sanctions regimes currently in force. They are aimed at attaining different foreign policy goals, such as preventing the financing of international terrorism,[1] obstructing the development of Iran's nuclear proliferation programme,[2] reacting against the persistent violations of fundamental rights perpetrated by certain authoritarian regimes,[3] persuading Russia to bring to a close the unlawful violation of Ukraine's territorial integrity[4] and so forth. All these sanctions regimes include so-called smart sanctions targeting natural and legal persons who are believed to be involved,

[1] Council Common Position 2001/931/CFSP of 27 December 2001 on the application of specific measures to combat terrorism [2001] OJ L344/93; Council Regulation (EC) 2580/2001 of 27 December 2001 on specific restrictive measures directed against certain persons and entities with a view to combating terrorism [2001] OJ L344/70 and subsequent amendments; Council Regulation (EC) 881/2002 of 27 May 2002 imposing certain specific restrictive measures directed against certain persons and entities associated with Usama bin Laden, the Al-Qaida network and the Taliban, and repealing Council Regulation (EC) No 467/2001 prohibiting the export of certain goods and services to Afghanistan, strengthening the flight ban and extending the freeze of funds and other financial resources in respect of the Taliban of Afghanistan [2001] OJ L139/9 and subsequent amendments.

[2] Council Decision 2010/413/CFSP of 26 July 2010 concerning restrictive measures against Iran and repealing Common Position 2007/140/CFSP [2010] OJ L195/39 and subsequent amendments; Council Regulation (EU) 267/2012 of 23 March 2012 concerning restrictive measures against Iran and repealing Regulation (EU) No 961/2010 [2010] OJ L332/31 and subsequent amendments.

[3] Council Decision 2011/101/CFSP of 15 February 2011 concerning restrictive measures against Zimbabwe [2011] OJ L42/6 and subsequent amendments; Council Regulation (EC) 314/2004 of 19 February 2004 concerning certain restrictive measures in respect of Zimbabwe [2004] OJ L55/1 and subsequent amendments.

[4] Council Decision 2014/145/CFSP of 17 March 2014 concerning restrictive measures in respect of actions undermining or threatening the territorial integrity, sovereignty and independence of Ukraine [2014] OJ L78/16 and subsequent amendments; Council Regulation (EU) 269/2014 of 17 March 2014 concerning restrictive measures in respect of actions undermining or threatening the territorial integrity, sovereignty and independence of Ukraine [2014] OJ L78/6 and related and subsequent acts.

directly or indirectly, in the activities against which the measures are directed. Smart sanctions typically include assets freezes and travel bans on the targeted individuals and companies. More recently, the EU has mixed targeted sanctions with broader restrictions on certain types of trade and transactions.[5] In terms of policy instruments, these restrictions are similar to more traditional forms of international economic sanctions against States, such as embargoes.

Although targeted sanctions have been successfully challenged in other jurisdictions,[6] the EU is definitely the legal order where judicial challenges have been more numerous, and more groundbreaking. Therefore, it comes as no surprise that EU sanctions cases have been the subject of considerable controversy, resulting rapidly in a copious body of literature.[7] However, there are still a number of unresolved issues that are likely to arise in the cases currently pending before EU Courts.

The aim of this chapter is to examine such issues in an attempt to provide the reader with a thorough summary of the current state of play. The chapter will depart (section II) from the early case law, in which the Court of Justice (ECJ), then followed by the General Court (GC), set out the basic principles applicable. Although the core elements of those principles are—by and large—still applied today, the second part of this chapter (section III) will explore how they have been clarified, and enriched with new elements, in the course of the last few years. The third part of this chapter (section IV) will be devoted to the analysis of those issues that remain

[5] See (n 2) as regards sanctions against Iran; but also Council Decision 2014/386/CFSP of 23 June 2014 concerning restrictions on goods originating in Crimea or Sevastopol, in response to the illegal annexation of Crimea and Sevastopol [2014] OJ L183/70 and subsequent amendments.

[6] Anti-terrorist sanctions have been successfully challenged in Canada, where domestic courts have quashed the listing of individuals suspected of being associated with Al-Qaeda; see Supreme Court of Canada, *Abousfian Abdelrazik v Department of Foreign Affairs and Attorney General*, 2009 CF 580; see also *Charkaoui v Canada*, 2007 SCC 9, commented by T Poole, 'Recent Developments in the War on Terrorism in Canada' (2007) 7 *Human Rights Law Review* 633. See also s IV below for an overview of judicial decisions taken by Member States' domestic courts.

[7] See, among many, I Cameron, 'European Union Anti-Terrorist Blacklisting' (2003) 3 *Human Rights Law Review* 225; H Keller and A Fischer, 'The UN Anti-terror Sanctions Regime under Pressure' (2009) 9 *Human Rights Law Review* 257; L Paladini, 'Le Misure Restrittive Adottate nell'Ambito della PESC: Prassi e Giurisprudenza' (2009) 14 *Diritto dell'Unione Europea* 341; M Lugato, 'Sono le Sanzioni Individuali del Consiglio di Sicurezza Incompatibili con il Rispetto delle Garanzie Procedurali?' (2010) 93 *Rivista di Diritto Internazionale* 309; B Fassbender (ed), *Securing Human Rights?: Achievements and Challenges of the UN Security Council* (Oxford, Oxford University Press 2011); M de Goede, 'Blacklisting and the Ban: Contesting Targeted Sanctions in Europe' (2011) 42 *Security Dialogue* 499; A Vines, 'The Effectiveness of The Effectiveness of UN and EU Sanctions: Lessons for the Twenty-First Century' (2012) 88 *International Affairs* 867; I Cameron (ed), *EU Sanctions: Law and Policy Issues Concerning Restrictive Measures* (Antwerp, Intersentia, 2013); F Giumelli, *The Success of Sanctions: Lessons Learned from EU Experience* (Farnham, Ashgate 2013); F Giumelli, 'How EU Sanctions Work: A New Narrative' (2013) Chaillot Paper no 129, EU Institute for Security Studies.

currently unresolved. In the fourth and concluding part (section V), some general conclusions will be presented.

However, this chapter will only take into consideration those aspects of EU sanctions regimes that, from a purely internal perspective—ie from an EU law perspective—raise issues of the protection of fundamental rights and of the rule of law. As for other questions—such as the systemic interplay between different legal orders, the responsibility of international organisations and so forth—the reader is referred to the other chapters of this book, as well as to other relevant scholarly writings.[8]

II. SETTING THE SCENE: FROM *PMOI* TO *KADI I*

The first case in which EU sanctions were successfully challenged was brought by the People's Mojehedin Organization of Iran (PMOI).[9] In this judgment of the GC one can find all the basic principles that the ECJ further developed in the landmark *Kadi I* some months later.[10] In short, the GC found that the listing of PMOI did not satisfy the rule of law in the (then) Community. In particular, the absence of a statement of reasons indicating the actual and specific grounds justifying the inclusion of the applicant in a list of suspected terrorists violated its right to a fair trial, and to an effective judicial remedy against the measures.[11] As is well known, at that time the same court had dismissed many similar claims, including Mr Kadi's first claim.[12] The reasons behind such change of case law had probably to do with the origin of the measures at stake: unlike in *Kadi*

[8] See, among many, M Nettesheim, 'U.N. Sanctions against Individuals—A Challenge to the Architecture of European Union Governance' (2007) 44 *Common Market Law Review* 567; L Gradoni, 'All'ombra delle Nazioni Unite' in G Gozzi and P Manzini (eds), *L'Occidente e l'Ordine Internazionale* (Turin, Giappichelli 2008); J D'Aspremont and F Dopagne, '*Kadi*: The ECJ's Reminder of the Elementary Divide between Legal Orders' (2008) 5 *International Organizations Law Review* 371; R Wessel, 'The Kadi Case: Towards a More Substantive Hierarchy in International Law?' (2008) 5 *International Organizations Law Review* 326; J W van Rossem, 'Interaction between EU Law and International Law in the Light of *Intertanko* and *Kadi*: the Dilemma of Norms Binding the Member States but not the Community' (2009) 40 *Netherlands Yearbook of International Law* 196; D Halberstam and E Stein, 'The United Nations, The European Union, and the King of Sweden: Economic Sanctions and Individual Rights in a Plural World Order' (2009) 46 *Common Market Law Review* 13; A Aust, 'Kadi: Ignoring International Legal Obligations' (2009) 6 *International Organizations Law Review* 293; G De Búrca, 'The European Court of Justice and the International Legal Order After Kadi' (2010) 51 *Harvard International Law Journal* 1.

[9] Case T-228/02, *Organisation des Modjahedines du peuple d'Iran v Council of the European Union* [2006] ECR II-04665.

[10] Case C-402/05 P, *Kadi and Al Barakaat International Foundation v Council and Commission* [2008] ECR I-06351.

[11] See *Organisation des Modjahedines du peuple d'Iran v Council of the European Union* (n 9) para 165.

[12] Case T-315/01, *Kadi v Council and Commission* [2005] ECR II-03649.

and other similar cases, the GC was confronted in *PMOI* with sanctions imposed autonomously by the EU. To put it differently, in *PMOI* the primacy of a UN Security Council resolution was not at stake: and this may have encouraged the GC to take what, at that time, can be seen as quite a bold and innovative stand.[13] Be that as it may, the fact remains that *PMOI* breached the castle walls: the basic principles developed therein marked the end of an era where security issues systematically won over fundamental rights concerns, paving the way for further developments.

Indeed, the apogee of this early case law was reached in 2008 when in *Kadi I*, on appeal from the GC, the ECJ annulled EU restrictive measures.[14] The number of scholarly writings devoted, directly or indirectly, to the analysis of that judgment is gargantuan.[15] Any comment of that decision would, therefore, be redundant. Suffice it to say that in *Kadi I* the ECJ broke the taboo relating to the unimpeachable nature of sanctions imposed in implementation of UN Security Council resolutions. The Court made it clear that, regardless of their origin, targeted sanctions in the EU are decisions made by EU institutions. As such, they are subject to judicial review in the same way as any other piece of EU legislation. This, in turn, requires that restrictive measures imposed by the EU comply with the core principles of EU law. Failure to comply with those principles will lead EU Courts to declare the measures unlawful.

PMOI and *Kadi I* both concerned restrictive measures imposed on natural and legal persons suspected of being involved in international terrorism. That is, to situations where the listed entities had no connection

[13] See eg: C Eckes, 'Case T-228/02, "Organisation des Modjahedines du peuple d'Iran v. Council and UK (OMPI)", Judgment of the Court of First Instance (Second Chamber) of 12 December 2006' (2007) 44 *Common Market Law Review* (note) 1118 ff; T Andersson, 'Developing Multiple EU Personalities: Ten Years of Blacklisting and Mutual Trust' in Cameron (ed), *EU Sanctions* (n 7) 74 ff.

[14] *Kadi and Al Barakaat International Foundation v Council and Commission* (n 10).

[15] See, among many, L M Hinojosa-Martinez, 'Bad Law for Good Reasons: the Contradictions of the *Kadi* judgment' (2008) 5 *International Organizations Law Review* 339; L van den Herik and N Schrijver, 'Eroding the Primacy of the UN System of Collective Security: the Judgment of the European Court of Justice in the Case of Kadi and Al Barakaat' (2008) 5 *International Organizations Law Review* 329; A Gattini, 'Yassin Abdullah Kadi v. Council and Commission' (2009) 46 *Common Market Law Review* 213 (note); P J Cardwell, D French and N White, 'European Court of Justice, Yassin Abdullah Kadi and Al Barakaat International Foundation v Council and Commission (Joined Cases C-402/05 P and C-415/05 P) Judgment of 3 September 2008' (2009) 58 *International and Comparative Law Quarterly* 229 (note); M Zgonec-Rožej, 'Yassin Abdullah Kadi and Al Barakaat International Foundation v. Council and Commission, Joined Cases C-402/05 P & C-415/05 P' (2009) 103 *American Journal International Law* 305 (note); T Tridimas, 'Terrorism and the ECJ: Empowerment and Democracy in the EC Legal Order' (2009) 15 *European Law Review* 103; F Salerno, 'Quale «comunità di diritto» per il signor Kadi?' (2009) 92 *Rivista di diritto internazionale* 110; E Cannizzaro, 'Security Council Resolutions and EC Fundamental Rights: Some Remarks on the ECJ Decision in the Kadi Case' (2010) 29 *Yearbook of European Law* 533; S Cassella, 'Les suites de l'arrêt "Kadi" de la CJCE: quel équilibre entre protection de la sécurité internationale et respect des droits de l'homme?' (2010) 56 *Annuaire Français de Droit International* 709.

whatsoever with a third country. As we shall see in the next section of this chapter, it would take a few years more before the principles developed in *PMOI* and *Kadi I* were extended to other sanctions regimes, in particular to inter-State smart sanctions. However, the two decisions already contained all the basic principles that the EU Courts developed, and further clarified, in the subsequent flood of sanctions cases. These principles can be briefly summarised as follows.

A. Statement of Reasons

First, EU authorities are under an obligation to give a detailed statement of the reasons for the entity's being placed on the list. Such reasons cannot be too general, excessively vague or lacking in sufficient detail.[16] As the ECJ put it, the 'statement of reasons identifies the individual, specific and concrete reasons why the competent authorities consider that the individual concerned must be subject to restrictive measures'.[17] The purpose of this obligation is twofold. On the one hand, it is aimed at guaranteeing the person's rights of defence, in that it enables the targeted person to understand what are the allegations made against it and to set up its defensive strategy accordingly. On the other, it makes it possible for the EU Courts to carry out an effective judicial scrutiny of the measures. If the reasons given are too vague, to borrow from the ECJ's own words, the Courts would be unable 'to undertake the review of the lawfulness of the contested' measures.[18] The obligation to give reasons can perhaps be considered the core element of the right to a fair trial of listed persons under EU law.[19]

B. Obligation to Provide Evidence

This obligation is intimately related to the previous one. The statement of reasons is essentially made of assertions that need to be substantiated by supportive evidence. As the ECJ put it, 'respect for the rights of the defence and the right to effective judicial protection requires that the competent Union authority disclose to the individual concerned the evidence against that person available to that authority and relied on as the basis

[16] Case C-539/10 P, *Al-Aqsa v Council and Pays Bas* (ECJ, 15 November 2012) paras 140–42.

[17] Case C-584/10 P, *Commission and Others v Kadi* (ECJ, 18 July 2013) para 116.

[18] See *Kadi and Al Barakaat International Foundation v Council and Commission* (n 10) para 351.

[19] See L Pantaleo, 'La protection des droits fondamentaux de la défense dans l'application des mesures ciblées. L'apport des juridictions à la gouvernance des problèmes sécuritaire' in L Balmond and M Arcari (eds), *La gouvernance globale face aux défis de la sécurité collective* (Naples, Editoriale Scientifica, 2012) 154 ff.

of its decision'.[20] The ECJ has in principle accepted that such evidence may not be disclosed before a person is listed. This is so in order to take advantage of the 'surprise effect' and to prevent targeted persons dispersing their assets.[21] However, after designation, there is no reason that can justify undue delays in communicating inculpatory evidence to the person concerned. The ECJ has also admitted that the communication of certain matters, such as classified materials, may be as of principle excluded because of overriding security considerations. However, this cannot go so far as to render judicial review of the measures ineffective.[22]

C. Right to be Heard and to an Adversarial Procedure

This right is part and parcel of the right to a fair trial. It includes the person's right to be informed of the case against them and to be able to comment on it. After the ECJ found the designation process incompatible with the right to be heard in *Kadi I*, EU authorities fulfil this obligation in the following way: once the decision concerning the listing of a natural or legal person is taken, the Commission sends out an individual notice to the person. In this communication, the person is invited to request access to the statement of reasons justifying her/his/its inclusion in the list, and to submit comments in order to make her/his/its point of view known.[23] This sort of pre-judicial phase is little more than a formality, since there are no cases—to my knowledge—of persons delisted at this point.

D. Comprehensive Judicial Review

Judicial review of the measures 'cannot be restricted to an assessment of the cogency in the abstract of the reasons relied on, but must concern whether those reasons, or, at the very least, one of those reasons, deemed sufficient in itself to support that decision, is substantiated'.[24] This means that matters of both fact and law must be scrutinised by the EU Courts in order to assess whether the inclusion of a person on the list is justified.

[20] See *Commission and Others v Kadi* (n 17) para 111.

[21] See *Kadi and Al Barakaat International Foundation v Council and Commission* (n 10) para 340.

[22] Ibid paras 342–43. The issue concerning the classified nature of certain evidence will be addressed in-depth in s IV below.

[23] See eg 'Notice for the attention of Mr Uthman Omar Mahmoud concerning his inclusion in the list referred to in Articles 2, 3 and 7 of Council Regulation (EC) No 881/2002 imposing certain specific restrictive measures directed against certain persons and entities associated with Usama bin Laden, the Al-Qaida network and the Taliban', OJ C80/12.

[24] See *Commission and Others v Kadi* (n 17) para 119.

In other words, the Courts must be able to assess whether the person involved falls within the listing criteria relevant to the sanctions regime in question: that is, that the person in question is actually supportive of international terrorism, is involved in the perpetration of serious violations of human rights and so forth.

These are the basic principles set out by the ECJ in the early case law concerning smart sanctions imposed on persons suspected of being involved in international terrorism. However, anti-terrorism sanctions are relatively few in comparison to the much larger number of so-called bilateral sanctions regimes—that is, sanctions imposed on third countries—that are currently in force. It is in this context that EU Courts have handed down a multitude of decisions in the last few years. Most of the still unresolved issues have arisen in that context. The next section shall focus on the developments that followed the early anti-terrorism case law.

III. THE APPLICATION OF *KADI* STANDARDS TO BILATERAL SANCTIONS REGIMES AND OTHER POST-*KADI* DEVELOPMENTS

A disputable distinction that emerged from the early anti-terrorism case law concerned the alleged difference between sanctions imposed on terrorists and bilateral sanctions regimes. The latter are different from anti-terrorism measures in that the sanctions are aimed at reacting to a State's conduct, in order to persuade the concerned State to bring to an end the contested behaviour. Despite this difference, they share the same nature: under both regimes, targeted persons are placed on a list and subjected to restrictive measures such as assets freezes and travel bans. The reasons justifying the designation of each person are connected with the role allegedly played by that person in the contested State's conduct. This may include participation in serious violations of human rights and humanitarian law (Ivory Coast),[25] the use of children or women in situations of armed conflict (Democratic Republic of the Congo),[26] unlawful nuclear proliferation (Iran),[27] brutal repression of dissent and violation of human

[25] Council Decision 2010/656/CFSP of 29 October 2010 renewing the restrictive measures against Côte d'Ivoire [2010] OJ L285/28 and subsequent amendments; Council Regulation (EC) 174/2005 of 31 January 2005 imposing restrictions on the supply of assistance related to military activities to Côte d'Ivoire [2005] OJ L29/5.

[26] Council Decision 2010/788/CFSP of 20 December 2010 concerning restrictive measures against the Democratic Republic of the Congo and repealing Common Position 2008/369/CFSP [2010] OJ L336/30 and subsequent amendments; Council Regulation (EC) 889/2005 of 13 June 2005 imposing certain restrictive measures in respect of the Democratic Republic of Congo and repealing Regulation (EC) No 1727/2003 [2005] OJ L152/1.

[27] See (n 2).

rights (Syria)[28] and so on. In the first place, the GC argued that entities targeted under bilateral sanctions regimes were not entitled to the same fundamental rights as suspected terrorists. Put shortly, the GC argued that, since the addressee of a decision establishing a bilateral sanctions regime was the third country in question, that decision was not of direct and individual concern to the listed entities within the meaning of Article 263 of the TFEU.[29]

It was clear to the observer that such distinction was untenable and that it was only a matter of time before the Courts acknowledged it.[30] The first decisions in which the principles set out in the context of anti-terrorism measures were applied to bilateral sanctions regimes were handed down by the GC in the *Bamba* case,[31] followed by the ECJ in *Tay Za*.[32] In those decisions, the EU Courts quashed the listing of individuals under bilateral sanctions regimes, granting those individuals the same fundamental rights standards established in *Kadi*. They made it clear that private natural or legal persons sanctioned under a bilateral regime could only be listed in reliance upon precise and concrete evidence adequate to justify their listing, and permitting the Courts to assess whether they fell within the listing criteria relevant to the regime in question.[33]

A slightly different, but related, question that emerged from Iranian sanctions cases is whether (private) State-owned entities, such as banks or financial and commercial actors, are entitled to fundamental rights protection in the same way as privately owned entities. According to the position taken by the Council and the Commission in *Bank Mellat*, State-owned entities were not entitled to such protection because such entities should be considered direct emanations of the State, which did not itself possess individual fundamental rights. However, and rightly so, the GC held that State-owned entities could be excluded from fundamental rights protection if, and only if, EU institutions provided evidence that the

[28] Council Decision 2012/739/CFSP of 29 November 2012 concerning restrictive measures against Syria and repealing Decision 2011/782/CFSP [2012] OJ L330/21 and subsequent amendments; Council Regulation (EU) 36/2012 of 18 January 2012 concerning restrictive measures in view of the situation in Syria and repealing Regulation (EU) No 442/2011 [2012] OJ L16/1.

[29] Case T-181/08, *Tay Za v Council* [2008] ECR II-01965. See, for a critical appraisal of the decision, L Pantaleo, 'Sanzioni "mirate" dell'Unione Europea contro uno Stato terzo e tutela dei diritti fondamentali degli individui' (2010) 93 *Rivista di diritto internazionale* 1143 (note).

[30] See Pantaleo, 'La protection des droits fondamentaux' (n 19) 160 ff.

[31] Case T-86/11, *Bamba v Council* [2011] ECR II-02749, commented by L Pantaleo, 'Sanzioni mirate dell'Unione europea contro uno Stato terzo e tutela dei diritti fondamentali nella sentenza Bamba: un passo avanti ed uno indietro?' (2011) 5 *Diritti umani e diritto internazionale* 657 (note).

[32] Case C-376/10 P, *Tay Za v Council* (ECJ, 13 March 2012), commented by L Pantaleo, 'Case C-376/10 P, Pye Phyo Tay Za v. Council, Judgment of the European Court of Justice (Grand Chamber) of 13 March 2012' (2012) 49 *Common Market Law Review* 1769 (note).

[33] See *Bamba v Council* (n 31) para 67.

entity participated in the exercise of governmental powers, or ran a public service under governmental control. Absent such evidence, the standard of judicial review and protection of fundamental rights remained the same. In other words, the fact of State ownership is not, as such, sufficient ground to remove an entity's fundamental rights.[34] As we shall see below, however, this line of reasoning does not apply to entities carrying out fundamental public policy functions (such as a central bank), irrespective of the ownership.

Another questionable distinction that emerged at some point is that between the supposedly different intensity of judicial review to be exercised in respect of EU autonomous sanctions, as opposed to UN-derived sanctions. The Council, along with the Commission and certain Member States, has often supported this position.[35] Put shortly, when it comes to restrictive measures imposed by the EU to implement UN Security Council resolutions, the judicial review performed by the EU Courts ought not to be comprehensive, that is to say focused on both the merits and the overall procedural fairness of the listing. Rather, according to this view, full scrutiny should be confined to sanctions imposed by the EU on an autonomous basis. Advocate General Bot endorsed such a position in his Opinion in *Kadi II*, grounding it on a twofold base. At first, he held that lesser judicial scrutiny was needed to give due deference to the Security Council.[36] In this sense, the Advocate General's argument seemed to attempt to resurrect the GC's core argument in *Kadi I*, killed off by the ECJ's judgment on appeal.[37] Moreover, in his view, a less intense standard of review—as opposed to the thorough *PMOI*-like review—was justified by the developments that had occurred at UN level as regards listing and delisting. In particular, the Advocate General opined that, given 'the important role played by the Ombudsperson in the decisions taken by the Sanctions Committee, … the procedure before it can no longer be regarded as purely diplomatic and intergovernmental'.[38] Hence, a less intrusive review by the EU Courts would not breach individual rights. Indeed, this

[34] Case T-496/10, *Bank Mellat v Council* (GC, 29 January 2013) paras 35–46.

[35] See eg Case T-85/09, *Kadi v Commission* [2010] ECR II-05177, paras 86–111.

[36] Case C-584/10 P, *Commission and others v Kadi* (ECJ, 18 July 2013) Opinion of AG Bot, paras 69 ff.

[37] As is well known, the GC in *Kadi I* argued that it could not review the internal lawfulness (ie against the Treaties) of an EU decision adopted to implement a resolution of the UN Security Council. It only accepted to check the resolution's legality against *jus cogens* norms. The resolution's immunity from judicial review was based on a sort of deference due to the Security Council, and to its primary responsibility to maintain international peace and security. See *Organisation des Modjahedines du peuple d'Iran v Council of the European Union* (n 12). For a comment favourable to such position, see C Tomuschat, 'Kadi v. Council and Commission, judgment of the Court of First Instance of 21 September 2005' (2006) 43 *Common Market Law Review* 537 (note).

[38] See *Commission and others v Kadi* (n 36) para 82.

represented the main, and by far the most interesting, part of Advocate General Bot's position, which seemingly suggested the existence of a rebuttable presumption of conformity of UN anti-terrorism sanctions with EU fundamental rights standards. Hence, it was argued, the EU Courts should do nothing more than verify the overall procedural fairness of the designation decision. In this, Advocate General Bot's position seems to be an evident application of a *Bosphorus/Solange*-like argument,[39] also known as the doctrine of equivalent protection, which the ECJ had itself alluded to in *Kadi I*.[40]

The Council put forward a similar argument in the context of sanctions against Iran. As is well known, these are originally UN-derived sanctions, yet EU sanctions, as well as US sanctions, go further than has the UN.[41] In the *Iran Transfo* case, the Council could not invoke the doctrine of equivalent protection, as the UN Ombudsperson is only competent to review Al Qaeda designations.[42] However, it suggested that the standard of review ought to be less intrusive with regard to bilateral sanctions regimes because the imposition of restrictive measures in that context was grounded on classified material that could not be made public. In addition, the Council pointed out that the object of judicial review in such situations would be, in essence, the policies of a State, and not the conduct of private persons, as in the case of terrorism. We must assume that the idea behind

[39] See *Bosphorus Hava Yolları Turizm ve Ticaret Anonim Şirketi v Ireland* App no 45036/98, ECHR 2005-VI; Case 11/70, *Internationale Handelsgesellschaft mbH v Einfuhr- und Vorratsstelle für Getreide und Futtermittel* (*Solange I*) Case No 2 BvL 52/71 International Law Reports 93, 362; *Wünsche Handelsgesellschaft* (*Solange II*) Case No 2 BvR 197/83 International Law Reports 93, 403.

[40] Before annulling the internal regulation which implemented UN sanctions for violating Mr Kadi's fundamental rights, the ECJ examined thoroughly the UN system as regards individual (quasi-)judicial protection—namely, the delisting procedure instituted by the SC. Only after finding this system unable to protect individual rights, did the Court conclude for the annulment of the regulation. As has been noted, '[b]y accepting the recognition of primary competence of a hypothetical mechanism for the protection of human rights within the UN, and by accepting the curtailing of its own competence in respect thereof, the ECJ seems to conceive of the UN system as being connected to the Community legal order'. See Cannizzaro, *Kadi*: The ECJ's Reminder of the Elementary Divide between Legal Orders' (n 8) 378, who note that the ECJ in *Kadi I* did 'exactly what the German and Italian Constitutional Courts did more than three decades ago when interpreting their relationship with the EC legal order which they deemed at odds with the human rights standards of their respective municipal legal order'. As is well known, the ECJ excluded any equivalent protection due precisely to the intergovernmental and diplomatic nature of the delisting procedure in force at that time.

[41] In particular, this holds true in respect of general prohibitions on certain types of trade and transactions.

[42] As is well known, the Office of the Ombudsperson was created by Security Council Resolution 1904, adopted on 17 December 2009, and its mandate was extended by Resolution 1989, adopted on 17 June 2011, and Resolution 2083, adopted on 17 December 2012. It is competent to review delisting requests from individuals and entities placed on the Al Qaeda sanctions list.

the Council's reasoning was that a judicial organ should avoid making judgements on discretionary—and highly sensitive—matters of foreign policy. Accordingly, the Council proposed that the appropriate standard of review was limited to an assessment of the overall plausibility of the reasons justifying the designation.[43] Insofar as it suggested that persons targeted under inter-State sanctions regimes were not entitled to the same fundamental rights standards as suspected terrorists, the Council's proposals were reminiscent of the GC's decision in *Tay Za*.[44] However, they perhaps also reflected criticisms of the EU Courts' case law made by those, primarily the US Government, who were reportedly unhappy with the Courts demanding disclosure of all the evidence relied upon by the Council in certain Iranian cases.[45]

Both the ECJ in *Kadi II* and the GC in *Iran Transfo* rejected these arguments. On the one hand, the ECJ did not take into consideration Advocate General's Bot equivalent protection doctrine. It also ignored the existence of the Ombudsperson, who was not even mentioned in the decision. As a result, the ECJ carried out a full review of the measures imposed on Mr Kadi, thus making it clear that a less intense judicial scrutiny was not an option. On the other hand, the GC stated that a judicial review limited to the overall plausibility of the allegations was incompatible with EU fundamental rights standards.[46] On this basis, it also quashed the applicant's listing. It follows from what precedes that, in the EU legal order, different standards of judicial scrutiny of restrictive measures are simply not possible. The EU Courts have considered, but ruled out, such a possibility several times, deciding instead on a single standard of judicial review for all EU sanctions. The EU Courts will review whether the reasons adduced by the Council are well founded and supported by evidence, including classified evidence. However, a different, although related question concerns the adjudication of sensitive cases in a secure manner; that is, the review of classified material in closed hearings where the evidence is provided to the judges but not disclosed to the applicant. We will deal with this issue in the following section of this chapter.[47]

Another interesting issue which has arisen before the ECJ concerns whether persons who are removed from sanctions lists before their cases are decided still have an interest in the proceedings for annulment. As is well known, there is settled case law stating that an applicant's interest to

[43] Case T-392/11, *Iran Transfo v Council* (GC, 16 May 2013) paras 32–33. The Commission supported it.
[44] See *Tay Za v Council* (n 29).
[45] See E Ferrari, 'When Push Comes to Shove: U.S. Not Happy With EU Sanctions These Days' (Sanction Law, 27 March 2013) available at: http://sanctionlaw.com/when-push-comes-to-shove-u-s-not-happy-these-days-with-eu-sanctions/
[46] See *Iran Transfo v Council* (n 43) paras 34–38.
[47] See s IV.

bring proceedings must exist not only at the stage of lodging the action, but also continue until a final decision is reached. Should such interest disappear in the course of proceedings, a decision would bring no benefit to the applicant. Hence, the court should dismiss the case by stating that there is no further need to adjudicate upon it.[48] However, there are a number of good reasons to maintain that persons removed from sanctions lists retain an interest in the proceedings even after removal. First of all, the removal of an entry from sanctions lists is tantamount to the repealing of an act, which takes effect *ex nunc*; whilst with an annulling judgment the act in question is removed retroactively, as if it never existed. Secondly, the nature of a judgment can be twofold: it can have declaratory, as well as constitutive elements. While the removal of an entry from a sanctions list may be equivalent to an annulling decision as regards its constitutive effect, the same does not hold true so far as the declaratory effect is concerned. An annulling judgment declares the unlawfulness of a given act. Its repealing does not. Such declaration can consequently be seen as a form of non-material compensation for the damage caused to the applicant's reputation. Thirdly, under Article 87(6) of the Rules of Procedure, where a case does not proceed to judgment, the allocation of costs is in the discretion of the Court. In theory, this could lead to a situation where a person removed from the list is ordered not only to bear their own costs—which would be unjust in and of itself—but also to pay other parties' costs. Finally yet importantly, an annulling judgment could serve the purpose of facilitating an action for compensation. It is true that, on a procedural level, an action for compensation does not have necessarily to be preceded by an action for annulment. However, especially where proceedings for annulment are close to coming to an end, it is clear that an annulling decision may make the applicant's job of seeking redress easier.

To begin with, the GC refused to continue proceedings in several sanctions cases where applicants, pending the judgment, had been removed from sanctions lists. None of the arguments put forward above were deemed to be convincing.[49] The ECJ did not have the opportunity to rule on the question for a long time. The first case where an appeal was brought challenging the GC's decision to declare an action of a delisted person devoid of purpose was in the *Abdulrahim* case. In his Opinion, Advocate General Bot held that the GC's case law in question was moot. According to him, at least two of the arguments put forward above were correct. In the first place, a favourable annulling decision would, at the very least, have contributed to the restoration of the appellant's reputation.

[48] See, among others, Joined Cases T-494/08, T-500/08 and T-509/08, *Ryanair v Commission* [2010] ECR II-05723, paras 42–43.

[49] See, among many, orders in T-142/11, *SIR v Council* (GC, 13 July 2011); Case T-285/11 *Gooré v Council* (GC, 3 February 2012); Case T-131/11 *Ezzedine v Council* (GC, 4 June 2012).

And secondly, a decision in favour of the appellant would have served as a basis for an action for damages.[50]

The Court of Justice largely followed Advocate General Bot's suggestions. First, it made it clear that it was a necessary, but also a sufficient condition for an applicant to demonstrate that there continued to exist at least one interest in the proceedings.[51] By saying so, it might be assumed that the ECJ wanted to advise the GC (to which the case was referred back) not to set too high a test for determining the existence of an interest in continuing proceedings, as the particularly rigorous nature of the scrutiny undertaken by the GC was one of the complaints made by the appellant. Secondly, the Court held that the question whether an applicant retains an interest in an action must be assessed in light of the specific circumstance of the case.[52] In this respect, the ECJ seemed to suggest that the case law concerning the retention of an interest must be interpreted to accommodate the specific context of restrictive measures, by taking into account, in particular, the stigmatising nature of such measures. Finally, the Court acknowledged that, in the case in point, recognition of the illegality of the contested act could help to rehabilitate the appellant, constituting a form of reparation for the non-material harm suffered by him.[53] Such symbolic compensation was sufficient to mean that the appellant's action for annulment was not devoid of purpose.

An additional interesting issue emerging from the case law concerns sanctions imposed by the EU upon proposals by Member States. This issue has arisen in particular in relation to the Iranian sanctions regime, where, as illustrated by the diplomatic cables leaked on the internet, Member States were subject to considerable pressure from the US Government to ensure the adoption of restrictive measures against certain Iranian entities.[54] In that context, the GC has stated that where the listing of entities is based on proposals by a Member State, the Council is under an obligation to undertake its own assessment of the accuracy and validity of the evidence relied on by the Member State for proposing the inclusion of the entities in the sanctions list. In *Bank Saderat*, the GC held that the Council had failed to comply with this obligation by omitting to double-check the precise extent of the Iranian State's holding in the applicant's share capital, which turned out to be other than the figures put before it.[55]

[50] Case C-239/12 P, *Abdulrahim v Council and Commission* (ECJ, 28 May 2013), Opinion of AG Bot, paras 65–67.

[51] Case C-239/12 P, *Abdulrahim v Council and Commission* (ECJ, 28 May 2013) para 66.

[52] Ibid para 65.

[53] Ibid para 72.

[54] See J Treanor, 'WikiLeaks cables: US pressured British regulator to act against Iranian banks' *The Guardian*, 13 December 2010, available at: www.theguardian.com/business/2010/dec/13/wikileaks-us-fsa-iran-banks.

[55] Case T-495/10, *Bank Saderat v Council* (GC, 20 March 2013) paras 91–102.

Finally, EU Courts have affirmed a number of principles governing evidential issues in the field of sanctions. In *Turbo Compressor Manufacturer (TCMFG)*, the Council maintained that the imposition of restrictive measures was justified by an allegation that the applicant was involved in the secret purchase of a cruise missile for the Islamic Republic of Iran in 2001 and 2002 (that is to say, four years before the adoption of Resolution 1696 (2006) by the UN Security Council, and 10 years before the imposition of sanctions against the applicant). The GC found that the sanctioning of the applicant could not be justified solely on a single event that occurred so far in the past. This was so because: (1) past misconduct could not be sufficient to hold that the applicant constituted a current threat; and (2) a single and remote event could not automatically imply that the applicant was a potential future threat.[56] The principle set out in *TCMFG* fits squarely into the case law concerning the obligation to provide reasons and evidence. The Council must be able to prove that listed entities are actually and concretely involved in the activity that constitutes the object of the relevant sanctions regime. Surely, that is not possible if the material relied on by the Council is obsolete. Along the same lines, the GC held that the Council could not take into account, in the course of proceedings, any material additional to that relied on at the time of designation.[57] The reasons behind this principle are self-evident: by putting forward evidence additional to that previously communicated to the persons involved, and which is, in all likelihood, unknown to them, the former's rights of defence would be severely prejudiced. A final principle regarding the law of evidence concerns the applicants' right to provide evidence. In particular, the Courts held that not only are the EU institutions under an obligation to provide supportive evidence, and the Courts under an obligation to assess its accuracy, but the persons concerned have also the right to produce exculpatory evidence, which must be taken into account by the Courts when reviewing the lawfulness of restrictive measures.[58]

IV. OPEN QUESTIONS AND REMAINING CHALLENGES

The case law discussed above has developed a considerable body of principles governing the field of targeted sanctions. Affected persons can now rely on sufficient and clear judicial protection, which, in turn, makes

[56] Case T-404/11, *Turbo Compressor Manufacturer (TCMFG) v Council* (GC, 17 April 2013) paras 17–44.

[57] Case T-128 and 182/12, HTTS *Hanseatic Trade Trust & Shipping GmbH v Council* (GC, 12 June 2013) paras 29–43.

[58] See *Commission and Others v Kadi* (n 17) paras 135–37; Case C-280/12 P, *Council v Fulmen and Mahmoudian* (ECJ, 28 November 2013) paras 55–56.

it possible to challenge restrictive measures in a less arbitrary way than previously. However, still quite a few problems remain unsolved.

To begin with, new rules applicable to classified evidence have recently come into force.[59] So far, the ECJ had admitted that the communication of certain matters, such as classified materials, could, in principle, be excluded on the basis of overriding security considerations. The ECJ had tried to reach a balance between, on the one hand, legitimate security considerations and, on the other, applicants' due process rights. The technique developed by the ECJ was that of assessing whether the reasons preventing disclosure adduced by the EU institutions were well founded. Should this not be the case, the Courts would review the lawfulness of restrictive measures solely on the basis of the evidence disclosed to the applicant, which were on most occasions insufficiently detailed. Hence, the decision would predictably conclude that the measures were unlawful. When the ECJ instead found that disclosure was effectively precluded by overriding security considerations, other possibilities were to be considered, such as disclosing to the applicant a brief summary outlining the evidence relied upon by the EU institutions.[60]

As was previously mentioned, the Courts' attitude in relation to evidence disclosure in certain Iranian cases had been criticised. The US Government had reportedly urged the EU to find a way to allow judges to review classified material in a secure manner. In the USA, this is done by means of closed hearings (*ex camera*), where evidence is shown to the court, but not disclosed to private parties and their counsel.[61] In the UK, a similar scheme permits so-called closed material procedures (CMP) when the disclosure of certain material is deemed contrary to the public interest.[62] The interpretation and application of the CMP provisions have given rise to considerable controversy in the UK.[63] Unlike the USA and the UK, however, in the EU judicial system there was no such thing as secret hearings.

[59] Rules of Procedure of the General Court [2015] OJ L105/1.

[60] See eg *Commission and Others v Kadi* (n 17) paras 125–29.

[61] See Ferrari, 'When Push Comes to Shove' (n 45).

[62] See Counter-Terrorism Act 2008, esp s 66 ff.

[63] The Counter Terrorism Act 2008 permits CMPs in the High Court and Court of Appeal, but is silent on the Supreme Court. In *Bank Mellat v Her Majesty's Treasury* [2013] UKSC 38, and [2013] UKSC 39 concerning the validity of a Treasury Order preventing people operating in the financial sector in the UK from doing transactions with the Bank, the Supreme Court was to decide whether it had jurisdiction to hold closed hearings. On the one hand, the Supreme Court held that it did have such jurisdiction. On the other, it held by a very narrow majority to exercise such jurisdiction in the case in point. However, dissenting judges drew up some very critical remarks, confirming the highly controversial nature of the issue in question. While eg Lord Hope stated that the Rubicon had 'been crossed' (para 88), Lord Kerr bitterly noted that 'sadly, but all too predictably, when the closed judgment was considered in the course of a closed material procedure, it became abundantly clear that it was quite unnecessary for us to have done so' (para 130).

However, the increasing pressure from international and internal criticism has produced the desired effect. The new Rules of Procedure of the GC (the rules) have come into force as of 1 July 2015. Chapter 7 of the rules contains only one provision (Article 105) devoted exclusively to the issue of classified evidence. Such provision sets out a general exception to the adversarial principle laid down in Article 64 of the rules. In brief, where a party to the proceedings intends to make use of information whose disclosure is deemed to harm the security of the Union or of the Member States, it has to submit to the GC such information in a separate document accompanied by an explanation of the overriding reasons justifying confidentiality. The GC will assess the relevance of the information provided and whether or not the request for confidentiality is well founded. Should the GC find that confidentiality is not necessary, the party that submitted the information will be requested its consent to disclose such information to the private party. If consent is refused the information will be returned to the party that submitted it and the information will not be taken into account in the determination of the case. Should the GC find that confidentiality is justified, the GC is authorised to base its judgment upon it if the material in question 'is essential in order for it to rule in the case'.[64] In such instance, Article 105(6) stipulates that the GC 'shall make a reasoned order' specifying an alternative way to present the information to the private party,

> such as the production by the party concerned [...] of a non-confidential version or a non-confidential summary of the information or material, containing the essential content thereof and enabling the other main party, to the greatest extent possible, to make its views known.

However, Article 105(7) gives the opportunity to the party that originally submitted the request for confidentiality to withdraw the material in question in full or in part. The withdrawal has to be requested within two weeks after the GC's decision to order disclosure of a non-confidential summary. In this case the information will not be taken into account by the GC.

The new rules on confidential evidence seem to incorporate—by and large—the ECJ's case law described above. Nonetheless there are a few points that should not go unmentioned. To begin with, it is worth noting that the draft initially proposed by the GC differs from the final version.[65] The changes implemented are all slightly in favour of the party that submits the request for confidentiality. This circumstance suggests that they may have been inserted or otherwise requested by the Council.

[64] See Rules of Procedure of the General Court, Art 105(8).

[65] See Draft Rules of Procedure of the General Court published on the Council's website: http://data.consilium.europa.eu/doc/document/ST-16724-2014-INIT/en/pdf.

For example, the possibility to withdraw the information within two weeks was not included in the draft.[66] The same holds true in respect of the closing sentence of paragraph 1, according to which where

> the information or material in respect of which confidential treatment is sought has been transmitted to the main party by one or more Member States, the overriding reasons put forward by the main party to justify the confidential treatment of that information or material may include those provided by the Member State(s) concerned.

Such sentence is a clear indication that the final version of the rules is more concerned with the interests of the Member States. Secondly, the determination of the actual security rules governing the handling of classified material is left to a later decision of the GC. Despite the silence of Article 105, it is, however, implicit that the rules will only apply after the publication of such decision. Thirdly, it seems apposite to recall that the rules will only apply to the GC's proceedings. Their impact on a hypothetical appeal judgment may, however, be significant. In fact, the GC enjoys jurisdiction on both the facts and the law, whilst the ECJ is as of principle empowered to review the GC's decisions on point of law only. From this perspective, the ECJ may not have the possibility to review the merits of the GC's decision concerning confidential information.

It seems fair to affirm that the implications of the rules on the fair trial standard applied to sanctions cases may turn out to be quite significant. It may be hard to reconcile closed hearings with the applicants' right to know the reasons for their designation and the supportive evidence relied on by the EU institutions; the right to comment on their case in an adversarial procedure; and, most importantly, the right to produce exculpatory material. The idea that applicants are entitled to produce counter-evidence is grounded on the basic principles governing the burden of proof. A procedure based on undisclosed evidence could be in breach of those principles, since it would make it impossible for applicants to disprove (unknown) inculpatory material with more convincing exculpatory evidence. The very idea of more cogent evidence presupposes that the party is aware of the less convincing evidence adduced against her/him/it. A sensible, compromise solution could be to allow full disclosure of evidence only on appeal, or only to the private party's counsel. However, that would require the adoption of new amendments. Finally, the fact that the information may be withdrawn by the party requesting confidentiality could also negatively affect applicants' due process rights. It is true that in such case the GC cannot base its ruling on the material

[66] The fact that such issue was a point of contention among Member States is a confirmation thereof. See M Lester, 'New EU Court Rules to be Adopted without UK Approval' (European Sanctions, 23 January May 2015) available at: www.europeansanctions.com/2015/01/23/new-eu-court-rules-to-be-adopted-without-uk-approval.

withdrawn. However, when withdrawal is made the material has already been scrutinised, and considered relevant, by the judges. It is difficult to maintain that it will exercise no influence whatsoever on them.

A second open question concerns the role that Member States courts play in reviewing the legality of EU sanctions. This is not an issue as regards UN anti-terrorism sanctions imposed under the auspices of Security Council Committee 1267 (the so-called Al Qaeda Sanctions Committee).[67] As is well known, the listing of individuals and entities by the Committee is based upon proposals of UN Member States, which take the form of official acts, such as orders, directions, decrees and so forth.[68] The right to challenge national acts concerning the proposal for inclusion of people in the Al Qaeda sanctions list has never been questioned. Indeed, there are a number of domestic judgments handed down by Member States' courts relating to these sanctions. Some of them are well known for their contributions to the judicial dialogue leading to the overall improvement of the anti-terrorism sanctions regime.[69] However, the justiciability of EU autonomous measures before domestic courts is much more controversial. For these measures, the decision to include people on the list is taken by the Council, albeit it is based on proposals from Member States. Under EU law, confirmed by well-settled ECJ case law, domestic courts do not have the power to declare Union acts invalid. They only have the power to assess the plausibility of invalidity claims brought before them, and to reject such claims should they find them manifestly unfounded. Should they instead consider that the acts in question might be invalid, they are under an obligation to pass the issue onto the ECJ, asking for a preliminary ruling.[70] This state of affairs is referred to as the *Foto-Frost* principle, after the main ECJ ruling affirming it. The reasons behind such jurisprudence involve the uniform interpretation and the very coherence of the EU legal order. Should domestic courts decisions diverge from one another, that coherence would be jeopardised.

However, why should a listed entity choose to challenge EU sanctions before domestic courts, instead of, or simultaneously with, challenging them before the EU Courts? The reasons why domestic courts might be preferred are various. In the first place, domestic courts can have a wider variety of remedies at their disposal. For example, in the *Vinck-Sayadi* case the Brussels Court of First Instance ordered the Belgian Government to

[67] See www.un.org/sc/suborg/en/sanctions/1267.

[68] See K Prost, 'Fair Process and the Security Council: a Case for the Office of the Ombudsperson' in A M Salinas De Frías, K L H Samuel and N D White (eds), *Counter-Terrorism: International Law and Practice* (Oxford, Oxford University Press, 2012).

[69] See, to name but the most famous ones, *HM Treasury v Mohammed Jabar Ahmed and others* [2010] UKSC 2 and 5, and the decision of the Brussels Court of First Instance, which ended up before the UN Human Rights Committee (n 71). See also Pantaleo (n 19) 164 ff.

[70] Case C-314/85, *Foto-Frost v Hauptzollamt Lübeck-Ost* [1987] ECR 04199, paras 13 ff.

request from Security Council Committee 1267 the applicants' removal from the list of suspected terrorists, 'à peine d'une astreinte de 250 euros par jour de retard, à compter de l'expiration du délai de 30 jours à partir de la signification du présent jugement'.[71] Such a creative remedy could hardly be given by the EU Courts, whose available instruments seem to be limited to annulment and, at the utmost, compensation of damages. As regards damages, another reason why domestic courts might be preferred is precisely connected with the applicants' chance to obtain reparation for material and non-material losses. In theory, the EU Courts can require EU institutions to pay compensation. In practice, in the field of sanctions they have awarded (non-material) damages only in one case, and the amount granted was significantly lower than what was claimed.[72] In this respect, domestic courts may also appear more attractive, especially in view of the fact that such courts may be more familiar than the EU Courts with questions concerning the non-contractual liability of the State. Another reason justifying the bringing of domestic proceedings relates to the EU Courts' reluctance to grant interim measures. As a matter of principle, the Courts have stated that they have the power to grant such measures.[73] However, this has never occurred in practice so far. Finally, a very simple, yet quite relevant factor that may justify preference for domestic courts is that cases in Luxembourg may take years to be adjudicated. In certain Member States—but certainly not in all of them—judicial decisions can be obtained much more quickly.

To begin with, domestic courts—mostly in the UK—rejected challenges of EU restrictive measures for want of jurisdiction over the Union's acts. In dismissing an application for interim measures brought by an Iranian company, the English High Court famously held that the applicant had 'taken the wrong point in the wrong court with the wrong defendant'.[74] However, the English courts' attitude towards EU restrictive measures may be changing. In an action brought by Mr John Bredenkamp, a businessman who was listed in the sanctions regime against Zimbabwe upon proposal from the UK, the English High Court has already issued two preliminary judgments. Mr Bredenkamp is seeking to obtain a declaration that the proposal was unlawful as a form of reparation.[75] In the first

[71] The decision in question is not published. However, some excerpts are reported and commented by M Arcari, 'Sviluppi in tema di tutela degli individui iscritti nelle liste dei comitati delle sanzioni del Consiglio di Sicurezza' (2007) 90 *Rivista di Diritto Internazionale* 659.

[72] Case T-384/11, *Safa Nicu Sepahan v Council* (GC, 25 November 2014) paras 45–152.

[73] See Order of the President in Case T-5/13, *Iran Liquefied Natural Gas v Council*, case in progress.

[74] *Melli Bank Plc v Her Majesty's Treasury* [2008] EWHC 1661 (Admin) para 82.

[75] For a summary of the factual and legal background of the case, see *John Arnold Bredenkamp v The Secretary of State for Foreign and Commonwealth Affairs* [2012] EWHC 3297 (Admin) paras 1–39.

judgment, which concerned the possible lack of jurisdiction pursuant to the *Foto-Frost* principle, the High Court retained jurisdiction over the case. In principle, it acknowledged the validity of the *Foto-Frost* principle. However, it found that the principle would not be infringed if the Court retained jurisdiction in the case in point. This was so because the judgment concerned the legality of the UK's proposal, and of its refusal to request delisting, which was a purely domestic issue that did not imply an automatic, inevitable ruling on the lawfulness of the EU's measures.[76] In the second preliminary judgment, the High Court ordered the Government to disclose documents and material relied upon by it in proposing the claimant's designation.[77]

The significance of this case may be limited by the fact that the EU Courts have in the meantime changed their position concerning the interest of delisted persons to continue proceedings. Mr Bredenkamp had his action dismissed by the GC because, pending the judgment, he had been delisted.[78] As already noted, some months later the ECJ overruled the GC on the point, stating that delisted persons still have an interest in seeking a final judgment precisely for the reasons put forth by Mr Bredenkamp in his claim before the English courts (ie as a form of non-material reparation). However, the potential impact of the High Court's ruling on the ECJ's exclusive jurisdiction ought not to be underestimated. In my view, the High Court's findings are largely misplaced, and should be overruled in the final judgment. The High Court based its understanding of the *Foto-Frost* principle on a Supreme Court judgment handed down in the context of Al Qaeda sanctions, where jurisdiction over the measures was retained.[79] As already pointed out, there are substantial differences between those sanctions and EU-autonomously imposed sanctions. First, in the Al Qaeda sanctions regime, the proposal for designation takes the form of a national decision, which is—materially and conceptually—separated from that of the Committee. This does not hold true in respect of EU autonomous measures, where designation is made directly by the Council. Indeed, the High Court itself acknowledged the situation, stating that there

> was in practice no workable distinction between the Council Decision itself and the participation of the Foreign Secretary or UK officials in a decision-making

[76] Ibid paras 49–50.

[77] See *John Arnold Bredenkamp v The Secretary of State for Foreign and Commonwealth Affairs* [2013] EWHC 2480 (Admin) paras 21–50. At the time of writing, the case is still pending and awaiting a final decision.

[78] See Order in Case T-145/09, *Bredenkamp and Others v Commission*. It is worth noting that Mr Bredenkamp has apparently lodged another application at the GC's registry (Case T-66/14, *Bredenkamp and Others v Council and Commission*, in progress). Although the content of his request has yet to be made public, it seems plausible that Mr Bredenkamp is seeking some sort of compensation for his unlawful listing.

[79] See *HM Treasury v Mohammed Jabar Ahmed and others* (n 69).

process involving all Member States. There was no prior decision-making by the Foreign Secretary, followed by a separate Council decision-making process.[80]

Secondly, the Supreme Court judgment referred to one of the main reasons for retaining jurisdiction was that there was no judicial remedy available at UN level. If there had been, the Supreme Court appeared to suggest that it would have applied—or, at least, considered—a sort of equivalent protection doctrine, thus declining jurisdiction.[81]

The assumption on which the Supreme Court based its reasoning—the lack of judicial remedies at the UN level—does not apply to the EU. To paraphrase the High Court, it seems safe to conclude that, when it comes to EU-autonomously imposed sanctions, the right place to challenge them is Luxembourg, and the right defendant is the Council. This is the case no matter what the position of the Member State concerned was in the Council at the time of designation, and what steps has it taken afterwards. The Council is a collegiate body and the positions of its components are not severable, either technically or conceptually. Any fictitious separation between the Council and Member States action in this field, in addition to jeopardising the coherence of the EU legal order, could lead to an undesirable forum shopping.

Another issue has emerged in recent times in the context of bilateral sanctions regime. It appears that the standards of review applied by European Courts are not always massively consistent. In particular, there have been a few recent instances where the standards applied were seemingly less strict both in reviewing the evidential basis for designation of individuals, and in assessing the existence of their actual involvement in the contested State's conduct. As is well known, the basic principles for reviewing the lawfulness of bilateral sanctions regimes were set out in *Tay Za*. In that case, the ECJ stated that the link between the affected person and the relevant State's conduct had to be established by means of precise, concrete and individualised evidence. In particular, the Court rejected the idea that listing decisions could be based on assumptions. In the case in point, the assumption was that family members of those who were in charge of businesses that benefited from the government's repressive policies were necessarily linked to those contested policies.[82] The Courts have been following *Tay Za* more or less constantly for quite some time. In this sense, they have exercised a full factual and legal scrutiny of the measures, often ordering the annulment of the measures at stake for want

[80] See *John Arnold Bredenkamp v The Secretary of State for Foreign and Commonwealth Affairs* (n 75) para 48.

[81] See *HM Treasury v Mohammed Jabar Ahmed and others* (n 69) paras 78 ff.

[82] See *Tay Za v Council* (n 32).

of sufficient evidence or actual involvement of the affected persons in the contested State's conduct.[83]

However, this rigorous review seems to be absent in some recent decisions. In *Anbouba*, the applicant was placed on the Syrian sanctions list for being president of an agro-industrial company, which the Council deemed to be supportive of the Syrian Government by providing it with financial and logistic assistance. The applicant claimed that the Council's allegation was based on a mere presumption, since it did not provide any inculpatory evidence. According to him, vague allegations like those put forward by the EU institutions resulted in an inadmissible shift of the burden of proof, and were in breach of his due process rights. His actual participation in the contested government policies needed to be proved.[84] As one can easily see, the applicant's argument resembled quite clearly the ECJ's findings in *Tay Za*. However, surprisingly the GC upheld the Council's allegations. It did so by stating that, given the circumstances of the case, it was reasonable to ground the listing on a presumption, or 'règle d'expérience commune' as the GC put it.[85] In particular, the GC held that it was justified to presume that a businessman, in a repressive regime like Syria, could not really prosper unless he benefited from the regime's favour, giving in exchange of this favour some kind of support. The judgment has recently been confirmed on appeal by the ECJ.[86] The same line of reasoning was applied by the GC in another Syrian ruling concerning the *Makhlouf* case. In the case in point the applicant was listed for being the uncle and an associate of President Bashar Al-Assad. The applicant objected, among other things, that the decision to place him on the list was unlawful in view of the fact that it was only based on consanguinity. His involvement in the violent repression of individual rights perpetrated by the Syrian regime was not proved. The GC, however, rejected the applicant's argument on the ground that 'l'extrême proximité de liens' between him and the President would in itself justify his placing on the list.[87] In my view, the type of assumptions admitted in *Anbouba* and *Makhlouf* are exactly the same ones that the ECJ had itself meant to rule out in *Tay Za*.[88]

The GC also took a similar view in the *Gossio* judgment. In the case in point, the applicant was listed for being the general director of Abidjan's

[83] See, among many, Case T-489/10, *Islamic Republic of Iran Shipping Lines and Others v Council* (GC, 16 September 2013) paras 56–61.

[84] Case T-592/11, *Anbouba v Council* (GC, 13 September 2013) paras 35–39.

[85] Ibid para 48. The judgment is currently only available in French.

[86] Case C-605/13 P, *Anbouba v Council* (ECJ, 21 April 2015) paras 80–83.

[87] Case T-509/11, *Mohammad Makhlouf v Council* (GC, 21 January 2015) para 75. At the time of writing, the judgment is only available in French.

[88] The same approach has emerged in other Syrian cases. See, among others, Case T-593/11, *Al Chihabi v Council* (GC, 30 April 2015).

harbour. Since the harbour was controlled by Laurent Gbagbo's illegal administration, the applicant was automatically deemed to be supportive of the regime. Mr Gossio claimed that the Council failed to prove his support for Gbagbo's administration. He also claimed that vague and stereotyped allegations—the Council designated other persons on identical or very similar grounds—were equivalent to no motivation at all. However, the GC found that the applicant, given his position, could not be unaware of the fact that resources coming from Abidjan's harbour contributed to the financing of Gbagbo's administration. That circumstance was already enough to justify his designation, and the Council did not have to prove the nature and the extent of the support provided by the applicant.[89] In my view, the *Tay Za* principle, as further developed in later cases, clearly requires the EU institutions to provide evidence of the actual involvement of targeted persons in the State's conduct that generated the sanctions. It is not easy to see the link between the fact of being director of Abidjan's harbour and the serious violations of human rights and humanitarian law perpetrated by Laurent Gbagbo and his acolytes. Nor is it easy to see, in the mere fact of being director of a harbour, a wish to contribute financially to a government's policies.

The ECJ has added another piece to this puzzle in the recent *Kala Naft* case. This case concerned Iranian sanctions imposed on a company, owned by National Iranian Oil Company (NIOC), for being allegedly the central purchasing body for the oil, gas and petrochemical divisions of the NIOC group. The Court held that trading in key equipment and technology for the gas and oil industry was, in itself, 'capable of being regarded as support for the nuclear activities of the Islamic Republic of Iran', in view of the fact that the concept of 'support' 'implies a lesser degree of connection to Iran's nuclear activities than "engagement" or "direct association", and that it is capable of covering the procurement of or trade in goods and technology linked to the gas and oil industry'.[90] Hence, the link between the company's activities and nuclear proliferation was sufficiently established. This decision appears questionable. The ECJ seemed to have assumed that an assertion contained in the preamble to Security Council Resolution 1929 (2010) provided, among other things, the basis for concluding that trading in the oil and gas sector was, in itself, necessarily linked to nuclear proliferation.[91] As it has been correctly pointed out, the ECJ erred both in grounding its decision on an assertion in the

[89] Case T-130/11, *Gossio v Council* (GC, 25 April 2013) paras 39–53. The listing of Mr Gossio has been quashed in a later judgment but on different grounds. See Case T-406/13, *Gossio v Council* (GC, 14 January 2015) paras 81–90.

[90] Case C-348/12 P, *Council v Manufacturing Support & Procurement Kala Naft* (ECJ, 28 November 2013) paras 80–83.

[91] Ibid para 81.

preamble of a resolution, which was not reiterated in its operative part, and in applying such interpretation retrospectively to pre-existing EU measures—namely, Regulation 423/2007.[92]

This strand of decisions seems to be a step backwards away from the ECJ's previous own case law concerning bilateral sanctions regimes. In my view, the principle that the EU institutions must demonstrate the actual and specific involvement of listed entities in the contested State's conduct should not be departed from. Otherwise, any activity of economic relevance can potentially be regarded as supportive of a certain State policy. One might fear, however, that the EU Courts' lax position taken in some recent cases, is expressive of an undesirable change in the European Courts' approach towards restrictive measures.[93]

V. CONCLUSIONS

This chapter has tried to provide the reader with a comprehensive summary of the current state of play concerning EU case law in the field of international economic sanctions. On the one hand, the EU judicature has greatly contributed to the progressive application of principles of the rule of law to such sanctions. On the other hand, there are still several unresolved issues, and perhaps more will arise in the future.

In these conclusions I would like to point out what appear, in my view, to be possible symptoms of a regression. Two events are worth mentioning. First, in October 2010 the Central Bank of Iran (CBI) was subjected to restrictive measures. CBI has challenged the measures and won the first battle.[94] The GC quashed its listing because the reason adduced by the Council, namely CBI's involvement in activities to circumvent sanctions, was inadequate in that it lacked sufficient detail. In particular, the GC stated that the statement of reasons contained 'no details of the names of persons, entities or bodies, [...] whom the applicant assisted in circumventing sanctions or of when, where and how that assistance took place'. The GC seemed to apply a *Tay Za*-like standard. In October 2012, CBI was re-listed and the Council included 'financial support to the Government' as an additional reason. In the resulting, later judgment rendered

[92] See P-E Dupont, 'The ECJ and (Mis)interpretation of Security Council Resolutions: The Case of Sanctions Against Iran' (EJIL: Talk!, 23 December 2013) available at: www.ejiltalk.org/the-ecj-and-misinterpretation-of-security-council-resolutions-the-case-of-sanctions-against-iran.

[93] In a more recent GC's judgment the concept of 'logistical support' was also interpreted very broadly. See Case T-95/14, *Iran Offshore Engineering and Construction Co v Council* (GC, 25 June 2015) paras 80–83.

[94] See Case T-262/12, *Central Bank of Iran v Council* (GC, 18 September 2014).

against CBI the GC endorsed a very broad interpretation of the notion of 'support'. It stated that such notion includes

> any activity of the person or entity concerned which, regardless of any direct or indirect link established with nuclear proliferation, is capable, by its quantitative or qualitative significance, of encouraging that proliferation, by providing the Government of Iran with support in the form of resources or facilities of a material, financial or logistical nature which allow it to pursue nuclear proliferation.[95]

The GC recognised that the statement of reasons in such case 'refers implicitly but necessarily to the functions and powers of the applicant as the central bank of the Islamic Republic of Iran'.[96]

Without going into too much detail, suffice it to say that the designation of a country's central bank seems to contradict the very idea of targeted sanctions. Central banks normally serve as depositary of States' reserves. In this sense, it would be difficult to deny that—but at the same time otiose to ask whether—a central bank financially supports a certain State's conduct, including nuclear proliferation. It is not easy to see how targeted, or smart, can the sanctioning of the central bank be, or, indeed, that of the stock exchange, railway company, motorways agency and so forth of a given country (in other words, the core administrative structures of that country). It would be tantamount to the imposition of general sanctions but with identified targets. This is not to say that branches of a State's administration should always, and by definition, be exempted from targeted sanctions. If there are individualised reasons to designation of, say, a central bank, the latter should be listed on those grounds. The suspicion, however, is that the EU institutions are increasingly using alternative forms of sanctions, possibly in the attempt to attenuate the impact of judicial challenges.[97] In such case the listing criteria inevitably become

[95] See Case T-563/12, *Central Bank of Iran v Council* (GC, 25 March 2015) para 66.

[96] Ibid para 85.

[97] The same holds true in respect of the recent placing on the list of the European subsidiary of the State-owned North Korea National Insurance Company (KNIC). It is meaningful that the reasons for listing state that KNIC is generating resources that '*could* contribute to the DPRK's nuclear-related, ballistic missile-related or other weapons of mass destruction-related programmes' (emphasis added). See Commission Implementing Regulation (EU) 2015/1062 of 2 July 2015 amending Council Regulation (EC) No 329/2007 concerning restrictive measures against the Democratic People's Republic of Korea [2015] OJ L174/16. Indeed, whatever revenue the State generates through its agency and offshoots *could* in theory be used for unlawful purposes. The fact remains that KNIC is, among other things, also supposed to compensate—perhaps not according to massively fair rules—North Korean victims of natural disasters. It is clear that the imposition of sanctions will affect also its ability to operate as insurer. The collateral effects of such sanctions on the potential beneficiaries of KNIC insurance policies could therefore be severe. In this sense, it becomes more and more difficult to see the differences between targeted and general sanctions.

broader and the judicial scrutiny less intense. In my opinion, however, these developments are at odds with the need for fairer and more accountable sanctions regimes.

Second, the EU is increasingly resorting to more traditional forms of sanctions, such as general prohibitions on certain types of trade and transactions. This has already been done in the Iranian and Syrian regimes.[98] Both the GC and the ECJ have declined jurisdiction in challenges to these sanctions under Article 275 of the TFEU.[99] As is well known, smart sanctions were created as a response to the criticism attracted by comprehensive sanctions, which caused considerable collateral damages to the civilian population, without being very effective in terms of policy results obtained.[100] To borrow from a prominent scholar, general sanctions were seen as taking 'hostage the population in order to force the leadership' to take the desired action.[101] Created as a policy tool susceptible of overcoming fundamental rights issues raised by traditional measures, targeted sanctions have been challenged on similar grounds, namely fundamental rights concerns. The difference is that, in the case of targeted sanctions, those challenges have taken place at the judicial level. Comprehensive sanctions seem to have the advantage of not being subject to judicial review, but only to moral and political review.

It would be a curious, and perhaps sadly ironic, twist of fate if the attempt to apply principles of the rule of law to international economic sanctions would result in a comeback of less targeted—and less equitable—forms of sanctions, which would take us some 25 years backwards.

[98] Council Decision 2010/413/CFSP of 26 July 2010 concerning restrictive measures against Iran and repealing Common Position 2007/140/CFSP [2010] OJ L195/39. As for Syria, Council Decision 2013/255/CFSP of 31 May 2013 concerning restrictive measures against Syria [2013] OJ L147/14.

[99] Case T-509/10, *Manufacturing Support & Procurement Kala Naft v Council* (GC, 25 April 2012) paras 34–39.

[100] See the thorough analysis of M Shervin Majlessi, 'Economic Sanctions in the United Nations Security System: Recent Developments' in L-A Sicilianos and L Picchio Forlati (eds), *Les sanctions économiques en droit international / Economic Sanctions in International Law* (Leiden, Martinus Nijhoff, 2004).

[101] See L-A Sicilianos, 'Sanctions Institutionnelle et Contre-Mesures: Tendances Récentes' in Sicilianos and Picchio Forlati (eds), *Les sanctions* (n 100) 81. The original French text, translated by the author, reads 'prendre la population en otage pour forcer la volonté des dirigeants'.

9

United States Sanctions: Delisting Applications, Judicial Review and Secret Evidence

RACHEL BARNES

I. INTRODUCTION

THIS CHAPTER PROVIDES an overview of the legal structure of domestic US sanctions. There are differences between the standards of due process available to those whose cases are determined solely by reference to the rules established under the sanctions' statutory schemes and those with sufficient connections to the US that they can also rely on the greater protections of the US Constitution. This chapter identifies and discusses those differences and offers some brief comparisons with approaches adopted by both English and EU courts.

The United States of America has had an unbroken record since the Second World War (WWII) of using economic sanctions as a tool of foreign policy. Accompanying this is a long-standing perception within US government circles that, as the USA is the major player within the global economy, restricting access to US markets can effectively augment diplomatic efforts to achieve particular foreign policy goals. Especially over the past 15 years, the US has provided an example to which other States and international organisations have looked when developing their own economic sanctions regimes. Accordingly, the US has had significant influence in the modern development of economic sanctions as tools of collective security and foreign policy within the UN and EU systems and in the municipal laws of other States. An understanding of the US domestic sanctions regime can inform the debates about sanctions in those other settings.

That said, the development of the applicable legal frameworks of targeted economic sanctions over the past decade has been driven largely by domestic and regional litigation outside the US, notably within the European Union Courts. Immediately after 2001, the debate focused on the extent to which judicial or even quasi-judicial protections were or should be available to individuals and entities named on sanctions blacklists. Now, however, the debate engages more detailed questions about the content of the protections that are or should be available. This includes the use of classified material (ie secret evidence) to justify listing decisions and how that material is managed in the course of legal challenges to such decisions. This chapter provides an overview of this issue in the context of US financial sanctions and listing decisions by the US Treasury's Office of Foreign Assets Control (OFAC). It considers recent US case law and draws some comparisons with approaches in the EU and the UK.[1]

Like the EU and the UK, the US domestic sanctions regimes are draconian asset freezing measures backed by criminal penalties as well as significant civil fines and forfeiture for regulatory breaches. Each breach of the OFAC regulations may attract a civil penalty of US$250,000 or twice the amount of the transaction at issue, while a wilful breach of the regulations is a criminal offence carrying a maximum penalty of 20 years' imprisonment and a US$1 million fine.[2] Sanctions listing decisions themselves do not directly result in individuals being held in detention. Nonetheless, they have profound, draconian effects on the lives of listed individuals, who have not necessarily been convicted of any criminal offence, and those closely connected to them, such as cohabiting family members.[3] Where the listed person is a commercial and charitable entity, those who rely on that entity for employment or social assistance such as education or health care can also be significantly affected. Although these draconian effects have been recognised by courts in both the EU and the US, the extent of judicial deference to executive decisions has been markedly different. The deference of the US courts to executive decision-making in sanctions cases and consequently, the circumscribed nature of legal challenges to those

[1] This chapter considers the financial sanctions regime only (the OFAC regime) and not the separate export or trade sanctions regime.

[2] Title 50 of the United States Code, s 1705 ('50 USC §1705'). By way of example, in 2012 civil penalties were levied against the European banks, HSBC and ING Bank, NV in the sums of US$375 million and US$617 million respectively. See OFAC Enforcement Action Information for 11 December 2012 and 12 June 2012 respectively, available at: www.treasury.gov/resource-center/sanctions/CivPen/Pages/2012.aspx.

[3] Observations by members of the UK Supreme Court in *Ahmed v HM Treasury* [2010] UKSC 2 on the draconian nature of counter-terrorism sanctions are now familiar. Lord Brown described it thus, at 192: 'The draconian nature of the regime imposed under these asset-freezing Orders can hardly be over-stated. … [T]hey are scarcely less restrict of the day to day life of those designated (and in some cases their families) than are control orders. In certain respects, indeed, they could be thought even more paralysing'. Lord Hope, at 60, referred to listed persons as, by operation of the sanctions against them, 'effectively prisoners of the state'.

decisions, is explained, at least in part, by the wartime inception of OFAC and its unbroken institutional development thereafter in the context of international conflict and situations characterised internally as national emergencies.

This chapter describes *how* classified material is managed rather than *whether* secret evidence should ever be used to justify administrative decisions. It considers classified material in general rather than the distinct issues that may arise from particular types of classified material, such as intelligence obtained through torture. In respect of US constitutional rights, this chapter focuses only on due process rights arising under the Fifth Amendment, which provides that 'no person shall be … deprived of life, liberty, or property, without due process of law'. A number of the recent US sanctions cases also examine rights under the Fourth Amendment (searches and seizures without warrants) and the First Amendment (freedom of speech and association); these give rise to significant and distinct issues and space does not permit their consideration in this chapter.

II. OFAC SANCTIONS—A MODEL OF ECONOMIC WARFARE

WWII is a convenient historical starting point, although the use of economic sanctions as a tool of US foreign policy and security precedes it. For example, the Joint Resolution of Congress of 22 April 1898 empowered the President to establish trade embargoes and enabled restrictions on exports of coal and war material immediately prior to the Spanish-American War; President Theodore Roosevelt later relied on the 1898 Resolution as the legislative authority for the US embargo of the Dominican Republic in 1905 when the US intervened against the revolutionaries there.[4] Another early twentieth-century example of the US use of economic sanctions—this time not in a conflict in which the US was directly involved—was the Joint Resolution of Congress and Presidential Proclamation of 28 May 1934, which established an arms embargo on the belligerents in the Chaco War (Bolivia and Paraguay) to foster a pacific resolution of the conflict. The breach of this arms embargo was an offence under US law.[5]

OFAC's forerunner was created in WWII under the name of the Office of Foreign Funds Control (OFFC). Its wartime role was to freeze the US-based assets of Nazi-occupied States and their nationals to prevent

[4] K Alexander, *Economic Sanctions: Law and Public Policy* (Basingstoke, Palgrave Macmillan, 2009) 13.

[5] *United States v Curtiss-Wright Export Corp.*, 299 US 304, 325 (1936).

enforced repatriation and seizure by Germany[6] and, when the US entered the war, to freeze enemy assets and block foreign trade and financial transactions with or for the benefit of the enemy.[7] OFFC worked closely with its British counterpart, the Ministry of Economic Warfare (MEW).[8] OFFC and MEW developed and administered complex, comprehensive and sophisticated regimes of asset freezing and other economic control measures which included extensive use of blacklists of economic actors deemed to be part of or otherwise assisting enemy nations. Prior to the official declarations of war President F D Roosevelt established the 'Proclaimed List of Certain Blocked Nationals', by which persons named on the list would be treated as if they were nationals of Germany or Italy and so subject to the asset freezing and blocking measures established under the Trading With the Enemy Act 1917 (TWEA) and Executive Order (EO) 8389.[9] The List published on 17 July 1941 ran to 17 pages of the Federal Register and named hundreds of natural and legal persons based in Latin American countries.[10] Similarly, in the UK the Board of Trade issued lists of Specified Persons under the Trading with the Enemy Act 1939.[11] In both the US and the UK, dealing with the assets of or transacting with these listed persons without a licence was a criminal offence.[12]

After WWII, the US maintained the institutional capacity it had developed during the war and continued its asset freezing and financial blocking measures, now in the context of the Cold War. In December

[6] This first happened on 10 April 1940 when, pursuant to s 5(b) of the Trading with the Enemy Act 1917 (40 Stat 411), President Roosevelt prohibited the transfer of property in which Denmark or Norway or any national thereof had an interest without Treasury approval; see Executive Order (EO) 8389 (5 Federal Register (FR) 1400). As German occupation in Europe expanded, so did the sanctions to cover property in which interests were held by, or by nationals of, the Netherlands, Belgium or Luxembourg (EO 8405, 10 May 1940, 5 FR 1677); France (EO 8446, 17 June 1940, 5 FR 2279); Latvia, Estonia and Lithuania (EO 8484, 15 July 1940, 5 FR 2586); Romania (EO 8565, 10 October 1940, 5 FR 4062); Bulgaria (EO 8701, 4 March 1941, 6 FR 1285); Hungary (EO 8711, 13 March 1941, 6 FR 1443); Yugoslavia (EO 8721, 24 March 1941, 6 FR 1622); and Greece (EO 8746, 28 April 1941, 6 FR 2187). See EO 8785 of 14 June 1941 (6 FR 2897) in relation to other countries including Germany and Italy.

[7] For a concise but detailed description of the TWEA asset freezing and economic warfare programme in the US during WWII, see M Malloy, 'US International Banking and Treasury's Foreign Assets Controls: Springing Traps for the Unwary' (1989) 8 *Annual Review of Banking Law* 181, 186–87.

[8] By 1940 the MEW was staffed by over 1000 civil servants; see HC Deb 23 July 1940, Vol 363 Col 572.

[9] Proclamation 2497 (17 July 1941, 6 FR 3555–56). On 26 July 1941 all Japanese assets in the US were frozen, following the Japanese occupation of French Indo-China on 24 July 1941; see EO 8832 (29 July 1941, 6 FR 3716).

[10] 6 FR 3557–73.

[11] See eg the Trading with the Enemy (Specified Persons) Order of 13 Sept 1939 (SR&O, 1939, No 1166); the Trading with the Enemy (Specified Persons) (Amendment) (No 4) Order of 23 Dec 1939 (SR&O 1939 No 1875).

[12] TWEA 1917 (50 USC App III, ss 3, 16); Trading with the Enemy Act 1939 c 89, s 1, respectively.

1950, TWEA was again invoked when President Truman declared a national emergency following the entry of China into the Korean War, blocked all Chinese and North Korean assets subject to US jurisdiction and established the Division, later the Office, of Foreign Assets Control.[13] Thereafter, TWEA continued to be used since the legislation permitted the President to establish economic sanctions both '[d]uring the time of war or during any other period of national emergency declared by [him]', until its amendment in 1977.[14]

Following the enactment of the National Emergencies Act 1976 and the limitation of emergency powers available to the President under TWEA to times of war only, Congress adopted the International Emergency Economic Powers Act 1977 (IEEPA), which in large part replicated the President's TWEA emergency powers, applicable in peacetime crises.[15] Like the TWEA, this other main legislative plank of OFAC powers post-WWII requires a declaration of national emergency by the President before he may impose financial transactions controls.[16] By definition therefore, almost every episode of the imposition of financial sanctions in the US is in response to a declared national emergency, which is relevant to understanding the courts' traditional deference in sanctions cases.[17]

The IEEPA envisages control over presidential actions by way of Congressional oversight. It requires the President to report to Congress whenever he exercises any of the delegated powers under the statute, to explain and justify his actions and to provide six-monthly reports thereafter.[18] US courts have not been receptive to arguments that this Congressional oversight function is an insufficient control on delegated executive power and that the Act is an unconstitutional delegation of legislative authority to the Executive.[19]

Far from robustly scrutinising and limiting this exercise of draconian executive power designed to deal with times of extraordinary national

[13] Proclamation No 2914 of 16 December 1950. See Malloy, 'US International Banking and Treasury's Foreign Assets Controls' (n 7) 188; National Archives of the United States, *Guide to Federal Records: Records of the Office of Foreign Assets Control*, www.archives.gov/research/guide-fed-records/groups/265.html#top; US Dept of Treasury, *Frequently Asked Questions and Answers: Sanctions*, available at: www.treasury.gov/resource-center/faqs/Sanctions/Pages/answer.aspx.

[14] TWEA 1917, s 5(b)(1), reproduced in *Regan v Wald*, 468 US 222, 227; 104 S Ct 3026, 3030 (1984) fn 2 (re OFAC's Cuban sanctions regulations).

[15] Malloy (n 7) 189–93. Supreme Court Justice Blackmun gave a detailed account of the legislative history of the IEEPA in his dissenting judgment in *Regan v Wald* (n 14) 244 ff.

[16] PL 95-223 (91 Stat 1626) codified at 50 USC §§ 1701 ff.

[17] This observation excludes those more recent sanctions programmes established by direct legislation rather than pursuant to the President's delegated powers under TWEA or IEEPA.

[18] 50 USC 1703(b), (c).

[19] *US v Amirnazmi*, 645 F 3d 564 (3d Cir 2011), cert denied 132 S Ct 347 (2011); *US v Mirza*, 454 Fed Appx 249 (5th Cir 2011).

crisis, Congress has instead co-opted this model of emergency legislation. Since 1977, the TWEA and IEEPA model has been replicated in numerous legislative instruments to establish additional economic sanctions programmes. These are often sponsored by Congressional groups acting independently of the presidential administration and in some instances promoting sanctions regimes that are stricter than those that have been promoted by the Executive.[20] In addition, the IEEPA itself has continued to be used as the basis for a variety of new sanctions programmes established by presidential Executive Orders, resulting in a constant state of emergency.[21] The upshot of this historical development of sanctions law and practice in the US is that a wartime model has become the norm. Notwithstanding the original legislative requirement of the existence of an 'unusual and extraordinary threat … to the national security, foreign policy, or economy of the United States' in respect of which the President must declare a national emergency,[22] this is a model that is now employed in normal, rather than extraordinary, times. It is against this background that the relatively sparse US case law has developed which has, in general, shown significant deference to the Executive in its actions relating to financial sanctions.

III. CHALLENGING A US SANCTIONS LISTING

A. Procedural Protections

The procedural protections available to a targeted person who challenges their listing decision and the level of judicial scrutiny that will be applied to such decisions differ according to whether the person can pray in aid

[20] eg Cuban Democracy Act 1992; Cuban Liberty and Democratic Solidarity Act 1996, PL 104-114 (the Helms-Burton Act) (codified at 22 USC 6021-6091); Iran and Libya Sanctions Act 1996, PL 104-172 (110 Stat 1541); Anti-terrorism and Effective Death Penalty Act 1996 (codified at 8 USC 1189, 18 USC 2339B); Foreign Narcotics Kingpin Designation Act 1999 (codified at 21 USC 1901–1908); Tom Lantos Block Burmese Jade (Junta's Anti-Democratic Efforts) Act 2008, PL 110-286; Comprehensive Iran Sanctions, Accountability, and Divestment Act 2010 (CISADA) PL 111-195 (124 Stat 1312) (codified at 22 USC 8501 ff); National Defense Authorization Act for Fiscal Year 2012 PL 112-81 (125 Stat 1298 at 1647) s 1245 (NDAA); Iran Threat Reduction and Syria Human Rights Act 2012, PL 112-158 (codified at 22 USC 8701 ff); Russia and Moldova Jackson-Vanik Repeal and Sergei Magnitsky Rule of Law Accountability Act of 2012, PL 112-208 (126 Stat 1496) ss 401–407; National Defense Authorization Act for Fiscal Year 2013, PL 112-239 (126 Stat 1632) ss 1241–1255 (incorporation of the Iran Freedom and Counter-Proliferation Act 2012).

[21] Recent examples include sanctions concerning North Korea (EO 13466, 27 June 2008, 73 FR 125); Persons undermining Democratic Processes or Institutions in Zimbabwe (EO 13288, 10 March 2003, 68 FR 46); Certain Persons Contributing to the Conflict in the Democratic Republic of the Congo (EO 13413, 31 October 2006, 71 FR 210); Transnational Criminal Organizations (EO 13581, 25 July 2011, 76 FR 144).

[22] 50 USC 1701(a).

the US Constitution. US persons (eg citizens, residents and companies incorporated within the US) have the protection of the Constitution, as do a small class of non-US persons. Non-US persons may only be able to raise constitutional claims in sanctions delisting cases if they can show substantial connections to the US,[23] which have predominately been interpreted as the acquiring or holding of property within the US.[24]

If the person does not have recourse to the US Constitution, he has only the minimal process provided by statute. Conversely, if he is able to assert constitutional rights these will augment the statutory scheme. This distinction contingent upon a listed person's nexus with the US can be contrasted with the situation under EU law. In the *Bank Mellat* and *Bank Saderat Iran* sanctions cases before the EU courts, the Council submitted that legal persons who were emanations of non-Member States could not rely upon the fundamental rights protection and guarantees of EU law. This submission was rejected by the General Court, the Advocate General and ultimately, by the Court of Justice in its decision in the *Bank Mellat* case.[25]

The conventional position in US case law, developed in the federal courts of the District of Colombia (DC), is that the extent of the additional constitutional due process protections that have been applied in OFAC cases has been relatively limited. As discussed below, in these cases the US courts have tended to focus on the flexible nature of due process rights under the Fifth Amendment to limit its scope. This conventional position has been unsettled slightly by some more recent decisions but it remains to be seen whether this will have any significant effect upon OFAC's procedure and practice in relation to listed persons who are, in contrast, unable to assert any constitutional rights.

[23] *People's Mojahedin Organization of Iran v US Depart of State* 182 F 3d 17, 22–23 (DC Cir 1999), cert denied, 120 S Ct 1846 (2000) ('*PMOI* (1999)'); applying *United States v Verdugo-Urquidez* 494 US 259, 268–71 (1990).

[24] *Kadi v Geithner* 2012 WL 898778 *21–22 (D DC), app dis 2012 WL 3243996 (DC Cir 2012) ('*Kadi* (2012)'). The *Kadi* Court also noted that in *Al-Aqueel v Paulson* 568 F Supp 2d 64 (D DC 2008), the substantial connections test was met so as to allow the petitioner who had frequently visited the US, was an officer of a US corporation and had assisted that corporation in acquiring property in the US, to raise a claim under the due process clause of the Fifth Amendment. Al-Aqueel could not, however, raise a Fourth Amendment claim in respect of the blocked assets which were overseas. See also *Ibrahim v Dept of Homeland Security* 669 F 3d 983 (9th Cir 2012) (as a consequence of inclusion on a terrorist 'No Fly' list, the plaintiff's US student visa was revoked when she was visiting her home country. The Court of Appeals held she was able to assert constitutional rights in challenging her inclusion on the 'No Fly' list due to her continuing substantial voluntary connections to the US including professional collaborations with US academics and personal friendships).

[25] Case T-496/10, *Bank Mellat v Council* [2013] All ER (D) 182 (Feb) paras 35–46; Case T-494/10, *Bank Saderat Iran v Council* (decision of 5 February 2013) paras 33–43; Case C-176/13 P, *Council v Bank Mellat* and Case C-200/13 P, *Council v Bank Saderat Iran* (AG's Opinion (26 February 2015) paras 43–44); Case C-176/13 P, *Council v Bank Mellat* (CJEU decision of 18 February 2016) paras 42–52.

B. Administrative Reconsideration of a Listing Decision—the Statutory Scheme

The Federal Regulations codify the mechanisms for seeking delisting from an OFAC blacklist.[26] This administrative reconsideration process must be exhausted before a designated person may seek judicial review of the decision to retain him on a blacklist. These OFAC regulations contain the statutory designation and delisting procedures but provide little substantive detail. For example, while the delisting procedures set out that the designated person 'may submit arguments or evidence that the person believes establishes that insufficient basis exists for the designation' or that the person 'also may propose remedial steps on the person's part, such as corporate reorganisation, resignation of persons from positions in a blocked entity, or similar steps, which the person believes would negate the basis for designation', there is no transparency regarding the factors that will be taken into account or the standards that will be applied during an administrative reconsideration of the designation.[27] This constructive ambiguity works to ensure OFAC's discretion under the regulations remains unfettered to the greatest extent possible.

There are three grounds upon which a request for administrative reconsideration may be made, namely where: (1) a party to blocked transactions claims that the funds in question have been blocked due to mistaken identity;[28] (2) a person believes that a sufficient basis for their designation does not exist;[29] or (3) a person proposes to take remedial measures which they believe would negate the basis for their designation.[30] Under the regulations there is no right to obtain a statement of reasons for the listing decision. Similarly, there is no statutory right to disclosure of unclassified material upon which the listing decision was based. After the applicant has submitted arguments and information to support his request, OFAC may request additional or corroborating information and clarification of certain issues,[31] initiating what could be a relatively lengthy dialogue between the two parties. This is in

[26] The Federal Register contains standard procedures across the economic sanctions programmes implemented and administered by OFAC: 31 CFR 501.101. These procedures apply to all persons on OFAC's consolidated list, the Specially Designated Nationals and Blocked Persons List (the SDN List) and on the Part 561 List of Foreign Financial Institutions subject to CISADA or NDAA prohibitions or conditions (see 31 CFR 561.801). The current version of the list is available at: www.treasury.gov/resource-center/sanctions/SDN-List/Pages/default.aspx.

[27] 31 CFR 501.807(a).

[28] 31 CFR 501.806.

[29] See (n 27).

[30] Ibid.

[31] 31 CFR 501.807(b).

many respects similar to the dialogue phase in the UN Ombudsperson's delisting process.[32]

During this administrative reconsideration process, the applicant has no right to an oral hearing before OFAC, although he or she may request one.[33] Whether that request will be granted is determined by officials within OFAC on a case-by-case basis. The *Kadi* case provides an example of this process, although it is an unusual case insofar as Mr Kadi could afford to instruct proactive and well-resourced US lawyers. Mr Kadi submitted three lengthy witness statements and numerous exhibits, his lawyers had at least four face-to-face meetings with OFAC officials between 2002 and 2003, and OFAC asked detailed questions in writing to which Mr Kadi submitted a 41-page response.[34]

Since at least the early-2000s, OFAC has compiled an unclassified Statement of the Case in respect of each listing decision both for internal government use and for the State Department to use in its negotiations with interested countries and international organisations (such as the UN Security Council) to persuade those actors to take parallel listing decisions.[35] There is no statutory requirement for this to be disclosed to the listed person, although in practice it may be in part. The disclosed document usually amounts to only a brief description of the alleged facts and will not provide the designee with detailed descriptions of the allegations against them, or describe the underlying information or evidence. This means that although a listed person has an opportunity to submit information, evidence and arguments in support of his application for reconsideration, any disclosed statements of reasons very often do not provide sufficient details necessary to enable listed persons to rebut with particularity very broad allegations.

The DC Court of Appeals is in the federal circuit in which the majority of OFAC cases are brought. It has described the administrative reconsideration process provided in the OFAC regulations as 'unlike the run-of-the-mill administrative proceeding, here there is no adversary hearing, no presentation of what courts and agencies think of as evidence, no advance notice to the entity affected by the Secretary's internal deliberations'[36] and there is no requirement for the Executive to provide procedures approximate to a trial, such as a right to confront and cross-examine witnesses.[37]

[32] A description of the Ombudsperson's 3-phase process for delisting requests is available at: www.un.org/sc/suborg/en/ombudsperson/procedure.

[33] 31 CFR 501.807(c).

[34] *Kadi* (2012) (n 24) *24.

[35] Testimony of Richard Newcomb (then Director of OFAC) before the House Financial Services Subcommittee on Oversight and Investigations, 16 June 2004, transcript ref. JS-1729, available at: www.treasury.gov/press-center/press-releases/Pages/js1729.aspx.

[36] *PMOI* (1999) (n 23) 19.

[37] *Holy Land Foundation for Relief and Development v Ashcroft* 333 F 3d 156, 164 (DC Cir 2003) ('*HLF* (2003)').

In other words, listed persons are often in a position in which they are unable to refute rather than simply to deny the essential allegations made against them.[38] In contrast to the courts in the UK and the EU, although they have noted these shortcomings the US courts have not required that a like process is made available to a listed person unless that person can rely on US constitutional rights.[39]

The decision whether to grant an applicant's request for delisting is generally made through an inter-agency process. This inter-agency process may include the Departments of Treasury, State, Defense, Homeland Security and Justice, the Federal Bureau of Investigation, the Central Intelligence Agency, the Drug Enforcement Agency and the White House.[40] Although the IEEPA regulations identify only OFAC as the decision-making body,[41] in some instances this inter-agency process has been formalised. For example, in respect of foreign terrorist organisation listings, the relevant legislation identifies the Secretary of State, in consultation with the Secretary of the Treasury and the Attorney General, as the decision-maker.[42] Similarly, under the Magnitsky Act sanctions against certain Russian officials, the responsibility for issuing a list of designated persons is delegated to the Treasury Department in consultation with the State Department.[43]

An applicant will be informed of a decision on a request for delisting in writing, if not the reasons for it.[44] In practice, OFAC may sometimes provide an unclassified memorandum of reasons at this stage. Again using the *Kadi* case as an example, when OFAC decided to refuse Mr Kadi's request for reconsideration in March 2004, it did provide an unclassified memorandum of reasons, running to 30 pages.[45]

C. Administrative Reconsideration—Additional Due Process Requirements of the US Constitution

As described above, under the statutory regime alone procedural rights are extremely limited: OFAC is under no statutory obligation to inform

[38] *Cf Bank Mellat v HM Treasury* [2010] EWCA Civ 483, [2012] QB 91, 97C, 6.

[39] For the US constitutional rights that may be available to some applicants for delisting from US sanctions lists, see section C below.

[40] See (n 35).

[41] 31 CFR 501.807(d).

[42] Anti-terrorism and Effective Death Penalty Act (AEDPA) s 302 (110 Stat 1214 at 1250), codified at 8 USC 1189(d)(4).

[43] Presidential Memorandum 'Delegation of Functions Under Sections 404 and 406 of Public Law 112-208' (5 April 2013) available at: www.whitehouse.gov/the-press-office/2013/04/05/presidential-memorandum-delegation-functions-under-sections-404-and-406-. The Magnitsky list was first published by OFAC on 12 April 2013, available at: www.treasury.gov/resource-center/sanctions/OFAC-Enforcement/Pages/20130412.aspx.

[44] 31 CFR 501.807(d).

[45] *Kadi* (2012) (n 24) *2.

the listed person of the basis for the designation and there is no right to request such information during the administrative reconsideration process.[46] In contrast, the position of those persons able to raise constitutional claims has improved over the past decade or so. The constitutional protections and the US courts' recourse to them are closer to, although by no means aligned with, the EU and UK jurisprudence in sanctions listing cases. However, it still seems that litigation or the threat of litigation is necessary before OFAC will act in accordance with this more rigorous process.

i. Disclosure of Non-Classified Portions of the Administrative Record

The due process clause of the Fifth Amendment of the US Constitution provides that no person shall be deprived of his property without due process of law. This requires the Executive to provide an applicant with notice of the non-classified information underpinning the designation decision and provide the designee with an opportunity to present in writing information, evidence or arguments to rebut the allegations made against them.[47] This notice must be pre-designation absent an assertion that this would endanger national security, in which case post-designation notice is sufficient, together with an opportunity for the listed person to present in writing information, evidence or arguments to rebut the allegations made against them.[48] In *People's Mojahedin of Iran v US Dept. of State*,[49] the DC Court of Appeals held that the Secretary of State had violated PMOI's due process rights by failing to grant it access to the non-classified portion of the administrative record and to allow it to make submissions in respect of that material prior to her decision to re-designate PMOI as a foreign terrorist organisation. Rather than quashing the listing outright, the Court remitted the case to the Secretary of State for a fresh listing decision in which she was required to take the decision after she had (1) made the non-classified information available to PMOI; (2) indicated which parts of it she considered sufficiently credible to rely upon; and (3) given the organisation an opportunity to comment upon the material.[50]

[46] 31 CFR 501.807. This difference between the statutory regime and the requirements of the due process clause of the Fifth Amendment are alluded to in *Al Haramain Islamic Foundation v US Treasury Dept* 660 F 3d 1019, 1029 (9th Cir 2011) ('*Al Haramain* (2011)').

[47] *National Council of Resistance of Iran v State Dept*, 251 F 3d 192, 208–09 (2001) ('*NCRI* (2001)'); *Global Relief Fund v O'Neill* 315 F 3d 748, 754 (2002) cert denied 2003 WL 21692662 ('*GRF* (2002)'). See also *Holy Land Foundation v Ashcroft* 219 F Supp 2d 57 (2002), aff'd 333 F 3d 156 (DC Cir 2003) ('*HLF* (2002)'); *Kadi* (2012) (n 24) *24.

[48] Ibid.

[49] *People's Mojahedin of Iran v US Dept of State* 613 F 3d 220, 230–31 (DC Cir 2010) ('*PMOI* (2010)').

[50] Ibid 230.

In the UK, the Supreme Court considered the question of pre- and post-designation notice in *Bank Mellat v HM Treasury (No 2)*. The Court held that the Bank had a common law right to prior notification of HM Treasury's intention to make it subject to economic sanctions and should have been given an opportunity to make representations before that decision was made.[51] In an attempt to maintain some margin of judgement or appreciation for the Executive and in recognition that in some situations financial restrictions might only effectively be applied without notice, the majority of the Supreme Court held that whether a right to prior consultation arose under the UK legislation should be determined on a case-by-case basis. The similarity between the US and UK law on this issue is that both the US Constitution and the English common law adopt a default position that requires pre-designation notice. The distinction lies in the judicial scrutiny that would be applied to a decision by the Executive that the circumstances are such that there should not be pre-designation notice. In the US, the courts will accept the Executive's bald assertion that pre-designation notice would endanger national security, whereas English courts will apply some measure of scrutiny, although in practice adopting a deferential approach to Executive decisions relating to national security.[52]

ii. Statement of Reasons

In two US sanctions cases it has been held that constitutional due process does require OFAC to provide notice of the reasons for a designation in addition to disclosure of the unclassified record.[53] In its 2012 decision in the *Al Haramain* litigation, the Ninth Circuit Court of Appeals rejected OFAC's argument that the flexible nature of constitutional due process meant that, relying upon earlier DC Court of Appeals decisions, those requirements could be met without providing notice of the reasons for a listing decision.[54] The Court stated that 'the opportunity to guess at the factual and legal bases for a government action does not substitute for actual notice of the government's intentions'.[55]

[51] *Bank Mellat v HM Treasury (No 2)* [2013] UKSC 39, 28–49, 178–92. In their dissenting judgments, Lords Hope and Reed highlighted that the construction of the statute strongly implies that Parliament envisaged a review mechanism only for those affected by HM Treasury directions and not a right of prior consultation, although the majority rejected the assertion that this was a necessary implication of the statutory language.

[52] See *R (Lord Carlile of Berriew QC) v Secretary of State for the Home Department* [2014] UKSC 60, [2014] 2 WLR 1404, 1418D–1426G at paras 21–34 per Lord Sumption JSC (citing *Bank Mellat (No 2)* (n 51) at para 21).

[53] *PMOI* (2010) (n 49); and *Al Haramain Islamic Foundation v US Treasury Dept* 686 F 3d 965, 986 (9th Cir 2012) ('*Al Haramain* (2012)').

[54] *Al Haramain* (2012) (n 53) 986.

[55] Ibid 986–87.

The *PMOI* and *Al Haramain* cases were both distinguished by the DC District Court in *Kadi* (2012).[56] Although Mr Kadi was not given a statement of reasons to which he could respond during the administrative reconsideration process, the District Court found that there was no breach of due process because his lawyers had met with OFAC officials face-to-face and OFAC had provided a five-page letter containing detailed questions relating to 12 'continued areas of concern—"the answers to which will help us issue a determination on the petition"'. The Court concluded that

> [t]he March 2004 OFAC Memorandum and the administrative record, including the back and forth exchanges with Kadi, show that OFAC considered all of Kadi's submissions and *explained its assessment of the evidence*. Therefore, it is clear that the requirements of due process were satisfied.[57]

One could attempt to reconcile *Kadi* (2012) with *PMOI* (2010) and *Al Haramain* (2012) on the basis that the District Court appeared to consider that, on the facts of the case, OFAC's explanation of its assessment of the evidence was equivalent to a statement of reasons. However, this is one of the difficult aspects of the *Kadi* decision and it bears emphasis that the Court was equivocal on the issue of whether Mr Kadi had standing to raise any constitutional claims in the first place. The District Court seemed untroubled by the fact that if an *ex post facto* justification for a listing decision (the March 2004 Memorandum) can be an adequate substitute for a pre-decision notice of reasons, it allows the Executive to move the goalposts in response to a listed person's representations rather than presenting a clear case for the listed person to answer. It is a classic exemplar of a shift in the usual burden of proof.

D. Judicial Review

i. Standard of Review

If the applicant is unsuccessful in his request for an administrative reconsideration of his designation and the application of economic sanctions against him, he may apply for judicial review of the decision. For sanctions designations under the IEEPA, the statutory standard of review limits the courts' determination to whether a decision was 'arbitrary, capricious, an abuse of discretion, or otherwise not in accordance with law'.[58] The same statutory standard is employed in respect of foreign

[56] *Kadi* (2012) (n 24).
[57] Ibid, emphasis added.
[58] 5 USC § 706(2)(A) (IEEPA).

terrorist organisation designations,[59] but as one of five discrete bases of review. When reviewing FTO designations, the statute requires that courts consider whether they are:

(A) arbitrary, capricious, an abuse of discretion, or otherwise not in accordance with law;
(B) contrary to constitutional right, power, privilege, or immunity;
(C) in excess of statutory jurisdiction, authority, or limitation, or short of statutory right;
(D) lacking substantial support in the administrative record taken as a whole or in classified information submitted to the court under paragraph (2), or
(E) not in accord with the procedures required by law.[60]

Neither statute provides a review of the merits of the administrative decision. For example, in the context of the various terrorist sanctions programmes, the question whether a listed person actually is a terrorist or an associate of a terrorist organisation (and so appropriately listed under the terms of those programmes) is non-justiciable.[61] Instead, the question for the courts is whether the Executive rationally made such a finding on the material before it. Similarly, whether that establishes a threat to US nationals or national security remains 'an unreviewable political question'.[62] In sanctions cases, the US courts have repeatedly underscored the highly deferential nature of their review.[63]

In comparison, in England and Wales the merits of HM Treasury's autonomous designation decisions are reviewed by the High Court on an application under section 26 of the Terrorist Asset-Freezing etc Act 2010 to assess whether it is: (1) reasonable to believe that the listed person is or has been involved in terrorist activity, or is owned, controlled or acting on behalf of such a person; and (2) necessary for purposes connected with protecting the public from terrorism that financial restrictions should be applied.[64] In such cases, the High Court can substitute its view on these questions for that of the Executive.

Other financial restrictions decisions by HM Treasury are reviewed by the High Court according to principles applicable to an application

[59] 8 USC 1189(c)(3)(A), codifying the relevant provisions of the Anti-Terrorism and Effective Death Penalty Act of 1996, Pub L No 104-132, 110 Stat 1214 (AEDPA). See eg *HLF* (2002) (n 47); *HLF* (2003) (n 37).

[60] 8 USC 1189(c)(3).

[61] *PMOI* (1999) (n 23) 23, 25; *People's Mojahedin Organiztion of Iran* 327 F 3d 1238, 1240, 1244 (2003) ('*PMOI* (2003)'); *HLF* (2003) (n 37) 159.

[62] *PMOI* (2010) (n 49) 223.

[63] See eg *Regan v Wald* (n 14) 242–43; *Paradissiotis v Rubin* 171 F 3d 983, 987 (5th Cir 1999); *Islamic American Relief Agency v Gonzalez* 477 F 3d 728, 732, 734 (DC Cir 2007) ('*Islamic American Relief Agency* (2007)'); *Holder v Humanitarian Law Project* 130 S Ct 2705, 2727–29 (2010); *Kadi* (2012) (n 24) *4.

[64] The standard for a final designation under the Act (see Terrorist Asset-Freezing etc Act 2010, s 2(1)).

for judicial review.[65] That standard does encompass a rationality review although, importantly, it is not limited to an assessment of the Executive's administrative record. In *Bank Mellat v HM Treasury*, an application to set aside HM Treasury's decision to impose financial sanctions against the Iranian Bank Mellat, the courts had to consider whether that decision was a proportionate response to the risk to the national interest that had been identified. In so doing, both the High Court (Mitting J) and the Court of Appeal gave 'great weight to the views of the Treasury endorsed by Parliament, about the risk to the national interests of the United Kingdom'.[66] These courts' judgments upholding HM Treasury's decision were overturned on appeal by the UK Supreme Court. Nonetheless, in his speech on the substantive issues in that case, Lord Sumption (with whom the majority of the Court agreed) reiterated the observations of Maurice Kay LJ in the Court of Appeal that the case lay in the areas of foreign policy and national security in which HM Treasury must be allowed a large margin of judgement in any assessment of the proportionality of its decision-making.[67] Indeed, the majority of the Supreme Court quashed HM Treasury's decision on procedural grounds and not on the substantive question. Similarly, in those cases in which the EU courts have been in a position to assess the lawfulness of autonomous EU listing decisions (because procedural requirements such as the disclosure of evidence have been met), those courts have generally adopted a relatively deferential approach to the Council's assessments and when considering the proportionality of the restrictive measures at issue.[68]

ii. Review is Limited to the Administrative Record

Consistent with this circumscribed review, a US court will make its determinations solely on the basis of the administrative record, which is submitted by the Executive and comprises the information upon which the designation decision was made.[69] This means that the administrative reconsideration process prior to litigation is the only opportunity that a listed person has to augment the administrative record with material that supports his case. Accordingly, in the *Kadi* litigation the District Court in

[65] Terrorist Asset-Freezing etc Act 2010, s 27; Counter-Terrorism Act 2008, s 63(3).

[66] *Bank Mellat v HM Treasury* [2011] EWCA Civ 1, [2012] QB 101, 121, 43, quoting Mitting J in the first instance decision.

[67] See (n 51) 21 per Lord Sumption; see also Lord Sumption's judgment in *R (Lord Carlile of Berriew QC)* (n 52) 21–35.

[68] See eg Case T-49/07, *Fahas v Council of the European Union* [2010] ECR II-05555, 83. See also Case C-380/09 P, *Melli Bank plc v Council of the European Union* (ECJ Grand Chamber, 13 March 2012) 53–64; Case C-548/09 P, *Bank Melli Iran v Council of the European Union* [2011] ECR I-11381, 111–17.

[69] 8 USC 1189(b)(2); *HLF* (2003)(n 37) 162; *PMOI* (2003) (n 61) 1242. See also *NCRI* (2001) (n 47) 196.

DC refused to consider decisions of courts in other jurisdictions quashing the application of financial sanctions against Mr Kadi because they were not part of the administrative record upon which the challenged decision by OFAC was made (these foreign decisions having post-dated the OFAC listing decision of March 2004).[70]

The administrative record may include hearsay evidence, intelligence data from US and foreign sources and information dated years earlier.[71] As described by the DC Court of Appeals, it may consist of little more than 'third hand accounts, press stories, material on the Internet or other hearsay regarding the [designated] organization's activities' without impairing the lawfulness of the government's decision.[72] Under the OFAC regulations classified information within the administrative record is presented to the court *in camera* and *ex parte*[73] (as discussed below, where listed persons can rely on constitutional claims there may be some relaxation of this strict approach).

In the equivalent English High Court proceedings to challenge HM Treasury designations, evidence is not limited to an administrative record but then disclosure of all the documents comprising that record would not be required, subject to the government's duty of candour. That duty requires that the defendant public authority in judicial review proceedings make full and fair disclosure necessary for the fair determination of the application, which would ordinarily include a document significant to its decision, subject to the specific procedure relating to closed material.[74]

iii. US Courts' Approaches to their Limited Review Function

The US courts have not shied away from highlighting the circumscribed nature of both the administrative process and their judicial review. The DC Court of Appeals has, for example, described the statutory scheme based as:

> unique … [in] the dearth of procedural participation and protection afforded the designated entity. At no point in the proceedings establishing the administrative record is the alleged terrorist organization afforded notice of

[70] *Kadi* (2012) (n 24) 8.

[71] *HLF* (2003) (n 37); *32 County Sovereignty Committee v Department of State*, 292 F 3d 797 DC Cir (2002).

[72] *PMOI* (1999) (n 23) 18; *NCRI* (2001) (n 47) 196.

[73] IEEPA, codified at 50 USC 1702(c); this subsection was added by the USA Patriot Act 2001, Pub Law 107-56 (115 Stat 272) s 106. The equivalent provision in the AEDPA 1996, now codified at eg 8 USC 1189(a)(3)(B), was included in that legislation as originally enacted; see PL 104-132 s 302(a) (110 Stat 1214 at 1249); *PMOI* (1999) (n 23) 18; *NCRI* (2001) (n 47) 197; *GRF* (2002) (n 47) 754; *PMOI* (2003) (n 61) 1240.

[74] *R (Bredenkamp) v Secretary of State for Foreign and Commonwealth Affairs* [2013] EWHC 2480 (Admin), paras 16–18, applying *Tweed v Parades Commission* [2006] UKHL 53, [2007] 1 AC 650.

> the materials used against it, or a right to comment on such materials or the developing administrative record.[75]

Thus, the Court continued, in any subsequent judicial review:

> the entity does not have the benefit of meaningful adversary proceedings on any of the statutory grounds [upon which a court may find the designation to be unlawful], other than procedural shortfalls so obvious a Secretary of State is not likely to commit them.[76]

To ensure that its denial of the applicant's complaint could not be interpreted as 'allowing the reputation of the Judicial Branch to be "borrowed by the political Branches to cloak their work in neutral colors of judicial action"', the DC Court of Appeals in the first *PMOI* case emphasised the limited nature of its review in these terms:

> We reach no judgment whatsoever regarding whether the material before the Secretary [the administrative record] is or is not true. As we wrote earlier, the record consists entirely of hearsay, none of it was ever subjected to adversary testing, and there was no opportunity for counter-evidence by the organizations affected.[77]

In its 2004 judgment in another PMOI-related case, *National Council of Resistance of Iran v State Department*, the DC Court of Appeals similarly observed that:

> it bears repeating that AEDPA does not permit us, in exercising our limited judicial review, to make any 'judgment whatsoever regarding whether the material before the Secretary is or is not true,' but allows us to inquire only whether the Secretary 'had enough information before [him] to come to the conclusion' [that he did].[78]

Despite these various remarks, some developments in the level of scrutiny applied to the Executive's determinations based on the administrative record can be detected over the past decade. In *Al Haramain* (2012), the Ninth Circuit Court of Appeals interpreted the 'arbitrary and capricious' standard of review as requiring a review of the administrative record for

[75] *NCRI* (2001) (n 47) 196; *PMOI* (2003) (n 61) 1240.

[76] *NCRI* (2001) (n 47) 197. See also *HLF* (2003) (n 37), in which the DC Court of Appeals described the 'arbitrary and capricious' standard of review in cases challenging Specially Designated Terrorist (SDT) and Specially Designated Global Terrorist (SDGT) designation under EO 12947 and EO 13224 respectively, as 'highly deferential'.

[77] *PMOI* (1999) (n 23) 25 (quotations omitted). The Court reiterated that its function was merely to determine whether the Secretary of State was rational in coming to her decision that the organisations were (1) foreign and (2) engaged in terrorist activities, on the basis of the information before her. It noted that '[h]er conclusion might have been mistaken, but that depends on the quality of the information in the reports she received—something we have no way of judging'.

[78] *NCRI*, 373 F 3d 152, 158 (DC Cir 2004) ('*NCRI* (2004)').

substantial evidence to support OFAC's factual findings,[79] although the relevant statute does not, unlike the AEPDA, specify a lack of 'substantial support in the administrative record' as a ground for striking down a listing decision. The DC Court of Appeals has also now more robustly scrutinised the Executive's decisions than in previous sanctions cases. In its judgment in *NCRI* (2004), the DC Court of Appeals refused to engage in any assessment of the credibility of the material in the administrative record. However, in its judgment in *PMOI* (2010), the Court of Appeals re-characterised this slightly. First, it repeated that the judicial review available under the AEDPA meant that 'it is emphatically not our province to second-guess the Secretary's judgment as to which affidavits to credit and upon whose conclusions to rely', quoting its decision in *NCRI*. However, the Court then went on to hold that because it had been charged by Congress with the task of assessing whether there was 'substantial support' in the administrative record for the designation, the fact that the Secretary had not indicated whether she regarded as credible those reports within the administrative record that on their face expressed doubts about the veracity or strength of the facts stated therein, her decision could be impugned on due process grounds.[80] Similarly, the Court held that although it would not substitute its judgement for the Secretary's in deciding which sources were credible, without knowing how the Secretary had evaluated the material in the record and upon which sources she had relied, it was unable to determine whether that record 'provides "a sufficient basis for a reasonable person to conclude" that the statutory requirements have been met'.[81] The Court remitted the case back to the Secretary of State with the order that she (1) indicate which sources within the (unclassified portion of the) administrative record she regarded as sufficiently credible that she relied upon them and (2) explain to which part of the statutory test for designation they applied (ie whether in her view they demonstrated that the organisation engaged in terrorist activities or retained the capability and intent to do so).[82]

iv. Treatment of Classified Material in the US

The first question in legal proceedings in which the Executive withholds classified material is whether the material is properly characterised as classified. Federal regulations require the Executive, when it is party to litigation in which classified material is in issue, to conduct a declassification review in which it asks the particular agency from which classified material originated whether the material can (in whole or part)

[79] *Al Haramain* (2012) (n 53) 976.
[80] *PMOI* (2010) (n 49) 229–30.
[81] Ibid 230.
[82] Ibid.

be declassified.[83] For example, twice during the *PMOI* litigation the State Department disclosed newly declassified material as a result of its declassification review.[84] In sanctions listings cases, the courts have generally accepted assurances from the government lawyers that this declassification review has been conducted[85] and will not substitute their own view of whether any material ought to remain classified. Accepting the argument that the courts are not best placed to determine which items of information should remain classified and which could be disclosed without risking national security, the DC Court of Appeals has stated that 'items of classified information which do not appear dangerous or perhaps even important to judges might "make all too much sense to a foreign counterintelligence specialist"'.[86]

This sentiment that the Executive is best placed to make assessments concerning classified material is not unique to the US. For example, it was expressed in an English sanctions case *R (Youssef) v Secretary of State for Foreign and Commonwealth Affairs*,[87] albeit in a slightly different context, when the High Court rejected the claimant's submission that the Court should adopt a full merits review of the Secretary of State's decision in 2005 that the UN Security Council's criteria for designation had been met and which resulted in the UK dropping the 'hold' it had placed on the claimant's listing by the UN Security Council's Al-Qaida Sanctions Committee. Giving the first judgment, Toulson LJ stated that:

> 57. Deciding whether a person meets the criteria for designation is likely in many cases to involve an evaluation of intelligence material which in the nature of things the Foreign Secretary is likely to be in a better position to make than a judge. Even those judges of the Administrative Court who deal with a lot of cases involving sensitive security issues cannot hope to have the same level of knowledge or sensitivity to surrounding security issues as the Foreign Secretary or Home Secretary of the day.
>
> 58. It is also a relevant factor, as Mr Swift [counsel for the defendant] properly reminded the court, that the courts customarily allow a wide measure of judgment to the Government in matters of security issues and foreign relations.

As noted above, under the US statutory schemes, the Executive may submit classified material in the administrative record to the court

[83] 28 CFR 17.17(a)(1).

[84] *PMOI* (2010) (n 49) 226.

[85] See eg *Islamic American Relief Agency* (2007) (n 63) 738.

[86] *NCRI* (2001) (n 47) 208. See also *PMOI* (2003) (n 61) 1242.

[87] *R (Youssef) v Secretary of State for Foreign and Commonwealth Affairs* [2012] EWHC 2091 (Admin) (Toulson LJ, Silber J). This was a judicial review of the Secretary of State's decisions, amongst other things, not to make representations to the EU Commission for the claimant's delisting from the EU Al-Qaida list, having determined that he did not currently satisfy the criteria for listing and having made such representations to the UN Security Council Sanctions Committee. It was not a statutory appeal against an autonomous listing decision by the UK.

for it to consider *ex parte* and *in camera*.[88] It is possible to detect some inconsistencies in the recent approaches adopted by different US courts to classified material in sanctions cases. However, the cases are few and far between, each is dependent in large measure on its own facts and, consequently, it is too early to talk of a clear split amongst the US federal circuits.

In the DC Circuit, courts have rejected submissions that consideration of secret evidence results in a denial of due process to listed persons and that due process requires disclosure of classified material. In these cases, the reviewing courts refused the claims on the basis that there was substantial support for the listing in the unclassified portion of the administrative record alone. According to the DC Court of Appeals, since constitutional due process is a variable standard which 'requires only that due process which is due under the circumstances of the case'[89] and the Executive did not need to rely on the classified portion of the records in order to resist the proceedings, the due process clause did not necessitate the disclosure of the classified material.[90]

The analysis by the majority of the DC Court of Appeals in *PMOI* (2010) of the Court's earlier decisions is the closest it has come to acknowledging that where the Executive has to rely on the classified material (because the unclassified material is of such low quality that it is, standing alone, insufficient to support a listing) some disclosure will be due to a listed person. Presently, the most that can be said is that the door in DC is ajar. In a subsequent decision in the *Kadi* case, the lower DC District Court only addressed the issue of classified information in its review under the statutory scheme[91] and not in its consideration of the constitutional due process claim, which was dismissed in a fairly perfunctory manner.[92] This is another difficult aspect of the *Kadi* decision and is difficult easily to reconcile with the observations of the majority of the Court of Appeals in *PMOI*.

Away from DC, both the Ninth Circuit Court of Appeals in the *Al Haramain* litigation and a federal District Court in Ohio (located in the Sixth Circuit) in the *Kindhearts* case have been more forthright.[93]

[88] 50 USC 1702(c); 8 USC 1189(a)(3)(B).

[89] *PMOI* (2003) (n 61) 1240; *HLF* (2003) (n 37) 164.

[90] *PMOI* (2010) (n 49) 230–31.

[91] *Kadi* (2012) (n 24) *18–19.

[92] Ibid *23–24.

[93] The Ohio-based charity Kindhearts for Charitable Humanitarian Development was subject to US financial sanctions following the US Treasury's determination that it was linked to Hamas (under the Specially Designated Global Terrorist sanctions programme). Protracted litigation ensued in which the charity challenged various decisions of the US Treasury related to its designation and the application of financial sanctions; see *In re Search of Kindhearts for Charitable Humanitarian Development* 594 F Supp 2d 855 (ND Ohio 2009), *Kindhearts for Charitable Humanitarian Development Inc v Geithner Kindhearts ('Kindhearts')* 647 F Supp 2d 857 (ND Ohio 2009), *Kindhearts* 676 F Supp 2d 649 (ND Ohio 2009) *Kindhearts* 710 F Supp 2d 637 (ND Ohio 2010).

Both courts applied the *Matthews* balancing test which requires the Executive to consider additional safeguards to mitigate potential unfairness to a plaintiff by the non-disclosure of classified material. Both courts indicated a willingness to apply procedures for managing classified information that are used in criminal and immigration cases. These safeguards can—but not necessarily—include providing unclassified summaries of the classified material (the exercise of 'gisting' that is familiar in English proceedings), allowing security-cleared defence counsel to view the classified material subject to protective orders or admitting relevant facts that the classified information would prove.[94] In its *Al Haramain* judgment, the Court of Appeals envisaged that this process could be supervised by the District Court.[95]

In US criminal proceedings, the process of managing classified information under the Classified Information Procedures Act (CIPA) generally starts with the supervising court holding an *inter partes* CIPA hearing prior to determining how the classified material is to be managed.[96] For the purposes of this CIPA hearing, it may be that the defence is given only a limited, generic description of the material at issue, and there may also be additional CIPA hearings in the absence of the defence during which the details of the classified material are considered by the court. In the *Al Haramain* case the process was different and the District Court did not appear to adopt such a proactive stance, as would be the case in criminal proceedings. Instead, the Court was prepared to let OFAC determine how it intended to comply with the Court of Appeals' directions and, in December 2012, the Court refused as premature an application by Al Haramain designed to compel OFAC to provide a summary of the classified material or allow security-cleared defence counsel to view it.[97] In contrast, in the *Kindhearts* litigation the District Court did adopt a more proactive case management stance. It proposed hearing OFAC *in camera* and *ex parte* to determine what then classified information would provide the charity with adequate notice under the due process clause and whether that material was capable of being declassified or summarised

[94] The use and disclosure of classified information in criminal proceedings is governed by the Classified Information Procedures Act 1980, PL96-456 (94 Stat 2025), codified at 18 USC App III. Rules governing the use of classified material in immigration proceedings are set out at 8 CFR 1240.11(c), 1240.33(c), 1240.49(c), 8 CFR 103.2(b)(16)(iv); see also US Dept of Justice, Operating Policies and Procedures Memorandum 09-01: Classified Information in Immigration Court Proceedings (5 February 2009). The disclosure requirements in criminal proceedings are more onerous than those in immigration proceedings.

[95] *Al Haramain* (2012) (n 53) 984: 'We expect the agency (and, if necessary, the district court) to consider, at a minimum, the nature and extent of the classified threat to national security, and the possible avenues available to allow the designated person to respond more effectively to the charges'.

[96] 18 USC App III §6.

[97] *Al Haramain* 2012 WL 6203136 (D Or 2012).

in a non-classified form. The Court went on to state that if the Executive determined that declassification or summarising would be impossible, it would order the Government to allow security-cleared counsel for the charity to view the material. This issue was never resolved in the case because the Government settled prior to the substantive hearings.[98]

To sum up, the position in respect of listed persons who can assert constitutional due process claims is more nuanced than the simple assertion that US law allows the Executive to make listing decisions on the basis of classified material which is not made available to listed persons in any form. Whether constitutional due process will require disclosure of any classified material is a fact-dependent exercise since it is a variable standard which 'requires only that due process which is due under the circumstances of the case'.[99] To date, the US courts have in general adopted an extremely restrictive approach in sanctions listings cases. However, in a limited number of cases, courts have indicated a willingness to borrow mechanisms formalised in other areas of US law to provide some measure of disclosure, despite there being no formal process governing the treatment of classified information in administrative reconsideration proceedings save for its *ex parte* and *in camera* consideration by the reviewing court.

v. Treatment of Classified Material: Comparisons with the UK and the EU

The lack of a formal process for the disclosure of classified information in US OFAC sanctions cases stands in contrast to the mechanisms in the UK to challenge autonomous listings decisions by HM Treasury. In the UK, the use of closed material procedures (CMPs) in legal challenges to sanctions designation decisions is on a statutory footing in respect of proceedings in the High Court and Court of Appeal.[100] In addition, on 20 March 2013, the Supreme Court by a majority decided that it had the power to use a CMP in the absence of an express statutory provision.[101] The English CMPs provide for open and closed hearings and judgments, and for the appointment of special advocates to represent the interests of the listed persons where the government is required to disclose classified material (either because it wishes to rely on the material or because it undermines its case or supports another party's case).[102] Like the security-cleared

[98] The settlement resulted in the Kindhearts charity being delisted but wound up and neither party admitting any wrongdoing. See ACLU, 'Government Settles Charity's Lawsuit Over Unconstitutional Terrorism Probe' (1 May 2012) available at: www.aclu.org/national-security/government-settles-charitys-lawsuit-over-unconstitutional-terrorism-probe.

[99] *PMOI* (2003) (n 61) 1240; *HLF* (2003) (n 37) 164.

[100] Counter-Terrorism Act 2008, s 67–70; Terrorist Asset-Freezing etc Act 2010, s 28(4); Civil Procedure Rules (CPR), pt 79.

[101] Statement of Lord Neuberger, President of the UKSC, 21 March 2013; *Bank Mellat v HM Treasury (No 1)* [2013] UKSC 38, [2013] 3 WLR 179.

[102] CPR, pt 79.18–19.

defence counsel appointed in US proceedings, English special advocates are unable to discuss the case with the listed person or his representatives following service of closed material, although they may be given specific permission to do so from the court.[103] In addition, a certain irreducible amount of disclosure must be given to the listed person that provides sufficient information about the evidential case against him to enable him to give instructions to his lawyers (not the special advocates) in respect of it and to refute rather than simply deny those allegations.[104]

Originally, there was no mechanism in the EU Courts for consideration of classified material that was not disclosed to all the parties in a case. On 1 July 2015, amendments to the Rules of Procedure of the General Court of the EU to allow for this came into effect. These amendments were prompted by a raft of decisions in which restrictive measures were annulled because the Council of the EU failed to submit evidence to justify its listing decisions on the basis that to do so would result in the disclosure of that material obtained from confidential sources. Consequently, the EU Courts held that they were unable to review the lawfulness of those decisions and so quashed them. This approach was confirmed by the CJEU in Case C-280/12 P, *Council of the European Union v Fulmen and Mahmoudian* (2013).[105] The General Court's earlier decisions in the Iranian bank cases, *Bank Mellat* and *Bank Saderat Iran*, are other examples (ultimately upheld by the CJEU).[106] These annulments caused particular agitation in Washington, DC, prompting diplomatic pressure from the US

[103] CPR, pt 79.20.

[104] *Bank Mellat v HM Treasury* [2010] EWCA Civ 483, [2012] QB 91, 6, 18 per Lord Neuberger MR (as he was then) applying *AF (No 3)* [2010] 2 AC 269; see also, Bank Mellat v HM Treasury [2016] 1 WLR 1187. In *Mastafa v HM Treasury* [2012] EWHC 3578 (Admin), Collins J held that Art 6 of the European Convention on Human Rights applies to appeals against listing decisions under the Terrorist Asset-Freezing etc Act 2010, and disagreed with the finding of Mitting J to the contrary in *R (Bhutta) v HM Treasury* [2011] EWHC 1789 (Admin).

[105] Case C-280/12 P, *Council of the European Union v Fulmen and Mahmoudian* [2013] All ER (D) 38 (Dec) see in particular, paras 70–80.

[106] See (n 25). A central plank of the General Court's decisions annulling the EU's restrictive measures against the applicant banks was the Council's failure to submit for review by the Court the evidence upon which the listing proposals and subsequent listing decisions were based. The AG's Opinion in the appeal addressed the Council's submissions regarding confidential information in two stages. The first was that the Council as a whole had not considered the confidential information, which had been available only to the Member States that proposed the banks' listings. The AG concluded that this was inadequate and the 'Council cannot content itself with rubber-stamping' (para 152). Secondly, she rejected the Council's unsubstantiated assertions that disclosure might endanger the provider(s) of the information or undermine international relations (paras 153–54). The Council of the EU appealed the decisions on, inter alia, the ground that the General Court failed to take due account of the fact that the evidence underpinning the allegations that the banks supported Iran's nuclear proliferation activities came from confidential sources. In its *Bank Mellat* judgment, the CJEU ruled this ground inadmissible because it was raised for the first time in the appeal (para 117). The Court went on to uphold the General Court's decision on substantially the same grounds. As of the date of writing, the CJEU had not handed down its decision in the *Bank Saderat Iran* appeal.

to introduce a mechanism to allow judicial consideration of closed material although the discussion within Europe pre-dated the General Court's decisions in these cases.[107] Advocate General Sharpston in her Opinion in Case C-27/09 P, *France v People's Mojahedin Organization of Iran* (2011), put this squarely in issue when she called for 'serious consideration' to be given to amending the Courts' rules of procedure to provide 'for the production of evidence that is truly confidential for consideration by [the EU courts] in a way that is compatible with its character without doing unacceptable violence to the rights of the other party or parties to the action'.[108] Following this, in its second *Kadi* decision, the CJEU observed that where overriding security concerns preclude the disclosure of some information or evidence to a listed person, it will be the task of the Courts:

> to apply, in the course of the judicial review to be carried out, techniques which accommodate, on the one hand, legitimate security considerations about the nature and sources of information taken into account in the adoption of the act concerned and, on the other, the need sufficiently to guarantee to an individual respect for his procedural rights, such as the right to be heard and the requirement for an adversarial process.[109]

The CJEU made the same observation in *Fulmen* and then went on to consider how such a process might occur in practice.[110] This conjecture has now been overtaken by the adoption of the amended Rules of Procedure for the General Court.

Article 105 of the Rules of Procedure allows a party to provide the Court with confidential information or material when its communication to the other main party in the litigation would harm either (1) the security of the EU or (2) that of one or more of its Member States or (3) the conduct of their international relations. The submitting party must apply to the Court for confidential treatment of the information or material

[107] See 'US Urges EU Action to Overcome Iran Sanctions Courts Appeals' *Reuters*, 25 March 2013, available at: www.reuters.com/article/2013/03/25/eu-iran-usa-idUSL5N0CH2WP20130325. The so-called 'US Diplomatic Cables' published by Wikileaks also disclose discussions about the possible provision of classified material to EU Courts reviewing the legality of listing decisions. See eg cable reference 09BRUSSELS41 (13 January 2009) available at: wikileaks.org/cable/2009/01/09BRUSSELS41.html, message subject 'EU TERRORISM FINANCE LISTINGS: TROUBLE AHEAD'.

[108] Case C-27/09 P, *France v People's Mojahedin Organization of Iran* (AG's Opinion) [2013] All ER (EC) 347, 384 at para 186; see generally 381–94, paras 177–255.

[109] Joined Cases C-584/10P, C-593/10P and C-595/10P, *European Commission v Kadi* (CJEU Grand Chamber, 18 July 2013 unrep) 125 (citations omitted) ('*Kadi* (2013)').

[110] Case C-280/12 P, *Council of the European Union v Fulmen and Mahmoudian* (CJEU Fifth Chamber, 28 November 2013 unrep) 70–74, citing *Kadi* (2013) (n 108), and, by analogy, Case 300/11, *ZZ (France) v Secretary of State for the Home Department* [2013] QB 1136 (a preliminary ruling by the CJEU in an English immigration case).

setting out the 'overriding reasons which, to the extent strictly required by the exigencies of the situation, justify the confidentiality ... being preserved and militate against its communication to the other main party'.[111] If the Court decides that the information or material is relevant for it to rule in the case and is not confidential vis-à-vis the other party, it will not take it into consideration if the submitting party objects to its disclosure.[112] Where the Court decides the information or material is both relevant and confidential it shall conduct a balancing exercise, weighing the requirements linked to the right to effective judicial protection against the security interests asserted. It shall then specify what procedures are to be adopted such as the production of a non-confidential version or summary of the information or material 'containing the essential content thereof and enabling the other main party, to the greatest extent possible, to make its views known'.[113] If the submitting party disagrees with the Court's decision and procedural requirements, it has two weeks within which to withdraw the confidential information or material, which shall not then be taken into account by the Court in reaching its ruling on the case.[114] Where a non-confidential version or summary of the information or material is disclosed to the other party in accordance with the Court's ruling, the Court may then base its judgment on the confidential information or material itself if it considers this to be essential to enable it to rule in the case and only to the extent it is strictly necessary. When assessing the confidential information or material, the Court must take into account the fact that the other party has been unable to make his views on it known.[115]

The new rules do not provide for any type of closed hearing or a special advocate procedure to enable security-cleared advocates to view and make submissions upon the confidential information or material. This raises questions over whether the Court will be able to test either the reasons put forward for the confidentiality of the information or material or for its necessity in the case or the information or material itself in any meaningful way. Although the UK's Minister for Europe indicated to the UK's parliamentary European Scrutiny Committee that he envisaged these special measures would only be used in a limited number of cases, the extent to which they are relied upon remains to be seen.[116]

[111] Rules of Procedure of the General Court, Art 105(1).
[112] Ibid Art 105(4).
[113] Ibid Art 105(5), (6).
[114] Ibid Art 105(7).
[115] Ibid Art 105(8).
[116] House of Commons European Scrutiny Committee, *Twenty-Ninth Report* (HC 2014–15, 63) para 13.8.

vi. US Remedies for Due Process Violations: 'Harmless Error' Analysis and Remission for Further Administrative Consideration

Although some US courts in recent years have found OFAC to have breached its constitutional obligation to provide due process, in no case has this resulted in the immediate quashing of the impugned decision. Instead, in cases in which a 'harmful error' has been identified, the matters have been remitted back to the Executive for further consideration.

First, the courts have employed the 'harmless error' test in evaluating the effect of the Executive's violations of due process and the remedy available to the listed persons. The question contained within the harmless error test is whether the lack of due process has prejudiced the administrative proceedings. There are inconsistencies in the US courts' application of the harmless error analysis in sanctions cases. In the *Al Haramain* case, the Ninth Circuit Court of Appeals held that the burden of proof fell on the plaintiff to prove that the Government's error was harmful. This required AHIF to show that had it been provided with the process it was due, it could and plausibly would have been able to resist the re-designation and either OFAC would not have made the re-designation decision or that decision would not have been supported by substantial evidence in the administrative record.[117] In contrast, in the *Kindhearts* case the District Court in Ohio held that the burden rested on the Government to show beyond reasonable doubt that its error in failing to provide due process was harmless.[118] The approach of the DC Court of Appeals in its 2010 *PMOI* decision was in line with *Kindhearts* insofar as it was not prepared to presume that the Government's lack of due process was harmless.[119]

Secondly, where harmful due process violations have been found, the US courts have rejected submissions that the breaches in due process in administrative reconsideration proceedings are 'structural errors' undermining the decision-making process per se such that the listing ought to be immediately quashed. The courts have instead consistently remitted the cases back to the Executive for further decision-making, whilst maintaining the listings on an interim basis. For example, in its judgments in both *NRCI* and *PMOI*, the DC Court of Appeals explained that it was leaving the designations in place and remanding the case back to the Secretary of State with instructions that the petitioners be provided with an opportunity to review and rebut the unclassified portions of the administrative record because it 'recognize[d] the realities of the foreign policy

117 *Al Haramain* (2012) (n 53) 988–89.
118 *Kindhearts* 710 F Supp 2d, 654–55 (2010).
119 *PMOI* (2010) (n 49) 228–29.

and national security concerns asserted by the Secretary in support of the designation'.[120] This is similar to the approach of the European Union Courts in decisions annulling designation decisions, which frequently suspend the effect of the annulment for a period to enable the Council to correct the irregularities found in their judgments. For example, in *Kadi I* the CJEU decided that the impugned regulation should be maintained against Mr Kadi for a three-month period rather than immediately annulled, to enable the Council 'to remedy the infringements found'.[121] Another example is the General Court's decision in *Sharif University of Technology v Council* to suspend the effect of its judgment annulling the restrictive measures against the applicant for two months.[122]

IV. SOME CONCLUDING REMARKS ABOUT THE US OFAC REGIME AND CHALLENGES TO LISTING DECISIONS

This chapter has identified some features of the US sanctions delisting process that from an English or European perspective are striking. The first of these is the extremely limited procedural protections available under the statutory schemes. Under the OFAC regulations, a listed person has no right to be informed of the reasons for a listing decision or even disclosure of the unclassified portion of the administrative record upon which the decision is based; the Executive may submit to the reviewing courts classified material to justify its decisions *ex parte* and *in camera*; and the judicial review is so limited that it is likely to impugn only 'procedural shortfalls so obvious a Secretary of State is not likely to commit them'.[123]

Another striking feature is the distinction between the process that is available to a listed person who can pray in aid any US constitutional protections and those who cannot. Even where a listed person may claim

[120] *NCRI* (2001) (n 47) 209; *PMOI* (2010) (n 49) 230. See also, *Kindhearts* 710 F Supp 2d, 658 (2010).

[121] Joined Cases C-402/05P and C-415/05P, *Kadi v Council of the European Union* [2008] ECR I-6351, [2009] 1 AC 1225, 1308C-D, 375–76. In the CJEU's second *Kadi* decision this issue was moot because Mr Kadi's name had already been removed from the UN and the EU sanctions lists before the Court delivered its judgment in July 2013. See Joined Cases C-584/10P, C-593/10P and C-595/10P, *European Commission v Kadi* (AG's Opinion, 19 March 2013) 42; and *Kadi* (2013) (n 108).

[122] Case T-181/13, *Sharif University of Technology v Council of the European Union* (General Court, 3 July 2014, unrep) 76–83.

[123] *NCRI* (2001) (n 47) 197. See also *HLF* (2003) (n 37), in which the DC Court of Appeals described the 'arbitrary and capricious' standard of review in cases challenging SDT and SDGT designation under EO 12947 and EO 13224 respectively, as 'highly deferential'.

rights under the due process clause of the Fifth Amendment, these have been applied by the US courts in a circumspect manner with limited substantive remedies and do not accord with the due process standards applied in the English or EU Courts. This chapter has focused on the more recent US case law in which the listed persons were able to rely on constitutional due process protections because in these cases it is possible to identify some developing jurisprudence. The courts have indicated in these cases that the Executive cannot rely on classified material without any form of notice or safeguards for the listed persons. Nonetheless, there is still no formalised procedure in US sanctions cases for the disclosure of relevant classified material to a legal representative whose function is to act on the listed person's behalf (whether a listed person's primary lawyer or a specially appointed security-cleared defence advocate). This is in contrast to the CMP system established in England and Wales in appeals of HM Treasury's designation decisions under the Terrorist Asset-Freezing etc Act 2010 or applications for the setting aside of other financial restrictions decisions by HM Treasury.

Over the past decade, the US Government has made considerable efforts to encourage other jurisdictions to adopt its model of financial sanctions. Its diplomatic efforts in Brussels are just one example of this; another is the US's central role in the development of the targeted sanctions programmes of the UN Security Council, notably the al-Qaida sanctions (the Resolution 1267 (1999) programme) and the general counter-terrorism sanctions under Resolution 1373 (2001). The standards of the statutory regimes administered by OFAC are not the only standards applied by the US courts in sanctions cases and this is pertinent in the face of US diplomatic efforts to promote particular models for further development of the legal frameworks of international economic sanctions (for example, the UN Ombudsperson's procedures).[124] This chapter has sought to show that consideration of the US constitutional requirements is more apt and it is important to note that US law in this area is developing, albeit

[124] Kimberley Prost, the first UN Ombudsperson, publicly highlighted the difficulties she faced in obtaining confidential information from designating Member States. The status of negotiations with States for access to such information can be found on the Ombudsperson's website at www.un.org/en/sc/ombudsperson/accessinfo.shtml. In his report on the UN's Al-Qaida sanctions programme published in September 2012 Ben Emmerson QC, the UN Special Rapporteur on the promotion and protection of human rights and fundamental freedoms while countering terrorism, called for a number of amendments to the Ombudsperson's process to enhance procedural protections for listed persons and to satisfy international minimum standards of due process; see UN Doc A/67/396 (26 September 2012) available at: http://daccess-dds-ny.un.org/doc/UNDOC/GEN/N12/522/54/PDF/N1252254.pdf?OpenElement.

at a slow pace that still falls short of the English and EU jurisprudence. In the recent cases of *PMOI* and *Kindhearts*, certain US courts have looked to the well-established methods of managing classified information that are employed in criminal proceedings under the US Classified Information Procedures Act (CIPA) and indicated a willingness to import them into sanctions cases. It seems unlikely that this will be put on a statutory footing in the near future and instead, this incremental development may continue through the case law. That said, the cases in which plaintiffs can assert US constitutional claims are limited and, as occurred in the *PMOI* and *Kindhearts* litigation, may well be settled by the government before any robust judicial precedent is set.[125]

[125] In relation to *Kindhearts*, see ACLU press release 1 May 2012: 'Government Settles Charity's Lawsuit Over Unconstitutional Terrorism Probe', and settlement agreement dated 29 November 2011, available at: www.aclu.org/national-security/government-settles-charitys-lawsuit-over-unconstitutional-terrorism-probe. In relation to *PMOI*, see *In re People's Mojahedin Organization of Iran*, 680 F 3d 832 (DC Cir 2012); State Department press release 28 September 2012 'Delisting of the Mujahedin-e Khalq' (PRN: 2012/1558), available at: www.state.gov/r/pa/prs/ps/2012/09/198443.htm. In a similar vein, the US Solicitor-General decided not to appeal the Ninth Circuit's decision in *Al Haramain*, thus avoiding a Supreme Court decision.

10

Sanctions and Commercial Law

PENELOPE NEVILL

I. INTRODUCTION

THIS CHAPTER EXPLORES the legal effect of sanctions (imposed by the UN, the EU or unilaterally by States) in English commercial law. Their legal effect arises primarily through three devices used in sanctions legislation which originate in rules on trading with the enemy and treatment of enemy subjects: restrictions on standing, prohibitions on concluding and performing contracts and prohibitions on assisting the enemy through commerce in any way. Where recent sanctions legislation is new is in the substantial regulatory demands it makes on the commercial sector, especially financial institutions.[1] Financial institutions are used not only to cut off funds, but to monitor and track the flow of funds to and from target States and individuals, identify and prevent unlawful transactions by third parties processed through electronic transfers, and report suspect transactions. Failure to comply with these obligations can lead to prosecution, fines and even imprisonment.

The English private law rules for determining the effect of a sanction on a contract (frustration, illegality) are the same as those used in previous centuries to determine the effects of war, reprisals or self-defence and the measures employed by sovereigns to prosecute them: blockades, contraband measures, trade embargoes and requisitions of property. Similarly, the standard form clauses developed by industry in response to wars and reprisals (restraint of princes, trading limits, war clauses) are often relied on by commercial actors in cases concerning UN and EU sanctions, even when on first impression they would not appear to apply. Indeed, regardless of the 'outlawing' of war and forcible reprisals and their replacement by collective mechanisms for peace and security in the twentieth century, the UN and EU sanction has a similar impact on commercial activity: commercial relationships must be severed, goods cannot be delivered

[1] This is alongside obligations under anti-money laundering and anti-corruption measures.

or insured and they may be seized. It is thus unsurprising that the old commercial law and standard form contracts have not much changed in response to the 'new' international law.

Section II of this Chapter provides a brief sketch of the historical background to the subject of this chapter. The modern legal framework is addressed in section III, including the implementation of UN and EU sanctions into EU and UK law and common sanctions provisions in EU and UK legislation. Section IV then looks at the treatment of sanctions in contract law, the interpretation of sanctions and the market impact of increased risk avoidance by banks and insurers.

II. HISTORY AND BACKGROUND

The 31st edition of *Chitty on Contracts*, published in 2014, opens with a reference from Sir Joseph Chitty's four-volume *Treatise on the Laws of Commerce and Manufactures and the Contracts Relating thereto*, published nearly 200 years earlier:

> As Sir Joseph Chitty observed, the law affecting commerce can be seen both in 'the law of nations [and] those municipal institutions of our own country, which are of a public and general nature, and which form the basis of that commercial intercourse which takes place between individuals' and in the law 'which relates to commerce itself, strictly so called, as contradistinguished from those measures of state policy by which it is secured and protected'. In the modern law, it remains useful to distinguish between laws which create the legal environment within which parties conclude their contract (which may broadly be termed market regulation) and laws which relate specifically to the conclusion of contracts, their terms, the relative rights and obligations which they create and the remedies which arise on breach (contract law in the narrow and usual sense).[2]

The distinction drawn by the authors of *Chitty* between the international law and domestic public or constitutional law that creates the legal environment, and the private law that operates within it, provides a useful framework for understanding the interrelationship between sanctions (and armed conflict) and commercial law today.

The first volume of *A Treatise on the Laws of Commerce and Manufactures and the Contracts Relating thereto* is devoted to an explanation of the 'commercial law of nations', the treatment of alien merchants and how the 'commerce and contracts' of belligerents and neutrals might be legally affected by war. The 'commercial law of nations' to which Sir Joseph was referring was a body of primarily maritime law which traced its origins

[2] At para 1-001, quoting from Sir J Chitty (the elder, 1776–1841), *A Treatise on the Laws of Commerce and Manufactures and the Contracts Relating thereto* (1824) Vol III, 1.

back to a set of laws compiled by the island of Rhodes in around 900 BC, and included the *Consolato del Mare* (thirteenth century), the Laws of Oleron (circa twelfth century), the Black Book of Admiralty, ordinances of the merchants and masters of Wisburg (thirteenth century), laws of the Hanseatic League (the late-sixteenth century) and the ordinance of marine of Louis XIV published in 1681 codifying maritime practices.[3] The subjects covered included reprisals, lawfulness of capture of enemy vessels, sharing prize[4] and the effect of restraint of princes on a voyage,[5] a mixture of what we might now categorise as rules of private commercial law, national public law and international law, but which were then conceived of as simply the 'law of nations'. Law reflected the prevalence of war. Indeed, the first 'multilateral treaty', the Pact of Paris of 1856, addressed the rules on the capture of enemy goods in neutral vessels and blockade.[6] Capture and treatment of enemy and neutral vessels and cargo and blockade received more extended treatment in the 1899 and 1907 Hague Peace Conferences,[7] and prize law received domestic legislative treatment in English law in the

[3] See M D A Azuni, *The Maritime Law of Europe* (1806) Vol I, 330–31, and Chitty, *A Treatise on the Laws of Commerce and Manufactures and the Contracts Relating thereto* (n 2) 35–38. It cannot be said there was one uniform maritime 'law of nations'. Nor was the law applied by any particular court seised of a maritime dispute necessarily the same throughout Europe and the Mediterranean; the law applied depended on the jurisdiction. This was not national jurisdiction in its modern sense, but the jurisdiction of the particular court in question, whether a merchant or city court or a consulate court established to deal with foreign traders. There was, however, a shared conception of a customary maritime and merchant law and shared sources considered to represent best law and, to that extent, a certain uniformity existed. It is generally accepted that there was a customary maritime law of nations across Mediterranean, Northern and Western Europe but whether there was a non-maritime *lex mercatoria* is contested: see C Donoghue Jr, 'Medieval and Early Modern *Lex mercatoria*: An Attempt at the *probatio diabolica*' (2004–05) 5 *Chicago Journal of International Law* 21–37.

[4] See *A Translation of the Chapters CCLXXIII and CCLXXXVII of the Consolato del Mare Relating to Prize Law* (1800), translated from an Italian translation used by the Casa Regis and reprinted at Venice in 1737. Lord Mansfield CJ in *Luke v Lloyd [or Lyde]*, 1 January 1759, 96 ER 102, 103, cited, inter alia, the Rhodian Law, Consolato del Mare, the Laws of Oleron and the ordinance of Louis XIV of 1681 as laying down the established 'law in these cases' concerning a freight claim where the vessel had been taken by a French privateer and retaken by an English man of war, which took half the goods for salvage (ie payment for recapture, called 'prize' when taken in war and subject to the law of prize).

[5] The Laws of Oleron, as published in *Black Book of Admiralty*, T Twiss ed, (1873) 89–132, 123.

[6] Large-scale blockades by naval powers became a feature of warfare and measures falling short of war from the 18th century, enabled by bigger and better naval fleets: S Neff, *War and the Law of Nations* (Cambridge, Cambridge University Press, 2005) 93.

[7] Of which the Hague Conventions (VI) on Enemy Merchant Ships 1907, (XI) on Restrictions on the Right of Capture and (XIII) on Neutral Powers in Naval War 1907 entered into force. Attempts to conclude a treaty for an international prize court to hear appeals from national courts and an agreed set of uniform rules of prize law failed (Convention (XII) relative to the Creation of an International Prize Court, 1907 and the Declaration of London concerning the Law of Naval War 1909. Both failed to attract sufficient ratifications) suggesting that there was not necessarily agreement between States as to the content of the rules of the law of nations on prize applied by their national courts.

1864 Naval Prize Act.[8] The continued relevance of the rules of naval warfare and neutrality as part of the *jus in bello* (notwithstanding the initial doubt after the 'outlawing' of war in the UN Charter) was affirmed in the 1994 San Remo Manual on the International Law Applicable at Sea[9] and, more recently, the various official enquiries into the 2010 flotilla incident in the Israeli blockade of Gaza.[10] English law still contains rules on prize[11] and its courts retain prize jurisdiction in section 27 of the Senior Courts Act 1981.

It was accepted as customary under the law of nations and English law that during war relations between subjects and hostile enemy subjects would come to an end.[12] Trading with enemy subjects was illegal unless under licence, and any property unlawfully traded was subject to confiscation.[13] Enemy aliens lacked standing before the courts, unless *pro hac* or in the 'King's peace'.[14] As a matter of English constitutional law, whether a state of war existed was a matter for the royal prerogative. Once a declaration of war had been published, the rules on trading with the enemy and the standing of enemy aliens applied. The common law was given legislative footing on the outbreak of the First World War in the 1914 Trading with the Enemy Act.

Enemy merchants within the realm were also the subject of regulation. The 1215 Magna Carta affirmed that those within the kingdom at the time of the outbreak of war with their country could be detained along with their goods, pending advice as to the standard of treatment received by English subjects in enemy territory.[15] The treatment of alien merchants in the territory and commerce in times of peace and war was frequently the subject of treaty from the sixteenth century onwards,[16] known as

[8] Prize law governs the seizure of enemy vessels or contraband cargoes by warships or privateers and passing of property therein. It has a long heritage. Rules on distribution of prize were included in the 14th-century *Black Book of Admiralty* (n 5) Vol I.

[9] A Roberts and R Guelff, *Documents on the Laws of War* (3rd edn, Oxford, Oxford University Press, 2000) 573.

[10] Report of the international fact-finding mission to investigate violations of international law, including international humanitarian and human rights law, resulting from the Israeli attacks on the flotilla of ships carrying humanitarian assistance, UN Doc A/HRC/15/21 (2010), UNSG Panel of Inquiry Report on the 31 May 2010 Flotilla Incident, September 2011, available at: www.un.org/News/dh/infocus/middle_east/Gaza_Flotilla_Panel_Report.pdf.

[11] Parts of the 1864 Act are still in force, amended by Acts of 1916 and 1939.

[12] W E Hall, *Treatise on International Law* (3rd edn, Oxford, The Clarendon Press, 1890), 382, para 124, 387, para 126; Chitty (n 2) 377–78.

[13] See *The 'Hoop' (Cornelius, Master)*, 13 February 1799, 165 ER 146, affirmed in *Janson v Driefontein Consolidated Mines* [1902] AC 484 (HL), where Sir Walter Scott considered the rule reflected a 'universal principle of law' as well as 'the law in most countries in Europe'.

[14] Ibid 148. See further the discussion on standing in *Porter v Freudenberg* [1915] 1 KB 857 below.

[15] Magna Carta 1215, para 41 of the English translation, A Beebe White and W Notestein (eds), *Source Problems in English History* (New York, Harper and Brothers, 1915); see also Chitty (n 2) Vol I, 134.

[16] According to G F von Martens, *A Compendium of the Law of Nations* (1802) 153–54.

'commercial treaties' or 'treaties of commerce, friendship and navigation'.[17] Common treaty provisions included an exemption from seizure for enemy merchants and their property and a period of time to leave the country, or terms on which they could remain and even continue trading throughout the war.[18] Internment of civilians with enemy nationality resident in the country at the outbreak of war became widespread practice in the First and Second World Wars.[19] Their property was subject to confiscation under the Trading with the Enemy Acts[20] to eliminate their 'commercial influence'.[21]

In World War I the premise underpinning the treatment of enemy nationals shifted from the 'conception that all subjects owing allegiance to the Crown were at war with subjects of the State at war with the Crown'[22] to one of public policy. According to Lord Reading CJ in the 1915 case of *Porter v Freudenberg*, public policy

> forbids the doing of acts that will be or may be to the advantage of the enemy State by increasing its capacity for prolonging hostilities in adding to the credit, money or goods, or other resources available to individuals in the enemy State. This consideration equally applies to a claim sought to be established in our Courts by a resident in enemy-occupied territory, for if the claimant succeeds, an asset in the form of an award or a judgment is created which the occupying power can appropriate and which is calculated to increase the enemy's resources.[23]

Under section 1(2) of the 1939 Trading with the Enemy Act (still in force) a person was deemed to trade with the enemy if he had 'any commercial, financial or other intercourse or dealings with, or for the benefit of, an enemy', including supplying any goods to the enemy or receiving any goods from an enemy, paying or transmitting any money, negotiable instrument or security for money to or for the benefit of an enemy or to a

[17] Chitty (n 2) Vol I, 42–43. The term 'FCN' treaty was coined in the 18th century.

[18] Ibid.

[19] Under the Alien Restrictions Act 1914, as amended in 1919 (provisions of which are still in force). On the more generous position regarding enemy aliens before WWI, see Hall, *Treatise on International Law* (n 12) 389–93, suggesting the law had moved away from allowing capture and detention of all enemy aliens on the territory at the outbreak of war.

[20] Of 1914, as amended in 1916, 1919 and 1939. German enemy property could also be vested in the public trustee and distributed under the provisions of the Distribution of Enemy Property Act 1949.

[21] R Roxburgh (ed), *Oppenheim's International Law* (3rd edn, London, Longmans, 1920) Vol II, 'War', para 88. German property was not confiscated but 'preserved' with a view to arrangements made on the conclusion of peace, namely satisfaction of war reparation claims: see R Roxburgh, 'German Property in the War and the Peace' (1921) 37 *Law Quarterly Review* 46.

[22] *Porter v Freudenberg* [1915] 1 KB 857, 868.

[23] Ibid. This resonates in the general 'catch-all' prohibition in EU sanctions on making available, directly or indirectly, economic resources to listed persons, eg Council Regulation (EU) No 267/2012 of 23 March 2012 concerning restrictive measures against Iran and repealing Regulation (EU) No 961/2010 [2012] OJ L 88/1, Art 23(2).

place in enemy territory, or performing or discharging any obligation of an enemy, even if the obligation was undertaken before the onset of war.[24] The definition of enemy in section 2 of the Act (as amended) does not include individuals by reason only of their being an enemy subject, but does include any individual resident in enemy territory, and any corporate persons carrying on business in any place if incorporated under the law of the enemy state or controlled by an individual resident in enemy territory, or any person incorporated under the laws of a State at war with Her Majesty.

Thus a state of war created a new legal environment affecting commercial relations as a matter of both international law and domestic law. Measures falling short of war, such as reprisals or 'peaceful blockades' might have the same effect. In short, the effect of the rules of international law and domestic law was that in certain circumstances, property might lawfully be forcibly taken (or destroyed in the attempt) and title might pass, and it was illegal to conclude or perform contracts with enemies unless authorised to do so. This is still the case today. However, while the law on trading with the enemy is still current, these days a merchant is much more likely to be faced with a sanction and related enforcement measures[25] or an armed conflict[26] than a war—the last formal declaration of war, a prerequisite for the application of the common law on war,[27] was during the Second World War.

Compliance with a prohibition on future trading with the enemy was straightforward enough. Questions over the effect of war on contracts

[24] Section 7 addresses the collection of enemy debts and custody of enemy property, providing that property may be vested in the custodian of enemy property. Section 3A confers the power to control and wind up certain businesses. Section 4 concerns standing; subsection 1 provides that no assignment of a chose in action (or transfer of a negotiable instrument) by or on behalf of an enemy shall be effective to confer on any person any rights or remedies in respect of the chose in action (or negotiable instrument), except with Treasury consent.

[25] As to which, see P Nevill, 'Military Sanctions Enforcement in the Absence of Express Authorization' in M Weller (ed), *The Oxford Handbook on the Use of Force* (Oxford, Oxford University Press, 2014) 272–292. If the sanctions relate to an armed conflict, the laws of armed conflict or international humanitarian law, including those governing war at sea covering blockade and contraband measures, apply, which may affect commercial operators. If the sanctions are not imposed in the context of an armed conflict, eg those countering proliferation or terrorism, the legal basis for boarding vessels and searching for and seizing sanctioned goods lies in the rules governing the jurisdiction of States under the law of the sea and any relevant treaty or Security Council resolution. Sanctioned goods within a State's jurisdiction are subject to the rules governing territorial jurisdiction. Outside the case where the rules of armed conflict apply, Security Council resolutions may authorise the seizure and destruction of sanctioned goods found within a State.

[26] This may be a war in layperson or merchant terms, but not in international law or domestic constitutional law. The 1939 Act does not specify when it applies, presumably on a declaration of war under the royal prerogative. A person may be deemed an enemy by the Board of Trade and Secretary of State under s 2(2) of the Trading with the Enemy Act 1939.

[27] *Halsbury's Law of England*, 'Armed Conflict and Emergency', Vol 3 (2011) para 6, 'Existence and Non-existence of a State of War'.

entered into with enemy aliens before the outbreak of war and contracts with non-enemies that might nonetheless be affected by the war (eg where the subject matter was destroyed or confiscated or the means of transport requisitioned, or performance was delayed because a longer route had to be taken to avoid a combat zone) were addressed through the contract law doctrines of illegality and frustration. Any contract made in breach of the prohibition on trading with the enemy or in furtherance of illegal trading was void for illegality.[28] Where a contract had been entered into with an enemy alien before the outbreak of war, the contract did not automatically become illegal, but the rights under the contract and the right to enforce them were suspended in full[29] or in part[30] until the war was over. However, where a contract made before the outbreak of hostilities could not by its nature be suspended, it would be treated as abrogated. For example, a partnership with enemy nationals was terminated on the grounds that the rights and duties of a partnership rendered assistance to the enemy and were therefore inconsistent with a situation of war.[31] A charterparty would be treated as at an end where the shipment had become illegal because purchased by an enemy or as contraband of war.[32]

More difficult questions might arise as to the allocation of risk and loss where a contract involving neutral trading was interrupted or prevented, for example by a lawful or unlawful seizure of contraband goods, or where the contract concerned might indirectly support the enemy war effort, for example the insurance or reinsurance of enemy concerns or their vessels. The outcome in each case depended on the nature of the contract and the facts. It might also be affected by changing views on what assisted the enemy, or the need to protect an important industry that would be affected by a successful plea of illegality or alien enemy. Insuring the enemy did not become an unlawful trade until an Act of 1793, because it was considered that holding otherwise would have too big an impact on the London insurance market.[33]

[28] eg *Potts v Bell* (1800) 101 ER 1540. See further L Scott, 'The Effect of War on Contracts' (1914) 30 *Law Quarterly Review* 77–90, 77–84 and the cases cited therein. Views and policy might change over time as to what is considered to assist the enemy.

[29] eg *Janson v Driefontein Consolidated Mines* (n 13), in respect of a claim under an insurance contract for a loss incurred before the war.

[30] eg *Leiston Gas Company v Lesiton-Cum-Sizewell Urban District Council* [1916] 1 KB 912, in which a claim of frustration was made in respect of a 5-year deal signed by a local authority to furnish street lamps and connect them to the gas mains. The Defence of the Realm Regulations 1914 prohibited the use of much street lighting. The claim was rejected because the Regulations did not render the contract wholly illegal or wholly incapable of performance. For a similar result in WW2, see *Cricklewood Property and Investment Trust Ltd v Leightons Investment Trust Ltd* [1945] AC 221.

[31] *Griswold v Waddington* (1818). For post-WWI jurisprudence on the point, see *Rodriguez v Speyer Brothers* [1919] AC 59 (HL).

[32] *Draddy v Deacon* (1691) 23 ER 757; *The Teutonia* (1872) LR 4 PC 171.

[33] See W R Willson, 'The Insurance of Foreign Property in War Time I' (1916) 32 *Law Quarterly Review* 373–83, at 373–74.

The Law Reform (Frustrated Contracts) Act 1943 and the House of Lords' decision in *Fibrosa Spolka Akcyjna v Fairbairn Lawson Combe Barbour Ltd*,[34] which ameliorated the impact of frustration by allowing the recovery of sums paid or payment for part performance, were a direct response to the impact on war on contractual relations.[35] The commercial response, then as now, was to provide certainty through standard form clauses in commercial contracts such as insurance policies and charterparties covering restraint of princes, requisition, war risks and trading limits,[36] and by taking out war and political risk insurance.

The new collective security system agreed at the 1919 Paris Peace Conference employed the same tools as States had in the wars and disputes falling short of war that had preceded it. Article 16 of the 1919 Covenant of the League of Nations provided that in the event of act of war by one of the members of the League (which included failing to submit disputes to peaceful means of settlement), the others undertook to impose a complete trade ban. They would:

> immediately subject it to the severance of all trade or financial relations, the prohibition of all intercourse between their nationals and the nationals of the covenant-breaking State, and the prevention of all financial, commercial or personal intercourse between the nationals of the covenant-breaking State and the nationals of any other State, whether a Member of the League or not.

In the event of breach, Article 16 further provided for blockades and other maritime measures:

> It shall be the duty of the Council in such case to recommend to the several Governments concerned what effective military, naval or air force the Members of the League shall severally contribute to the armed forces to be used to protect the covenants of the League.

III. THE MODERN LEGAL FRAMEWORK

A. UN Sanctions and Unilateral Sanctions

The 1945 United Nations Charter likewise made provision for collective trade bans in Article 41:

> The Security Council may decide what measures not involving the use of armed force are to be employed to give effect to its decisions, and it may call upon the Members of the United Nations to apply such measures. These may include

[34] [1943] AC 32 (HL).

[35] Unless the contract provides otherwise. The Frustrated Contracts Act 1943 is not applicable to charterparties, insurance contracts or certain contracts for the sale of goods: see s 2(5).

[36] The jurisprudence and standard form clauses concerning carriage by sea are detailed in K Michel, *War Terror and Carriage by Sea* (London, Informa, 2004) (war risks clauses, war cancellation clauses and war-related exceptions).

> complete or partial interruption of economic relations and of rail, sea, air, postal, telegraphic, radio, and other means of communication, and the severance of diplomatic relations.

Apart from two isolated instances,[37] the Cold War paralysis of the Security Council prevented the use of collective sanctions. States of course had not lost their traditional power to impose sanctions, and continued to do so after 1945. Between 1945 and 1990, 91 unilateral sanctions regimes were established, mostly by the US.[38] The first UN sanctions after the Cold War were imposed in 1990, in response to Iraq's invasion of Kuwait.[39] There has been a more or less constant stream of UN sanctions ever since. States continue to employ sanctions on a unilateral basis. Notable recent examples include sanctions in response to conflicts in Syria (2011–) and the Ukraine (2014–), where the P5 veto has prevented the Security Council from acting.[40]

For States that are members of the European Union (EU), the decision to impose unilateral (ie non-UN) sanctions and the implementation of UN and unilateral sanctions is largely carried out under the EU Treaties and through the EU legal system.[41] It is also common for the EU when implementing UN sanctions to go beyond the measures required in the resolution and add additional EU measures; for example, in the case of measures against Iran to counter proliferation of nuclear weapons, sanctions also targetted the Iranian oil and gas sector.[42] The EU now ranks alongside the United States as very active in the use of sanctions. Thus a very large volume of commerce and related services are affected by sanctions. Even transactions involving non-US nationals outside the US may be caught by US measures, because of the worldwide practice of using US dollars as the currency of the transaction which relies on correspondent banking relationships with US institutions.[43]

[37] South Africa, in response to apartheid in 1963 (UNSC Res 181 and 182); Rhodesia in 1965, in response to the white minority government of Ian Smith (UNSC Res 216, 217 and 216 (1966)).

[38] K Alexander, *Economic Sanctions: Law and Public Policy* (Basingstoke, Palgrave Macmillan, 2009) 9.

[39] UNSC Res 661 (1990).

[40] For the measures adopted by the EU and Member States, see the principal legal instruments, Council Regulation (EU) No 36/2012 (Syria) and amendments implementing Council Decisions 2011/782/CFSP and Council Implementing Decision 2012/37/CFSP and subsequent Council Decisions, and Council Regulations (EU) No 833/2014 and 692/2014 (Ukraine), implementing Council Decisions 2014/512/CFSP, 2014/145/CFSP, as amended.

[41] Under the Common Foreign and Security Policy (CFSP) of the Treaty of the European Union (TEU) and Art 215 of the Treaty on the Functioning of the European Union (TFEU).

[42] Implemented in Council Regulation (EU) No 961/2010 [2010] OJ L 281/1, repealed and replaced by No 267/2012 [2012] OJ L 88/1.

[43] On this point, see *Libyan Arab Foreign Bank v Bankers Trust* [1989] QB 728; *Soeximex SAS v Agrocorp International Pte Ltd* [2011] EWHC 2743 (Comm), [2012] 1 Lloyd's Rep 52, paras 17–18 (letter of credit in US dollars caught by US sanctions); *Sea Glory Maritime Co v Al Sagr National Insurance Co (The Nancy)* [2013] EWHC 2116 (Comm), [2013] 2 CLC 114 (freight payment in US dollars was caught by the US revocation of its 'U-turn authorisation' of 10 November 2008, making an exception from sanctions coverage for transactions involving trade with Iran where the only connection with the US was the currency).

B. Implementation into EU and Domestic Law

Whether a sanctions regime originates in the UN or the EU, it is implemented and enforced by the national authorities of EU Member States through their national legal systems. UN or EU sanctions measures are first adopted by the Council Decision under the CFSP and then, where the measures falls within Union competence under the Treaty on the Functioning of the European Union (TFEU), implemented through regulation. Even though regulations are directly applicable in the legal systems of Member States, they will require additional domestic implementing legislation to establish criminal penalties for breach.[44] Furthermore, not all measures adopted in CFSP decisions fall within the EU's legislative competence under the TFEU (ie sanctions involving travel bans or wholly internal measures).[45] UN Security Council sanctions measures and/or Council Decisions under the CFSP falling outside Union legislative competence under the TFEU are implemented directly by Member States.

English law on the reception of international law treats UN Security Council resolutions in the same way as treaties, requiring implementation into domestic law through an Act of Parliament or order in council.[46] The United Nations Act 1946 makes provision for implementation of Security Council resolutions by order in council. UN measures may also be implemented through orders under the Export Control Act 2008.[47] However, UN sanctions measures implemented through EU regulation (that is, those involving financial or trade measures) take effect under the European Communities Act 1972. Additional national implementing regulations for EU financial sanctions are made under the European Communities Act 1972 by HM Treasury, whilst the Department of Business, Innovation and Skills is responsible for measures involving sale or export of sanctioned goods and related contracts, and passes any necessary additional domestic regulation under the Export Control Act 2008 or the European Communities Act 1972.

Thus, to take an example from the Iran sanctions regime countering proliferation of nuclear weapons, UN Security Council Resolution 1929

[44] This is because the EU has limited competence in criminal matters.

[45] Some measures involving weapons may also fall outside Union competence by virtue of TFEU, Art 346: see Q Michel, 'Arms Trade Exception to The EU Common Commercial Policy: a Soft Law Exception to a Hard Law Principle' available at: http://local.droit.ulg.ac.be/jcms/service/file/20140209183637_Exception-to-the-EU-Common-Commercial-Policy-rev.pdf.

[46] How SC resolutions are received into the domestic law of each State depends on their domestic law. For a survey of national jurisdictions, see V Gowlland-Debbas, *National Implementation of United Nations Sanctions: A Comparative Study* (The Hague, Martinus Nijhoff, 2004).

[47] Financial restrictions may also be made under pt 2 of the Anti-Terrorism, Crime and Security Act 2001 and the Counter-Terrorism Act 2008.

(2010) of 9 June 2010[48] led to the European Council declaration of 17 June 2010, followed by the adoption of EU Council Decision 2010/413/CFSP of 26 July 2010, which was implemented by Council Regulation (EU) No 961/2010 (published in the Official Journal on 27 October 2010).[49] In the United Kingdom, the criminal penalties for breach of the financial measures were established by the Iran (European Union Financial Sanctions) Regulations 2010,[50] which came into force on 11 December 2010; and the criminal penalties for sale and export-related measures were established by the Export Control (Iran) Order 2011,[51] which came into force on 13 June 2011.[52] Sanctions with extraterritorial effect (sale or purchases of weapons of mass destruction (WMD) or military goods to or from Iran, the use of ships and aircraft for transport of WMD and military goods to or from Iran) were implemented by the Iran (United Nations Sanctions) Order 2009.[53]

As this illustration shows, there can be lengthy time lags between passing sanctions legislation and its implementation. This creates a peculiar lacuna in that a person may be bound by, and in breach of, a directly effective EU regulation, but may not have committed a criminal act. While prosecution may often be precluded in such cases,[54] any contractual party will be able to rely on the regulation. It should be noted too that regulations usually provide that transitional and savings provisions will only apply to contracts concluded before the date of the Council Decision, which may be some months earlier. Commercial operators therefore need to keep up to date with and implement Council Decisions under the CFSP, even if they do not yet have effect in domestic law.

[48] Council Decision 2010/413/CFSP of 26 July 2010 concerning restrictive measures against Iran and repealing Common Position 2007/140/CFSP [2010] OJ L195/39 expanding the sanctions regime in UNSC Res 1737 (2006), 1747 (2007) and 1803 (2008). These were implemented through earlier EU legal acts, Common Positions 2007/140/CFSP, 2007/246/CFSP, 2008/652/CFSP and Council Regulations under the EC Treaty (now TFEU), Regulation (EC) No 423/2007 as amended.

[49] Following the successful conclusion of the Joint Comprehensive Plan of Action on 14 July 2015, if certain requirements are met, the UN Iran sanctions will be terminated, subject to certain exemptions and licensing requirements: UNSC Res 2231 (2015), 20 July 2015, esp paras 7, 21–23.

[50] SI 2010/2937.

[51] SI 2011/1297.

[52] At the date of writing, the legislation was Council Regulation (EU) No 267/2012 and the principal UK regulations were the Iran (European Union Financial Sanctions) Regulations 2012 (SI 2012/925), the Export Control (Iran) Order 2007 (SI 2007/1526), the Export Control (Iran Sanctions) Order 2012 (SI 2012/1243) and the Iran (United Nations Sanctions) Order 2009 (SI 2009/886), as amended. This legislation has been amended in light of the agreement reached with Iran reflected in UNSC Res 2231 (2015). The point for present proposes is that a careful search of all relevant regulations must be carried out, as not all the implementing regulations are in the same instrument.

[53] SI 2009/886.

[54] Even if there is not a specific order implementing an EU measure, export-related sanctions may be prosecuted under general provisions in the Customs and Excise Act 1979.

C. Content of Sanctions—Bans and Limits on Commercial Activity

Security Council Resolution 661 (1990) imposed a complete trade embargo on Iraq, reflecting the traditional State practice during war of banning all trade and commercial relations with the enemy, including enemy nationals.[55] While it made exceptions for 'supplies intended strictly for medical purposes and, in humanitarian circumstances, foodstuffs',[56] the tremendous suffering of the Iraqi population under the embargo led to the development of the 'targeted' or 'smart' sanctions we are now familiar with, ie travel and asset-freezing bans on designated individuals, and embargoes and trade bans on arms and specified commodities or sectors which contribute to or finance a war or armed conflict or other activities threatening international peace and security. The growth in the number of sanctions measures since 1990 has been exponential. According to a study of the period 1990–2005, 74 UN arms embargoes were introduced[57] and as of mid-2009 1,186 individuals were listed under UN and EU sanctions regimes.[58] In 2006, HSBC estimated there were 6,000 individuals, companies and other entities listed on US, UN and EU lists.[59]

There are significant variations between the different UN sanctions regimes in the number and detail of the measures imposed.[60] The sanctions against Iran are amongst the most detailed. Not only do they call on States to prevent the supply, sale, transfer or export of WMD, related materials and arms to and from Iran and authorising their seizure and destruction, but they require Member States (if there are reasonable grounds to believe such activities contribute to Iran's proliferation activities) to freeze the assets of and prevent the provision of financial services (including insurance and reinsurance) to the Iranian State or listed individuals, to prevent Iranian banks from opening new branches, subsidiaries or correspondent banking relationships or their nationals from doing the same in Iran, and prevent bunkering by their nationals of Iranian-owned or contracted vessels.[61] They also impose vigilance obligations to monitor Iranian activities.

[55] UNSC Res 221 (1966) referred to its 'call to all States to do their utmost to break off economic relations with Southern Rhodesia, including an embargo on oil and petroleum products'.

[56] At para 3(c), reflecting obligations under the law of armed conflict, in eg Geneva Convention IV, Arts 21 and 55 and Additional Protocol I, Art 70.

[57] M Erikkson, *Targeting Peace: Understanding UN and EU Targeted* Sanctions (Farnham, Ashgate, 2011) 33.

[58] Ibid 105.

[59] Ibid 206.

[60] UNSC Res 1929 (2010) (Iran) totals 35 pages, compared with the 2 pages of Res 661 (1990).

[61] Ibid paras 18, 21, 23 and 24.

The EU Iranian sanctions regime implementing the UN sanctions imposes significant additional measures. These include bans on the import or purchase of Iranian crude oil, petroleum products and petrochemical products, the transport of such products and the provision, directly or indirectly, of financing or financial assistance (including derivatives), insurance or reinsurance related to the import, purchase or transport of crude oil and petroleum products.[62] Another is the requirement for authorisation for transfers of funds to and from any Iranian person or, if with a certain euro range,[63] a requirement to notify the transaction.[64] If the funds are being transferred through electronic transfer, the notification and authorisation obligation falls not on the contracting parties, but the banks processing the payment.[65] Prior authorisations are required for the sale, supply, transfer or export of certain goods and technology.[66] Financial institutions are also required to monitor Iranian and Iranian-related activities under an 'enhanced vigilance' obligation.[67] EU sanctions measures typically target not only designated persons and trades directly, but second and third tier contracts and transactions that are ancillary to and enable the sanctioned activities, ie financing, insurance, transportation, electronic processing of payments related to transactions and so on. The catch-all limitation on making funds or economic resources available directly or indirectly to listed persons has a particularly wide reach, especially where, as in the case of Iran and Syria, the listed persons include the State, the government and related entities.[68]

An EU sanctions regulation thus employs the same tools and rules as the common law on trading with the enemy applicable during war. While not all commercial activity with Iranian nationals is banned as it was with enemy nationals under the common law, parallels can be seen in the measures targeting all commercial activity that could contribute to the proliferation of WMD and the requirement of notification or authorisation in respect of the transfer of funds to or from *all* Iranian nationals.[69] Where the modern sanctions measures move beyond the trading with the enemy rules is in the use they make of credit and

[62] The current regulation is Council Regulation (EU) No 267/2012, Arts 11 and 13

[63] Previously €10,000–40,000; now, following limited relief agreed under the Joint Plan of Action by the E3+3 (UK, US, Russia, China, France and Germany), €100,000–400,000 (in place until 30 June 2015).

[64] These are made to the 'competent authorities' designated by each Member State (Art 48). The designated authority in the UK is HM Treasury.

[65] See Council Regulation (EU) No 267/2012, Art 30(3).

[66] Listed in Annexes I–III or the common military list: see Arts 3, 5 and 7. Applications in the UK are made to BIS.

[67] Council Regulation (EU) No 267/2012, Art 32.

[68] Ibid Art 23(3).

[69] Ibid Art 30.

financial institutions to monitor sanctions compliance by everyone else, to collect information and report suspicious activities through their obligations of 'enhanced vigilance'.[70] In doing so, sanctions impose a significant regulatory compliance burden and cost on financial institutions, alongside their obligations under anti-money laundering and corruption legislation.[71]

D. Prohibitions on Standing and Enforcement

Like the English law on the standing of enemy aliens in war, an EU sanctions regulation prohibits the enforcement of claims by designated persons and entities. According to Article 38(1) of EU Council Regulation No 267/2012 on Iran:

> [n]o claims in connection with any contract or transaction the performance of which has been affected, directly or indirectly, in whole or in part, by the measures imposed under this Regulation, including claims for indemnity or any other claim of this type, such as a claim for compensation or a claim under a guarantee, notably a claim for extension or payment of a bond, guarantee or indemnity, particularly a financial guarantee or financial indemnity, of whatever form, shall be satisfied if they are made by:
>
> (a) designated persons, entities or bodies listed in Annexes VIII and IX;
> (b) any other Iranian person, entity or body, including the Iranian government;
> (c) any person, entity or body acting through or on behalf of one of the persons, entities or bodies referred to in points (a) and (b).

The limitation extends to all claims where the existence or content of the claim results directly or indirectly from the sanctions measure and the burden is on the claimant to establish that their claim is not prohibited.[72] The link between the sanctions rules on standing and the common law rules on the effects of war is made explicit in *Amin v Brown*,[73] in which the defendant raised the preliminary plea of alien enemy against the Iraqi claimant. Rejecting the defence, Lawrence Collins J observed that '[t]o the extent that there is a public policy against enriching a person who is resident in a foreign State with which there are hostilities, that policy was

[70] Ibid Art 32.

[71] As noted by the Court in *Dahabshiil Transfer Services Ltd v Barclays Bank Plc* [2013] EWHC 3379 (Ch), [2014] UKCLR 215, para 16.

[72] Council Regulation (EU) No 267/2012, Arts 38(2)–(3). Judicial review of the legality of the non-performance of contractual obligations under the Regulation is safeguarded in Art 38(4), but the likely success of such a claim in cases concerning the freezing or not making available of funds or economic resources is severely curtailed by Art 42(1), which provides a defence where the measures are taken in good faith and not withheld by gross negligence. Establishing bad faith or gross negligence is likely to be an insuperable obstacle.

[73] [2005] EWHC 1670 (Ch).

satisfied in the case of Iraq by the Iraq (United Nations Sanctions) Order 2000'.[74] The Order did not preclude standing in the case.

However, where it does apply, a prohibition on standing may be permanent. The House of Lords in *Shanning International Ltd v Lloyds*[75] held that the preamble and the *travaux* of the EU's Iraq sanctions regulation showed the legislator's intention was to 'protect operators permanently from ...claims' arising as a result of the embargo and there was nothing in the regulation lifting the prohibition on enforcing claims after the embargo was lifted. Lord Hope considered that anything less than a permanent prohibition would not relieve economic operators in the EU from the damaging effects of the embargo.[76] Lord Bingham emphasised the careful thought that had gone into considering the best way to protect innocent economic operators. It remains to be seen whether, or to what extent, this interpretation remains unchallenged or is confined to its facts in light of the recent judgments of the Luxembourg and Strasbourg courts in *Kadi*[77] and *Nada*.[78] It may well turn on the facts of each case. Relevant factors may include whether the claim concerns funds or assets clearly belonging to an Iranian national, or whether the contract is of a type that could be suspended during the life of the sanctions, for example a bank account.[79] As regards title to property, there is nothing in the regulations to suggest that property may be confiscated and title lost or passed, except

[74] Ibid para 46.

[75] [2001] UKHL 31, [2001] 1 WLR 1462, concerning European Council Regulation (EEC) No 3541/92. The contract in question was an agreement by Shanning, a UK company, to sell medical supplies to a buyer in Iraq, who made an advance payment of 20% of the purchase price. An Iraqi bank issued a guarantee in reliance of a counter-guarantee by Lloyds in favour of the Iraqi bank. Lloyds' counter-guarantee was secured by a counter-indemnity in its favour from Shanning and a deposit by Shanning in an amount equal to the advance payment. Shanning had almost completed supply when Iraq invaded Kuwait and consequently was unable to complete the contract. Shanning claimed repayment of the deposit plus interest. Lloyds refused on the basis that it was under a potential liability to the Iraqi bank under the counter-guarantee. As the EU sanctions provision was to be interpreted as permanent ban on enforcement by Iraqis, the buyer and the Iraqi bank were permanently prohibited from pursuing their claims, allowing Shanning to recover.

[76] Ibid para 38, per Lord Hope.

[77] C-402/05 P, *Kadi v Council of the European Union* [2008] ECR I-6351, [2008] 3 CMLR 41, [2009] 1 AC 1225, [2009] 3 WLR 87.

[78] *Nada v Switzerland* (2013) 56 EHRR 18. See also *Al-Dulimi and Montana Management Inc v Switzerland* App no 5809/08 (ECtHR, 26 November 2013), which has been referred to the Grand Chamber.

[79] Unilateral sanctions imposed by a third State would not have that effect: see *Libyan Arab Foreign Bank v Bankers Trust* [1989] QB 728, where Staughton J, following the wartime cases, held, inter alia, that the correspondent banking contract between UK and Libyan banks was not frustrated or impossible of performance by reason of US sanctions, which had the effect of preventing processing of US dollar transactions. The parties had not altogether been discharged from future performance. Bankers Trust was still required to repay one day and in the meanwhile to credit interest to the account.

in the case of goods seized and destroyed in accordance with UN Security Council Resolutions.[80]

E. Scope of Application of Sanctions

The EU Iran sanctions regulation covers the territory of the Union, on board any aircraft or any vessel under the jurisdiction of a Member State, any person inside or outside the territory of the Union who is a national of a Member State and any legal person, entity or body incorporated or constituted under the law of a Member State.[81] It also extends to 'any legal person, entity or body in respect of any business done in whole or in part within the Union',[82] arguably extending beyond the limits of States' prescriptive jurisdiction as a matter of public international law.[83] However, the UK implementing regulations creating the accompanying criminal offences and penalties extend only to conduct wholly or partly outside the UK by UK nationals or bodies incorporated or constituted under the law of any part of the United Kingdom.[84]

F. Common Approach across Sanctions Legislation

There is significant variation between the substantive restrictions imposed by the different EU sanctions regimes—each must be carefully read, together with the (usually frequent) amendments. The use of a standard form legislative template is nevertheless apparent. The same secondary articles are used across all the sanctions regimes whether or not originating in a UN Security Council resolution, including the scope of application article, and the limits on standing and enforcement.[85]

[80] eg UNSC Res 1929 (2010) paras 14–16. See also Case C-177/95, *Ebony Maritime SA v Prefetto della Provincia di Brindisi* [1997] ECR I-1111, paras 43–49, upholding domestic Italian legislation implementing the EC's regulation implementing UN sanctions against the Federal Republic of Yugoslavia (FRY) and imposing a penalty of confiscation of cargoes, even though the EC legislation did not make provision for confiscation.

[81] Council Regulation (EU) No 267/2012, Art 49(a)–(d).

[82] Ibid Art 49(e). The claim to a broad jurisdiction is reminiscent of the excessive exercises of extraterritorial jurisdiction by the US in its Cuban and Libyan sanctions regimes in the D'Amato and Helms-Burton Acts, vigorously contested by other States and the EC which introduced blocking legislation in Council Regulation (EC) No 2271/96, 22 November 1996, [1996] OJ L309/1.

[83] To the extent a crime could not be said to fall within a State's objective or subjective territorial jurisdiction.

[84] The Iran (European Union Financial Sanctions) Regulations 2012, reg 1(2)–(3); the Export Control (Iran Sanctions) Order 2012, reg 1(3)(b).

[85] See eg Council Regulation (EU) No 36/2012 [2012] OJ L16/1 (Syria), Council Regulations (EU) No 833/2014 [2014] OJ L229/1 and 692/2014 [2014] OJ L183/9 (Ukraine).

The same observation and caution applies to the UK secondary legislation implementing UN and EU sanctions measures.

IV. SANCTIONS, CONTRACTS AND COMMERCIAL RELATIONS

While the UN Charter followed Article 16 of the Covenant in Article 41, where it made a clean break from the past was in the prohibition on the use of force in Article 2(4). The question that consequently vexed international lawyers was whether the law of war, in particular the rules conferring belligerent rights, had survived.[86] Thus in *Amin v Brown* the plea of alien enemy was rejected on the basis that

> the disability of alien enemies is a part of the rules of English law relating to the traditional laws of war, and that there is no warrant for extending it to modern armed conflict not involving war in the technical sense.[87]

However, although 'war' may have disappeared from the lexicon of public international law, it did not disappear from commercial law because it did not disappear in fact. Even before Article 2(4) and the *jus ad bellum*, judges rejected arguments that war cancellation clauses in charterparties did not apply because there had been no declaration of war. In *Kawasaki Kisen Kabushiki Kaisha of Kobe v Bantham Steamship Co Ltd*,[88] Goddard J held the vessel owners could rely on a clause allowing cancellation of a charterparty 'if a war breaks out involving Japan', even in the absence of a declaration of war, because whether there was a 'war' within the meaning of the contract was a question of fact. Mr Justice Goddard dismissed the arguments based on public international law with the withering observation that '[i]t is not to be expected that business men can concern themselves with the extraordinarily nice distinctions which aredrawn by great international lawyers'.[89] Mr Justice Goddard's reasoning and conclusions were later upheld by the Court of Appeal.[90]

[86] See Neff, *War and the Law of Nations* (n 6) 335–40.

[87] *Amin* (n 73) para 46.

[88] [1938] 61 131.

[89] At 138. '[T]he parties meant in this charterparty that if there was a state of conflict going on... if a state of affairs broke out in which there was armed conflict between competing nations of which Japan was one, that would justify breaking off the contract': ibid 138. The Foreign Office, asked whether or not it recognised a state of war between China and Japan, replied that it was not prepared to say whether a state of war existed because the situation was indeterminate and anomalous, but suggested that 'the meaning attached to the term "war" as used in a charterparty may simply be one of interpreting the relevant clause, and that the attitude of Her Majesty's Government may not necessarily be conclusive on the question whether a state of war exists within the meaning of the term "war" as used in particular documents or statutes' (at 137).

[90] *Kawasaki Kisen Kabushiki Kaisha of Kobe v Bantham Steamship Co Ltd* [1939] 2 KB 544 (CA)

The intention of the parties, to be ascertained in light of what a reasonable person would have understood them to have meant in view of the situation they were in and with the background knowledge reasonably available to them, remains the governing rule of contract construction,[91] not the meaning of terms in international law. Accordingly, jurisprudence arising out of wars 200–300 years ago is still cited[92] and affirmed in cases concerning the effect of armed conflicts, wars, embargoes and blockades on contracts.[93]

A. Illegality and Frustration as Applied to Sanctions

The Court in *Al-Kishtaini v Shanshal*[94] held that a breach of the Control of Gold, Securities, Payments and Credits (Republic of Iraq) Directions 1990[95] rendered a share purchase agreement unenforceable on grounds of illegality. This did not infringe property rights guaranteed by Article 1,

[91] *Rainy Sky SA v Kookmin Bank* [2011] UKSC 50, [2011] 1 WLR 2900, headnote, 2901–02. '[W]here a term of a contract is open to more than one interpretation, it is generally appropriate to adopt the interpretation which is most consistent with business common sense' (para 30). For a more recent case concerning interpretation of a cancellation clause referring to 'war' relied on in the context of NATO's Kosovo Operation, see *The Northern Pioneer* [2003] 1 Lloyd's Rep 212.

[92] In *The Bamburi* [1982] 1 Lloyd's Rep 312, Staughton J noted that: 'The political and commercial history of the Western world for the last two hundred years is reflected in the cases on war risk insurance. The present dispute is concerned with the war between Iran and Iraq which started in September 1980. In the course of argument I was referred to cases arising during the Seven Years War (1756), the American Revolution (1778), the Napoleonic Wars (1793), the siege of Paris (1870), the war between Turkey and Greece in 1912, the Great War (1914), the Spanish Civil War (1936), The World War (1939) and the Vietnam War (1966)'.

[93] As regards frustration, the Court of Appeal, in *Arab Bank v Barclays Bank* [1953] 2 QB 527, affirmed jurisprudence arising out of the Second World War to the effect that '[t]he law, in its concern to prevent benefit to enemies, does not go to the length of confiscating enemy property'. It held that Israeli trading with the enemy legislation did not frustrate a bank account contract, but had only a suspensory effect. The credit balance held was a liquidated debt owed by the bank to the plaintiffs, and was not 'cancelled' by war, but merely in hiatus until its conclusion.

[94] [2001] EWCA Civ 264. But *cf Royal Boskalis Westminster NV v Mountain* [1997] CLC 816. There, the Iraqi Government had contracted with two companies to undertake dredging work along the Iraq-Kuwait border, insured against war risks by a contract which was subject to English law. When the First Gulf War began, Iraq seized the dredging equipment under its own national legislation, taking the operators hostage. A 'finalisation agreement' was made, negotiating the release of vessels and men in return for payments to the Iraqi Government, structured in such a way as to avoid breaching the ongoing sanctions. When the companies sought to recover under the insurance contract, a dispute developed. Clearly, the Iraqi Government would have been precluded from enforcing the 'finalisation agreement', given that the purpose was to evade sanctions which had been lawfully imposed. However, this merely precluded enforcement of the contract, it was not void for illegality, and was thus still recognisable for the purposes of an ancillary contract of insurance, and recovery was allowed by the Court.

[95] SI 1990/1616.

Protocol 1 of the European Convention on Human Rights or the Human Rights Act 1998, because it fell within the public policy limitation on property rights and was proportionate in light of the exemption scheme operated by HM Treasury.[96] However, a contract will not be discharged by frustration or supervening illegality, even where the party is a designated entity, where any licence given under the sanctions regime allows it to remain in effect in full or in part and for payments to be made. Thus in *Islamic Republic of Iran Shipping Lines v Steamship Mutual Underwriting Association (Bermuda) Ltd* the terms of a licence issued by HM Treasury precluded the insurers from treating as discharged the cover for liability for pollution for risks required to be insured under the International Convention on Civil Liability for Bunker Oil Pollution Damages 2001 and to meet all claims made in respect of those risks.[97]

Performance of a contract may not be rendered illegal or frustrated by unilateral sanctions imposed by a third State where the parties did not intend to evade those sanctions,[98] although the performance obligations may be suspended. In *Libyan Arab Foreign Bank v Bankers Trust*,[99] Staughton J, following the wartime cases, held that the correspondent banking contract between UK and Libyan banks was not frustrated or impossible of performance by reason of US sanctions which had the effect of preventing the processing of US dollar transactions. The parties had not altogether been discharged from future performance. Bankers Trust was still required to repay one day and in the meanwhile to credit interest to the account.

Libyan Arab Foreign Bank thus provides guidance as to what may be required in respect of freezing funds held on account, whether in a bank account or client account. In practice, it appears the funds are, as the name suggests, simply frozen. The EU regulations do not require the payment of interest or dividends, but expressly state that the obligation to freeze accounts shall not apply to the addition to frozen accounts of interest or other earnings, by implication reinforcing the position under the wartime cases that certain obligations are simply suspended in so far as they are

[96] The parties had not applied for an exemption.

[97] [2010] EWHC 2661 (Comm), [2010] 2 CLC 534. The Club terminated insurance on the ground of discharge by frustration or supervening illegality because of the Iran sanctions. 24 hours later one of the vessels insured, the 'ZOORIK' suffered a casualty in Chinese territorial waters causing bunker oil pollution. The part of the contract dealing with oil pollution was still lawful and not dependent on the other parts of the contract to be performed.

[98] *Sea Glory Maritime Co v Al Sagr National Insurance Co (The Nancy)* (n 43), applying *Foster v Driscoll*, a case concerning evasion of the US laws on prohibition. The sanctions breach was the payment of freight in US dollars, which was caught even though the transaction was outside the US and did not involve US nationals because of the 10 November 2008 U-turn authorisation.

[99] [1989] QB 728.

incompatible with the sanctions. In *DVB Bank SE v Shere Shipping Ltd*,[100] the Court noted that sanctions regulation 267/2012 did not preclude crediting frozen accounts with repayments due as a result of a breach of a loan agreement entered before the claimants were listed provided those accounts remained frozen.[101] Any other dealings with funds held in suspended accounts or other assets belonging to designated persons would, following the wartime practice, require further legislation.[102] The sanctions legislation does not, however, address limitation periods, nor difficulties that might arise if the entity holding the funds is no longer able to continue doing so for any reason. Nor is it clear what bearing *Shanning International Ltd v Lloyds* might have on any claims after sanctions have ended. The rarity of litigation over the long-standing Iraq sanctions might suggest problems rarely arose in practice.

Contracts may be terminated by frustration where the sanctions regime extends beyond a period contemplated by the parties. In *Saipem v Rafidain Bank*,[103] the Court had to consider a 1993 settlement agreement entered by the claimant and the Iraqi State Company for Oil Projects to settle issues arising from the interruption by the First Gulf War of a project agreement to construct a trans-Arabian pipeline. It was anticipated at the time the agreement was concluded that the Iraq sanctions would delay shipments of spare parts for the project as long as they were in place. Saipem was required to keep the parts in custody until such time as the sanctions were lifted and the parts could be transferred and paid for. The sanctions were not lifted until 2003. Saipem argued that the settlement agreement was terminated by frustration, which meant the provisions of the original project agreement which provided for frustration in the event of war applied and entitled it to payments for the parts and to draw on sums held in trust by the defendant bank. An express contractual provision dealing with the cause of the frustration, ie the settlement agreement addressing the sanctions, would ordinarily prelude reliance on frustration, but it was held that the length of the sanctions regime was outside the contractual intentions of the parties when concluding the settlement agreement. The judge observed that:

> it is hardly to be imagined that any of the parties to the agreement could have envisaged that the sanctions would continue in force for a further 10 years—a

[100] [2013] EWHC 2321 (Comm). The attempts by the defendants, also designated entities or related to designated entities, to rely on the sanctions regulation as a defence to enforcement of the loan agreement failed because the licensing system in the regulation enabled payments to be made by them.

[101] Ibid para 92. If the repayment obligations were incapable of being performed indefinitely due to the sanctions (which was found not to be the case), the result would not be suspension of the obligation but frustration of the contract, in which case the relief available under s 1 of the Law Reform (Frustrated Contracts) Act 1943 would apply (para 61).

[102] As adopted in the Distribution of Enemy Property Act 1949 and Trading with the Enemy Act 1939.

[103] [2007] EWHC 3119 (Ch).

> period which I understand to be unprecedented in the history of international sanctions. Such an agreement would seem to be quite outside the commercial contemplation of any of the parties.[104]

Whether it could still be said that 10-year sanctions regimes are unprecedented may be doubted: it would be unwise for commercial parties to make similar assumptions in respect of other sanctions regimes, for example those concerning the Democratic People's Republic of Korea.

B. Standard Form Contract Provisions and their Construction

Commercial contracts increasingly make provision for UN sanctions, although not always separately from war clauses. The BIMCO Conwartime 2004 and Voywar 2004 war risk clauses include a provision that the vessel shall have the liberty

> to comply with the terms of any resolution of the Security Council of the United Nations, the effective orders of any other Supranational body which has the right to issue and give the same, and with national laws aimed at enforcing the same to which the Owners are subject, and to obey the orders and directions of those who are charged with their enforcement.[105]

'War risks' clauses may have some application to sanctions, for example where they are enforced by blockade.[106] The question of construction which arises from a reference to UN sanctions in a war risks clause is whether it would extend to sanctions which are not imposed in the context of war or armed conflict but are preventative measures imposed to counter proliferation of WMD or terrorism, a relatively recent development in Security Council practice.[107] The English approach to commercial contract

[104] Ibid para 16. For a recent decision refusing to allow a statutory demand by a person subject to the Libyan sanctions regime, see *Maud v Libyan Investment Authority (also known as Maud (In Bankruptcy), Re* [2015] EWHC 1625 (Ch).

[105] Paras (g)(iii) and (f)(iii).

[106] eg BIMCO's Conwartime 2004 and Voywar 2004 clauses for time charters and voyage charters define war risks to include 'any actual threatened or reported: War; act of war; civil war; hostilities; revolution; rebellion; civil commotion; warlike operations; laying of mines; acts of piracy; acts of terrorists; acts of hostility or malicious damage; blockades (whether imposed against all vessels or imposed selectively against vessels of certain flags or ownership, or against certain cargoes or crews or otherwise howsoever); by any person, body, terrorist or political group, or the Government of any State whatsoever, which, in the reasonable judgement of the Master and/or the Owners, may be dangerous or are likely to be or to become dangerous to the Vessel, her cargo, crew or other persons on board the Vessel' (clauses (a)(ii) of both clauses). Conwartime 2013 contains the same wording: www.bimco.org/en/Chartering/Clauses_and_Documents/Clauses/War_Risks_Clause_for_Time_Charters.aspx.

[107] Notably Michel appears to treat responses to terrorism as part of war and the law (above n 36, paras 1.18–1.28, 1.33) and *Halsbury's Laws of England* deals with sanctions and war together in the volume on Armed Conflict and Emergency, Vol 3 (5th edn, 2011).

construction might suggest the parties would be able to rely on the clause, because sanctions have the same effect whether they are imposed in relation to an armed conflict or not; the intention of commercial parties is that all sanctions and related actions (embargoes, blockades) would be caught by the same provision and commercial actors would not be concerned with 'extraordinarily nice distinctions... drawn by great international lawyers'.[108]

In 2010, BIMCO published a specific sanctions clause for time charterparties, in response to a fourth round of UN sanctions against Iran and expanded US legislation.[109] Because time charters may be of several months' or years' duration, and sanctions can be imposed, extended or amended at any time with little warning, the provision is intended to give owners flexibility to respond to the uncertainties created by sanctions regimes by refusing any voyage order which in their reasonable judgement will expose the vessel or its insurers to any sanction. Intertanko has also published a sanctions clause deeming any trade unlawful which could expose the vessel, its owners, its crew or insurers 'to a risk of sanctions imposed by supranational governmental organisation' or the States listed in the clause.[110] The drafting is not a model of clarity, in that it suggests the sanctions covered are those *imposed on* the vessel, its owners, its crew or insurers, rather than exposing them to the application of or liability under sanctions. However, a commercial construction would likely be adopted.[111]

Another common contractual approach is to modify the provision for contractual warranties against dangerous goods, by requiring that cargo does not pose any risk, whether physical or legal, to the vessel or her

[108] *Kawasaki Kisen Kabushiki Kaisha of Kobe v Bantham Steamship Co Ltd* (n 90) 138.

[109] See the Explanatory Note. The 'Owners shall not be obliged to comply with any orders for the employment of the Vessel in any carriage, trade or on a voyage which, in the reasonable judgement of the Owners, will expose the Vessel, Owners, managers, crew, the Vessel's insurers, or their re-insurers, to any sanction or prohibition imposed by any State, Supranational or International Governmental Organisation'. It applies to the application of sanctions after the vessel has begun an employment under the charter: www.bimco.org/Chartering/Clauses_and_Documents/Clauses/Sanctions_Clause.aspx.

[110] 'Any trade in which the vessel is employed under this Charterparty which could expose the vessel, its Owners, Managers, crew or insurers to a risk of sanctions imposed by a supranational governmental organisation or the United States, {insert other countries} shall be deemed unlawful and Owners shall be entitled, at their absolute discretion, to refuse to carry out that trade. In the event that such risk arises in relation to a voyage the vessel is performing, the Owners shall be entitled to refuse further performance and the Charterers shall be obliged to provide alternative voyage orders'.

[111] See *Arash Shipping Enterprises Co Ltd v Groupama Transport* [2011] EWCA Civ 620, [2011] 2 Lloyd's Rep 607, para 59 (Tomlinson LJ) on the interpretation of a sanctions clause in an insurance contract. It was not 'happily drafted' because it suggested it would be triggered only where the *acts of the assured* exposed the insurer to risk whereas 'sanctions are often aimed not so much at acts of the target nationals but rather at the acts of those dealing with target nationals'.

owner. The Shelltime 4 Time Charter includes the proviso at clause 4 that the charter is 'for the purpose of carrying lawful merchandise'. This puts the onus onto cargo interests, a particularly heavy warranty given the complexity of dual-use technologies and materials which fall under modern sanctions regimes.[112] Clause 28 of the Shelltime 4 form also provides that: '[n]o voyage shall be undertaken, nor any goods or cargoes loaded, that would expose the vessel to capture or seizure by rulers or governments'. Clauses 4 and 28 were considered by Colman J in *Ullises Shipping Corp v Fal Shipping Co Ltd ('The Greek Fighter')*.[113] The tanker owners had claimed against time charterers for an indemnity when the vessel and its cargo were confiscated and sold by the UAE authorities as contraband Iraqi oil transported in breach of UN sanctions. Colman J gave judgment for the owners on the basis that the charterers were in breach of the lawful merchandise warranty in clause 28, even though they were unaware of the origin of the oil. The subsequent detention of the vessel did not frustrate the contract. The charterers were liable for damages for the difference between the charter rate and the reduced rate paid during the detention because their breach of clause 28 was the consequence of their shipment of Iraqi oil. If the charterers had not been in breach of the oil embargo, the UAE authorities would not have been entitled to detain the vessel, and the charterers could have relied on the restraint of princes provision.

Parties may also seek to rely on trading limits clauses. This could be risky because the clauses are not drafted with modern targeted sanctions in mind. Many refer to a traditional trade embargo enforced by a blockade of a port or ports, such as those imposed by the early Rhodesia and Iraq sanctions regimes, not the approach taken in targeted sanctions regimes which have now been in use for several years.[114]

[112] In this respect the annexes to EU regulations listing items subject to sanctions read like GATT lists of customs tariffs, which may provide some guidance to construction.

[113] [2006] EWHC 1729 (Comm), [2006] 2 CLC 497.

[114] eg:

> Vessel is not allowed to trade *to ports/areas which are or may become during the currency of this Charter party sanctioned* by USA, European Union and/or the United Nations and/or organizations of the United Nations;
>
> or
>
> World-wide safe ports, always afloat within IWL, excluding Cambodia … and other countries/dangerous zones by actual threatened war, hostilities and/or war-like operation or the like acts *and countries banned and/or boycotted by the United Nations.* Subject always to instruction and/or recommendation by the country of the Vessel's flag from time to time …
>
> Equally should circumstances change for the worse in any countries and areas currently included in the trading limits, the Charterers agree to review the clause with a view to excluding such certain countries and areas.

C. Lack of Clarity in Sanctions Measures—Implications for Contracts

The lack of clarity in EU or national legislation or their failure to reflect the practice of the industry which they purport to regulate also give rise to difficulties in construction. A party terminating a contract in the mistaken belief that it is covered by a sanctions measure may expose itself to an unlawful breach of contract claim, as was the case in *Arash Shipping Enterprises Co Ltd v Groupama Transport*.[115] The insurer served a notice of cancellation of a policy covering hull and machinery risks under a sanctions clause. The sanctions clause entitled the insurers to cancel 'in circumstances where the Assured has exposed or may, in the opinion of the Insurer, expose the Insurer to the risk of being or becoming subject to any sanction'. The insured, a Cypriot company controlled by Iranian interests and insuring Iranian vessels, argued the policy was not covered by the EU sanctions regulation because it contained an automatic renewal provision.[116] The regulation prohibited the provision of insurance to Iranian legal persons and the extension or renewal of insurance, but did not prohibit compliance with contracts entered before that date. HM Treasury had been approached for advice and said the regulation did extend to automatic renewals, and the EU Commission apparently gave similar advice, although in cryptic terms.[117] The court below and Court of Appeal agreed with this interpretation, and held that, in any event, the insurer was entitled under the terms of the sanctions clause to make its own assessment of exposure to risk of sanctions, provided it did so reasonably and in good faith. The case illustrates the benefit of drafting sanctions clauses to provide certainty and a right of termination where sanctions legislation is unclear.

Another example is the 2012 case of *'The Alead'*, a Russian-owned vessel carrying Syrian helicopter gunships repaired in Russia back to Syria. The vessel stopped en route in the UK's territorial waters around Scotland and its UK-based insurers were urged to pull the vessel's cover. But it was not immediately apparent that the Syrian sanctions measures extended to the transport of arms and related insurance contracts because it prohibited only the provision of financing or financial assistance, directly or indirectly, 'including in particular grants, loans and export insurance' for any sale, supply, transfer or export of equipment which might be used for internal repression. The P&I club pulled its cover on 19 June 2012 in any event. On 26 June 2012, Council Regulation (EU) 545/2012 amended the prohibition to include the provision of insurance for any 'sale, supply, transfer or export'. An HM Treasury Financial Sanctions Notice

[115] [2011] EWCA Civ 620, [2011] 1 Lloyd's Rep IR Plus 42.

[116] Council Regulation (EU) No 961/2010, now No 267/2012.

[117] The Syrian Sanctions Regulation (36/2012) made express an exception from the prohibition on renewals for automatic renewals, perhaps in response to this case.

of the same date said '[t]his clarifies the provisions on direct or indirect insurance and reinsurance related to the sale, supply, transport or export of military technology'. The reference to 'clarification' seems rather euphemistic.

The current approach of the EU Courts to the interpretation of sanctions legislation can be summarised as taking a rigorous approach to the question of whether an entity ought to be designated or not, but interpreting the wording of sanctions measures widely in line with their preventative purpose and the strong public interest.[118] Account must be taken of the wording and purpose of the UNSC resolution which the EU regulation is designed to implement.[119] But it may be questioned whether even a strong teleological interpretation by the CJEU could or should result in reading a prohibition on the insurance of transport into a regulation in the absence of any express reference to transport or insurance as form of financial assistance, especially as earlier sanctions legislation included express provisions on transport and related insurance contracts.[120] The application of the principle of *ejusdem generis* and requirements of legal certainty argue against it. On the other hand, it can be argued that including the insurance of the transport of the arms within the meaning of financial assistance would achieve the objective of the sanctions—as was shown in this instance as *The Alead* turned around when its cover was withdrawn.[121]

[118] See Case C-177/95, *Ebony Maritime SA v Prefetto della Provincia di Brindisi* [1997] ECR I-1111, para 44; Case C-550/09, *E & F* [2010] ECR I-6213, paras 67–69 ('The notion of "funds, other financial assets and economic resources"... takes on... a wide meaning which covers assets of every kind, however acquired'; 'The expression "made available" has a wide meaning, encompassing all the acts necessary if a person, a group or an entity on the list is effectively to obtain full power of disposal in respect of the funds, other financial assets and economic resources concerned', 'That meaning [of "making available"] is independent of the existence or absence of a relationship between the perpetrator of the act of "making available" and the beneficiary'); Case C-117/06, *Möllendorf and Möllendorf-Niehuus* [2007] ECR-I 8361, para 56 (giving a wide meaning to the words 'making available an economic resource' so that registration of a completed sale of land in the land registry would be making a resource available to a designated person); Case C-72/11, *Afrasiabi* [2011] ECR-000, paras 44–49 ('making available' includes the provision of a sintering furnace that cannot be used because a key operating component has been held back).

[119] Case C 340/08, *M & Ors v HM Treasury* [2010] ECR 000, para 45. However, not every action will be construed so broadly. Making a court order for maintenance payments in Russia from a person listed in Russia will not amount to circumvention where the payment itself can be lawfully made with a licence within the UK, or, if no such licence is given, enforced after the sanctions come to an end: *R v R* [2015] EWCA Civ 796 (paras 27 and 29, per Arden LJ). The preliminary ruling reference in *R (Rosneft) v HM Treasury & Ors* [2015] EWHC 248 (Admin) is likely to provide further guidance on the interpretation of 'financing and financial assistance' in Council Regulation 833/2014 as amended (concerning restrictive measures in view of Russia's actions destabilising the situation in Ukraine).

[120] eg Council Regulation (EU) No 267/2012, Arts 11(1)(d) and 14(1)(b).

[121] 'Russian ship with helicopters for Syrian regime sets sail again' *The Telegraph*, 31 July 2012: available at: www.telegraph.co.uk/news/worldnews/middleeast/saudiarabia/9398597/Russian-ship-with-helicopters-for-Syrian-regime-sets-sail-again.html.

Problems also arise from the sheer volume of EU regulations, UK regulations and orders, amendments and subsequent amendments. This was highlighted in *R v PD & EB (Iraq Sanctions)*,[122] which involved a prosecution for exporting arms to Iraq in 2005–07 carrying a sentence of eight years' imprisonment. Despite extensive research by counsel during the hearing,[123] no one could find out whether the offence applied at the relevant time because it appeared that a central ingredient had been inadvertently omitted from the subordinate legislation during a round of amendments. The Court of Appeal refused to apply the principle of statutory interpretation that a court might correct obvious drafting errors, because it would not be right to put individuals at risk of loss of their liberty except under clear authority of law. Moreover, the courts 'should not countenance errors by a Secretary of State in the exercise of… broad Executive powers' to make subordinate legislation without parliamentary scrutiny. To do so would not be consistent with principles of good governance and the rule of law.[124]

D. The Freezing Effect on Economic Relations

A different commercial challenge arises from sanctions in cases where there is no contractual or other obligation to either enter into a contract with a person or continue relations with them. Sanctions have a 'freezing effect' on commercial dealings as banks and other businesses adopt a cautious, risk-averse approach.[125] Not only does this lead to complaints about banks causing loss by refusing to process transactions which are not caught by the sanctions, but it can lead to hardship where there is no market alternative to the service being withdrawn. This problem received particular attention in the case of sanctions targeting Al-Shabab. Banks across the market in 2012–13 withdrew the provision of services to money service businesses active in Somalia and rejected new applications.

[122] [2011] EWCA Crim 2082, [2011] Lloyd's Rep FC 610.

[123] It was recorded in the judgment that '[i]t became necessary to ask counsel at the conclusion of the oral hearing to conduct some further research, as no one could be sure that all the relevant subordinate legislation had been found and whether such as had been found was in force at the material time. The work done has revealed some serious and significant deficiencies in the system that the Executive branch of the State employs for the making and recording of the type of subordinate legislation in issue in this case' (ibid para 2).

[124] Ibid para 66.

[125] For a case where the bank's approach was considered to be justified (at least on a refusal of interim relief) on the basis that it had 'reasonable grounds to suspect' that leaving the claimant's accounts unfrozen would make 'funds or economic resources… available, directly or indirectly, to or for the benefit of' of a listed person under the UK regulations implementing the EU Syrian sanctions regime, see *Hmicho v Barclays Bank* [2015] EWHC 1757 (QB).

This effectively closed off or severely limited the available channels for the Somali community in the UK to send remittances back to families in Somalia. Some respite was given in *Dahabshiil Transfer Services Ltd v Barclays Bank Plc*.[126] Three money service businesses which had had their contracts with Barclays Bank terminated leaving them without any banking facilities.[127] They successfully secured urgent interim relief on the ground that it was seriously arguable that Barclays had abused a dominant market position in breach of Article 102 of the TFEU. It was common ground that the money service business sector was a high risk one, and that global banks like Barclays are subject to increasing and intensive regulation in this area and this impacts on the compliance costs of continuing to provide such services.[128] Nevertheless, the Judge held there was a question of law as to whether a dominant undertaking could commit an abuse by seeking to reduce its participation in the market and by cutting off supplies or goods or services to an existing customer without justification sufficient to support interim relief.[129]

This case highlights the conflicts that sanctions can cause between competing, valid commercial interests, which are capable of inflicting real and unintended hardship on individuals and communities. There are no easy answers, but in this instance it does appear the parties were able to reach an agreement following the injunction for the continued provision of services until an alternative solution could be found.[130]

V. CONCLUSION

UN sanctions may appear to be a relatively recent creation in the 1945 Charter, but they have a long pedigree in the laws of war. The modern-day sanction and the measures used to enforce them are direct descendants of the measures employed in war or reprisal and the related rules of international and domestic law on trading with the enemy, trade embargoes, blockades, contraband measures, reprisals, letters of marque, prize

[126] [2013] EWHC 3379 (Ch), [2014] UKCLR 215.

[127] Under 'at will' provisions; it was agreed Barclays had no contractual obligation to continue to provide banking services.

[128] Ibid para 16.

[129] Ibid paras 73–74. For proceedings concerning a claim for damages as a result of a unilateral UK financial sanctions measure successfully challenged in judicial review proceedings, see *Bank Mellat v HM Treasury (No 2)* [2013] UKSC 39, [2014] AC 700 and *Bank Mellat v HM Treasury* [2015] EWHC 1258 (Comm). For claims for damages as part of a successful action for annulment of a listing under EU law, see eg Case T-384/11, *Safa Nicu Sepahan Co v Council*, 25 November 2014, unreported, on appeal, C-45/15 P.

[130] 'Barclays Settles Dispute with Money Transfer Company Dahabshiil' *Wall Street Journal*, 16 April 2014, available at: www.wsj.com/articles/SB10001424052702304626304579505661804336976.

and commercial treaties. Commercial actors and English commercial law apply the same principles of illegality and frustration and the same standard form clauses to sanctions as were applied to war and reprisals. In the words of Chitty, sanctions are part of the law of nations which form the basis of the commercial intercourse which takes place between individuals and part of the legal environment within which commerce takes place. Sanctions do hinder commerce and may give competitors from other jurisdictions which have not imposed the same sanctions an advantage. But they are an inevitable fact of commercial life because they are one of the few tools of law enforcement and prevention available in international law.

Index

Footnotes are indicated by the letter 'n' following the page number

Lightning Source UK Ltd.
Milton Keynes UK
UKOW01n1323191017
311251UK00009B/246/P

9 781849 465908